The Foundation of the Unconscious

The unconscious, cornerstone of psychoanalysis, was a key twentieth-century concept and retains an enormous influence on psychological and cultural theory. Yet there is a surprising lack of investigation into its roots in the critical philosophy and Romantic psychology of the early nineteenth century, long before Freud. Why did the unconscious emerge as such a powerful idea? And why at that point? This interdisciplinary study breaks new ground in tracing the emergence of the unconscious through the work of philosopher Friedrich Schelling, examining his association with Romantic psychologists, anthropologists and theorists of nature. It sets out the beginnings of a neglected tradition of the unconscious psyche and proposes a compelling new argument: that the unconscious develops from the modern need to theorise individual independence. The book assesses the impact of this tradition on psychoanalysis itself, re-reading Freud's *The Interpretation of Dreams* in the light of broader post-Enlightenment attempts to theorise individuality.

MATT FFYTCHE is a lecturer at the Centre for Psychoanalytic Studies, University of Essex. His research focuses on the history of psychoanalysis, and critical theories of subjectivity in the nineteenth and twentieth centuries. He is a co-editor of the web-based digital archive, 'Deviance, Disorder and the Self'.

The Foundation of the Unconscious

Schelling, Freud and the Birth of the Modern Psyche

Matt ffytche

CAMBRIDGE
UNIVERSITY PRESS

CAMBRIDGE UNIVERSITY PRESS
Cambridge, New York, Melbourne, Madrid, Cape Town,
Singapore, São Paulo, Delhi, Tokyo, Mexico City

Cambridge University Press
The Edinburgh Building, Cambridge CB2 8RU, UK

Published in the United States of America by Cambridge University Press,
New York

www.cambridge.org
Information on this title: www.cambridge.org/9780521766494

First published 2012

Printed in the United Kingdom at the University Press, Cambridge

A catalogue record for this publication is available from the British Library

Library of Congress Cataloguing in Publication data
Ffytche, Matt.
  The foundation of the unconscious : Schelling, Freud, and the birth of the
  modern psyche / Matt Ffytche.
    p.   cm.
  Includes bibliographical references and index.
  ISBN 978-0-521-76649-4 (hardback)
  1. Subconsciousness.   2. Psychoanalysis – History.   3. Schelling,
  Friedrich Wilhelm Joseph von, 1775–1854.   4. Freud, Sigmund,
  1856–1939.   I. Title.
  BF315.F53 2011
  154.209–dc23
  2011031544

ISBN 978-0-521-76649-4 Hardback

For Andrea
Light cast over our camp as if in day by reason
and seeks cover underground.

Contents

Acknowledgements

I would like to thank John Forrester and the editorial team on *Psychoanalysis and History* for publishing an earlier draft of some of the arguments in Chapter 6 as '"The Most Obscure Problem of All": Autonomy and its Vicissitudes in *The Interpretation of Dreams*', *Psychoanalysis and History*, 9, 1 (2007), 39–70, and Joel Faflak for publishing a portion of my earlier researches on the Romantic psyche as 'F.W. J. Schelling and G. H. Schubert: Psychology in Search of Psyches', in the issue on *Romantic Psyche and Psychoanalysis* he guest edited for *Romantic Circles Praxis Series* (December 2008), and for his encouraging editorial comments.

I am very grateful to have had access to the collections at Senate House Library, the Wellcome Library and the British Library, throughout the period of my research, and for the patience and professionalism of the staff there. Also to the librarians and staff of the Albert Sloman Library, University of Essex, and the libraries at Queen Mary, and at the Institute of Germanic Studies (University of London). I am grateful to the Arts and Humanities Research Board who funded the beginnings of this project many years ago as a Ph.D. at Queen Mary, and to Paul Hamilton for his benign supervision and preparedness to enter the Schellingian abyss when it was still very dimly lit.

I count myself lucky, and am immensely grateful for the many expert and critical readers of parts of this manuscript in earlier forms, especially to John Forrester, Howard Caygill, Sonu Shamdasani and Andrea Brady who read and commented on the first draft of this book, and whose critical insights and practical support have been invaluable. Also to Daniel Pick, Jacqueline Rose, Peter Dews, Peter Howarth, Will Montgomery and Ben Watson who generously read and responded to sections of this work and offered valuable suggestions and help. I would like to thank Rowan Boyson, Molly MacDonald, Garry Kelly, Helen McDowell, Dominic ffytche, Michèle Barrett, David Dwan, Nikolay Mintchev, Angus Nicholls, Keston Sutherland, Ian Patterson, John Wilkinson and Jeremy Prynne, variously, for encouragement, support, critical dialogue and conversation on psychoanalysis, psychology, German philosophy, contemporary theory and many points beyond and between. I also particularly want to remember my fellow participants in the research student reading group on *The Interpretation of Dreams* run by Jacqueline Rose at Queen Mary in 1999–2001, a forum which played a big role in provoking my interest in that work, and in the Graduate Forum in 'Psychoanalytic Thought, History and Political Life' at London University, run by Daniel Pick and Jacqueline Rose, which continues to be useful and to inform my researches on the intellectual history of psychoanalysis.

Especial thanks go to my colleagues at the Centre for Psychoanalytic Studies, at the University of Essex, who have supported the final stages of this project, including in particular Roderick Main, Bob Hinshelwood, Andrew Samuels, Karl Figlio, Aaron Balick and Kevin Lu, and to Sanja Bahun and Leon Burnett in the department of Literature, Film and Theatre Studies, and Mike Roper in Sociology.

I owe a great debt to my parents, Tim and Bärbl, for their support and encouragement, for valuing the spaces of reading and thinking, and building the bridge with Germany.

Above all I wish to honour the love, work and friendship of Andrea Brady, careful and critical reader of this book, spur to my living and my thinking, and who has helped me to keep my thought in life.

This book will forever be associated with the birth of my daughters, Hannah and Ayla, who can only have experienced it as a mysterious void in my presence, and I thank them for the immeasurable joy they have given me, for which this work is a poor return.

Introduction: the historiography of the unconscious

> We want to make the I into the object of this investigation, our most personal I. But can one do that?[1]

The historiography of psychoanalysis needs radical revision. This book poses the question: where does psychoanalysis begin? Which is to ask both when can we begin with it historically, and how exactly does it emerge? The conventional answer to those questions has, for many decades, been the one provided by Freud himself: that it begins in Vienna, out of a combination of Freud's private clinical work with neurotics, his collaboration with Josef Breuer in the treatment of hysteria, and the period of depression which inaugurates his own self-analysis in the 1890s, all of which fed into the genesis of the *Interpretation of Dreams* – the work which for many marks the opening of the 'Freudian' century.[2] More recent scholarship has greatly extended our knowledge of Freud's formative contexts, including the publication of his correspondence with Wilhelm Fliess, and studies of the intellectual ambience of the Viennese medical school and Freud's earliest work on neuro-anatomy, as well as the crucial impact of his period of study with Charcot in Paris.[3] Psychoanalysis, evidently, has broader roots than Freud's own

[1] Sigmund Freud, *Studienausgabe*, vol. I: *Vorlesungen zur Einführung in die Psychoanalyse und Neue Folge*, ed. Alexander Mitscherlich, Angela Richards and James Strachey (Frankfurt am Main: S. Fischer Verlag, 1982), 497. The translation is that given by Andrew Bowie, *Aesthetics and Subjectivity: from Kant to Nietzsche* (Manchester University Press, 1990), 59.

[2] See, for instance, Lionel Trilling's Introduction to Lionel Trilling and Steven Marcus (eds.) and abridged, Ernest Jones, *The Life and Work of Sigmund Freud* (London: Penguin, 1964), 12: 'But the basic history of psychoanalysis is the account of how it grew in Freud's own mind, for Freud developed its concepts all by himself.'

[3] See, amongst others, S. Bernfeld, 'Freud's Earliest Theories and the School of Helmholtz', *Psychoanalytic Quarterly*, 13, (1994), 341–62; Ola Andersson, *Studies in the Prehistory of Psychoanalysis: The Etiology of Psychoneuroses and Some Related Themes in Sigmund Freud's Scientific Writings and Letters, 1886–1896* (Stockholm: Svenska, 1962); Peter Amacher, 'Freud's Neurological Education and Its Influence on Psychoanalytic Theory', *Psychological Issues* 4, 4, Monograph 16 (New York: International University Press, 1965); Jeffrey Moussaieff Masson (ed.), *The Complete Letters of Sigmund Freud to Wilhelm Fliess 1887–1904* (Cambridge, MA: Harvard University Press, 1985);

1

self-investigation. Two reassessments, George Makari's *Revolution in Mind* and Eli Zaretsky's *Secrets of the Soul,* both draw on such revisions in psychoanalytic scholarship and shift the focus of study away from Freud's own biography and towards colleagues, collaborators and the broader cultural climate. Even so, there remains a seemingly unshaken consensus that psychoanalysis is born out of the melting pot of late nineteenth-century Viennese modernity. According to Zaretsky, 'we have still not historicized psychoanalysis', but he takes this to mean exploring the breadth of its appeal and its contradictory impact on twentieth-century culture. Carl Schorske's *Fin-de-Siècle Vienna* is, for Zaretsky, still the greatest attempt to 'grasp psychoanalysis historically'.[4] Equally, for Makari, what is needed is a lateral broadening of the frame of inquiry in order to identify the many different fields from which Freud 'pulled together new ideas and evidence... to fashion a new discipline'.[5] None of these works, with the exception of Sonu Shamdasani's ground-breaking reassessment of the work of C. G. Jung,[6] pay any attention to the longer-range history of the 'unconscious psyche', or tie Freud's work back into the earlier nineteenth century's fascination with the obscure tiers, functions and forces at work below the level of consciousness, the secret histories of the self. It is as if these notions emerge wholly unannounced in the 1890s.

The object of this study is to provide a new and more complex account of the emergence of the idea of a psychic unconscious, and so to explore the possibility of giving psychoanalysis a much deeper historical context. There are good grounds for locating this moment historically at the threshold of the nineteenth century in Germany, under the wings of Romanticism and post-Kantian idealism. Here, at the very least, one finds the initial integration of a theory of the unconscious with the mind's inner medium, named as the 'psyche' or the 'soul' (*Seele,* the word still used by Freud to indicate the psychical apparatus). Both of these terms, already at this time, were set in the context of a psychological theory and a therapeutic practice which developed out of and alongside a concern with mesmerism and animal magnetism. Here, too, in the work of figures such as the idealist F. W. J. Schelling and

Mark Solms, 'Freud, Luria and the Clinical Method', *Psychoanalysis and History,* 2, 1 (February 2000), 76–109; Mark Luprecht, *'What People Call Pessimism': Sigmund Freud, Arthur Schnitzler, and Nineteenth-Century Controversy at the University of Vienna Medical School* (Riverside, CA: Ariadne Press, 1991).

[4] Eli Zaretsky, *Secrets of the Soul: a Social and Cultural History of Psychoanalysis* (New York: Alfred A. Knopf, 2004), 3–4.

[5] George Makari, *Revolution in Mind: the Creation of Psychoanalysis* (London: Gerald Duckworth, 2008), 3.

[6] Sonu Shamdasani, *Jung and the Making of Modern Psychology* (Cambridge University Press, 2003).

the nature philosopher and anthropologist G. H. Schubert,[7] one finds many of the characteristic idioms associated with psychoanalytic theory in the twentieth century: the notion of an internal mental division and a dialogue between a conscious and an unconscious self; the sense of concealed or repressed aspects of one's moral nature; a new concern with memory and the past, and with both developmental accounts of the self and reconstructions of the origins of consciousness. The first two items listed here – the unconscious and repression – are those suggested by Freud as the principle cornerstones of psychoanalytic theory, according to his 1923 Encyclopaedia article on 'Psychoanalysis', the other two being the theory of sexuality and the Oedipus complex.[8]

Moreover, though Zaretsky sees in Freud 'the first great theory and practice of "personal" life'[9] and Makari finds him trying to win for science 'the inner life of human beings',[10] both accounts strangely eclipse that moment, a hundred years earlier, which saw the production of Rousseau's *Confessions*, Fichte's theory of subjectivity, Goethe's *Wilhelm Meister* and Wordsworth's *Prelude*. This same period gave rise to both the various kinds of self-investigation practised by German Romantics such as Friedrich Schlegel, J. W. Ritter and Novalis, and also J. C. Reil's coinage of *psychotherapie*, Carl Moritz's *Magazine for Empirical Psychology* and many other similar initiatives, all organised around the secular investigation of personal and interior life.[11] Finally, there emerges at this time a specific theoretical focus on the foundation of consciousness in earlier, more primitive and unconscious stages (both from the point of view of individual development, and as an issue for cultural history as a whole), as well as a new kind of psychological interest in peculiar or pathological states of mind, including forms of madness, but also sleep, dreams and trances.

Various writers have at times suggested more distant points of inception for the basic concepts of psychoanalysis, including Lancelot Law Whyte in his slim 1960 volume *The Unconscious Before Freud*, and more importantly Henri Ellenberger, whose still unparalleled scholarship in *The Discovery of the Unconscious* traces the therapeutic contexts of depth

---

[7] Throughout this book, 'anthropologist' will be used in the early nineteenth-century sense of a general science of man.

[8] Sigmund Freud, 'Two Encyclopaedia Articles', in *The Standard Edition of the Complete Psychological Works of Sigmund Freud*, 24 vols., ed. James Strachey in collaboration with Anna Freud, assisted by Alix Strachey and Alan Tyson (London: Hogarth Press and the Institute of Psychoanalysis, 1953–74) (hereafter *SE*), vol. XVIII, 247. See also Stephen Frosh, *Key Concepts in Psychoanalysis* (London: The British Library, 2002), 11, for an account of the unconscious as the single key concept in psychoanalysis.

[9] Zaretsky, *Secrets of the Soul*, 5.

[10] Makari, *Revolution in Mind*, 3.

[11] For more details see Matthew Bell, *The German Tradition of Psychology in Literature and Thought, 1700–1840* (Cambridge University Press, 2005).

psychology back through various nineteenth-century trends to the vogue for mesmerism in the eighteenth century.[12] Ellenberger's work and that of Odo Marquard in the 1980s, both of which I will consider further below, provide important accounts of the way in which psychoanalysis links back to Romantic intellectual contexts.[13] Yet still surprisingly little work has been done on the interconnection of the various Romantic and idealist notions of the psyche and the unconscious, their links to an emerging field of psychology, or their relation to a 'Freudian unconscious' at the other end of the century.[14] Whatever contemporary interest there is in influences running between psychoanalysis and the epoch of Romanticism has come not from the history of ideas, or the history of psychology, but from contemporary debates in literary theory and continental philosophy. Two obvious examples are *The Indivisible Remainder* by Slavoj Žižek and *Schelling and Modern European Philosophy* by Andrew Bowie, both of which have wanted to make a case for the close links between the work of Schelling and the conceptual apparatus of psychoanalysis.[15] For Žižek, for instance, Schelling's *Ages of the World* [*Weltalter*] is 'a metapsychological work in the strict Freudian sense'.[16] Such publications undoubtedly brought this rather obscure backwater in intellectual history on to the contemporary agenda and were the first indications of a more recent Schelling revival.[17] More recently, Joel

---

[12] Lancelot Law Whyte, *The Unconscious Before Freud* (New York: Anchor Books, 1962); Henri F. Ellenberger, *The Discovery of the Unconscious: the History and Evolution of Dynamic Psychiatry* (London: Fontana Press, 1994).

[13] For parallels in historical work on psychiatry, see the suggestion in F. G. Alexander and S. T. Selesnick, *The History of Psychiatry: an Evaluation of Psychiatric Thought and Practice from Prehistoric Times to the Present* (New York: Harper & Row, 1966), 135, that: 'In their new and enthusiastic concern over the nature of the psyche, the Romantics brought psychiatry to the threshold of modern concepts and techniques'.

[14] Angus Nicholls and Martin Liebscher (eds.), *Thinking the Unconscious: Nineteenth-Century German Thought* (Cambridge University Press, 2010) is a recent work which brings together essays by Sonu Shamdasani, Paul Bishop, Matthew Bell and others, as an attempt to start to piece together perspectives on the nineteenth-century field.

[15] Slavoj Žižek, *The Indivisible Remainder: An Essay on Schelling and Related Matters* (London: Verso, 1996); Andrew Bowie, *Schelling and Modern European Philosophy* (London: Routledge, 1993).

[16] Žižek, *The Indivisible Remainder*, 9.

[17] Žižek wrote a major interpretive essay to accompany the first translation of Schelling's 1813 draft of *Ages of the World* (Slavoj Žižek/F. W. J. von Schelling, *The Abyss of Freedom/Ages of the World*, trans. Judith Norman, Ann Arbor: The University of Michigan Press, 1997) (hereafter, Schelling, *Ages*) and since then there have been a spate of publications fostering dialogue between the work of Schelling and that of Freud, Lacan and also Heidegger, Deleuze and Levinas, and between Romantic philosophy and postmodern theories of the subject. See, for instance, Judith Norman and Alistair Welchman (eds.), *The New Schelling* (London and New York: Continuum, 2004), and Jason M. Wirth (ed.), *Schelling Now: Contemporary Readings* (Bloomington, IN: Indiana University Press, 2005).

Faflak's *Romantic Psychoanalysis* has advanced similar theoretical arguments, this time drawing on the work of British Romantic writers such as Wordsworth, Coleridge and De Quincey.[18]

There are, however, a number of reasons why such works are not particularly helpful to this investigation. One is that the idea of psychoanalysis which they seek to identify in the works of Romantic authors is not so much Freud's, but Freud read through the lens of Lacanian and postmodern continental theory. (For Bowie, psychoanalysis is one out of many areas of modern theory in relation to which he is keen to establish Schelling as a foundational thinker – others include deconstruction, Marxism and the postmodernism of Richard Rorty.) This is not just a dispute over the roots of psychoanalysis – 'Lacan versus Freud'. The problem is rather that psychoanalysis is assimilated too directly to the terms of the European philosophy of the subject. It is frequently a question of mapping post-Lacanian theory on to an older idealist and post-idealist philosophy (by which it had already been informed via figures such as Alexandre Koyré and Alexandre Kojève) rather than investigating the way in which proto-psychoanalytic concepts themselves emerge in the early nineteenth century, and what their original implications were. Faflak's *Romantic Psychoanalysis* is an intricate and thoughtful study, thoroughly immersed in the task of unearthing the relevance of Romantic forms of psychological and aesthetic reflection for contemporary debates on the 'fragility' or structural elusiveness of subjectivity. However, he uses the term 'psychoanalysis' in the wider sense given it by the philosophers and literary critics of deconstruction, for whom it means submitting the grounds of subjectivity to a process of infinite inquiry. Such analyses are in turn directed towards establishing the historical groundlessness of subjectivity, or an 'interiority inconsistent with itself'.[19] What is at stake in such texts, then, is really an argument about the postmodern 'de-centred subject', and a (plausible) attempt to locate certain anticipations of this debate within Romanticism. Likewise Žižek and Bowie equate the terms and structures of Romantic philosophy directly with those of contemporary theory. But in making the connection between psychoanalysis and German idealism, such works are not primarily pursuing the genealogy of psychoanalytic concepts at all. What is missing is a concern with how and why the terminology of the unconscious psyche emerges in this Romantic context in the first place.

---

[18] See Joel Faflak, *Romantic Psychoanalysis: The Burden of the Mystery* (Albany, NY: State University of New York Press, 2008).
[19] Ibid., 13.

Where does it emerge from, and how and why does it begin to function so centrally within psychological theory?[20]

A second problem is that such works tend to deal with psycho-theoretical questions in a way that abstracts them from frameworks of historical enquiry, beyond the bare essentials of descriptive contextualisation. This means that they fail to incorporate a dynamic and critical sense of the shifting cultural connotations of such crucial terms as 'psyche', 'personal identity', 'spirit' and 'individual existence', over the course of one or two centuries, likewise the striking shift in assumptions about the nature of 'self-consciousness', 'independence', 'individuality' itself, and so on. They fail, that is, to give an adequate representation of the ideological pressures which, over time, have pulled the 'unconscious' and the 'psyche', one way or another, into different signifying contexts which fundamentally change their meaning. Positioning Schelling's work in relation to Kant, Žižek is nonetheless keen to read Schelling's work radically out of context as exhibiting a 'double non-contemporaneity to his own time'.[21] But though formal accounts of the structure of psychic and subjective life may beg to be read philosophically and trans-historically, there are serious problems with such an approach. Do terms such as 'subjectivity' and 'psyche' mean the same things in the nineteenth, twentieth and now twenty-first centuries? What would 'metapsychology' have meant for Schelling, and could he ever have intended it in the Freudian sense?

By abstracting such concepts from wider debates in nineteenth-century psychology, anthropology, political theory, religion and from metaphysics, or from cultural and aesthetic theory, one loses crucial interpretive factors. What is really being argued through the notion of an unconscious? What issues are thinkers attempting to resolve as they reorganise their theory of mind? It may be that cultural and socio-political factors are crucial in accounting for the way the notion of a psychic unconscious moves centre-stage at this point in time, casting its shadow back over the Age of Reason. When Žižek describes Schelling's ideas as emerging in a brief flash, which 'renders visible something that was invisible beforehand and withdrew into invisibility thereafter',[22] he may

---

[20] Faflak is most concerned not with psychology at all, but with the 'poetics of psychoanalysis', meaning these broader questions of identity linked to post-structuralist philosophies of the subject. He argues that these trends are implicitly there in Freud, though repressed beneath 'his confirmed scientism', *Romantic Psychoanalysis*, 14.

[21] Žižek, *The Indivisible Remainder*, 8.

[22] Ibid., 8.

be suggesting that the historical emergence of new concepts must itself sometimes be modelled on the obscure and unknowable irruptions of the unconscious itself, but such an assumption forecloses any attempt to give the unconscious itself a history.

The broader unconscious

In wanting thus to recognise how concepts of the psyche and the unconscious function in more general currents of intellectual and cultural history in the early nineteenth century, I am not aiming simply to temper contemporary perspectives with a more sensitive reconstruction of the past. Rather my concern is that the angle of vision has been much too narrow. The study of the unconscious – which Buchholz and Gödde have termed the '*Zentralmassiv* of psychoanalysis'[23] – requires to be opened up, vastly, before we can begin to make sense of such issues as the emergence of a strictly 'psychoanalytic' unconscious and the rationale for its appearance in modernity. We need to look beyond the Freudian and Jungian paradigms, let alone the Lacanian or Derridean, to the outlines of a broader nineteenth-century interest in the unconscious for which there is no single logic and no single history. The unconscious we associate with psychoanalysis – and which remains one of the most fundamental concepts in contemporary psycho-dynamic theory, of whatever persuasion – is a fragment of a much larger puzzle. By the end of the century, it had in fact become so ubiquitous a concept that the question is not so much 'did Freud inherit the unconscious from earlier in the century', but which versions of it did he inherit?

Already in the late eighteenth century there emerged notions of a life force which governs the organic and developmental functions of the body – described by Herder as 'the inner genius of my being'[24] – and which is either entirely distinguished from the soul, or imagined to represent unconscious capacities within it. As the nineteenth century advances, such ideas are partly translated into the discourse of an 'unconscious', an example being the writings of Carl Gustav Carus, whom C. G. Jung cited as a forerunner to his own work. Besides such vitalist ideas there is the Romantic medical and philosophical interest in the phenomena of mesmerism and somnambulism, documented by

---

[23] Michael B. Buchholz and Günter Gödde (eds.), *Macht und Dynamik des Unbewussten: Auseinandersetzungen in Philosophie, Medizin und Psychoanalyse*, in the series *Das Unbewusste*, 3 vols. (Gießen: Psychosozial-Verlag, 2005), 11.

[24] Johann Gottfried Herder, cited in Stefan Goldmann, 'Von der "Lebenskraft" zum "Unbewussten"', in Buchholz and Gödde, *Macht und Dynamik*, 127.

Ellenberger and others, and connected with this are various attempts to theorise the different unconscious forces, functions and powers governing trance and hypnoid states reported in the burgeoning literature on psychopathology. On a different front there are philosophical debates running throughout the century, from the immediate post-Kantians to figures such as J. S. Mill and later Franz Brentano, which are concerned to establish the limits of reason, or to argue for or against the possibility of unconscious ideas. Yet another avatar of the unconscious, which increases its hold as one moves through the century, is the evocation of the buried past of the mind, to which we could add a broader sense of the unconscious as the primeval, the inherited, or the deep historical past. Also of great importance to any survey of the nineteenth-century unconscious is Schopenhauer's more metaphysical portrait of nature as a vast organism with its own unconscious will, which was further developed in the light of evolutionary theory by Eduard von Hartmann in his *Philosophy of the Unconscious* which ran to eleven German editions between 1868 and 1904 and was first translated into English in 1884.[25] Another crucial tributary of the concept is Johann Friedrich Herbart's descriptions of the way ideas in the mind are thrust above or below the threshold of mental perception according to particular degrees of mental force – notions which fed through into Gustav Fechner's psychophysical investigations of the 1850s. Both of these writers influenced some of Freud's earliest ideas on repression in terms of the vicissitudes of quantities of psychical energy. Somewhere we must also take into account Romantic theories of genius and creativity as emanations of unconscious life, as well as such poetical and spiritual descriptions of the unconscious as 'the darkness in which the roots of our being disappears, the insoluble secret in which rests the magic of life'.[26]

Many of these languages of the unconscious tend towards the overtly religious or metaphysical – at times the unconscious signals nothing less than the immanent and mysterious power of a divine creator, or of 'nature' or the 'absolute' which come to stand in for this in only partly secularised ways. But equally, and from early on in the century, the unconscious is used in a more limited and empirical way to indicate automatic functions such as reflexes. Further into the Victorian period, neurological and physiological usages emerge, such as 'unconscious cerebration', and finally from the 1880s onwards there are the new psychiatric and psychological coinages emerging in the work of

[25] Eduard von Hartmann, *Philosophy of the Unconscious*, trans. William Chatterton Coupland (London: Kegan Paul, Trench, Trubner, 1931).
[26] Friedrich Schlegel, cited in Buchholz and Gödde, *Macht und Dynamik*, 105.

Pierre Janet, F. W. H. Myers and others, including the subconscious, the subliminal, and the dissociated aspects of the self.[27]

Attempts to trace the impact of these instances of the unconscious through to Freud and to Jung have been necessarily piecemeal. Jung openly acknowledged his debt to many of these precursors, particularly the work of Schelling, Schopenhauer, Nietzsche and Carus. But there are also obvious traces in Freud's writings of the legacy of mesmerism and psychophysics, Romantic literature and the philosophy of nature. As Buchholz and Gödde argue, 'Freud was in no way prepared to content himself with a clinical psychology. The claims of his metapsychology aim far beyond that and lay claim to a terrain that had been traditionally leased to theology and philosophy'.[28]

A complete understanding of the rationale for the development of the unconscious in the nineteenth century would require nothing less than a cultural history of the nineteenth century itself, and a sensitivity not only to 'influences' of various generations of thinkers on each other, but also to confluences between radically different yet cognate terms, and various permutations and infiltrations across disciplinary fields. This would hardly amount to a 'tradition' – certainly, nothing so clear as a tradition linking Freud to the Romantics. Such a study could at most sketch the evolution of a set of ideas and problems, linked to a term distributed across quite far-flung contexts. The unconscious pervades psychiatry, medicine and psychology, but also philosophy, religion and metaphysics and theories of nature and history, as well as more popular psychological and cultural elaborations in novels, poems and moral essays, in such a way that one can hardly begin to describe its 'specific' provenance. Did Freud imbibe the term in a medical context, or from student discussions of Nietzsche or Schopenhauer, from his interests in myth and Victorian anthropology, or even from youthful readings in Jean-Paul Richter, E. T. A. Hoffmann and Ludwig Börne.[29]

For these reasons, this book is not so directly concerned with tracking a specific 'line of influence' from Schelling to Freud. But why, then, turn to intellectual shifts in Germany in the early 1800s? What specifically can be found there to inform us of what is going on later in the century? My conviction is that there is something instructive about

---

[27] For details of Janet's work on the subconscious and dissociation, see Ellenberger, *Discovery*, 331–417; for subliminal consciousness, see F. W. H. Myers, 'The Subliminal Consciousness', *Proceedings of the Society for Psychical Research*, 7 (February 1892), 289–355.

[28] Buchholz und Gödde, *Macht und Dynamik*, 18.

[29] See Freud's brief 'A Note on the Prehistory of the Technique of Analysis', *SE*, vol. XVIII, 265.

examining the inception of a concern with the unconscious. It is true that one can trace instances of this concern back indefinitely, and certainly late eighteenth-century thinkers interested in an unconscious were aware of certain specific precursors – most obviously Leibniz's notion of *petites perceptions*, the mass of smaller details which go to make up the quality of more general sense perceptions, but of which, taken individually, we may be unconscious. However, something happens in the early nineteenth century which introduces some dramatic changes to the way in which such a discourse of the unconscious functions. Its usage and usefulness is greatly expanded – many of the different versions of the unconscious listed above are already in operation in this early phase, as subsequent chapters will show. The term is also already tied to a new interest in the psyche and starts to take on a quite novel central role within psychological, philosophical and metaphysical argument about the nature and development of subjective identity. From having been a side issue, the unconscious becomes a fulcrum for certain tendencies within the natural and human sciences, and Friedrich Schelling is central to this development.

Certain things are also apparent in the early 1800s that will be harder to make out one hundred years on, partly because by then, even though it remains a highly contested idea in some fields, aspects of the unconscious (conceptually, ideologically and metaphorically) will have become part of the general background of late Victorian cultural and scientific understanding. By going back to the beginning of the century it is possible not only to trace more clearly the logic by which philosophical and psychological notions of the unconscious emerge and begin to interact, but also to learn from informative debates on the necessity of the unconscious as a core principle for the human sciences, and even more particularly in psychology. In examining such arguments, we can see that the unconscious is not just implicated in psychology insofar as psychology becomes interested in acknowledging and investigating phenomena on or beyond the fringe of consciousness – such as dreaming and madness. Right from the start, an unconscious within the individual is central to psychology for additional reasons, one of which is the role it plays in enabling philosophers and psychologists to conceive of autonomy, spontaneity, creativity or self-development within individuals. Here Zaretsky's insight that Freud 'gave expression to possibilities of individuality, autonomy, authenticity and freedom that had only recently emerged' is perhaps crucial.[30] Where Zaretsky is at fault, though, is in his timing which places the emergence of these concerns

---

[30] Zaretsky, *Secrets of the Soul*, 7.

in what he calls the second industrial revolution, 'roughly 1880s to 1920s'.[31] Although many individuals may only have gained practical experience of certain freedoms towards the end of the nineteenth century, the idea of those freedoms had been elaborated long before this in writings of the Romantic period.

I should emphasise here that, though I am making Schelling central to this investigation of the emergence of the idea of the unconscious, and of the moulding of this unconscious into forms which will be incorporated into an emergent Romantic psychology, Schelling would not have perceived himself as a 'psychologist', or have wanted to carve out a philosophical role for psychology in the modern sense.[32] He was, however, concerned to centralise the role of the 'psyche' – as opposed to 'consciousness' or 'reason' – within a new ontology of the self, to the extent that some of his works develop a philosophy of the unconscious psyche. For this reason, and particularly in this period, it is important not to determine the boundaries of 'psychology' too exclusively, or to limit its meaning either to later notions of an experimental science, or to earlier ones which specifically announce themselves as 'psychologies'.[33] As we shall see, philosophical and psychological constructs were constantly impinging on each other, influencing each other's attempts to materialise the constitution of inner life. This is particularly the case where increased attention to the unconscious is concerned.

Methodological problems

If one accepts that an investigation into the development of Romantic and idealist concepts of the unconscious psyche will provide an extremely valuable framework for understanding the later emergence of psychoanalysis and its success within the human sciences, as well as locating these in relation to wider movements in European thought and culture, the task still poses some very particular difficulties for the historian of ideas.

First of all, as noted, the term 'unconscious' has a propensity to slip away as a coherent object for historical analysis, because of its diffusion

---

[31] Ibid., 5.
[32] See, for instance, Bell, *The German Tradition of Psychology*, 163.
[33] On the pitfalls of limiting the definition of the psychological in historical work, see Thomas Dixon, *From Passions to Emotions: the Creation of a Secular Psychological Category* (Cambridge University Press, 2003), 6–25: 'An historian of psychology who approaches the past looking for thinkers and thoughts that closely resemble present-day academic psychologists and their theories (in other words, looking for narrowly defined "precursors") will tend to overlook the rich variety of psychological discourses that have been produced in past eras, and which have (positively and negatively) shaped subsequent ideas', 24.

across a wide number of discursive contexts. The notion of an 'unconscious' was articulated, extended and correlated, this way and that, between philosophy, psychology, natural history, spiritualism and literature throughout the nineteenth century before it became more restrictively associated with the new science of psychoanalysis. Thus any attempt to stabilise its history within a particular institutional or cultural domain is bound to tell only a small portion of the story.

Secondly, there is the particular difficulty in historicising concepts of mind per se. It is one thing to deal with the broader repercussions of action in politics and society, where questions of internal motives can be relegated to the position of secondary and speculative features of a historical account. But it is another to deal with the 'ego', the 'soul' or the 'I' as themselves historical constructs. Can these, to mirror Freud's question in the *New Introductory Lectures*, be made into the object of an investigation?[34] Can they be extracted as historical objects, even if one is assured of their shifting historical definitions? How does one historicise or even locate the interchanges between modes of lived self-perception and, for instance, the broader transformations of religious and scientific languages?

Thirdly, there are still major obstacles to the interpretation of German idealism within the framework of materialism and empiricism which has so dominated Anglo-American intellectual history. Many aspects of the German conceptual terrain appear radically alien from the other side of this interpretive rift, and it is quite common for historians of mind, or of psychology, who are happy to attend to aspects of Kant and Schopenhauer's thought, to steer carefully around philosophers such as Schelling and Fichte because of the difficulties of reconstructing their assumptions. Work by Frederick Beiser, Terry Pinkard and Karl Ameriks has begun to rectify this situation to some extent as regards philosophy, but little impact has been made as yet on the historiography of psychology. Graham Richards in his survey of psychological ideas from 1600 to 1850 squeezes an allusion to German idealism from Fichte to Hegel into a half-paragraph, though he is able to devote much more space to the empiricist responses to Kant of Fries, Herbart and Beneke.[35] Edward S. Reed investigates the Romantic assumptions of the Shelleys, but makes only a few scant references to the idealists and the German Romantic *Naturphilosophen*.[36] This, despite the fact that

---

[34] Freud, *SE*, vol. XX, 58.

[35] Graham Richards, *Mental Machinery: the Origins and Consequences of Psychological Ideas, 1600–1850* (Baltimore, MD: Johns Hopkins University Press, 1992), 298.

[36] Edward S. Reed, *From Soul to Mind: the Emergence of Psychology from Erasmus Darwin to William James* (New Haven, CT: Yale University Press, 1997). Michel Henry's *The*

Schelling exerted a very broad influence over the continental development of natural and biological science and psychology in the first half of the nineteenth century, as well as on the post-Romantic concept of the imagination and, as I will argue, the psychic unconscious. For Stefan Goldman it is Schelling in 1800 who uses the term 'unconscious' as a substantive for the first time, in the context of his analysis of the unconscious conditions of self-consciousness and the sources of art.[37]

Fourthly, there are difficulties in establishing a neutral set of reference points for such an enquiry, given the complex ideological conflicts waged over languages of mind even now, in which the various schools of psychoanalysis are themselves vociferous protagonists. As Irma Gleiss argues, 'the psychoanalytic movement has taken great pains to marginalise its Romantic companions – for instance, C. G. Jung and Georg Groddeck'.[38] Psychoanalysis already has various internal narratives concerning the historical inception of psychoanalytic structures – including those outlined by Freud in *Totem and Taboo*, *Civilization and Its Discontents* and *Beyond the Pleasure Principle* – which generally identify this inception with distant moments in cultural, if not species, prehistory. Leaving these aside, there is the fiercely guarded tendency, already noted, to associate the prehistory of psychoanalytic concepts with the prehistory of Freud's own career leading up to the publication of *The Interpretation of Dreams*. At one extreme, there are those studies which equate the emergence of psychoanalysis entirely with the process of Freud's own self-analysis and investigation of his dream life (for instance by Anzieu and Grinstein).[39] In looking beyond Freud for the beginnings of nineteenth-century interest in a psychical unconscious, one is moving somewhat critically against the tide. Historical investigations which seek to establish alternative contexts for the emergence of psychoanalytic structures cannot help but present themselves, in some way, as acts of delegitimation. Frank J. Sulloway's *Freud: Biologist of*

Genealogy of Psychoanalysis (Stanford University Press, 1993) also leaps from Kant to Schopenhauer, and emphasises a lineage from Descartes to Husserl, bypassing German Romanticism.

[37] Goldmann, 'Von der "Lebenskraft" zum "Unbewussten"', in Buchholz and Gödde, *Macht und Dynamik*, 138. See also Klaus Doerner, *Madmen and the Bourgeoisie: A Social History of Insanity and Psychiatry*, trans. Joachim Neugroschel and Jean Steinberg (Oxford: Basil Blackwell, 1991), 234–5 for an account of Schelling's dominating influence over mid-century academic psychiatry.

[38] Irma Gleiss, 'Der romantische Weg in die Tiefe', in Buchholz and Gödde, *Macht und Dynamik*, 95.

[39] Didier Anzieu, *Freud's Self-Analysis*, trans. Peter Graham (Madison, CT: International Universities Press, 1986); Alexander Grinstein, *Sigmund Freud's Dreams* (New York: International Universities Press, 1980).

the Mind, for instance, bears the subtitle 'Beyond the Psychoanalytic Legend'.[40]

One major exception to the occlusion of Romantic and idealist contributions to psychoanalytic concepts, within psychoanalytic historiography, must be made for Henri Ellenberger's landmark volume on the *Discovery of the Unconscious*, which is still unsurpassed in its historical range and the multiplicity of perspectives it sheds on the emergence of what he identifies as 'dynamic psychiatry' or 'dynamic psychotherapy'. That book traces the origins of such dynamic theories of mental life 'through a long line of ancestors and forerunners', going all the way back to the eighteenth century, where Ellenberger pursues the fortunes of the mesmerist movement into Germany and thus into transformative contact with Romantic philosophy. He provides brief accounts of the psychological theories of Schelling, G. H. Schubert and C. G. Carus, as well as comparisons with the framework of Freudian metapsychology.[41] However, Ellenberger is examining a particular aspect of the psychoanalytic phenomenon – 'the mystery of the mechanism of psychological healing' from exorcism to hypnotism to talking cure. He investigates why 'certain patients respond to a certain type of cure while others do not', a phenomenon 'of great theoretical importance to the study of psychiatry as the basis of a new science of comparative psychotherapy'.[42] In this case, approaching the 'problem' of the psyche means being able to set the therapeutic claims of psychoanalysis in a wider framework of historically identifiable practices, including mesmerism, hypnotism and Romantic psychiatry. But in focusing on the history of therapy, he gave less attention to the history of conceptual developments around the ego, the psyche and the unconscious – concerns which only partly overlap with his own.

All these hindrances to study – the diffuse application of the concept of an unconscious; the difficulty of historicising concepts of mind; paradigmatic confusion over the terms of German idealism; and the resistance of psychoanalysis to its historicisation – have in one way or another impaired historians' ability to assess the significance of the intersection between theories of the unconscious and theories of the psyche in the early nineteenth century, or of the links running forwards to new accounts of individuality and interiority in modernity. With this in mind, the object of this study is simply to establish a more developed understanding of the relationship between the terms of psychoanalysis

---

[40] Frank J. Sulloway, *Freud, Biologist of the Mind: Beyond the Psychoanalytic Legend* (New York: Basic Books, 1979).

[41] See particularly Ellenberger, *Discovery*, 202–8.

[42] Ibid., 3.

and their historical inception in the context of post-Kantian idealism and Romanticism. But it is also my belief that broadening the framework for thinking about the emergence of the psychic unconscious does more than enable one merely to uncover further historical reaches of Freud or Jung's cultural inheritance. These contexts reveal unrecognised historical implications of the psychoanalytic project itself. That is, by disturbing the roots of psychoanalytic historiography we can allow new perspectives and wholly new questions to emerge. In this light I want to consider two major theoretical studies which *have* situated the unconscious in just such a way – not in relation to medical positivism in *fin de siècle* Vienna, but to a nexus of issues emerging at the beginning of the century. One of these works establishes a genealogical relation between Freudian psychoanalysis and German idealism, the other relates the unconscious – as theoretical object of psychoanalysis – to a paradigmatic upheaval at the end of the eighteenth century that gave birth to the modern human sciences. In both cases this greater temporal reach makes the unconscious diagnostically central within a broader account of modern culture and its distinctive ideological transformations.

Marquard

The first text is Odo Marquard's highly original and provocative study, *Transzendentaler Idealismus, Romantische Naturphilosophie, Psychoanalyse*, which, though now twenty years old, has yet had little impact on historical research on psychology in the Anglo-American world.[43] The book is concerned with the philosophical genealogy linking psychoanalysis to the project of German idealism – as Marquard puts it, 'The point was to show that certain elements of psychoanalysis were actually "philosophical" ones'.[44] He begins with a description of how Kant's transcendental philosophy was drawn towards the terrain of aesthetics in *The Critique of Judgement* in an attempt to reconcile the structure of rational thought, as Kant conceived it, with the idea of human freedom. In Marquard's reading, the path taken by philosophy at this juncture led in a particularly unpromising direction – towards a decline or enchantment of the Enlightenment commitment to self-awareness and political self-determination. Marquard suggests, in

---

[43] Odo Marquard, *Transzendentaler Idealismus, Romantische Naturphilosophie, Psychoanalyse* (Cologne: Jurgen Dinter, 1987). An exception to this neglect is Shamdasani's *Jung and the Making of Modern Psychology*.
[44] Ibid., 2.

part, that the turn to aesthetics, in order to theorise a model for the spontaneous operation of judgement, disengaged thinking and acting from the terrain of social and political conflict in which the nature of freedom – and the possibility of its historical production – is ultimately to be defined. There was, as it were, a dangerous hiving-off of the enquiry into subjective freedom from historical and social contexts within which such questions are immediately implicated, and, at the same time, the substitution of a more illusory and gratifying terrain for study (that of aesthetic consumption). On the other hand (and it is this development with which Marquard is particularly concerned) Kant's allied attempt to speculate on the teleological structure of nature as an organic whole threatened to bolster the transcendental account of human freedom in another way. The danger for the Enlightenment project was that it would illicitly substantiate an account of human potential – potential freedom and potential harmony – by giving it a speculative basis in 'nature', at the very same time as these ideals were failing to materialise in human history. For all its seeming concreteness and 'materiality', the turn to a philosophy of nature was in danger of shoring up a grand metaphysical illusion. Marquard's target is not so much Kant himself as the propensity, in post-Kantian philosophy, for transcendental projections of the structures underlying human experience to be formulated as an aesthetics, and for such aesthetic theories to embed themselves in speculative theories of natural history: 'Where historical reason has become "transcendental", that is, indeterminate as to its goal and means ... the hope emerges that nature will replace that which is failing.'[45]

It is this tendency in the development of German thought to 'transport the political definition of history, into a definition of history split off from the political' which particularly arouses Marquard's critical concern.[46] A similar analysis is made of Schiller's *Letters on Aesthetic Education*: they 'break off without having resolved the dilemma posed between beauty and the political'. Marquard sees this as symptomatic of a political resignation so decisive that the dilemma can only be forgotten. In Schiller's later *On Naive and Sentimental Poetry*, the role of the artist is solicited 'no longer in relation to history and the state, but in its relation to "*Natur*"'.[47]

But how does this relate to the history of psychology? These are the first steps in Marquard's complex narrative about ideology in early nineteenth-century Germany which shows German philosophy

---

[45] Ibid., 155.   [46] Ibid., 155.   [47] Ibid., 150.

shifting its engagement with cosmopolitan political history towards a concern with transcendental aesthetics, and then on to theories of nature and natural teleology. The second stage in the argument explores the consequent flourishing of a Romantic philosophy of nature – Marquard has Schelling and his disciples primarily in mind – which develops a metaphysical account of the unconscious grounds of human life in nature as a counterweight to the instabilities originally diagnosed in history and politics. Again, he reads this further 'falling away from the historico-political framework towards nature' as an affliction born of historical pessimism: 'Where the transcendental philosophy fails to ground the historical hopes of humanity, historico-philosophically, on political reason, the attempt of natural philosophy forces them to be grounded on the unconscious grounds of "nature".'[48] Translated into natural-historical, rather than political-historical terms, transcendental philosophy – its theory of man, of subjectivity and of human freedom – is elaborated in the early 1800s in terms of unconscious grounds and 'unknown history'. That is to say, this subjectivity and this freedom are thought to exist as a potential, and this potential is elicited via speculative constructions of the natural history thought to precede it. Human freedom is something continually evolving out of its origins in nature. Their muse is 'a Mnemosyne who no longer recollects history but rather prehistory'. Ironically, for the generation writing in the first quarter of the nineteenth century, the philosophy of development now 'becomes predominantly a philosophy of the past'.[49]

The final step in Marquard's argument is that psychoanalysis is simply a modification of the methods of thinking originally adopted by transcendental philosophy and then transformed into such a philosophy of nature: 'One could say that psychoanalysis is a disenchanted Romantic *Naturphilosophie*, that's why it thinks in the manner of this *Naturphilosophie*.'[50] In support, he provides a list of various conceptual features the two ideologies hold in common, for instance, the turn from mind to 'nature', the stress on recollection and clarifying the prehistory of the ego, as well as the project of consciously retrieving unconscious histories. He suggests that the relationship between the two periods has remained unnoticed largely for the reason that Schelling's writings are no longer read.

Marquard's account of the emergence of such terms as 'repression' and 'unconscious nature', and his identification of their ideological

[48] Ibid., 156.   [49] Ibid., 158.   [50] Ibid., 163.

function in this early nineteenth-century context, is penetrating and persuasive and adds immensely to our perception of the relationship between psychoanalysis and its prehistory within other disciplinary fields. However, from the point of view of a history of psychology, his final negative judgement on that set of ideological transformations is distorted. His work becomes a polemic directed by philosophy against the emergence of nineteenth-century anthropology and psychology. In his reading, psychoanalysis is a final symptom of transcendental philosophy's falling away (implicitly through lack of critical nerve) from an engagement with political reason. For Marquard, psycho-analytic psychology is shot through with appeals to historical experi-ence – to the past, to recollection, to unconscious grounds – which function culturally as a way of displacing conscious historical experi-ence (social and political) into these speculatively constructed and somewhat mythical unconscious dimensions of human life. But what from Marquard's standpoint of 'political reason' appears as a narrative of *Verfall*, might be recast, from an alternative disciplinary perspec-tive, as a narrative about the emergence of new sciences of human life and experience. For surely, what he is charting, without ever acknow-ledging it in such terms, is also the emergence of a more empirical and secular psychology, which draws on medicine and philosophy as well as aesthetics and new theories of organic nature in order to develop an account of human being adequate to the post-Enlightenment age. What happens when such a narrative is retold from the perspective of a history of psychology, as a discipline which, rather than merely per-verting the course of political philosophy, is seeking its own new foun-dations by transforming the moral and spiritual languages of body, soul and mind?

Foucault

The second work to situate psychoanalysis in relation to the idealist period is Michel Foucault's *The Order of Things*, which gives the 'uncon-scious' a special role within Foucault's account of an 'epistemic shift' in modernity.[51] The middle section of this work sketches a portrait of the classical period (i.e. the seventeenth and eighteenth centuries) in which knowledge was perfectly homogenous: 'All knowledge, of what-ever kind, proceeded to the ordering of its material by the establishment of differences and defined those differences by the establishment of an

[51] Michel Foucault, *The Order of Things: an Archaeology of the Human Sciences* (London: Tavistock, 1980).

order.'[52] The field of knowledge – its reflection of the 'order of things' in the world – was co-extensive with certain practices of representation inherent in the production of taxonomies, tables and systems of classification. According to Foucault, there was as yet no sense of a 'gap' between the power to arrange and connect such systems and notions of the structure of the world itself, nor of the constructive input of humankind as the agent of such organised knowledge. But at the end of the eighteenth century, the argument runs, this efficiently functioning paradigm broke down. Questions were raised about the origin of representation as a specific form of thinking, and representation itself lost 'the power to provide a foundation ... for the links that can join its various elements together'.[53] At the same time, 'man', the newly perceived agent of knowledge, became the object of a new kind of investigation – that of the 'human sciences'. These sought to replace 'representation' with a set of more foundational principles, derived from examination of the productive activities of human life itself: 'on the horizon of any human science there is the project of bringing man's consciousness back to its real conditions.'[54]

To some extent Kant is again the major exemplum of this epistemological turn. His *Critique of Pure Reason* 'sanctions for the first time ... the withdrawal of knowledge and thought outside the space of representation'.[55] But, as a result, a problematic duality is installed within the human sciences at their very inception. On the one hand, they have as their object the life, histories and cultures of empirical human beings; but on the other hand, because human life is now to provide a basis for the theory of knowledge in general, human experience becomes the focus of a new kind of foundational project, to be pursued beneath and beyond the merely empirical and descriptive investigations of human culture and history. The connective power which had, in the classical epoch, been attributed to representation itself, must now be sought 'outside representation, beyond its immediate visibility, in a sort of behind-the-scenes world even deeper and more dense than representation itself'.[56] Seen in this way, the emergence of the 'problem of the unconscious', for Foucault, is not a contingent theoretical issue that happens to appear in the nineteenth century; rather it is 'ultimately coextensive' with the very existence of the human sciences and is the shadow cast by the human sciences themselves.[57]

Foucault's interest in the unconscious centres on the ways in which society, emerging self-consciously as itself the agent of representation,

---

[52] Ibid., 346. [53] Ibid., 238–9. [54] Ibid., 364.
[55] Ibid., 242. [56] Ibid., 239. [57] Ibid., 364.

attempted to establish a hypothetical relationship to the deeper or foundational basis of its own practice, whether this was viewed in logical, historical or evolutionary terms. But this means that the unconscious indicates a very diverse set of ideological phenomena. At some points Foucault seems to use it as shorthand for the whole project of German idealism itself – 'A transcendental raising of level that is, on the other side, an unveiling of the non-conscious is constitutive of all the sciences of man'.[58] At other points, his concern is with those aspects of human phenomena which escape the rationalising drive for self-consciousness of a cogito. It represents the 'unthought' aspects of human life and production. In yet other moments, Foucault alludes to the attempt to ground human existence through the intellectual recovery of distant historical origins. Foucault assimilates all these different versions of the unconscious to a single principle which forms a powerful undertow within his account of the nineteenth century as a whole. Psychoanalysis, in this story, is the point at the threshold of the twentieth century where the necessary relation between the human sciences and an 'unconscious' breaks out into the open as a named theoretical object, just as in Foucault's earlier scheme of the eighteenth century 'representation' became a conscious issue for the nineteenth century. The twentieth century becomes conscious of the unconscious – which is not the same as saying that the unconscious is dissolved. Rather, it appears for the first time: 'Whereas all the human sciences advance towards the unconscious only with their back to it ... psychoanalysis points directly towards it, with a deliberate purpose ... towards what is there and yet is hidden.'[59] Psychoanalysis sets itself the task of 'making the discourse of the unconscious speak through consciousness'.

This account of the emergence of the unconscious raises some intriguing questions. For a start, it sheds some light on Foucault's own implicit methodological assumptions – namely, that intellectual phenomena in the nineteenth century are being re-read through the lens of French structuralist debates in the 1950s and 1960s. The unconscious which the human sciences struggle towards is revealed (in the light of the work of Saussure and Levi-Strauss) as being the inferred prior system of signification underlying discursive performance: 'the system is indeed always unconscious since it was there before the signification, since it is within it that the signification resides and on the basis of it that it becomes effective.'[60] But if the unconscious is something that is everywhere implicit in the nineteenth century, but emerges into consciousness in the twentieth (and becomes clearer still in the

[58] Ibid., 364.   [59] Ibid., 374.   [60] Ibid., 362.

1950s), then what do we make of the emergence of the 'psyche' and the 'unconscious' at the *beginning* of the epoch under review? What of the contribution of figures such as Schelling who, taking up and transforming Kant's transcendental concerns, was already altering the notion of epistemology to incorporate an explicit principle of unconsciousness? And what of Carus' mid-century assertion that 'The key to an understanding of the nature of the conscious life of the soul lies in the sphere of the unconscious'?[61]

What is missing from Foucault's account is first of all a more adequate evocation of the German, as opposed to the French, intellectual context stretching from the mid eighteenth century to the mid nineteenth century (thus developing across the period in which Foucault posits his epistemic break). That context is concerned precisely with such transcendental objects as consciousness, knowledge, structure, groundedness and, eventually, the unconscious and history – the very objects which Odo Marquard examines. One would want, at the least, a more careful depiction of the relationship between the emergence of the human sciences and these already complex speculations on the nature of knowledge and justification. But in fact, beyond Kant, Foucault makes very little reference to the German context. Jürgen Habermas noted the absence of Fichte's *Wissenschaftslehre* in *The Order of Things*, and also suggested Schelling as evidence of a much earlier awareness of human being 'as the remote product of a history ... of which it is not master'.[62]

But there is a second kind of omission in Foucault's account, which one might describe as the moral and political pressures bearing down upon the terms of the discursive shift which he isolates as an autonomous epistemological occurrence. This is of course an intentional product of the structuralist approach which is concerned to abstract and isolate the structures of discourses as agents of their own history – the 'folding over of each separated [epistemological] domain upon its own development', is the way Foucault describes the transitional process.[63] But by concentrating on the emergence of epistemological structures as in some sense free-standing entities, he precludes any investigation of how representation, order, connectedness and grounds were entangled in particular ideological commitments and projections. Early

---

[61] Carl Gustav Carus, *Psyche, On the Development of the Soul. Part One: The Unconscious* (Dallas, TX: Spring Publications, 1970), 1.

[62] Jürgen Habermas, *The Philosophical Discourse of Modernity* (Cambridge: Polity Press, 1990), 262–3. Habermas notes too that Schelling's conception of madness as the other of reason had again been absent from *Madness and Civilisation*.

[63] Foucault, *The Order of Things*, 369.

nineteenth-century debates about the 'order of things' inherit not only the mantle of an epistemological crisis, but also an ontological mission linked to concrete moral and political claims. The formative debates of idealism and Romanticism occurred during the period of the French Revolution; their convictions were tested, in Germany, by the subsequent invasion of German states by Napoleonic forces. Alongside their radical questioning and refounding of epistemological structures, German thinkers explicitly applied themselves to the question of human freedom and to the possibility of describing a human order on grounds finally detached from the heritage of political absolutism. As will emerge in Chapter 1, the task of probing the transcendental origins and coherence of knowledge for a thinker such as Fichte is substantially bound up, first of all, with reaction against a perceived dogmatism or moral slavery in human experience, and secondly with the pursuit of an alternative basis on which to theorise human unity, one which, as with Kant, is to be found within oneself, rather than imposed from above or patterned on the unrationalised conventions of the past.

The liberal unconscious

The first Idea is naturally the notion of *my self* as an absolutely free being.[64]

Both Foucault and Marquard are concerned to make a point about the emergence of modernity. They both bring psychoanalysis back into contact with a period in which the unconscious began to carry a new structural weight in the depiction of individual life, and they redefine the significance of psychoanalysis itself within that broader historical framework. And yet they detach their accounts from what one would think are the most prominent and long-lasting features of ideological shift in this period: the socio-political pressure to overcome the vestiges of feudalism and absolute government; and the revised moral and spiritual vocabularies occasioned by Enlightenment pressure on religious tradition. This book argues that any changes in the way the structure of experience, subjectivity and inner life is theorised at the opening of the nineteenth century must be read in that double context. By doing so, I believe one can gain a new perspective on the foundation of the unconscious, and the unconscious *as* a foundation, which is worked theoretically into the heart of processes affecting the life of the individual.

---

[64] 'Oldest System Programme of German Idealism' [1796], authorship attributed variously to F. W. J. Schelling, G. W. F. Hegel or Friedrich Hölderlin, trans. Andrew Bowie, in Andrew Bowie, *Aesthetics and Subjectivity*, 265.

In particular, this book sets out to demonstrate the close relationship between the invention of a psychic unconscious and the new clamour in the Romantic period for descriptions of an autonomous, self-creating individual, which was to be so significant for later forms of liberal ideology.[65]

The unconscious, insofar as it forms the basis for a new science of the individual mind (in part philosophical and transcendental, in part natural-scientific, in part a form of moral self-description) is prima facie not detachable from nineteenth-century attempts to give an account of autonomy, originality and independence in the individual, or the wider desire to find new languages and new conceptions of human and social order. It is useful to look again at Zaretsky's suggestion that people have drawn on Freudian psychoanalysis in the twentieth century 'to help recast the promise of individual autonomy', which encompasses 'the freedom to think one's own thoughts and to decide for oneself what to do with one's life', and, furthermore, that autonomy is no longer restricted to the sphere of morality but applies as well to 'creativity, love and happiness'.[66] The freedom of thought and the self-direction and creation of one's own life, as well as the idealisation of love, are of course the *leitmotifs* of Romantic philosophical, moral and aesthetic debate. Already in the 1790s, writers in Germany were strenuously pursuing the implications of subjective freedom raised by the Enlightenment, and particularly the ramifications of that idea for personal and psychological life. The core argument of this book is that the increasing interest in an unconscious psyche reflects not simply the attempt to produce an adequate account of the phenomena of interior life, but also a concern with establishing the possibility of a self-caused self, or a self the logic of whose development is irreducibly detached from more systematic forms of explanation, or from the idea of its manipulation by external authorities or other determining causes. Such ideas would have an immense (if contested) appeal, particularly within liberal theories of individuality, and thus at the broadest level this book is concerned with attempts to describe a stable 'basis' to the self in the nineteenth century and beyond, into the domain of psychoanalysis itself.

---

[65] See, for instance, Steven Lukes, *Individualism* (Oxford: Basil Blackwell, 1973), 67, 125: 'the notion of self-development is … typically Romantic in origin' and furthermore represents one of the 'three faces of liberty or freedom'. Likewise Andrew Vincent remarks on the 'fortuitous alliance of Romantic self-choice (*Bildung*) with the traditions of epistemological individualism and classical liberalism' in modernity. Andrew Vincent, 'Liberalism and Postmodernism', in James Meadowcraft (ed.), *The Liberal Political Tradition* (Cheltenham: Edward Elgar, 1996), 142.

[66] Zaretsky, *Secrets of the Soul*, 9.

Many accounts of liberalism, and of an associated concern with the free development of individual life in Western thought, mark a transformation in the culture of individuality effectively at this same point in post-Revolutionary Europe – where freedom and self-development become constellated as part of an emerging vocabulary of self, in reaction against eighteenth-century absolutism and rationalism. Importantly, this shift in the envisaged role of individuality concerns not so much the emergence of political movements (though it has inevitably accompanied them) but the elaboration of a complex set of ideas – moral, metaphysical, ontological – about the qualities of selfhood, which are gradually worked into traditions of broader liberal theory, becoming part of the world view of post-Enlightenment modernity.[67] For John Gray, essential to an understanding of liberalism is an insight into its background in modern European individualism – the conception of ourselves 'as autonomous rational agents and authors of our own values'.[68] These features 'are fully intelligible only in the light of the several crises of modernity' which include the dissolution of the feudal order in Europe and the French and American revolutions at the end of the eighteenth century.[69] Likewise, Charles Taylor finds that 'The ethic of authenticity is something relatively new and peculiar to modern culture', building on earlier concepts of individualism (from Locke or Descartes) but essentially born at the end of the eighteenth century.[70] People 'in the culture of authenticity (who have adopted that ideal)' according to Taylor, 'give support to a certain kind of liberalism'.[71] And again, this individualising freedom – ambivalent, for Taylor, but at least symbolic of modernity – 'was won by our breaking loose from older moral horizons', from the larger hierarchical order, in some cases 'a cosmic order', in which people used to see themselves.[72] Terry Eagleton has associated the emergence of 'bourgeois culture' and the middle class in modernity with a liberal humanism centred on the notion of an 'autonomous human subject'.[73] However ghostly its existence, this autonomous subject is no mere 'metaphysical fantasy' – it remains somehow indispensable to modern culture 'partly because the subject as unique, autonomous, self-identical and self-determining remains a political and ideological

---

[67] See Meadowcraft, *The Liberal Political Tradition*, 1.
[68] John Gray, *Liberalism* (Buckingham: Open University Press, 1995), 50.
[69] Ibid., xi.
[70] Charles Taylor, *The Ethics of Authenticity* (Cambridge, MA: Harvard University Press, 1991), 25.
[71] Ibid., 17.   [72] Ibid., 3.
[73] Terry Eagleton, *The Ideology of the Aesthetic* (Oxford: Basil Blackwell, 1990), 377.

requirement of the system'.[74] Alexis de Tocqueville famously parodied this individualising aspect of the emergence of modern democracy, in which 'people form the habit of thinking of themselves in isolation and imagine that their whole destiny is in their hands', and in which 'each man is forever thrown back on himself alone'.[75] However, this critique is nowadays commonly associated with its inverse, accepted as being part of the ontological core of liberalism, taken in this wider cultural sense, and a key aspect of the modern idea of freedom.

The important thing to note here is not that the nineteenth century sees the birth in Germany of a self-consciously political 'liberal' movement (what liberalising tendencies there are at this point are short-lived and remain tied to strong notions of the state), nor a sudden recognition of the fact of individuality as the self-evident starting point for moral and political forms of self-description (against this, one might consider the tendency for German or later British idealists, such as Bernard Bosanquet or F. H. Bradley, or monists such as Herbert Spencer, to begin with the idea of the state, society, or life in general, as a transcendent spiritual or organic fact). What does appear in the wake of the 'crises' of modernity is an intensification of a conjectural movement towards core notions – freedom, autonomy, vitality, self-development – which are recurrently emphasised in accounts of the self, particularly once such terms become detached from wider idealist and Romantic assumptions about holism and pantheism.[76] One thinks, for instance, of Wilhelm von Humboldt's contention that each person should strive to develop himself 'from his own inmost nature, and for his own sake', or 'by his own energies, in his perfect individuality',[77] which was taken up in J. S. Mill's defence of originality, 'individuality of power', and a person 'whose desires and impulses are his own',[78] and eventually in Hobhouse's belief that 'society can safely be founded on this self-directing power of the personality'.[79] But the

---

[74] Ibid., 374–5.

[75] Alexis de Tocqueville, *Democracy in America* (London: Fontana Press, 1994), 508.

[76] Taylor sums these emphases up in his notion of 'authenticity' or the moral ideal 'of being true to oneself', *The Ethics of Authenticity*, 15; Edward Shils, *The Virtue of Civility: Selected Essays on Liberalism, Tradition and Civil Society*, ed. Steven Grosby (Indianapolis, IN: Liberty Fund, 1997), 158, recognises a list of candidates attracting liberals with a collectivist bent, including 'creative' or 'true individuality' and the 'vital self'. For Lukes, *Individualism*, 125, the core liberal ideas of freedom, in modernity, are 'autonomy, privacy and self-development'.

[77] Wilhelm von Humboldt, *The Limits of State Action* (Indianapolis, IN: Liberty Fund, 1993), 13.

[78] J. S. Mill, 'On Liberty', in Mary Warnock (ed.), *Utilitarianism* (London: Collins, 1962), 186.

[79] L. T. Hobhouse, 'Liberalism', in *Liberalism and Other Writings* (Cambridge University Press, 1994), 59.

coherence or integrity of such conceptions of individuality – pitched ambivalently as they are between a commitment to 'individualism' and the search for a new kind of moral and political order – carries with it a new kind of crisis, which is the intellectual struggle within liberal theory over the security of its own ideological foundations. Partly this insecurity is prompted by the spectre of rampant individualism itself, as Andrew Vincent puts it: 'the bulk of liberal theory might be described as a half-conscious holding operation against the implicit threat of individualism'.[80] Or as Terry Eagleton observed, 'once the bourgeoisie has dismantled the centralising political apparatus of absolutism, either in fantasy or reality', the question arises as to 'where it is to locate a sense of unity powerful enough to reproduce itself by'.[81] Eagleton's presentation of this predicament is very close to Marquard's narrative of the travels of transcendental philosophy from political history to *Natur*, and both shed light on Tocqueville's earlier observation that 'the concept of unity becomes an obsession' in democratic culture, to such an extent that the Germans were 'introducing pantheism into philosophy'.[82] Schelling's own Romantic concern for 'creative life' and the power of 'asserting one's own individuality' is always counterbalanced by a metaphysics of nature as an organic whole, and by the 1830s will have been assimilated to a much more reactionary conception of social order and state authority.[83] He himself can hardly be classed as a liberal thinker.

Theories of liberalism wrestle with a second kind of insecurity, and this concerns more simply how individuality can actually be 'thought', how it can be conceived of and theoretically underpinned without being reabsorbed into overarching ideas of coherence, rational order or the system, but equally without unleashing the threat of fragmentation. Notions of individuality have to be defended not only in relation to the State, but also against the need to argue from universal principles, with little sensitivity for the kind of contingent or 'individual' factors which the demands for private, inward and autonomous development of the self seemed to require. Quite apart from nineteenth-century struggles over politically diverse freedoms such as the extension of the political franchise, the freeing of economic markets, or freedom of the press – all of which involve notions of the 'freedom of the individual' – there is a struggle over the

---

[80] Vincent, 'Liberalism and Postmodernism', 139.
[81] Eagleton, *Ideology of the Aesthetic*, 23.
[82] Tocqueville, *Democracy*, 451.
[83] F. W. J. Schelling, 'On the Relation Between the Plastic Arts and Nature', trans. A. Johnson, *The Philosophy of Art; an Oration on the Relation Between the Plastic Arts and Nature* (London: John Chapman, 1845), 4.

concept of individuality itself. How should one ground the *descriptions* of such self-creating individuals and their moral bases? From the start, the ideologues of liberal freedom were forced to draw on notions of 'constitution' which lay beyond the sphere of practical politics in the realms of art and literature, nature philosophy, metaphysics and psychology.

The unconscious

The unconscious and the psyche are deeply implicated in the constructions of selfhood which emerge from these foundational debates about freedom and individuality. The psychological individual is not suddenly 'revealed' beneath the tattered cloak of religious orthodoxy at the beginning of the nineteenth century as a self-evident empirical framework for understanding mental life. It, too, is implicated in the ideological search for new foundations, which accompanies 'the conception of ourselves as autonomous rational agents and authors of our own values'.[84] Because of this, the unconscious and the psyche are quickly caught up in speculative cross-currents of scientific, aesthetic, moral and political thought, where they are linked in diverse ways to the fortunes of the individual. First of all, they take on a role within psychological description and psychiatric investigation. There are processes within our minds and bodies which seem to operate unconsciously, and there are states of mind (dream, madness, poetic invention) of which we are not wholly consciously in control. The unconscious psyche, in this sense, is something to be reckoned with because it is part of the psychology of the empirical individual, the component unit of liberal theory – and a part, moreover, which stirs anxieties over the liberal belief in the societal role of reason.

Secondly, the unconscious and the psyche also function as tacit forms of holism operating across a community of individuals: there are psychic and unconscious aspects of mind which reveal our groundedness in wider processes of nature, empirically (theories of instinct, for instance) or spiritually and mystically. Once the individual is notionally amputated from the organic body of society,[85] versions of the unconscious start to reconceive that greater organic body in such a way that moral and political anxieties concerning fragmentation are allayed, though without wholly compromising the experience of self-directedness within the individual.

[84] Gray, *Liberalism*, 50.
[85] See Noberto Bobbio's account in *Liberalism and Democracy* (London: Verso, 1990), 43.

Thirdly, the introduction of irrationalism into philosophical models – by Schelling in particular – enables the conceptual altercation between 'freedom' and 'control', 'individuality' and the 'system', to fall out differently. The very notion of system becomes complex, dynamic, organic and in certain ways obscure. The psychic unconscious thus provides boundaries and borders for thinking the consistency of individual life in all sorts of new and different ways. Most importantly, it provides a solution to the problem of thinking independence, spontaneity, particularity, originality and self-authorship against, or alongside, the universal legislation of reason. At the same time, the unconscious is itself in the process of being given an empirical and scientific body, insofar as it is involved in scientific accounts of the self-developing structures of individual life – in nature philosophy, in embryology and biology, and above all in psychology.

The argument

What is proposed here is a way of thematising the origin of modern concepts of the psyche such that they are not detached from this wider set of crises in the understanding of subjective identity at the threshold of the nineteenth century. I will argue for the emergence of an unconscious, and forms of unconsciousness, as a mediator in descriptions of freedom and individuality, and thus indirectly but recurrently in liberal and modern ideas of the self. The persistence of the unconscious as an idea across the epoch is not solely a question of anticipation or regression (Marquard) or untimeliness (Žižek) or the latent structure of an episteme (Foucault). When it appears at the beginning of the nineteenth century, the unconscious is already mediating the problem of self-founding and self-authorship, and it continues, characteristically, to straddle two important aspects of modern liberal identity – belief in a robust and original independence of the self and its powers of self-development, and the attempt to give the individual a universalising moral and ontological basis with which to master fears of socio-political fragmentation. Crucially, the traumatic experience of selfhood explored in the foundational vocabularies of nineteenth-century German psychology and psychiatry, and the more conceptual trauma surrounding the theory of individuality, bear upon each other, constantly and unwittingly, throughout the century.

This study is necessarily interdisciplinary, exploring cross-currents between various philosophical theories of mind, as well as their expressions in literature, anthropology and psychology. Its methodological framework must be flexible enough, in the first place, to allow

propositions from transcendental philosophy – 'The first Idea is naturally the notion of *my self* as an absolutely free being'[86] – to be viewed
alongside the ideals of individuality developed by mainstream liberal
thinkers in the early to mid nineteenth century. This will enable us to
observe how insistence on the 'free development of individuality', coming from both philosophy and political thought, starts to endow this
individual with hidden, inner sources of growth and development, as
evidence of its moral freedom. For liberal philosophy (itself resistant to
the idea of an unconscious, which removes choice from the conscious
individual), these might take the form of 'the inward forces which make
[human nature] a living thing' (Mill),[87] or the development of the 'basal
factors of personality' (Hobhouse),[88] or, as parodied by Bosanquet, the
post-Wordsworthian idea that 'The dim recesses of incommunicable
feeling are the true shrine of our selfhood'.[89] While such political theories of the individual are becoming increasingly interested in hidden
moral or psychological dimensions of the person, psychology – particularly in Germany – is exploring ideas of individuality and autonomy and
working them as principles into psycho-dynamic descriptions of the
mind. Thus for many Romantic and modern theorists of the psyche,
'The unconscious is precisely our ownmost and most genuine nature'
(Carus);[90] the human being is, in the ideal case, 'creator of himself'
(Rank);[91] 'Each of us carries his own life-form within him, an irrational
form which no other can outbid' (Jung).[92]

Such assumptions also converge in early twentieth-century literary
writing. For instance, modernist writers involved in the reception of psychoanalysis in Britain emphasise exactly the same interlinked notions
of individuality, self-development and the unconscious, and draw on
the same complex mixture of psychology, idealism and post-Romantic
moral vocabularies in their descriptions of the self.[93] D. H. Lawrence's

[86] Bowie, *Aesthetics and Subjectivity*, 265.
[87] Mill, 'On liberty', 188.
[88] Hobhouse, 'Liberalism', 63.
[89] Bernard Bosanquet, *The Value and Destiny of the Individual* (London: Macmillan, 1923), 36. Bosanquet's critique of this assumption that the self is most itself when alone, or must be absorbed in its own exclusiveness, sees it as mired in the 'pathos and bathos of sentimentalism'.
[90] C. G. Carus, 'Über Lebensmagnetismus und über die magischen Wirkungen über-haupt', in *Denkwürdigkeiten aus Europa* (Hamburg: Marion von Schröder, 1963), 153.
[91] Otto Rank, *Truth and Reality* (New York and London: W. W. Norton, 1964), 2.
[92] C. G. Jung, 'The Aims of Psychotherapy', *The Collected Works of C. G. Jung*, ed. Sir Herbert Read, Michael Fordham, Gerhard Adler and William McGuire, vol. XVI, *The Practice of Psychotherapy: Essays on the Psychology of the Transference and Other Subjects* (London and Henley: Routledge & Kegan Paul, 1966), 36–52, 41.
[93] For more on the reception of psychoanalysis by modernist writers, see Matt ffytche, 'The Modernist Road to the Unconscious', in Peter Brooker, Andrzej Gasiorek,

writings on Freudian psychoanalysis constantly make assertions along the lines that: 'Every individual creature has a soul, a specific individual nature the origin of which cannot be found in any cause-and-effect process whatever ... There is no assignable cause, and no logical reason for individuality.'[94] May Sinclair explored Jungian and Freudian theory in articles for *The Medical Press*, arguing that sublimation represented 'the freedom of the Self in obedience to a higher law than preceding generations have laid upon him'.[95] At the same time she was responding to Samuel Butler and Henri Bergson, reviewing idealism, monism and the new Freudian psychoanalysis, in order to try and comprehend the 'secret of Personal Identity and Individuality' and the nature of acts of will, which had become obscure or paradoxical in the light of evolutionary theory and psychology.[96] Whatever is at stake in the unconscious in the nineteenth century develops both within and beyond psychology. But even within its strictly psychological and psycho-dynamic applications, the unconscious is linked into questions concerning the foundation of the life of the individual, with all the moral and ideological implications this question entails. Theoretical changes in the psychological sphere cannot help but reflect, channel, or displace transformations in that wider project of the liberal self. In retrospect, perhaps this will turn out to be key: that the unconscious in Romanticism, and later on in psychoanalysis, pits against abstract and invariant notions of 'individual psychology' a more complex, dynamic and obscure elaboration of process, within which certain core ideals for liberal moral theory – spontaneity, particularity, privacy, autonomy – can still be thought. As Adorno observed, 'while psychology always denotes some bondage of the individual, it also presupposes freedom in the sense of a certain self-sufficiency and autonomy of the individual'.[97]

The main part of this book is given to an examination of how all these kinds of assumptions – metaphysical concerns with the ontology of individuality, ethical and political concerns with freedom, and theoretical and empirical concerns with unconsciousness – interpenetrate in

Deborah Longworth and Andrew Thacker (eds.), *The Oxford Handbook of Modernisms* (Oxford University Press, 2010).

[94] D. H. Lawrence, 'Psychoanalysis and the Unconscious', in *Fantasia of the Unconscious and Psychoanalysis of the Unconscious* (Harmondsworth: Penguin, 1971), 214.

[95] May Sinclair, 'Clinical Lectures on Symbolism and Sublimation', part II, *Medical Press*, 153 (16 August 1916), 142–5, 144.

[96] May Sinclair, *A Defence of Idealism: Some Questions and Conclusions* (London: Macmillan: 1917).

[97] Theodor Adorno, 'Freudian Theory and the Pattern of Fascist Propaganda', in Andrew Arato and Eike Gebhardt (eds.), *The Essential Frankfurt School Reader* (New York: Continuum, 1993), 118–37, 136.

Schelling's work, and of how they develop together in reaction to the theoretical languages of the eighteenth century, and as part of an attempt to found a new account of individual identity. It is this interpenetration of philosophical, moral and psychological concerns that in turn shapes key conceptual components in the psychodynamic tradition. After elaborating these relationships, the book investigates whether, and in what sense, the terms of this engagement between notions of individuality and psychology are still applicable within Freud's conceptualisations of the unconscious, and what it means to place Freud in the context of those earlier debates. This way of reading the unconscious and exploring its role in the early nineteenth century, without isolating it from broader ideological currents, will yield new insights into the prehistory of psychoanalysis.

Along the way, I have sought to track the curious interplay between the unconscious, used to ground the concept of individual life, and the unconscious functioning empirically and descriptively in accounts of psychic illness – to explore, that is, the way in which unconsciousness, repression and forgetting, which appear from the point of view of psychoanalytic investigation to be aspects of a particular empirical entity, the psyche, have at the same time an ulterior logic and an anterior history. These accounts of psychological phenomena, which have found their way into a modern science of the individual mind, also have a key role to play in providing ontological justifications of the idea of independent, self-developing individuality itself. Seeing the unconscious psyche in this way can help us to understand how psychoanalysis is complexly beset by attempts to draw its theoretical insights into psychical trauma towards broader questions of moral and existential ontology. I am referring here partly to the extended and often transformed life of psychoanalytic principles within contemporary theory and philosophy of various hues. But of course, this wider cultural resonance of psychoanalytic ideas feeds back into the self-representation of psychoanalytic theory itself, and is also present as a tension at its inception.

The book is divided into three main sections. Chapter 1 begins by examining a crisis in late eighteenth-century notions of the self through the eyes of the idealist philosopher J. G. Fichte. Writing in the wake of the revolutionary philosophies of Rousseau and Kant, and experiencing the upheaval of the French Revolution, Fichte attempted to develop a philosophical description of the 'I', beyond the dominant eighteenth-century languages of mechanism and determinism, and founded on the notion of freedom. However, each time Fichte attempted a rational account of identity the project foundered on an internal contradiction between the freedom of the individual and the systematic nature of

Fichte's conceptual approach. This is true whether Fichte begins with logical justifications, or with an act of subjective introspection. I show that these contradictions are only able to be resolved by the introduction of metaphors of darkness or unconsciousness into his theoretical descriptions. Such metaphors draw a veil over the imagined nature of the bonds between the self and the system of rational consciousness, though we have not yet arrived at a concept of 'the unconscious'. Chapter 2 examines the way in which Schelling transferred Fichte's philosophical interest in autonomy over to a philosophy of nature, the goal of which is a portrait of human self-consciousness, emerging as the highest development of the evolution of nature itself. As with Fichte, Schelling's philosophical narratives hit a point of impasse over whether the system of nature can be fully explicated by consciousness, or whether the nature of consciousness itself must remain wrapped in obscurity, in order to preserve the possibility of certain notions of freedom, genius and the unconscious foundations of selfhood. These two chapters constitute the first phase of the book, which is concerned with the theoretical dilemmas of accounts of subjective identity which do not yet incorporate the unconscious as a specific principle.

The second part of the book is devoted to a deeper investigation of the foundation of the unconscious itself. I examine how, in the first decade of the nineteenth century, Schelling's philosophical approach turns the science of subjectivity on its head as he gives increasing weight to the mystery of nature and of origins, and prioritises the notion of the unconscious over that of consciousness. The central chapters of this book are occupied with a closer investigation of this shift, particularly as manifested in a series of drafts of an uncompleted project of 1811–15, entitled *The Ages of the World*. Chapter 3 traces the metaphysical path that led Schelling to assert the unconscious as an absolutely necessary part of the theorisation of human independence. Schelling shifts from acknowledging the need for a certain kind of mystery at the heart of the system of nature, to proposing the unconscious itself as a foundational concept. The theory of identity will rest on a stable premise, but that premise must be itself removed from consciousness. Schelling conceives of the absolute ground of life in various ways, as repressed, or passive, or hidden, but the logic is that a necessary 'unconsciousness', placed notionally at the origin of individual existence, preserves the concept of individual freedom, insofar as the individual cannot be shown to be bound by a pre-existing structure of cause and effect, or made the subject of an abstract system of laws. At this point there is a brief excursus on how such issues as to whether an individual can 'cause' itself, and what is the subject's relation to scientific necessity, have reappeared within French psychoanalysis. In Chapter 4 I examine how, having established the need for a realm of the unconscious, Schelling integrates this principle of unconscious foundations into various empirical accounts of individuality, particularly in the guise of 'buried' history, or an unconscious past, but also as an issue within psychology and anthropology. This is effectively where the narrative shifts away from the philosophy of identity and towards the unconscious as it emerges in other strands of the nineteenth-century human and life sciences. The chapter is split into five parts, the first four of which are concerned with various forms of the Romantic description of human existence. Tracing intellectual dialogues between Schelling and other Romantic writers in Germany I examine this fostering of the concept of the unconscious in accounts of (1) cultural prehistory (Schelling's dialogue with G. H. Schubert); (2) the revival of interest in negative theology (Franz von Baader's rediscovery and popularisation of the work of Jakob Böhme and Meister Eckhart); (3) Schelling's description of the formation of myth in terms of the 'uncanny'; and (4) the investigation of the nature of life processes (seen in the work of Schelling, G. H. Schubert and Friedrich Schlegel). Finally, I examine briefly the afterlife of such concepts of the unconscious and uncanny ground of reality in the work of Heidegger and Derrida, to show that Schelling's account resonates not only within liberal theory, but also with the philosophy of existentialism and later continental theories of the subject and 'otherness'.

Although my account suggests that ideas and concepts, familiar today through psychoanalysis (the unconscious, repression, the uncanny) emerged independently of the field of Romantic psychology in the early nineteenth century, this does not remain the case. From the point at which Schelling and his associates had become convinced of the need for an unconscious, one of the areas in which they sought for evidence of its existence and effects was in the field of psychopathology. Here they found physicians and psychiatrists who, for their part, were willing to absorb such metaphysical explanations as a way of supporting their interest in unconscious and pathological phenomena of the mind. Chapter 5 explores the fascinating cross-currents running between philosophy, mesmerism, psychology and literature in the period, looking at the impact of Schelling's ideas on figures such as G. H. Schubert, C. A. Eschenmayer and E. T. A. Hoffmann, as well as on the work of C. G. Carus in the next generation of psychologists, whose theories of unconscious and creative individuality influenced Jung.

Chapters 1–5, then, trace first of all the development of the unconscious in the field of philosophy, where it helps to ground the notion of autonomous individuality, and secondly track its movement as a formative principle into the fields of anthropology and psychology. Here it finds an appropriate niche at the core of the empirical science of the individual mind. The final chapters, which constitute the third part of the book, use this new perspective to re-examine the function of the unconscious in the work of Freud. They consider how, in psychoanalysis, the unconscious has served to maintain a principle of freedom at the heart of a theory of identity. Psychoanalysts such as Jung, Rank and also D. W. Winnicott inherit many Romantic assumptions about the self, including the emphasis on the unconscious as a field within which the autonomy of the self may or may not be developed. Looking closely at the various descriptions of process and individuality in *The Interpretation of Dreams*, it seems at first that Freud strove to keep his theory of the psyche clear of such ontological statements about the nature of identity. Even so, the unconscious does continue to play this functional role, and Freud's psychological writings are thoroughly embedded in assumptions concerning the health and autonomy of the liberal individual. Furthermore, the deeper one looks, the more one finds that Freud's concept of the ego, or I, is fraught with ambiguities which mask or distort the account of individuality in his work in ways familiar from those early nineteenth-century accounts. In conclusion, I suggest that the way this concept of the ego itself began to unravel as Freud's theoretical work progressed, returns us, in effect, to the crises with which the book began. In Freud's late work the nature of the individual itself appears to require a new theoretical basis – the concepts of the warring forces of Eros and the death drive. As the conditions of liberal identity in Germany slipped beyond crisis into catastrophe, Freud's attempt to shore up the account of the ego in many ways started to reproduce the metaphysical patterns of Schelling's Romantic nature philosophy.

Part I

The subject before the unconscious

1   A general science of the I: Fichte and the crisis of self-identification

'Gentlemen' he would say, 'collect your thoughts and enter into your-selves. We are not at all concerned now with anything external, but only with ourselves.' And, just as he requested, his listeners really seemed to be concentrating upon themselves. Some of them shifted their position and sat up straight, while others slumped with down-cast eyes. But it was obvious that they were all waiting with great suspense for what was supposed to come next. Then Fichte would continue: 'Gentlemen, think about the wall.' And as I saw, they really did think about the wall, and everyone seemed able to do so with success. 'Have you thought about the wall?' Fichte would ask. 'Now, gentlemen, think about whoever it was that thought about the wall.' The obvious confusion and embarrassment provoked by this request was extraordinary. In fact, many of the listeners seemed quite unable to discover anywhere whoever it was that had thought about the wall. I now understood how young men who had stumbled in such a mem-orable manner over their first attempt at speculation might have fallen into a very dangerous frame of mind as a result of their further efforts in this direction.[1]

The question now is whether a freedom such as I wish is even thinkable.[2]

There is a certain appeal in beginning this investigation into the lan-guages of modern subjectivity, individuality and the unconscious, with the German radical idealist philosopher Fichte. Though the grounds of most of Fichte's ideas – the problems he wrestled with and developed – lie, as for many Germans of his generation, in the terrain opened up by Kant's new critical philosophy, it was Fichte who sought to pull the vari-ous elements of the Kantian system into shape around a theory of the 'I' (*Ich*). Kant had famously left his system divided between very well-defined, but ultimately separate component investigations into how the

---

[1] Henrik Steffens, an account of Fichte's lectures in the winter semester of 1798–99, quoted in J. G. Fichte, *Introductions to the Wissenschaftslehre and Other Writings (1797–1800)*, ed. Daniel Breazeale (Indianapolis, IN: Hackett, 1994), 111.

[2] J. G. Fichte, *The Vocation of Man* (Indianapolis, IN: Hackett, 1987), 22.

self knows, how it acts morally and what the conditions of judgement are, and had sought, for reasons I will discuss below, to fend off any ultimate attempt to delineate the nature or coherence of the human subject as a whole.[3] Following the lead of Karl Leonhard Reinhold, the most important early interpreter and populariser of Kant's critical philosophy, Fichte sought very explicitly to close the gaps in the system, and to give a full moral and intellectual account of the foundations of selves. Not only this, but he translated Kant's concern with the technical constitution of knowledge, of the knowing subject, into a much grander theory of the 'I' and the production of its freedom and self-determination.[4]

For this reason, various contemporary Fichte commentators have wanted to claim for his work a foundational status in relation to modern conceptions of the self. Most conspicuously, for Dieter Henrich, 'anyone seeking a suitable concept of "self-consciousness" must go back to Fichte';[5] for Neuhouser, Fichte's goal was to develop an account of the nature of subjecthood;[6] and La Vopa finds Fichte's modern relevance in his capacity to 'conceptualise the inner sanctum of selfhood'.[7] This renewal of Fichte's fortunes has filtered through into the margins of psychoanalytic studies. For David E. Leary, it was on to Fichte's voluntarist interpretation of Kant, corroborated by insights from Schopenhauer and Nietzsche, that Freud grafted his evolutionary and dynamic conceptions of the psyche.[8] Frie and Reis, following Henrich, cite Fichte as being the first to demonstrate that the reflection model of self-consciousness is 'insufficient for explaining the knowledge we have of ourselves';[9] while for Andrew Bowie, the questions Fichte explores

---

[3] 'Kant had always insisted that reason is a unity … and that reason must take systematic form. But he failed to explain the source of this unity, leaving it a mystery for the speculation of his successors.' Frederick C. Beiser, *German Idealism: the Struggle Against Subjectivism 1781–1801* (Cambridge, MA: Harvard University Press, 2002), 233.

[4] Reinhold's preceding attempt to found the system on an elementary principle of consciousness had to some extent foundered on internal contradictions.

[5] D. Henrich, 'Fichte's Original Insight', in Darrel Christensen (ed.), *Contemporary German Philosophy*, vol. I (University Park, PA: Pennsylvania State University Press, 1982), 16.

[6] F. Neuhouser, *Fichte's Theory of Subjectivity* (Cambridge University Press, 1990), 2.

[7] Anthony J. La Vopa, *Fichte: the Self and the Calling of Philosophy, 1762–1799* (Cambridge University Press, 2001), 425.

[8] David E. Leary, 'Immanuel Kant and the Development of Modern Psychology', in William R. Woodward and Mitchell G. Ash (eds.), *The Problematic Science: Psychology in Nineteenth Century Thought* (New York: Praeger, 1982), 17–42, 31.

[9] Roger Frie and Bruce Reis, 'Understanding Intersubjectivity: Psychoanalytic Formulations and Their Philosophical Underpinnings', *Contemporary Psychoanalysis*, 37 (2001), 297–327, 302.

are a mirror image of the difficulties Freud encountered in his attempt to give an account of the overall structure of the psyche in his *New Introductory Lectures*.[10] Such attributions of continuity are lent force by the fact that Fichte in the 1790s was working with some of the same terms that Freud would later use in his metapsychology – for instance, *Ich* (I/ego) and *Trieb* (drive).

One has to be wary of inserting Fichte's 'I'/ego too readily into modern psychological contexts or equating his terms directly with accounts of empirical, psychological or psychoanalytic self-experience. Fichte's theory, like Kant's, concerns the 'transcendental subject' – that is, it explores and postulates the necessary structural and logical conditions of subjectivity, rather than the perceived nature of psychological experience. Such conditions will include empirical self-consciousness as part of the object of enquiry, but it does not follow that the everyday 'I' is conscious of its own logical grounds; these are being philosophically deduced, and for this reason, much Fichte criticism renounces any engagement at all with questions of overt psychology.[11]

At the same time, even though Fichte is working these questions out at a very abstract philosophical level, it is important not to isolate his engagement with consciousness and individuality from a set of much wider commitments and concerns. Take, for instance, the injunction that self-consciousness requires freedom, one that will be central to this chapter because of the way it yokes together questions concerning the mind and the nature of self-determining individuality. In one sense, Fichte's freedom of the 'I' implies something quite technical – a quality of spontaneity, or self-initiation, ascribed to the mind in terms of the way it thinks and constructs series of its 'own' perceptions out of the data of appearances. It would be wrong to identify this 'freedom' too closely with either the psychological or the political experience of the self and its freedom. And yet, these are precisely the kinds of extensions which are at stake in Fichte's project. The task of specifying scientifically the way self-knowledge functions, and the degree to which it could be ultimate and authoritative, was being urged by Fichte within a climate of general scepticism and suspicion regarding human authority. Thus his work is closely tied to the rationalist or humanist bids for self-determination, as it was then understood by an emerging but politically unempowered Third Estate. Culturally, the internalised claims

---

[10] Bowie, *Aesthetics and Subjectivity*, 60.

[11] Though Leary notes that Fichte's concepts of egoism, activism and voluntarism were used in psychological analyses by his followers including G. E. A. Mehmel and Karl Fortlage. Leary, 'Immanuel Kant', 31.

of 'subjectivity' are pitted against those of religious metaphysics on the one hand, and a fatalism concerning the insufficiency of the human will on the other, which was used to justify coercive applications of state power. Thus the war Fichte was waging against mysticism, dogmatism and scepticism under the banner of philosophical 'reason' was also a very political one, which sought to assert its radical implications in the broadest sphere of social self-consciousness. Part of the task of philosophy would be to re-shape and re-enthuse inner self-perception according to new conceptions of the source, nature and practical activity of consciousness. For Fichte, such a task was linked with a wider ethical and political mission; it required at the same time 'a means of arousing the courage of the individual amongst the throng to be neither master nor slave of anyone',[12] and this situates him clearly at the brink of that turn away from the old order and into modernity which Taylor and Gray identify with the emergence of liberal modernity. 'The whole content of Fichte's philosophy', wrote Max Horkheimer, 'consists in a call to be interiorly independent, to put aside all views and behaviours that are based solely on authority. For all bourgeois writers the most contemptuous description of a man is slave, and this holds especially for Fichte.'[13]

We should therefore not overlook the political dimensions of Fichte's work – most obviously his radical pamphleteering in the early 1790s, his forced resignation from Jena in the controversy over atheism in 1799, and his later delivery of *Addresses to the German Nation* in occupied Berlin, in the wake of the battle of Jena. But politics is there even at the heart of his attempt to deduce transcendentally the various functions of knowing and willing. In 1795 Fichte observed to Jens Baggesen that his system belonged to the French nation: 'It is the first system of freedom. Just as that nation has torn away the external chains of man, my system tears away the chains of the thing-in-itself, or external causes, that still shackles him more or less ...'[14] This radical equation of idealist epistemology with a battleground between the subjugated and the free became a key motif amongst radical thinkers in the immediate post-Kantian tradition. Schelling, for instance, in his Fichtean essay 'Of the "I" as Principle of Philosophy', equates the dead formulae of traditional metaphysics with a kind of epistemological Bastille which 'would function as just so many prisons of man's mind', and he mocked the current

---

[12] Quoted in La Vopa, *Fichte*, 282.
[13] Max Horkheimer, 'Authority and the Family', in *Critical Theory: Selected Essays* (New York: Herder and Herder, 1972), 74.
[14] Quoted in Frederick C. Beiser, *Enlightenment, Revolution, and Romanticism: the Genesis of Modern German Political Thought, 1790–1800* (Cambridge, MA: Harvard University Press, 1992), 60.

languid age for its faintheartedness in not shaking up 'the slaves of objective truth by giving them an inkling of freedom'.[15]

Above all, we must consider Fichte's encounter with Kant's *Critique of Practical Reason* – 'arguably the most powerful and consequential philosophical experience of his life'[16] – and the central role that work gave to the idea of autonomy. Kant had announced in his Preface that freedom, insofar as its reality is proved by an apodictic law of practical reason, 'constitutes the *keystone* of the whole structure of a system of pure reason'.[17] Fichte's subsequent intense pre-occupation with notions of autonomy and freedom led Leonard Krieger to identify him as one of the only intellectuals of stature able to integrate liberal ideas into the rise of German nationalism,[18] and Frederick Beiser to claim that, as difficult as it is to place Fichte according to modern political categories, 'It would be least misleading to consider him a liberal'.[19]

We can think of this liberal tendency in his philosophy in two ways. First of all, by proposing human reason as the sole determinant of moral action, and by making moral self-determination the prime focus of philosophy, Fichte takes these issues out of the hands of religious metaphysics and defends the individual against the imposition of external political controls. As Fichte proclaimed in his 1793 pamphlet *Reclamation of the Freedom of Thought*, 'The times of barbarism are gone, you people, when one dared to proclaim to you in God's name that you were a herd of cattle placed on earth by God to serve a dozen sons of God as bearers of their burdens, as servants and handmaidens of their comfort, and ultimately as cannon fodder.' People are to realise instead that they belong to no one but themselves.[20] It is in its very *abstractness*, and its aim to set out from *philosophical* first principles, that Fichte's epistemology intends to establish a moral foundation, apart from religion or politics, in human mental life. As La Vopa has described it: 'The task he assigned himself was to ground the human

---

[15] F. W. J. Schelling, 'Of the I as the Principle of Philosophy', in F. W. J. Schelling, *The Unconditional in Human Knowledge: Four Early Essays (1794–1796)* ed. Fritz Marti (Lewisburg, PA: Bucknell University Press, 1980), 67–8.

[16] Neuhauser, *Fichte's Theory of Subjectivity*, 13.

[17] Immanuel Kant, *Critique of Practical Reason* in *Practical Philosophy*, Mary J. Gregor (ed.), *The Cambridge Edition of the Works of Immanuel Kant* (Cambridge University Press, 1996), 139.

[18] Leonard Krieger, *The German Idea of Freedom, History of a Political Tradition* (Boston, MA: Beacon Press, 1957), 178.

[19] Beiser, *Enlightenment, Revolution*, 57.

[20] J. G. Fichte, *Reclamation of the Freedom of Thought from the Princes of Europe, Who Have Oppressed It Until Now*, trans. Thomas E. Wartenberg in James Schmidt (ed.), *What Is Enlightenment?: Eighteenth-Century Answers and Twentieth-Century Questions* (Berkeley, CA: University of California Press, 1996), 123–4.

right to freedom in a new way of conceiving the essentially human – a way that, by the self-evident status of its truth, would draw a line of defence for the moral self that the differentiating and distorting effects of power could not violate.'[21]

The commitment to autonomy is further implicated in Fichte's insistence that an audience of free and self-reflecting individuals must affirm the system for themselves. As philosophy, its proofs should be universally valid, hence the working title of Fichte's project *Doctrine of the Science of Knowledge* (hereafter, *Wissenschaftslehre*), which began as a lecture series in the early 1790s and was published in various shifting and augmented versions over the next decade. But the validity of the system cannot simply be imposed from without, as a finished intellectual construct: 'Everyone must freely generate it within himself.'[22] If humans have fallen prey to political systems which treat them as cattle, then, according to the *Reclamation of the Freedom of Thought*, philosophy can redeem them, because 'to be able to think freely is the most notable distinction between human understanding and animal understanding'.[23] Civil legislation, likewise, 'becomes valid for me only by my freely accepting it'.[24]

Fichte's call for freedom of thought is, then, a complex one. It is, in the first place, a practical call, concerned with free communication within a public sphere, but Fichte also seeks to foster within individuals an active sense of their own inalienable sources of reason and will. Hence Fichte's constant appeal to 'attend to yourself', to be concerned 'only with yourself'.[25] According to Anthony La Vopa, the *Wissenschaftslehre* was intended to 'ground knowledge in the interiority of selfhood and to give selfhood, through knowledge, a public voice'.[26] Much of Fichte's effort will be directed towards making philosophy's first principle into an *act* of thought, rather than a traditional proposition, which establishes the individual's self-consciousness of freedom.

The self as object

It is this moral and ontological appeal to determine the foundation of individuality which most concerns us, for it is on this ground that the concept of the unconscious emerges within idealism. However, before we can consider that emergence in detail through the work of Schelling,

[21] La Vopa, *Fichte*, 428.
[22] Fichte, *Introductions to the Wissenschaftslehre*, 14.
[23] Fichte, *Reclamation*, 126.   [24] Ibid., 125.
[25] Fichte, *Introductions to the Wissenschaftslehre*, 7.
[26] La Vopa, *Fichte*, 15.

it is necessary to examine the problems that arise in a theory of the subject which as yet has no principle of the unconscious. If one follows Beiser and La Vopa's lead in accepting the political implications of Fichte's epistemology, a question mark still stands over what kind of person his philosophy constructs. There are in fact two separate problems here. The first is one that arises repeatedly within modern moral and existential traditions: how does one delineate individual freedom using a set of tools geared primarily towards the demonstration of philosophical necessity, and which at one point Fichte urged should become 'as rigorous and self-evident as geometry'.[27] Can there be a geometry of freedom for individuals? The second problem is the ambiguity over transcendental and empirical (or universal and particular) levels of meaning in Fichte's appeal to the I. This second problem is only implicit, but it emerges in the confused reception of Fichte's thought throughout the nineteenth century. One might put it in this form: who, in practice, empirically, can claim the mantle of Fichte's much proclaimed autonomy?

There is a crucial ambiguity, for instance, over the subject of the term 'autonomy'. Charles Taylor traces the notion of 'autonomy' and 'self-determining freedom' from Rousseau to Kant and on through Fichte as a stream of modern thought which 'insists on an autonomous generation of the forms we live by'. But does this mean we as individuals, or we collectively, as humankind? To what degree are the forms of our ethical life necessarily shared? If the aspiration of this radical autonomy is 'ultimately to a total liberation', is this of the self or of society?[28] Elsewhere Taylor places German idealism in the context of the Enlightenment which made freedom central to the problem of 'self-defining subjectivity',[29] but does this mean the subjectivity of each self, or subjectivity conceived as somehow universally self-defining? For Taylor autonomy seems emphatically to imply in this Enlightenment context *self*-emancipation and *self*-experience, as well as the adoption of a Rousseauian inwardness as the point of reference for self-description; however, as the generation of 'the forms *we* live by' it at the same time implies at least general social mediation, if not a general social agent. In just the same way, 'self-defining subjectivity' appears to suggest a creative individualism; but Taylor also observes that the modern shift to a self-defining subject was bound up with a sense of control over the

---

[27] Beiser, *German Idealism*, 236.
[28] Charles Taylor, *Sources of the Self: The Making of the Modern Identity* (Cambridge University Press, 1989), 364.
[29] Charles Taylor, *Hegel* (Cambridge University Press, 1975), 24.

world – 'at first intellectual and then technological' – which seems to imply, at root, collective and social phenomena.[30]

This indeterminacy over the reference of terms so central to Fichte's project as 'autonomy' and 'subjectivity' begs some intriguing questions, because it is precisely such indeterminacy, and the accompanying spectre of social instability, that the philosophies of knowledge and freedom were designed to overcome. How does Fichte's philosophy configure human freedom and human necessity, social unity and human individuality, into a coherent system of freedom? Does it propose the autonomy of humanity as a collective moral agent, as in the Rousseauian 'general will'? Or does the emphasis remain with the independence of the individual which Fichte asserts as the first principle of the *Wissenschaftslehre*: 'the self [*Ich*] begins by an absolute positing of its own existence',[31] and again in the 'First Introduction' to the *Wissenschaftslehre*: 'one's supreme interest and the foundation of all one's other interests is one's interest in oneself'?[32]

I will return below to the difficult problem of deciding who is the subject of Fichte's new theoretical principle, the *Ich* (translated variously as I, self or ego), but for the time being I want to turn back to that other query which concerns the conditions imposed by attempting to state or know freedom philosophically, and the nature of the descriptive tools at Fichte's disposal. In an essay on the Romantic revolt against the eighteenth century, Alfred Cobban describes how political theories based on abstractions have a tendency to articulate themselves in terms of political extremes. Hence nineteenth-century politics, for Cobban, was vitiated by the tension between a theory of the absolute state and the theory of the absolute individual: 'The assertion of individual rights as such leads to anarchy, the attribution of all rights to the political state to tyranny.'[33] Whether or not one agrees with this reading of nineteenth-century political theory, it begs further questions concerning Fichte:

---

[30] Ibid., 7.

[31] J. G. Fichte, *Science of Knowledge: With the First and Second Introductions*, trans. Peter Heath and John Lachs (Cambridge University Press, 1982), 99. Neuhauser, *Fichte's Theory of Subjectivity*, 43, renders this as 'the I originally and unconditionally posits its own existence'.

[32] Fichte, *Introductions to the Wissenschaftslehre*, 18. The Introductions were written in 1797; aspects of the *Wissenschaftslehre* were presented in different versions, mainly as lecture courses, from 1794 onwards, when the original course on 'Foundations' of the *Wissenschaftslehre* was given at Jena. It is this text which is translated by Heath and Lachs as the *Science of Knowledge*. For a narrative of this and subsequent versions, see Daniel Breazale's Editor's Introduction to *Introductions to the Wissenschaftslehre*.

[33] Alfred Cobban, 'The Revolt Against the Eighteenth Century', in Harold Bloom (ed.), *Romanticism and Consciousness: Essays in Criticism* (New York: W. W. Norton, 1970), 144.

since freedom, for Fichte, is to be materialised by being *thought*, and in abstraction from everyday particulars, how will he avoid such polarisations? Given his own pronounced rationalism, what kind of description of individuality was he able to conceive per se?

The problem is expressed directly in Fichte's presentation of the intellectual choices with which anyone is faced. In his 1797 Introduction to the *Wissenschaftslehre*, Fichte explained that all philosophies were faced with a subject/object divide and could be reduced to one of two kinds – dogmatist or idealist – depending on whether they prioritised material reality or the free will of the self. Dogmatism, for Fichte, grounds the basis of experiential truth on some principle outside consciousness (truth is in some sense objectified), idealism, on some principle immanent to consciousness, or the I. Furthermore, for idealism the I is fundamentally free within its world (because experience derives from its own internal conditions), while for dogmatism it is passive, determinable according to some external law (such as God's or nature's). Of these two forms of philosophical grounding – in the self, or in some greater, external object – 'only one [term] can be the starting point, only one can be independent. The one that comes second ... necessarily becomes dependent'.[34] That is, if one concedes some external law of nature, as a foundation for philosophy, one will never arrive at a truly independent principle of subjectivity. This tension over priority between subject and object derives from Kant's recognition in the *Critique of Practical Reason* of a paradoxical conflict in the way subjectivity is led to think of itself – on the one hand, as having an empirical existence within the world of nature in which every object is determined in a causal series, and on the other, as a free being, a *noumenon*, with the power of self-determination, and the ability to act independently of coercion by sensuous impulses.[35]

Fichte has, in effect, extended this paradox into a forced choice covering all possible systems of thought. Ranged on the side of 'dogmatism', he was targeting a number of different opponents: in particular, the revival of interest in Spinoza in eighteenth-century Germany, and Spinoza's idea of a God who constituted the totality of reality, providing its unique and singular substance.[36] Such a God had been interpreted by Herder and others along more dynamic, vitalist lines – a God who lived and breathed through nature, rather than one codified for all time in a set of logical propositions – but for many Spinoza was still the symbol of a shockingly all-encompassing determinist and materialist system. Fichte

---

[34] Fichte, *Introductions to the Wissenschaftslehre*, 17.
[35] Kant, *Critique of Practical Reason*, 141. See also Beiser, *German Idealism*, 159: 'Spontaneity is impossible in the phenomenal realm where every event happens according to the category of causality.'
[36] Spinoza, corollary 2 of Proposition 14, *The Ethics*, 10.

was perhaps also targeting the post-Newtonian attempt to objectify experience along mechanical and corporeal lines, as well as the materialist systems of the French *philosophes*. D'Holbach, for instance, began his *Système de la nature* with the proposition that: 'Man is the work of Nature … he is submitted to her laws: he cannot deliver himself from them; nor can he step beyond them even in thought.'[37] As La Vopa has suggested, at issue for Fichte was 'whether selfhood as autonomous agency was an illusion and indeed whether the very notion of an integral self dissolved if the individual was merely one more object in a vast web of causes.'[38]

Fichte famously elaborated this dilemma of freedom versus the objectification and alienation of the self in the Introduction to the *Wissenschaftslehre* of 1797, and redeployed it to dramatic effect three years later in *The Vocation of Man*, Fichte's first attempt at a more popular exposition of his philosophy, after losing his academic position in Jena owing to charges of atheism in 1799. In the latter text, by way of illustrating the predicament, he gives a dizzying account of how a thinker who has once granted primacy to a world of objects – 'which I am constrained to regard as self-subsisting things'[39] – is drawn inexorably by their own search for validity towards the assumption of a fully determined world which surrounds their being in an immense causal net. To avoid placing himself within a world of meaningless and contingent events (the constant spur to Fichte's system is this fear that life might be empty, 'a mere game which comes from nowhere and goes nowhere'),[40] Fichte's hypothetical protagonist is led to posit a force of nature which guides and determines the unfolding of events. Each successive state of worldly affairs is deemed dependent on its predecessor while nature itself 'strides through the endless series of its possible determinations without rest'.[41] This conjunction of a logically necessary system with a material description of reality gives rise to the determinist vision of 'an unbroken chain of appearances' within which one could deduce all possible conditions of the universe backwards or forwards: 'you could shift no grain of sand from its spot' without thereby 'changing something in all parts of the immeasurable whole'.[42]

Though such a systematisation of nature appears to grant the thinker a sovereign vantage over the structure of reality, he has gained such certainty only through a Faustian exchange for his soul: 'I myself, along with everything I call mine' must also be a 'link in this chain of strict necessity'.[43] The sense of chains and subordination here echoes the language of the

[37] Baron d'Holbach, *The System of Nature, Volume One*, trans. H. D. Robinson (Manchester: Clinamen Press, 1999), 7.
[38] La Vopa, *Fichte*, 46.   [39] Fichte, *Vocation*, 5.
[40] Ibid., 71.   [41] Ibid., 7.
[42] Ibid., 10.   [43] Ibid., 11.

Reclamation pamphlet in which Fichte accused the German princes of placing 'feet in stocks, hands in chains' and paralysing 'the first principle of spontaneity' in men.[44] Fichte's point in the *Vocation* is that anyone following this train of thought to its absolute limit should be repelled by its consequences which go against the innermost root of individual existence.[45] It was not '*my own* freedom', his protagonist complains, but rather that of '*an alien force* outside me'. What is wanted instead is that '*I myself*, that of which I am conscious as my self, as my person' should be independent, not 'in and through another'. The thinker wants himself 'to be the fundamental cause of all [his] determination'; he wants to be 'the master of nature' not its servant.[46] Likewise the Introduction to the *Wissenschaftslehre* of 1797 argues that, 'Anyone, however, who is conscious of his own self-sufficiency and independence from everything outside of himself … will not require things in order to support his self, nor can he employ them for this purpose, for they abolish his self-sufficiency and transform it into mere illusion.'[47]

However, Fichte also admits that a system conceived on a purely subjective basis, on the inalienable *feeling* of free will in the person (by which he presumably intends Kant's depiction of the internal experience of moral law) also has its insurmountable flaws. Without the connective structures of knowledge there is no way of establishing the coherence of experience, and no convincing basis on which to extend one's own feeling of free will outwards into the world at large, or to hypothesise an integrated world of free beings. As Neuhauser notes, 'Rejecting the principle of sufficient reason may succeed in salvaging a kind of freedom, but it does so only at the expense of our self-comprehension as free agents'.[48] Thus Fichte suggests that, for anyone wishing to place themselves wholly beyond the iron cage of determinism, the perception of freedom will remain, to some extent, private and incapable of being more broadly validated, simply a vague aspiration towards unity.

This preliminary stand-off between philosophical options is left undecided. In the *Wissenschaftslehre* Fichte found that each position, idealist or dogmatist, nullifies the other and 'any system that tries to combine elements of both is necessarily inconsistent … at some point there arises an enormous gap'.[49] In *The Vocation of Man* he is left pondering the existential implications of this impasse, 'Which of the two opinions shall I adopt? Am I free and independent, or am I nothing in myself?'[50]

---

[44] Fichte, *Reclamation of the Freedom of Thought*, 131.
[45] Fichte, *Vocation*, 20.   [46] Ibid., 21.
[47] Fichte, *Introductions to the Wissenschaftslehre*, 18–19.
[48] Neuhauser, *Fichte's Theory of Subjectivity*, 5.
[49] Fichte, *Introductions to the Wissenschaftslehre*, 16.
[50] Fichte, *Vocation*, 24.

This is the paradox which Fichte's philosophy repeatedly constructs, and attempts to overcome. He wants a self that is secular, practical and self-determining, one that could be representative of the needs of the emerging Third Estate;[51] one also capable of being consciously grasped and known by the members of that class. In a post-theological twist on Cartesianism, individuals are to free themselves by looking inside, engaging in new kinds of self-apprehension and self-certainty, and discovering a self-sufficient internal basis for moral, intellectual and scientific truth. This political hope cannot be realised, however, if the only scientific tools for grasping the nature of that self, the tools of philosophical reason, would appear to render it passive, to dissolve its spontaneity and eradicate its will in favour of a compliant system of causes and effects. Bound by the extreme forms in which philosophy at that time was able to constitute descriptions of structure and freedom (forms which themselves derived from the immediate intellectual traditions of scientific modernity: the mechanism, rationalism and determinism of the seventeenth and eighteenth centuries), the free-thinking subject is unable to represent its own idea of self-determination except as an antinomy between a law that can be rationally demonstrated (but is morally repugnant) and a wilful assertion of the primacy of the self. If these are the consequences of the philosophical project, what kind of emancipation could it offer from religious dogmatism or political subjection? Are individuals to choose between even tighter and self-denying controls, or visions of anarchy? As La Vopa observes, this philosophical turn 'endangered the very concept of selfhood it was meant to secure'.[52]

How, then, did Fichte himself aim to circumvent these paradoxes of determinism? What new intellectual idioms could affirm the grounds of human autonomy such that the self could be represented as both real and free, both part of a nexus of rational and coherent causes *and* an independent, self-determining individual? What language, in effect, would allow the 'liberal self' to be described? This problem of self-description was structurally prominent in Kant's critical philosophy, but Kant's solution had been, in various ways, to make the I unknowable. At one level, this meant leaving the different facets of subjectivity divided between quite different forms of apprehension: the self must be regarded as free in relation to the moral law, but empirically bound in relation to its knowledge of natural laws – 'otherwise the self-contradiction of reason is unavoidable'.[53] In those few places where Kant is constrained to posit some very basic unity of the I – as the I which in

[51] See La Vopa, *Fichte*, 283.   [52] La Vopa, *Fichte*, 188.
[53] Kant, *Critique of Practical Reason*, 141.

some form thinks all its experiences, for instance, and without which it is hard to imagine any experiences being synthesised at all – he is quick to point out that this is merely a logical construct, without any substance in itself: 'Through this I, he or it (the thing) which thinks, nothing further is represented than a transcendental subject of the thoughts = X';[54] it is only 'the reference of the internal phenomena to their unknown subject'.[55] Likewise, when it comes to the internal sources of moral law, that aspect of the self which is *noumenal* or spontaneous cannot be known or represented, because that would require application of the categories of the understanding to the self, which would entail making the self passive, determined and objectified. Where Kant does deal more directly with the issue of psychological introspection (as opposed to the philosophical construction of the logical subject of thinking) he is again mistrustful. The section on 'Self-Observation' in *Anthropology from a Pragmatic Point of View*, is full of warnings against the 'studied compilation of an inner history of the involuntary course of our thoughts and feelings'. Such deliberate self-observation 'is the most direct path to illuminism and terrorism' in the confused belief that we 'are subject to unknown interior forces'.[56] Here it is the flux of experience, the difficulty of systematic observation, which renders such material harmful and misleading as a basis for self-knowledge.

Kant's resistance to comprehensive self-description was aimed at preserving the conditions for the reality of knowledge and of moral freedom, in themselves and from each other, because the principle of sufficient reason through which the understanding constructs the field of knowledge is incompatible with the possibility of spontaneity. But despite Kant's assurance that theoretical and practical reason form a unity, Fichte's generation recognised that here was an unreconciled antinomy at the heart of the subject, and that this jeopardised the moral and political mission of the critical philosophy. These divisions also implied that, although humanity is credited with the capacity to be morally self-determining, reason can give no final indication that the nature of the world itself will accord with human purposes. As Hegel characterised this dilemma in the *Phenomenology of Spirit*, the result is 'a *Nature* whose laws like its actions belong to itself as a being which is indifferent to moral self-consciousness, just as the latter is indifferent

---

[54] Immanuel Kant, *Critique of Pure Reason*, trans. Norman Kemp Smith (Basingstoke: Macmillan, 1993), 331.

[55] Immanuel Kant, *Prolegomena to Any Future Metaphysics*, ed. Beryl Logan (London: Routledge, 1996), 96.

[56] Immanuel Kant, *Anthropology from a Pragmatic Point of View* (Carbondale and Edwardsville, IL: Southern Illinois University Press, 1996), 16–17.

to it'.[57] This is the split which Kant had tentatively sought to bridge with his analysis of teleological judgement in the *Critique of Judgement* by asserting the need to proceed *as if* nature and reason formed a harmonious organic whole. It was this latter suggestion that Fichte, like many of his generation, took up for himself, finding Kant's hesitation over the actuality of human freedom too inconclusive. Furthermore, as far as Fichte was concerned, to assume that the source of the self, the basis of its ideas and actions, was some unknown 'thing' or 'x', implied that self-consciousness was determined by some cause alien to itself. Though for the moment I will trace the ways in which Fichte sought to overcome this aporia or ellipsis at the heart of the subject, it is its ineluctable return that forms one of the bases for the narrative of this book. In the longer term, intellectuals in the nineteenth century found they had to come to terms with this alien in the self – the unconscious – as the price for thinking their coherence, their individuality and their freedom.

The will of the I

Fichte's solution to these dilemmas has two important aspects. One is to go beyond Kant and radicalise the notion of the self and its unity – everywhere warded off by Kant as an object of knowledge, but in Fichte made absolutely central to the system of philosophy. Its task is now to show that, 'a single essential structure underlies and informs the whole of subjectivity'.[58] This need for a single principle stems not just from a desire for metaphysical 'completeness', the desire to have a 'system'. Rather, it reflects Fichte's more fundamental concern to ground the individual within an autonomous cosmos of human thought and agency – to make an absolute and Promethean case for the idea of human autonomy, in which all the conditions for the determination of human actions are potentially internal to its own capacity for knowledge, will and judgement. If successful, this would in effect ascribe to humanity the kind of absolute status and unconditional power of self-determination traditionally reserved for the deity or the metaphysical absolute. Such collective self-transparency would in turn sustain

---

[57] G. W. F. Hegel, *Phenomenology of Spirit*, trans. A. V. Miller (Oxford University Press, 1977), 365.

[58] Neuhauser, *Fichte's Theory of Subjectivity*, 63. Reinhold had been one of the first Kantians to press the need for philosophy to be systematic and to begin with a single self-evident first principle, as a way of 'saving the *Aufklärung* from its imminent collapse', Frederick C. Beiser, *The Fate of Reason: German Philosophy from Kant to Fichte* (Cambridge, MA: Harvard University Press, 1987), 226–8.

the individual's possibility of self-certainty, because nothing external to human being would impinge on the determinations of human will. Hence Fichte must also direct his efforts against the existence of a world which falls beyond the grasp of human consciousness – the not-I, as Fichte calls it. Putting a world of things-in-themselves beyond, or prior to the intellectual and moral reach of the self was, for Fichte, another blow against human autonomy. In contrast, the science of the 'I' proposes that 'the self, in all its determinations, must be absolutely posited by itself, and must therefore be wholly independent of any possible not-self'.[59]

This drive towards establishing the I as supreme principle and ultimate arbiter of reality does not mean that Fichte thought the self created the world, but that the human subject should come to think of itself as being responsible for the totality of the conditions of its own experience. Fichte argued that all we can experience or know is either immediate sensations (which are materialised according to our sensory constitution, thus falling within the content of our *own* experience), or our extrapolation from such sensations in the form of notional objects (an activity which, following Kant, depends fundamentally on the agency of the understanding and its own particular principles), or, thirdly, our inner feelings of necessity (following Kant's autonomy of the moral will). All three of these conditions of experience – constituting the elements of the objective and subjective world – can be construed as, in one way or another, internal to the self. As Fichte posed this insight initially in his collection of notes on Reinhold's *Elementar-Philosophie* of 1793–4: everything 'occurs in a single mind; therefore everything must be assimilable to this subjective unity'.[60] In *The Vocation of Man* he justified the idea as follows: 'My immediate consciousness is composed of two constituent parts, the consciousness of my passivity, the sensation; and the consciousness of my activity, in the production of an object according to the principle of causality; which latter is immediately annexed to the first.'[61] The self may appear passively to sense an object, but this very assumption of a 'cause in the object' is itself a product of the self's autonomous schematisation of a world of things and causes. 'Everything that occurs in consciousness is founded, given, and introduced by the conditions of self-consciousness';[62] thus 'all knowledge is only knowledge of yourself'.[63]

[59] Fichte, *Science of Knowledge*, 220.
[60] Quoted in Neuhauser, *Fichte's Theory of Subjectivity*, 38.
[61] Fichte, *Vocation*, 44.
[62] Fichte *Science of Knowledge*, 50.   [63] Fichte, *Vocation*, 45.

A heroic statement of this self-consciousness sets the ball rolling at the start of the *Wissenschaftlehre*: 'The self posits itself', or 'the I is posited absolutely'.[64] Fichte plays with the logic of this idea in various ways: '*I am absolutely, because I am*', or likewise 'I am I', which is equated in turn with the self-evidence of 'A = A'.[65] His aim is to make this self-referential moment of reflection foundational for all philosophical knowing, and it is evidently meant to develop the Cartesian '*Cogito ergo sum*'. Except that instead of establishing a dualism between mind and body, Fichte intends to get rid of that distinction altogether. As he would elaborate a few years later: 'What I am, thereof I *know*, because I am it ... Here no connection between subject and object is required; my own being is this connection. I am subject and object: and this subject-objectivity, this return of knowledge into itself, is what I designate with the concept "I".'[66] As we shall see, this is not a psychological statement about the way consciousness experiences itself, but it does have a bearing on the way in which self-consciousness, self-determination and individuality are conceived in relation to each other.

The second aspect of Fichte's solution to the dilemmas of the critical philosophy led him deeper into the theory of the will. The problem for Kant with attempts to unify subject and object worlds, spontaneity and necessity, was that their unity could not be co-ordinated by the understanding; it could not, in effect, be thought. But Fichte shifted the basis of his philosophical doctrine away from epistemology and the knowledge of unity, towards unity conceived as an act – a *Thathandlung* – that is produced, or willed, by subjects. For Kant, there are sources of the will which issue from humanity as *noumenon* (rather than from the nature of empirical objects) and thus escape consideration under the cause and effect categories of the understanding. They emerge instead as conditions of a mysterious inner spontaneity. However, Kant reserves this theorisation of self-determination specifically for the inner moral law, for conscience. What Fichte did was greatly to extend the philosophical role given to the will by hypothesising that the transcendental conditions of freedom and objectivity – of self-consciousness *and* the experience of external objects – are jointly posited by an act of will on the part of the subject. This act cannot be known as a fact, as a piece of inert knowledge but, according to Fichte, it can be demonstrated by being *produced*, as an act of will.

This solution, hinging on the will, performs a double feat. It ties together the fragments of the Kantian system by hypothesising a

---

[64] Fichte, *Science of Knowledge*, 97.
[65] Ibid., 99, 96.   [66] Fichte, *Vocation*, 48.

mysterious underlying activity performed by the subject itself, from which the conditions of moral freedom and of objective knowing both emerge. Potentially nothing in human experience is extraneous to this ongoing productive activity, or need in principle prevent the subject from fulfilling its will. At the same time the will, the organ of self-determination, is inserted hypothetically at the basis of subjectivity as a whole – thus centralising Fichte's radical ethical plea for self-assertion within the structure of philosophy. The self begins with an absolute *positing* of its own existence. Individuals are not called upon to acknowledge a proof of their autonomy, but to prove themselves capable of willing it.

Fichte's radical assertion of the autonomy of the I, its subsumption of all externalities and unknowns, is characteristically interpreted as Fichte's attempt to justify human mastery over nature – Taylor's autonomy as 'control over the world'.[67] The task is to constitute an idea of reality entirely according to human moral principles, so that objectivity is ultimately a condition of subjectivity, while the notion of a heterogeneous 'nature' is reduced to nothing more than a contentless check, or *Anstoß*, on the activity of the human subject. Nature becomes merely the occasion or stimulus for the subject's self-relation. The entire sensible world is now 'to be understood as the necessary condition for the self-consciousness of our freedom'.[68] As already suggested, this constitution of reality was conceived not only as a speculative act, but also as a practical task – perhaps never completely achievable, but providing an ideal around which the principles of human action could be oriented. This heroic statement of the mission of human consciousness echoed across the following century. Georg Lukács, for instance, acknowledged Fichte's influence on his own vision of collective subjectivity in *History and Class Consciousness*, one of the prime texts of Western Marxism.[69] But Fichte has also been criticised for providing a manifesto for human domination of the planet (for Karl Popper he was the man 'whose "windbaggery" has given rise to modern nationalism').[70] In this light, Schelling's turn against Fichte's omnipotent human subject and towards Romantic *Naturphilosophie* (as will be outlined in the next chapter) has been presented as a saving antidote to such aggravated

---

[67] Ibid., 21.   [68] Beiser, *German Idealism*, 273.

[69] Georg Lukács, *History and Class Consciousness: Studies in Marxist Dialectics* (London: Merlin Press, 1971), xi, 122–3.

[70] K. R. Popper, *The Open Society and Its Enemies*, vol. II: *The High Tide of Prophecy: Hegel, Marx and the Aftermath*, 2 vols. (London: Routledge, 1993), 54.

instrumentalism. Andrew Bowie, for example, suggests that Schelling's concern with nature prefigures the development of modern ecology.[71]

But such an interpretation of the I in totalitarian terms passes over an equally important condition of Fichte's argument, which is the way in which the grounds of absolute self-determination are ascribed not just to 'humanity' in general, but are to be realised by the particular self. Fichte writes, 'my own being' is the connection between subject and object, this 'is what I designate with the concept "I"'[72] – just as the anonymous 'Oldest System Programme of German Idealism' of 1796 proclaims the first idea of idealism to be 'the notion *of my* self as an absolutely free being'.[73] At one level, Fichte's beginning with the inner reflection of the individual merely ensures that nothing external (religion, custom, metaphysical suppositions concerning nature) can impinge on the elaboration of *human* autonomy, and nothing can coerce or anticipate the self's freedom of thought (in much the same way as Husserl will later introduce the *epoche*, a suspension of all experiential reference, as the first phenomenological act). It does not necessarily follow from this provisional statement of Fichte's aims that he is ascribing absolute importance to the self's passing whims, or even to its 'originality' as a self.[74] Here one would mark a division between Fichte's rationalist egalitarianism and the more humanist bent of Schiller and Wilhelm von Humboldt, who were interested in the free cultivation of selfhood as partly an aesthetic question, and therefore more clearly tied to the empirical aspects of individual feelings and perceptions.

Yet the appeal to the self is so unequivocally personal, the injunction to recognise the principle 'I am I' so urged as something practically to be realised within each self – '*I myself*, that of which I am conscious as my self, as my person'[75] – that the transcendental register is in danger of collapsing, uneasily, into the empirical experience of the person. This is particularly the case as self-reflection, transformed by Fichte's focus on the will, becomes not just a mechanical act of putting two and two together, or a passive mirroring of a world outside, but a wager on the self's powers of self-authorisation, its ability to reshape inner self-experience. This is nowhere so clear as in those moments where Fichte's readers or auditors were enjoined to perform an 'intellectual

---

[71] Bowie, *Schelling and Modern European Philosophy*, 46.
[72] Fichte, *Vocation*, 48.
[73] 'Oldest System Programme' (1796) in Bowie, *Aesthetics and Subjectivity*, 265.
[74] Compare Beiser's account of the Kantian 'I' in *German Idealism*, 151, as 'not my personal and private self but my impersonal and public self', although it seems equally misleading to align the transcendental self with the self's 'public face'.
[75] Fichte, *Vocation*, 21.

intuition' of their subjective self-consciousness, and in so doing to ratify independently the identification of subject and object, the absolute interconnection of will and perception.[76] This takes us back to the extraordinary report by the young Danish student Henrik Steffens, later a key exponent of the Schellingian *Naturphilosophie*, used as the epigraph to this chapter. Steffens in his autobiography recalls Fichte's dramatic request to think about a wall, and then to 'think about whoever it was that thought about the wall' – a request which provoked 'obvious confusion and embarrassment'.[77] This is effectively a first-hand report of how that directive in the *Wissenschaftslehre*, to 'attend to yourself; turn your gaze from everything surrounding you and look within yourself', was experienced. Whether his students, destined for careers as government bureaucrats, teachers and clergymen, were able to achieve the insight or not, no doubt they felt harried by Fichte's assertion that someone who has been 'enervated and twisted by spiritual servitude, scholarly self-indulgence, and vanity' will never be able to raise himself to the level of idealism.[78]

The problem, then, which threatened the validity of the entire project, was how the transcendental components of Fichte's description of the I were to be connected with empirical individualities and understood in relation to modes of personal self-consciousness. How were those claims regarding the self-generation of subjectivity ultimately to be interpreted? How, in particular, was the individual to straddle the gulf between a hypothetically absolute and autonomous logic of subjectivity, and a more limited, dependent or impoverished experience of selfhood? The young Schelling was one who obviously felt he *had* managed the act: '*I am*! My I contains a being which precedes all thinking and imagining. It *is* by being thought ... Thus it *is* because it alone is what does the thinking ... It produces itself by its own thinking – out of absolute causality.'[79] But in general, as the individual was urged towards acts of transcendental self-recognition, to co-ordinate the grander 'I' with the more vulnerable self, an impossible tension descended upon the consciousness of those unable to comprehend the finite and the absolute, the empirical and the transcendental, within themselves. Hence the remorseless parodying of Fichte by contemporaries such as Hegel,

---

[76] As Andrew Bowie, *Aesthetics and Subjectivity*, 64, remarks: 'Fichte is led to the demand for an immediate access to consciousness', commonly termed the 'intellectual intuition' of the I. 'He will spend the rest of his philosophical life failing to give an adequate account of this immediate access.'

[77] Cited in Fichte, *Introductions to the Wissenschaftslehre*, 111.

[78] Ibid., 20.   [79] Schelling, 'Of the I', 75.

who in his essay on *Faith and Knowledge* reports how Fichte's intellectual intuition 'has aroused general complaint, and we have sometimes heard tell of people who went mad in their efforts to produce the pure act of will and the intellectual intuition'.[80]

What concerns us here is how these philosophical arguments provoked debates about the real basis of subjectivity which filtered through the German intellectual classes. Fichte's ideas contributed to a climate of paradox and confusion in the languages of the self, particularly as regards the split between absolute, transcendental and empirical accounts of self-consciousness. The eccentric German novelist Jean Paul Richter, a disciple of Lawrence Sterne's and one of the major literary influences on E. T. A. Hoffmann (all three were favourites of Freud), satirised Fichte and the critical philosophy at great length in his comic novel *Titan* (1801–2). The book charts the downfall of Peter Schoppe whose sense of himself is unhinged by reading Fichte and Schelling, thrusting him into a crazed narrative of split and mistaken identities and an endless flight from his nemesis, the I: '"I can bear anything and everything," said Schoppe, "only not the *me*, – the pure, intellectual *me*, – the god of gods".'[81] Schoppe, in his paranoia, believes he is being chased by the I and finally dies in a duel with a *doppelgänger*. In a further comic supplement to the novel, a character called Leibgeber believes it is he himself who, since time immemorial, has unconsciously been creating the universe: '"I astonish myself," said I, casting a cursory eye over my System, while my feet were being bathed ... "to think I am the universe and the sum of all things; one can hardly do more in the world than become the world itself".'[82]

It is important to remember, then, that works such as Fichte's were widely read and discussed, and their moral, ethical and theological implications taken in earnest. If the terms are debated often in a confused way, or misunderstood, these confusions announced real crises in the attempt to shift from older metaphysical vocabularies to a newer, post-Enlightenment concept of the soul and the self. It is clear that, for all the comedy, Jean Paul also had a horror of the vacuum left by Kant's critical philosophy. In an earlier novel *Flower, Fruit and Thorn*, also admired by Freud, he described with some despair how, 'The whole

---

[80] G. W. F. Hegel, *Faith and Knowledge*, trans. Walter Cerf and H. S. Harris (Albany, NY: State University of New York Press, 1977), 157.

[81] Jean Paul Richter, *Titan: a Romance*, vol. II, trans. Charles Brooks (London: Trübner, 1863), 441.

[82] Jean Paul Richter, 'Clavis Fichtiana seu Leibgeberiana', in Timothy J. Casey (ed.), *Jean Paul: a Reader* (Baltimore, MD: Johns Hopkins University Press, 1992), 227.

spiritual universe is smashed by the hand of atheism and shattered in countless quicksilver dots of selfs, flashing, running, straying, converging, and scattering, without unity or consistence.'[83]

Fichte's principle of the 'I' was intended to integrate the realms of freedom and of objectivity and provide a new moral basis for the self in modernity. But on examination, it reveals a rift in the human subject every bit as disconcerting as that between freedom and nature which Fichte had sought to dissolve in the first place. Far from issuing a coherent vision of a new proto-liberal cosmos of the self, Fichte's attempt to isolate and emphasise the independence of the person *and* to uphold the overall notion of human integration *and* to be explicit about a sole principle governing the unity of this arrangement, produces a radically unstable point of reference for 'subjectivity'. Partly this is because the philosophy appears to inscribe absolute drives and capacities within the individuality of persons whose autonomy is in practice only provisional. *The Vocation of Man* refers to the self's drive towards 'absolute independent self-activity', as well as its self-perception as 'omnipresent knower and known',[84] and the self-origination of the 'I' in 'the absolute sovereignty of myself as intelligence'.[85] Likewise in the *Wissenschaftslehre* the issue of wholeness drives the depiction of the I towards 'absolute unity, constant self-identity, complete agreement with oneself'.[86]

The crisis here is not so much, or not only, an ethical one of ascribing absolute mastery to the individual, or even to humanity; rather, it is the ambiguity over the point of reference of the I and its autonomy – to the individual self, or to a meta-subject, such as the social totality – which is introduced by harnessing a universal and transcendental terminology of will and consciousness to an appeal to self-realisation on the part of empirical individuals. It is here that a lot of the confusion hanging over Fichte's philosophy, both in his time and in his modern reception, emerges. Beiser has noted the way in which critics have dwelled 'on the apparently anarchist consequences of making every individual the sovereign authority in matters of politics'.[87] But Fichte's subject, the 'I', has also frequently been interpreted in the opposite way, as a figure for a collective or universal social subject, or even a divine subject or

---

[83] Jean Paul in Casey (ed.), *Jean Paul*, 180. Freud not only read Jean Paul's *Flower, Fruit and Thorn* in his youth, but even suggested to his friend Eduard Silberstein that they themselves swap identities in imitation of the characters in that novel. Sigmund Freud, Letter to Eduard Silberstein, 13 June 1875, in Walter Boehlich (ed.) *The Letters of Sigmund Freud to Eduard Silberstein 1871–1881* (Cambridge, MA: Harvard University Press, 1990), 118.
[84] Fichte, *Vocation*, 68.   [85] Ibid., 69.
[86] La Vopa, *Fichte*, 221.   [87] Beiser, *Enlightenment, Revolution, and Romanticism*, 4.

ego encompassing all creation. Isaiah Berlin, for instance, envisioned Fichte's I either as 'an eternal divine spirit outside time and space, of which empirical selves are but transient emanations', or as a representation of a different kind of supra-personal self – 'a culture, a nation, a Church'.[88] Note the splits here not only between individual and universal, but also between transcendent (divine spirit) and empirical/historical (a culture, a nation). In either case, Fichte's project skates over the issue of how the actions of autonomous individuals can be co-ordinated with each other, or of how such a notionally unified and active subject could determine itself in reality. In Berlin's interpretations, the irony is that the system of human freedom falls back into the traces of theology and political absolutism from which it had announced such a resounding break.

In the next section I will examine the way in which Fichte allows degrees of mystery and unconsciousness to creep back into the science of self-consciousness, and will consider the implications of this for psychology. But first I want briefly to mention two reinterpretations of Fichte's project. Frederick Beiser has attempted to redeem Fichte, and rescue him from the various reductive or contradictory interpretations of his work, by stressing that the 'will' must be conceived not as something immediately actualised in self-reflection, but as a regulative ideal around which ethical principles can be organised, with the goal of developing social freedom in practice. Thus the 'I' is neither 'an absolute ego, which resides somehow in each and every finite or individual ego', nor an entirely solipsistic, subjective individual with no God other than itself.[89] Instead, it is a demand made towards the world by the finite self, which aims to create the conditions for a perfected human autonomy by projecting this ideal outwards as an infinite general task. The justification for this reading of Fichte's system lies in the third part of the *Wissenschaftslehre*, the 'Foundation of Knowledge of the Practical', in which Fichte describes the self-experience of the I in Romantic (and Protestant) terms as 'striving'. As Beiser interprets this, the only means of overcoming the despair of scepticism 'is to act rather than to think, for only in acting do we begin to surmount the subject-object dualism that is the chief obstacle to knowledge'.[90] As a corroboration of this reading *The Vocation of Man* culminates in a stirring vision of human activity which converges inexorably on the global unification of culture:

[88] Isaiah Berlin, 'The Apotheosis of the Romantic Will', in Henry Hardy and Roger Hausheer (eds.), *The Proper Study of Mankind: An Anthology of Essays* (London: Pimlico, 1998), 570.

[89] Beiser, *Enlightenment, Revolution, and Romanticism*, 61.

[90] Ibid., 74.

'Our species is destined to unify itself into one single body, thoroughly acquainted with itself in all its parts and everywhere educated in the same way.'[91] Savage tribes will be educated, class privileges overcome, and the practices of societies and nations eventually co-ordinated with each other.[92]

But, one can argue, this progressive interpretation of Fichte passes too quickly over the mechanisms for such absolute unification of freedom. It fails to recognise the uneasy void in human affairs that has been opened up by Fichte's absolute exclusion of 'natural', customary or imposed laws in favour of principles that are entirely self-given through the freedom of thought and philosophy. On the one hand, as Hegel early on suggested, Fichte's new theory of the I merely reproduces the forms of the world exactly as they already are, 'as if he were not in one and the same prison of his own condition, subject to the same necessity as before'.[93] In this case, all that Fichte has introduced with his sublimation of striving is the apprehension of an absolute ground that is precisely *not* present. This, as Hegel quipped, is like deducing money from an empty moneybag.[94] On the other hand, if this striving *is* to be taken positively as an emancipatory praxis, what will guarantee that human freedom issues in more than just a blind striving, or a war of all against all, or the French revolutionary terror?[95]

Terry Pinkard has, in a slightly different way, interpreted Fichte's I as a principle of normative judgement, implying neither the inner nor outer performance of self-identity but simply the capacity for individuals to make and internalise judgements bridging theory and practice.[96] The self-conscious subject 'must come to think of itself as having an absolute normative status that it confers on itself.'[97] Although Pinkard agrees that the key issue pursued by Fichte is the 'problem of self-authorisation', it is ultimately this *formal* capacity that Fichte is seeking to ground with the 'I', and which he wants the self to recognise in self-reflection. But again there are problems with Pinkard's reading which

[91] Fichte, *Vocation*, 85.

[92] Terry Eagleton describes Fichte as taking the Kantian moral subject and projecting it 'into a kind of dynamic revolutionary activism', *The Ideology of the Aesthetic*, 131.

[93] Hegel, *Faith and Knowledge*, 163.   [94] Ibid., 159.

[95] See Howard Caygill, *A Kant Dictionary* (Oxford: Basil Blackwell, 1995), 208: 'Fichte and Schelling transformed spontaneity and autonomy into subjective and objective absolutes – a practice which Hegel criticized for positing absolute and insatiable demands which remained empty and incapable of realisation except through destructive terror.'

[96] Terry Pinkard, *German Philosophy 1760–1860: The Legacy of Idealism* (Cambridge University Press: 2002), 118.

[97] Ibid., 116.

were already visible in Fichte's time. One is that, if the self-positing of the I concerns merely the ability to universalise ethical judgements in a certain way, irrespective of their content, then this once more opens up a division between the transcendental forms of subjective consciousness and the practical content of reality – or between the theory of knowledge and the theory of morals – which is exactly what Fichte sought to overcome. But if Pinkard is emphasising the *practical* role of normative judgements, as they are embedded in functional contexts in society, then the same caveats apply as with Beiser's notion of praxis.

The self may well identify itself with an 'absolute ethical task', but there can be no assurance that a world of such individuals will harmonise in practice or in their conceptions, once one returns from the philosophy of the I to the historical world of persons. What is exposed here is the underlying threat to social coherence discussed by Hegel in the final pre-ethical section of the *Phenomenology*, and analysed by Durkheim at the other end of the century under the rubric of *anomie*. Where social agents break free from the uniformity imposed by older socio-political and economic forms (the religious, ethical and governmental patterns of eighteenth-century Germany, still imprinted by feudal hierarchy) they may simply produce new inconsistencies of powers, positions and purposes – an unco-ordinated heteronomy of selves. As Schelling pointed out in his own *System of Transcendental Idealism*, published the same year as Fichte's *Vocation of Man*: 'If we think of history as a play in which everyone involved performs his part quite freely and as he pleases, a rational development of this muddled drama is only conceivable if there be a single spirit which speaks in everyone'. Not only this, but the playwright must already have 'so harmonised beforehand the objective outcome for the whole with the free play of every participant, that something rational must indeed emerge at the end of it'.[98] In Schelling's later *Philosophical Inquiries into the Nature of Human Freedom* (1809) (hereafter *Human Freedom*), he again noted the problems which Fichte stored up for himself by declaring that 'after all there are only individual wills each being a centre for itself'.[99] By testifying to the existence of such multiple and autonomous wills, and at the same time to the existence of 'unity' in the form of a moral order, Schelling argues that Fichte 'immediately fell into contradictions'.[100]

---

[98] F. W. J. Schelling, *System of Transcendental Idealism*, trans. Peter Heath (Charlottesville, VA: University Press of Virginia: 1978), 210.

[99] F. W. J. Schelling, *Philosophical Inquiries into the Nature of Human Freedom*, trans. James Gutmann (La Salle, IL: Open Court, 1985), 8–9.

[100] Ibid., 9.

Towards an unconscious

This question of the transcendental unity of the 'big' I of the moral order with the self-apprehension of the little I of empirical self-consciousness, and what might secure the ground between them, repeatedly generates anxieties in the early nineteenth century. All the more so because the ideology of individual experience and freedom thrives, but many of its actual political forms and practices have yet to be fully established. These insecurities show the obverse face of the early liberal ideal, which is beset by foundational anxieties even as it is theorising robustly independent and rational individuality. It is typical that Fichte's extreme commitment to rationalism (rather than faith, aesthetics or psychology, for instance), and his absolute demands for unity in the subject, steer him away from the exploration of more general social and intersubjective forms of mediation, so that at times one feels one is reading not the ground-plan for an enlightened republic but a strange hybrid of Berkeley and Luther. In contrast to this, many of the younger post-Kantian idealists, including Schelling and the thinkers assembled around him, elaborated theories of spirit or nature which sustained a sense of the coherence of human life at large.

These anxieties over social coherence are exemplified in the way *The Vocation of Man* goes beyond the *Wissenschaftslehre* in suggesting a further mystical or providential basis for the co-ordination of intersubjective activity. Beiser and Pinkard's pragmatic interpretations of Fichte do not acknowledge that he tends to circumvent the field of actual social behaviour and instead posits illicit or speculative mechanisms of harmonisation which operate in obscure ways *between* his solipsistically abstracted individuals, whose wills and self-authorised identities therefore remain intact. At points Fichte reaches formulations reminiscent of Adam Smith's invisible hand of the market, or Hegel's cunning of reason operating through history: 'it seems that the world's highest good grows and flourishes quite independent of all human virtues and vices according to its own law through an invisible and unknown power'; this power 'overwhelms what was undertaken for other purposes and uses it for its own purpose'.[101] The 'I' here does begin to slide towards the notion of an overarching providential power – a kind of World Subject. Fichte's transcendental analysis of the will becomes the pretext for an abstract and a priori resolution of all the problems of self-determination within a hypostatised realm of 'free will', which lifts clear of the body of the social and into the ideological ether.

---

[101] Fichte, *Vocation*, 92.

The mystical drift in *The Vocation of Man* is once more modelled on the distinction Kant draws between a 'supersensible' realm of the will and the conditions of the worldly interaction of things, or rather, between the nature of the will and the principles on which the understanding synthesises the world of appearances into chains of cause and effect. The fear of relinquishing the notion of self-determination to an external objective system led Fichte to the lonely proposition: 'Connect I must, but I cannot connect with another being', because a being 'which is *connected* to another being is ipso facto *caused* by this other being'.[102] But Fichte resolves the problem in this later text by developing an account of the will not as praxis, but as an *unrepresentable* principle, one which cannot be fully assimilated to conscious reflection. In this hypothetical realm of the will each individual is an absolute cause acting on the outside world (an *Urzweck*, as Kant had it), just as in Fichte's account of politics each individual is granted the fundamental right (*Urrecht*) to intervene in worldly affairs.[103] Because the individual's actions are thought to arise out of the depths of his *own* will, the world of moral duty it imposes on him implies no loss of identity but is absolutely self-given: 'My will is mine, and it is the only thing which is entirely mine and completely depends on me, and through it I am even now a citizen of the realm of freedom and rational self-activity.'[104] Fichte appeals to the individual's 'most authentic being' and 'most intimate purpose',[105] and presents himself as 'sole source of all my being' – 'I have life in myself unconditioned by anything outside myself'.[106]

Because the will cannot itself be described as an object, or using the concepts normally applied to objects, its agents are likewise redeemed from their bondage to a mechanical or natural determinism. The law to which the *will* is subject is 'a bond for living minds. It disdains to rule over dead mechanism.'[107] At the same time Fichte ascribes to humanity a principle of unity and co-ordination every bit as absolute as the system of nature was for the dogmatists, though it requires to be expressed in different terms. Not only is the will constituted 'like no law in any sensible world', but it cannot be thought of as given by any kind of agent to any other.[108] It is 'not given by my will nor by the will of any finite being nor by the will of all finite beings taken together', and yet this law is one 'to which my will and the will of all finite beings are themselves

---

[102] Ibid., 68.
[103] See the account in Krieger, *The German Idea of Freedom*, 183.
[104] Fichte, *Vocation*, 95.   [105] Ibid., 96.
[106] Ibid., 100.   [107] Ibid., 94.   [108] Ibid., 106.

subject'.[109] Evidently, Fichte has transferred the unknowable dimensions of selfhood from the mystery of the self's coherence in Kant, to a mystery of the will and its operations. How then is will to be conceived of? Only in quasi-religious terms, 'as a One, as a common spiritual source', as an 'infinite will which mediates all individuals' and through which all free beings have their consequences.[110]

We must pause here to take stock of this development of the concept of will, and the ways in which it appears to have resolved the contradictions between system and freedom, or universality and individuality, and to have brought Fichte's protagonist to the ultimate point of self-authorisation: 'I stand free and calm and unmoved, myself my own world'.[111] First of all, the transcendental structure of the will – that attempt to give categorical form to human self-determination – is, in effect, detached from the description of empirical social and historical existences. To borrow from Krieger's account, it hovers over that historical world as 'an integral world of spirit – the abode of the transcendental ego in its undifferentiated totality'.[112] Fichte's attempt to be rigorous and rational about the constitution of subjecthood – to give philosophical, rather than religious, expression to his egalitarianism, and to provide a foundational account rather than a compilation of empirical observations – at the same time forces a departure from the concrete differentiations of human life. This rift is compounded, rather than resolved, by the isolation of an autonomous sphere of reason from which to derive a model of human interaction, and this is because the structure of those interactions cannot itself be stated. Just as the principle of the 'I' ambiguously merged individual with universal subjects, the will, conceived in abstract terms, sustains an ambiguity over how connections and influences between people really occur, rather than laying out the logic of those relationships.

As Fichte searches for figurative ways of weaving the connotations of unity and freedom together, he can only do so by remaining strategically obscure over the functioning of will. The will, and by implication the principle of human autonomy, appears to divide between two conceptual axes, one of which 'lies hidden from all mortal eyes in the secret darkness of my heart'. This is the axis at which the individual is the absolute cause of itself and is as such 'the pure and sole first link in a chain of consequences which runs through the entire invisible realm of spirits, just as in the earthly world *the act*, a certain movement of matter, becomes the first link in a material chain which flows through the

[109] Ibid., 104.   [110] Ibid., 109.
[111] Ibid., 117.   [112] Krieger, *The German Idea of Freedom*, 179.

whole system of matter'.[113] On the other hand, the will is equally that axis governing the spiritual order as a whole, which 'I neither survey nor see' because 'I am only a link in *its* chain, and can judge the whole as little as a single tone of a song can judge the harmony of the whole'.[114] It seems that the self is only saved from that same unstable oscillation over self-authorisation, which shadowed the discussion of self-knowledge at the opening of *The Vocation of Man*, because it is now invested with a deeper, or ulterior, principle which is shrouded in obscurity and yet bridges and fuses the two different kinds of subjective unity – the empirical and the transcendental. One is within me 'hidden from all mortal eyes'; the other 'I neither survey nor see'.

At another point in the text Fichte's self-constituting protagonist concedes that 'what I ought to become and what I will be transcends all my thought ... It is visible only to one, the father of spirits'.[115] This brings us to a third point of weakness, which is that what appears at first as a bold and imaginative attempt to 'liberate' and secularise the individual self, has inexorably curved round into a kind of religious intuition. One already senses here the tendency that Feuerbach will later attack within German intellectual culture and Marx will in turn expose within Feuerbach, namely that philosophy is never completely disenchanted of theology; and even apparently secularised concepts, such as Feuerbach's transcendental anthropology, give rise to new 'enchantments' in the form of the sublimated essence of 'man', 'will', 'spirit', 'nature' or 'history'. Such abstract terms become the object of a new religious identification, with philosophers and anthropologists as priests. For La Vopa, Fichte's thought is a stage in the secularisation of Lutheranism, and for this reason it 'is not amenable to a neat distinction between the religious and the secular'; in fact, Fichte 'endowed the calling with a kind of sacred meaning in the very process of desacralizing it'.[116] One thinks here, too, of Adorno's contention that all the traditional metaphysical systems, while being critical of dogmatic or fixed ideas, have attempted 'to rescue, on the basis of thought alone, that to which the dogmatic or transcendent ideas referred' – that is, God or the 'absolute'. Such systems use concepts to 'form a kind of objective, constitutive support' for scattered, individual, existing things.[117]

---

[113] Fichte, *Vocation*, 94.   [114] Ibid., 107. My italics.
[115] Ibid., 115.   [116] La Vopa, *Fichte*, 439.
[117] Theodor W. Adorno, *Metaphysics: Concepts and Problems* (Cambridge: Polity, 2001), 8. La Vopa in his interpretation of Fichte's secularisation, endorses M. H. Abrams' notion that this process entails not 'the deletion and replacement of religious ideas' but rather their 'assimilation and reinterpretation', *Fichte*, 13.

We can think of these 'individual existing things' as both Tocqueville's individuals who 'form the habit of thinking of themselves in isolation and imagine that their whole destiny is in their hands', and Eagleton's bourgeois individuals 'in search of a unity powerful enough' to reproduce themselves by. In Fichte's case, it is the I which gathers, grounds and authorises the scattered empirical selves. If Fichte's individual has gained an absolute sense of self-determination, that self relies on a form of faith – if not in a world of spirits, then of 'free spirits'. Moreover, the differentiated chains of worldly and spiritual causation which Fichte delineates in *The Vocation of Man* evoke nothing so much as the perfect co-ordination of the Leibniz–Wolff system from which Kant had originally attempted to emancipate human experience and human knowledge. Now, however, it is the I, not God, who is 'Architect of the machine of the universe and Monarch of the divine city of Minds'.[118]

The even greater irony is that Fichte's quasi-religious apotheosis of the I and the will has a tendency to swallow up the particularity of individual freedom. Some idea of how this might happen can be gleaned from Schelling's apostrophe to the absolute in his early Fichtean work *Of the I* which dates from 1795:

The absolute I is the only Eternal; therefore the finite I, as it strives to become identical with it, must strive for pure eternity … In the finite I there is unity of consciousness, that is, personality. The nonfinite I, however, knows no objects at all and therefore no consciousness … Consequently, the ultimate goal of all striving can also be represented as an expansion of personality to infinity, that is, as its own destruction.[119]

Here the mingled overtones of Jena Romanticism, Pietist spiritual yearning and Lutheran self-abnegation usurp the original emphasis on liberal emancipation. At the same time, the ever more inflated and absolute concept of the I gives rise to visions of a moral totality in which the empirical individual becomes entirely inconsequential.

Correspondingly, when Fichte applies his theory of the I back to the phenomenal world of political rights and laws, there is a profound inversion in the nature of the project. Because the grounds of individual freedom are developed in principle through Fichte's theorisation of the supersensible operations of the will, the substance of that freedom evaporates once Fichte turns his attention to the concrete operations of the state. Thus Leonard Krieger notes that Fichte's theory of freedom ironically left the structure of the existing absolutism 'entirely intact'.[120]

---

[118] Gottfried Leibniz, *Philosophical Writings* (London: Dent, 1973), 193.
[119] Schelling, 'Of the I', 99.
[120] Krieger, *The German Idea of Freedom*, 181.

In the *Foundations of Natural Law* of 1796 and the *Closed Commercial State*, published the same year as *The Vocation of Man*, Fichte emerged with a vision 'quite in line with the traditional separation of a spiritual realm reserved to the individual and an actual realm surrendered to the state'.[121] As a result, the concept of autonomy threatens to fall apart once more into the unassimilable registers of individual and system, almost exactly as Cobban predicted of political theories based on abstractions. Krieger remarks that, in the last decade of the eighteenth century, Fichte's conception of society all but disintegrated 'between the sum of individuals that composed it and the State which it founded'. Although this world was authorised by a notion of individualism, its operative principles 'were themselves supra-individualistic relationships, at once necessary and problematic for personal freedom'.[122] It was assumed that once the state was formed, the individual would transfer the co-ordination of 'freedom' directly to it: 'The common will was represented as an operative force only in the sovereign ruler.'[123] In a note scribbled in the final margins of his copy of *The Vocation of Man* sometime in or after 1815, Coleridge observed that 'Fichte would have made a more pernicious & despicable Tyrant than Caligula or Eliogabalus. – Indeed the whole of these *Vernunft-gesetze* is but *Ego per me* – I by itself I – and everybody shall *obey me*!'[124]

The self's new interior

He expounded that Space and Time and Categories were nothing at all per se or to other creatures but everything to the human race and that with the help of those modes of thought we created for ourselves the whole material world ... Meanwhile, all these outward appearances created by us *within* related quite unexpectedly to true and genuine things per se, to real Xs, quite unknown to him ... and he himself, being his own optical illusion, related to one such X domiciled within himself, which was the very granite core and the self of his self. – But as he was never, not after death either, going to get to see any of this whole incognito universe ... he saw no reason why he should worry about a Something eternally hidden like the Nothing, an eternally invisible mirror foil of visible forms.[125]

[121] Ibid., 182.
[122] Krieger, *The German Idea of Freedom*, 183.
[123] Ibid., 184.
[124] S. T. Coleridge, *The Collected Works of Samuel Taylor Coleridge*, vol. XII, *Marginalia, Part 2: Camden to Hutton*, ed. H. J. Jackson and George Whalley (Princeton University Press, 1984), 622.
[125] Jean Paul Richter, *Palingeneses* (1798) extracted in Timothy J. Casey (ed.), *Jean Paul: a Reader* (Baltimore, MD: Johns Hopkins University Press, 1992), 196.

This chapter's account of the issues which surround, impinge on or threaten accounts of selfhood and interiority in modernity has been necessarily complex. In Fichte's work, the description of consciousness, interiority and absolute authority is constellated around a central demand for freedom and individuality, and draw on vocabularies of scientific determinism, feeling and increasingly and sublimely, the will. The overall point to be made here is not so much about political freedom, or the dangers of founding concepts of individuality in the abstract. It is about the problem of self-description per se, and where the points of contradiction or obscurity in such descriptions repeatedly emerge. We are confronted with the paradox that the very philosophy which announced the I, which both isolated and absolutised it, seems one way or another to result in the non-appearance or impossible appearance of the individual. The individual is still haunted by the need to be grounded in an absolute structure. Fichte had not thought his way beyond the eighteenth-century chains of determination; he divided and relocated them, but they continued to govern the individual, even after Fichte removed the whole notion of determination from the external world and reinserted it hypothetically in the structure of the I. Once reality becomes wholly internal to the self – 'myself my own world' – the self becomes ultimately unthinkable and, against the grain of Fichte's original intentions, split into contradictory registers of abstract identity, empirical existence and a notional absolute meta-ego. It wavers between Jean Paul's 'To think I am the universe!' and his 'quicksilver dots of selfs', and ultimately finds solace in something akin to an enigmatic basis, an 'X', 'eternally hidden like the Nothing' within his interior.[126] Such instabilities in description, as we will see in Chapter 5 on the Romantic psyche, easily become conflated with apprehensions of psychical illness, of pathology.

Yet there *are* signs that Fichte moved the problem of self-representation into new territory, so that questions of 'grounds' or 'basis' could be assimilated to forms of self-description in a different way. First of all, despite the criticism that Fichte's philosophy of the I does not fully extricate itself from either the religious ideology or the mechanistic thinking it was designed to overthrow, this is by no means a traditional religious metaphysic. Fichte was forced to resign from Jena just prior to writing *The Vocation of Man* precisely on the grounds that he had equated God with a self-willed moral order. We are not dealing with the soul's relation to God, with divine judgement, with afterlife and

---

[126] Jean Paul, in Timothy J. Casey (ed.), *Jean Paul*, 227, 180, 196.

punishment, but with internal principles of judgement and conscience, with individuals and their freedom, and a heaven which is 'not beyond the grave' but made real in the concept of will.[127]

Secondly, the voice of the will which Fichte's self hears internally as the voice of conscience may be represented as an 'oracle from the eternal world', but this eternal world is that of the human, self-determining I, and the dialogue established is now that between conscious understanding and *its* hidden basis. As Andrew Bowie has suggested, one can begin to perceive a structural similarity to Freud's characterisation of the psychoanalytic demand as: '*Wo Es war soll Ich werden*' – where it (id) was, there I (ego) shall be.[128] Thirdly, Fichte identifies the internal medium of the I as the psyche, replacing the Christian notion of the soul with something both classical, and newly modern and scientific. Until the self comes to comprehend the inner nature of its reality and its freedom, he writes, 'the immortal Psyche remains tethered to the earth with her pinions bound'. It is the philosophy of the I which 'will be the first power to free Psyche from her cocoon and spread her wings'.[129]

The last forty years have seen a number of recoveries and reinterpretations of Fichte which have identified these philosophical descriptions of the I with the birth of modern self-conscious interiority itself. Dieter Henrich effectively began this process of rehabilitation, arguing that it was Fichte who, on the brink of nineteenth-century modernity, discarded previous ontological categories in order to 'reach the experience of this soul, the processes of consciousness, the structure and flow of its experiences and thoughts'.[130] The implication is that Fichte turned inwards on himself and articulated the primacy of the aesthetic phenomena of mental life in a language which anticipates the flows of time and memory found in G. H. Lewes, Bergson or William James.[131] Though such studies have undoubtedly made Fichte once more relevant to contemporary philosophy, Fichte's I and its double chain of will and corporeality cannot so easily be equated with modern discourses of the self except by distorting Fichte's intellectual co-ordinates. If one wants to see a Fichtean psychology echoed on nineteenth-century terrain one could as well turn to the alien and phantasmagorical experience evoked in George Eliot's *The Lifted Veil* of 1859, which drew on

[127] Fichte, *Vocation*, 94.
[128] Bowie, *Aesthetics and Subjectivity*, 58–9; Freud, *New Introductory Lectures to Psycho-Analysis, SE*, vol. XXII, 1–182, 80.
[129] Ibid., 102, 115.
[130] Dieter Henrich, *Konzepte*, cited in Bowie, *Aesthetics and Subjectivity*, 58.
[131] See Rick Rylance, *Victorian Psychology and British Culture 1850–1880* (Oxford University Press, 2000), 10–12, for an account of the emergence of 'flows' of thought in the nineteenth century.

German idealism and contemporary mesmerist theory in its portrayal of a psychopathology of the mind: 'this double consciousness at work within me, flowing on like two parallel streams that never mingle their waters and blend into a common hue'.[132]

What is missed, by transcribing Fichte's philosophy of the 'I' into a more contemporary context, are the conditions within which the moral appeal to self-determination was originally made: that sense of the anxiously provisional existence of the proto-liberal self once it has stepped beyond the bounds of social relations as customarily organised. Returning to Fichte, we risk overlooking the way the problem of the individual's relationship to law, to theology, and political insecurity in general, was experienced. As Michelle Perrot and Alain Corbin have noted, although the sense of individual identity became more distinct and widespread in the nineteenth century, it was a long time before such notions translated into actual rights and powers.[133] As we saw from the example of Jean Paul, where Fichte's account of the I broke down the effects were extremely disturbing. Such crises of the self were hardly seen in their own time as the sign of an inner 'density' or obscurity of experience, which might testify to the self's inalienable aesthetic core, or symbolic plentitude. Modern philosophy of the subject is able to assume and naturalise such a richly meaningful and inalienable inner life within its theory of the individual, only because the individual's moral right to exist has long been established as an idea within Western culture.

The point is not so much about the need to locate the subject within specific historical and political contexts. It has more to do with the way two very distinct issues get superimposed. On the one hand there is the empirical description of the self and the story of the gradual emergence of a descriptive psychology oriented around the issue of inner self-experience. On the other hand, there is the defence and justification of the concept of individuality itself – in Fichte's case, the attempt to isolate and absolutise the possibility of self-identity, to conceive of the individual life as self-related and self-grounded. One can see that, in Fichte, it is the second of these two questions which predominates – and it is here, I think, that Bowie errs in reading Fichte too directly in terms of more modern conceptions of the aesthetics of individual 'self-consciousness' without considering the political and historical

---

[132] George Eliot, *The Lifted Veil/Brother Jacob* (Oxford University Press, 1999), 21.

[133] Michelle Perrot, 'Introduction' to Alain Corbin, 'Backstage', in Michelle Perrot (ed.), *A History of Private Life*, vol. IV: *From the Fires of Revolution to the Great War* (Cambridge, MA: Harvard University Press, 1990), 453.

fortunes of individuality itself, which in many ways needed to be positively affirmed before such interior aesthetics could become essential
or even relevant to a theory of the person. The structural conditions
of Fichte's I – even, or especially, those aspects such as striving and
unconsciousness – are very much bound up, not simply with the need
to look inwards, better to describe an interior empirical domain, but
precisely to construct a justification of the self as autonomous, as 'self-
formed', as wholly individual. It is important to make this distinction
clear, because it is on the latter front – the concern with autonomy and
determination – that the unconscious will intercede as a theoretical
solution.

This pressure to make the description of the self coincide with the
description of autonomy was key to Fichte's system of freedom, as it was
for the writers of the 'Oldest System Programme of German Idealism'.
But as we have witnessed in the accounts given by Gray, Taylor, Lukes
and others, this same idea of individuality exerted a crucial pressure on
the emerging discourses of liberal modernity in general, and perhaps
still does so. The philosopher Thomas Nagel finds that our unanalysed
sense of autonomy is something 'we can't get rid of, either in relation to
ourselves or in our relation to others'.[134]

The same idea was given a striking articulation by Jacques Lacan
in a psychoanalytic context: 'A certain mental breathing space seems
indispensable to modern man, one in which his independence not only
of any master but also of any god is affirmed, a space for his irreducible
autonomy as an individual, as individual existence … In a word, the
existence of a permanent discourse of freedom in the modern individual seems to me indisputable.'[135]

Nagel concludes, however, that 'We are apparently condemned to
want something impossible', while Lacan comments wryly: 'Here
there is indeed something that merits a point-by-point comparison
with a delusional discourse'.[136] The point is that the demand to locate

---

[134] Thomas Nagel, *The View from Nowhere* (Oxford University Press, 1986), 113.
[135] Jacques Lacan, *The Psychoses: The Seminar of Jacques Lacan Book III 1955–1956*, ed.
Jacques-Alain Miller (London: Routledge, 1993), 133.
[136] Nagel, *The View from Nowhere*, 113; Lacan, *Psychoses*, 133. Compare Sándor Ferenczi,
'Stages in the Development of the Sense of Reality', in *First Contributions to Psycho-
Analysis* (London: Karnac, 1994), 213–39, 232, 'Nevertheless, we possess in the
doctrine of the freedom of the will an optimistic philosophical dogma that can still
realise phantasies of omnipotence'. See also R. D. Hinshelwood, *Therapy or Coercion:
Does Psychoanalysis Differ from Brainwashing* (London: Karnac, 1997), 198: 'We
accept and aspire to independent self-creating status as individuals – because from
inside, too, our psychology may seek such an imagined closure.' But psychoanalysis
'can therefore support unwittingly that wishful illusion of an indivisible coherence'.

or substantiate the individuality of the self (where such individuality implies not only the most formal and abstract sense of identity, but also its autonomy, privacy, self-determination, sovereignty or creativity) appears for both authors to be unjustifiable and yet ideologically necessary within Western modernity.

But if the modern individual is condemned to want to supplement a psychology of consciousness with an ontology of 'the autonomous self' – to counter a certain lack of autonomy in the world with an increasingly emphatic idea of a person's self-directedness, or self-authorship – then we may begin to understand why the kinds of theoretical gestures and structures Fichte was drawn towards to preserve the concept of autonomy also become key within the new sciences of self-description.

Fichte's theory of the I is relevant for the future psychoanalytic project in two ways. First of all, the hiddenness, the blindness stemming from Kant's ban on attempts to know the nature of subjective coherence, was originally eschewed by Fichte in favour of transparency and self-consciousness, but then reinscribed by him as an obscure principle of the will, acting behind and constituting consciousness. One can see here the inception of a recurrent strategy in modernity which will complement empirical or scientific observation of the self with a quasi-metaphysical concept of an unconscious will. The direction of this tendency is pre-figured in Jean Paul's parodic description of the 'incognito universe', something eternally hidden within, 'like the Nothing', which is at the same time 'the very granite core and the self of his self'.[137] This same condition of obscurity will be theorised more explicitly in Schelling as the unconscious, but it also emerges in Schopenhauer's concept of the world as will. Schopenhauer, who had attended Fichte's lectures in 1811, inserted a negative principle, shorn of Fichte's providential and quasi-religious assumptions concerning harmonisation, into that same gap which Kant had maintained concerning the description of things in themselves, or the imperatives of the noumenal world.[138] Later in the century, Eduard von Hartmann's *Philosophy of the Unconscious* attempted to fuse insights from Schopenhauer, Schelling, and the Romantic psychologist C. G. Carus into a grand metaphysic of an 'unconscious will' at work in

---

[137] Casey, *Jean Paul*, 196.
[138] See note in Richard Askay and Jensen Farquhar, *Apprehending the Inaccessible: Freudian Psychoanalysis and Existential Phenomenology* (Evanston, IL: Northwestern University Press, 2006), 405, for an account of Herbart's perception that Schopenhauer's ideas were unoriginal and could be found already in Fichte.

the universe. Freud was certainly aware of Schelling and Hartmann's work (both of them are referenced in *The Interpretation of Dreams*), and he famously credited Schopenhauer with having established certain key psychoanalytic ideas before him – Schopenhauer's 'unconscious "Will" is equivalent to the mental instincts of psychoanalysis. It was this same thinker, moreover, who in words of unforgettable impressiveness admonished mankind of the importance, still so greatly underestimated by it, of sexual craving'.[139] C. G. Jung was also an inheritor of this German post-idealist tradition. He frequently alluded to Hartmann and Carus as forerunners and contextualised his own concepts in relation to Schopenhauer's work, for instance referring explicitly to Schopenhauer's designation of the will as 'a thing-in-itself' when developing his theoretical description of libido in 1911.[140] What is important here is not so much the awareness later psychologists had of such precursors, or their occasional citation of these, but the way in which a very broad tradition of thought about unconscious influences (as forms of human or natural will) enters nineteenth-century cultural and scientific discourse, forming a background context for the development of the later theories. For Philip Rieff, Fichte, Schelling, Hegel, Schopenhauer, von Hartmann and Nietzsche 'broached the meaning Freud finally gave to the term unconscious, by seeing it as "blind natural will"'.[141]

Secondly, there is a more structural observation to be made. This is that the 'hiddenness' in the will is not just an effect of the blind spots in Kantian epistemology (i.e. that there are unknowable or unrepresentable dimensions or forces at work in organic and subjective life, some of which will later emerge as the object of psychological investigation). Rather, we must remember that in Fichte the unconscious aspects of the will have a specific ideological role to play. They cover over the

[139] Freud, 'A Difficulty in the Path of Psychoanalysis', *SE*, vol. XVII, 135–44, 143. See also Freud's comment in reference to Schopenhauer and Nietzsche, in 'On the History of the Psychoanalytic Movement' (1914), that 'laborious psychoanalytic investigation can merely confirm the truths which the philosopher recognised by intuition, *SE*, vol. XIV, 15; James Strachey's Appendix on Schopenhauer in *SE*, vol. XIX, 223–4; and Thomas Mann's 'Freud and the Future', *International Journal of Psychoanalysis*, 37 (1956), 106–15, much of which is devoted to comparisons of Freud with Schopenhauer.

[140] C. G. Jung, *The Collected Works*, vol. V, 'Symbols of Transformation' (London: Routledge & Kegan Paul, 1956), 137. In the 1950s, Jung also tied his concept of synchronicity to Schopenhauer's notion of unified primal cause in existence. See C. G. Jung, *Synchronicity: An Acausal Connecting Principle* (London: Routledge, 2008), 16–20.

[141] Philip Rieff, *Freud: The Mind of the Moralist* (New York: The Viking Press, 1959), 35–6.

anxieties and the cracks that open up within attempts to assert the basic autonomy of individuals. This is why these formulations of an enigmatic causal principle, an obscure and untheorisable bond, or a hidden reservoir of the will in which the determinations of self-consciousness are themselves grounded, will become so central to other kinds of philosophical and non-philosophical accounts of the self, including the empirical psychology of individual life. The task which lay ahead for the liberal self was, as it were, to weave that self-authorising rationale into the very fibre of self-experience and self-description at personal and poetic, but also scientific levels. The usefulness of such transcendental notions of the unconscious is precisely that they were able to be incorporated as structural motifs into more mundane categories of existence, specifically into the emerging sciences of history and nature, and thus, as we shall see in the work of Schelling and G. H. Schubert, into the Romantic anthropology of the self. Chapters 4 and 5 will examine how these new idiomatic figures of obscurity and unconsciousness are drawn into an alliance, first of all, with concepts of natural and historical process, and then into the developing models of German Romantic psychology where they start to define the contours of a specifically psychic unconscious.

In tracing the relations between an ontology of the subject and emerging theories of the psyche, I am seeking to illuminate the way in which the latter both mediate the metaphysical problem of self-justification *and* present themselves as part of an empirical, natural-scientific and medical description of psychic life. As such, I am concerned not so much with the history of psychiatry or psychology as separate disciplines, nor with the philosophy of self-consciousness as an abstract problem, but with intersections between the empirical study of mental life and foundational assumptions about the nature of individuality. Both of these are in turn allied with the shifting moral and quasi-political demand to ground the stability, authority and agency of the person in modernity.

This chapter has focused on the failure of Fichte's science of the I, and the obscurity that necessarily befalls the doctrine of the transcendental subject once one tries to make assumptions about the primacy and functioning of freedom and self-determination more explicit. It has also been about the attempt to move beyond certain eighteenth-century figures of mechanism and determinism – the problems inherent in any account of the self modelled on the principle of sufficient reason. I will now move on to examine the way in which this very failure was turned to positive account in the philosophy of Schelling, and how, out of the conditions of a failure in knowledge itself, a new set of descriptive figures evolve: resistance, the withdrawal of grounds, non-being, and ultimately, principally, the unconscious. At the same time, I intend to show that, from the outset, and through each of its later transformations, the theory of the unconscious remains closely allied with that original idealist demand to represent the autonomy of the self, and to provide a foundational discourse for the self-determining individual.

2   Natural autonomy: Schelling and the divisions of freedom

> Every organic product carries the reason of its existence in itself, for it is cause and effect of itself.[1]

> There are no native sons of freedom.[2]

As with Fichte, the issue of freedom cuts across the whole of Schelling's work and its innumerable frames of reference. The *Ideas for a Philosophy of Nature* (originally published in 1797, hereafter *Ideas*) begins with the statement, 'Philosophy is throughout a work of freedom';[3] his more Fichtean work *The System of Transcendental Idealism* early on asserts that 'freedom is the one principle on which everything is supported';[4] in 1809 he published his *Philosophical Inquiries into the Nature of Human Freedom*; and, according to Michael Vater, all of Schelling's later work, from the 1815 *Ages of the World* to the lectures on mythology and religion of the 1840s to 1850s, show him to be 'in search of a principle of freedom and actuality not confined to and determined by reality as merely conceived'.[5]

In this light, the long-standing Anglo-American tendency to associate Schelling primarily with the philosophy of art or a poetic vision of nature, wrongly separates him from the ideological anxieties of liberalism and nineteenth-century social philosophy. As with Fichte, the question that plagued Schelling was once more how to fit individuality and unity, freedom and structure together into a convincing post-Enlightenment philosophy of man. As his biographer Gustav Plitt noted, 'the goal of his whole life's work was the ethical renewal of the people'.[6] When Schelling received a summons to Berlin in the 1840s

---

[1] F. W. J. Schelling, *Ideas for a Philosophy of Nature* [1797/1803] (Cambridge University Press, 1988), 31.

[2] Ibid., 10.   [3] Ibid., 9.

[4] Schelling, *System of Transcendental Idealism*, 35.

[5] Michael Vater, Introduction to Schelling, *System*, xx.

[6] Gustave Leopold Plitt, *Aus Schellings Leben in Briefen*, 3 vols. (Leipzig: Hirzel, 1869–70), vol. II, 91.

to take up the chair of philosophy which Hegel had occupied at his death ten years earlier, the Prussian government hoped he would be able to stem the threatening rise of Hegelianism amongst the Berlin students. However, the announcement of his lecture course on 'The Philosophy of Revelation', for all its orthodox and Christian overtones, in fact sent out a message to the youthful intelligentsia of Europe that Schelling had something epoch-making to reveal. He now promised to unveil the 'positive' philosophy of actuality, which the previous phases of idealism had only transcendentally critiqued. It was this expectation that drew a spectacular array of auditors, including the young Kierkegaard, Friedrich Engels, Jakob Burkhardt and Mikhail Bakunin, all of them hoping to hear how idealism's philosophy of freedom could be made real.

But the terms of 'freedom', capable of mediating so many different visions when left as a general rubric, could not possibly be actualised in such a way as to satisfy the diverse social ideals driving Schelling's youthful student audience – incipient existentialism, communism, cultural organicism and anarchism. Kierkegaard's diary relates how 'the embryonic child of thought leapt for joy within me' when, in his second lecture, Schelling mentioned the word 'actuality'.[7] But the initial burst of excitement was soon to dissipate. In February Kierkegaard wrote that 'Schelling talks the most insufferable nonsense'.[8] Likewise Engels, who had joined a study circle of Berlin Young Hegelians nicknamed 'The Free', responded with two scathing pamphlets – *Schelling, Philosopher in Christ* and *Schelling and Revelation* – which advised Germany to 'turn away from this waste of time'.[9]

The rejection of Schelling's philosophy by this most famous generation of radical intellectuals is well known – a spectacular downfall to match the narrative of his brilliant emergence as the new star of the critical philosophy in the mid 1790s, at the age of twenty. What has been neglected, until recently, is the more soul-searching intervening phase of the 1810s, and it is this period which is important for narratives of the unconscious. Over these years covering the Napoleonic invasion and its immediate aftermath Schelling began to question the whole notion of philosophical 'system' and grappled with ways of introducing obscurity and resistance into the structural programme of idealism.

---

[7] Søren Kierkegaard, *The Concept of Irony*, trans. Howard V. Hong and Edna H. Hong (Princeton University Press, 1989), xxi.

[8] Ibid., xxii.

[9] Friedrich Engels, 'Schelling and Revelation' [1842], in *Karl Marx Frederick Engels: Collected Works*, vol. II: *Frederick Engels 1838–42* (London: Lawrence & Wishart, 1975), 237.

This and the following chapter begin by looking at Schelling's earlier turn from Fichtean idealism to *Naturphilosophie* (the philosophy of nature), and then trace the further repercussions of this shift through to the 1810s and Schelling's concern with unconscious principles at the heart of human life. One effect of this turn to nature, as we shall see, is that the general 'chain of knowledge' which attains stability in some supreme, unconditioned uppermost point', assumed in his own early essay 'Of the I as Principle of Philosophy', converts into more complex idioms of polar tension, growth and equilibrium.[10] These, in their turn, fundamentally reconfigure the way individuality, connectedness and freedom can be thought. Against the very public vote of no confidence in Schelling's philosophy of the 1840s, there was then a more behind-the-scenes achievement over the prior decades in which Schelling was reworking eighteenth-century philosophical and structural idioms. In the longer term, this kind of shift appears more radical than it did in the light of practical demands in the revolutionary period. Schelling arrived at quite new descriptions of how entities in general, including human individuals, might interconnect – descriptions which resonated through the nineteenth century in the life sciences, aesthetics, philosophy and psychology.

The current brief chapter provides some necessary background to Schelling's theory of nature before I proceed to examine his turn to the unconscious in the middle section of this book. What I want to consider in particular is how nature initially serves Schelling much as the theory of the will had served Fichte. He takes a concrete and seemingly empirical area of existence (for Fichte, the will as a field of human practice; for Schelling, nature as a field of human knowledge) and invests it with alternative, metaphysical descriptions of identity in which the idea of human freedom can be founded. But just as Fichte could only preserve the notion of autonomy by making the operations of the will obscure, so Schelling was increasingly drawn beyond delineations of the 'system' of nature to a concern with the obscure generative or dialectical principles through which nature originally emerged. By focusing once more on the shifting configurations of individuality, unity and autonomy which lie concealed behind the general account of 'freedom', I will provide a new set of indices for understanding Schelling's gradual shift of concern from the I to nature, from nature to nature's origins, and, in the next chapter, from origins to unconsciousness. These shifts are implicated just as much in the problem of imagining the metaphysical foundations of the liberal self and its self-certainty as they are in their manifest enquiry into nature.

[10] Schelling, 'Of the I', 77.

The freedom of nature

How does nature, the term which for Fichte had conjured up the dog-matic web of external authority – the very factor to be excluded from the foundational account of the I – help Schelling to pose and resolve issues of human identity and freedom? Schelling made a number of very different inroads into the question of nature between the *Ideas* of 1797 and *Explanation of the True Relations of Naturphilosophie to the Revised Fichtean Teaching* of 1806. These ranged in form from geometric systems to transcendental critiques, from Neoplatonic dialogues to articles for the *Journal of Speculative Physics*. The key works here include *On the World Soul, a Hypothesis of the Higher Physics* (1798), *First Draft of a System of Naturphilosophie* (1799), *The System of Transcendental Idealism* (1800), *Of the True Concept of Naturphilosophie* (1801), *Bruno, or Concerning the Divine and Natural Principle of Things. A Conversation* (1802), *System of the Whole of Philosophy and of Naturphilosophie in Particular* (1804), and *Aphorisms Concerning the Naturphilosophie* (1805), all of which unfold a complex and varying set of relations between metaphysics, epistemology, ontology and natural scientific research. As a whole they encompass not so much a single line of development as a restless adjustment of perspective. Joseph L. Esposito has identified at least six major reformulations of Schelling's *Naturphilosophie* over this relatively short time period. As for many of his Romantic contemporaries, nature was not simply an object out there, or a set of physical materials with diverse properties, but a general medium for existence through which metaphysical, scientific, moral and spiritual questions could be explored.

As an idealist in the post-Kantian tradition Schelling initially sought to extend the notion of an a priori subjective structuring of reality beyond the most abstract or formal epistemological levels and into the heart of the natural scientific description of matter, in all its chemical and organic diversity. This was a direction which Kant himself had pursued in the late 1790s with his search for mediating concepts between the metaphysical principles of natural science and the actual content of empirical physical law. As Frederick Beiser has outlined, Kant became interested in conceptualising the forces behind phenomena such as solidification, magnetism and chemical affinity, which he credited with being both a priori and a posteriori, a bridge between formal possibility and actual reality.[11] Thus one aspect of Schelling's researches in the 1790s comprises his attempts to gather the details of new empirical research (Galvani and Volta's experiments with dynamic

---

[11] Beiser, *German Idealism*, 185.

forces, Lavoisier and Priestley's investigations into the composition of matter) and to equate these results with his own transcendental deductions of the principles inherent in nature. At the same time, Schelling was to some extent also forwarding Fichte's idea of nature as ultimately a construct of the human subject – nature should necessarily 'not only *express*, but *even realise*, the laws of our mind'.[12]

The nature and timing of Schelling's intellectual shifts are much debated.[13] What is clear is that at some point towards the end of the 1790s Schelling upended the assumptions of Fichtean idealism: instead of dissolving the concept of nature wholly into the transcendental subject of reason, he inaugurated a new kind of study of nature itself. His project was now to explore nature – at its most general and particular levels of organisation – as the manifestation of polar tensions between finitude and infinitude, contraction and expansion. Idealism no longer consisted in the complete subsumption of the external world under the terms of the transcendental I. Just as Fichte had posited a principle within the I which constituted both subjective consciousness and the conditions of the objective world, so Schelling sought to conceptualise a new absolute developmental principle, at work in nature and mind alike, but not necessarily ascribed to the 'I'. One way in which he conceived of this absolute principle was in terms of polarities – subjectivity and objectivity, light and gravity – which oscillate around the possibility of synthesis, rather than being integrated in a completed formal structure.

It is around this presentiment of a principle of development 'by which contrarieties in nature set in shifting but opposed polar positions eternally compelled their resolution', that a broad school of *Naturphilosophie* developed in the early 1800s exerting its own immense influence over nineteenth-century ideas of evolutionary and dynamic systems in both the human and natural sciences.[14] Kant had already asserted the necessity of such dynamic polarities within nature in *The Metaphysical Foundations of Natural Science* of 1786. But for Schelling, these contrary principles do more than simply reflect the categories of the understanding – they are inherent in nature itself, which is credited with its own powers of creative self-development. The emphasis of idealism thus shifted in Schelling's hands from the principles of human reason towards the reciprocal relation between nature and subjectivity – the presentiment that nature and mind are held in dynamic tension with

---

[12] Schelling, *Ideas*, 41–2.
[13] The final break in the friendship between Fichte and Schelling is usually dated around the years 1801–2. For a detailed account of their growing intellectual disagreement, see Beiser, *German Idealism*, 491–505.
[14] William Coleman, *Biology in the Nineteenth Century* (New York: John Wiley, 1971), 49.

each other. Ultimately, 'Nature should be mind made visible, mind the invisible Nature'.[15] As Bowie, Beiser and others have suggested, with the development of *Naturphilosophie*, Schelling 'began to question the whole Cartesian tradition of the knowing subject'.[16]

It is this attempt to theorise a 'system' of nature based around conflict, change and growth, rather than 'chains of determination', which mainly concerns us here. But one must at least be aware of some other important facets of Schelling's engagement with nature. There is, first of all, the crucial exchange of ideas between Schelling and Goethe during Schelling's Jena years (1798–1803) at a time when both thinkers were concerned with the possibility of nature's creative independence. It was Goethe who helped bring Schelling to Jena in the first place, and according to Robert J. Richards, it was Goethe who helped turn Schelling away from the influence of Fichte.[17] Schelling would repay the debt by describing *Faust* as the greatest poem of the Germans and a uniquely philosophical one: 'Let anyone wishing to penetrate into the true sanctuary of nature approach these tones from a higher world.'[18] What drew Goethe and Schelling together in particular was a mutual interest in applying the idea of archetypes, or *Urtypen*, to the world of nature. This would prove influential in the development of biological thought in Germany, culminating in the work of Lorenz Oken and Karl von Baer. It also signals, alongside the shift from consciousness to nature, an increasing ambiguity around the status of 'ideas' in Schelling's idealism. These are no longer just the regulative ideals of the Kantian doctrine. Rather, as we shall see in the *Ages of the World*, Schelling became attracted to the possibility of ideas as form-giving powers, somehow constitutive and formally present in the world.[19]

Secondly, one should note Schelling's immersion in the circle of the Jena Romantics and his absorption of the aesthetic and religious conceptions of the Schlegels and Novalis who were also reworking Fichtean subjectivism in novel ways. Schelling is most commonly associated with

---

[15] Schelling, *Ideas*, 42.

[16] Beiser, *German Idealism*, 471.

[17] Robert J. Richards, *The Romantic Conception of Life* (University of Chicago Press, 2002), 148, 179. See also Lukács' comment, *Goethe and His Age* (London: Merlin Press, 1979), 172, that 'Goethe never entirely associates himself with any one current of this philosophy, but he has a deep sympathy for young Schelling's attempts at a philosophy of nature'.

[18] F. W. J. Schelling, *The Philosophy of Art*, trans. Douglas W. Stott (Minneapolis, MN: University of Minnesota Press, 1989), 278.

[19] See also Beiser, *German Idealism*, 349–74, for an account of the impact of Platonism on the generation which included Hölderlin, Novalis, Hegel and Schelling, and also Werner Beierwaltes, *Platonismus und Idealismus* (Frankfurt am Main: Vittorio Klostermann, 1972).

such Romantic conceptions of nature, and indeed it is these aspects of his philosophy which were perhaps most easily assimilated beyond the circles of *Naturphilosophie*. Like the Romantics, Schelling appeared to embrace pantheism, asserting the existence of a 'world soul', a single active and organisational presence within the whole of nature, and he posited an absolute creative principle as a shared source for nature and the subject, manifested in the human world in the genius of art. Schelling's paean to the artist at the close of *The System of Transcendental Idealism* exemplifies such Romantic and idealist notions, which entered into the currency of Anglo-American aesthetic theory through Schelling's influence on Coleridge.[20]

What most deserves emphasis, however, is the way in which Schelling's continual investigation into the consistency of nature was provoked as much by the reverse side of this question, which is: 'What is the nature of consistency?' Schelling's turn to nature and away from a Fichtean pre-occupation with the I was not just a retreat from idealism's totalitarian claims for consciousness, nor merely an attempt to make idealism viable for a new epoch of natural-scientific research; it also sought a more tangible way of mediating those conflicting terms of autonomy and authority from which Fichte's philosophy took its departure. Nature is a field for empirical and scientific research, but it is also to provide a new basis for transcendental deductions of different forms of freedom and identity. As with Fichte, the issue appears at first to turn on a confrontation between the human desire for complete self-knowledge and a refractory world of nature. Nature in Schelling's hands is to realise mind, the structure of the world is to validate the speculative structures of human identity, with no remainder, for all the same reasons covered in the previous chapter: to establish human moral autonomy and exhibit security and stability in the secular field of knowledge. But at another level, the investigation of nature is not a confrontation, but a search for the elusive 'principle' of freedom which human rationality has not been able to articulate except in contradictory or ambiguous fashion, as chains of determination or the obscure source of the will. Nature was that which, following Kant's *Critique of Judgement*, appeared to be both purposive *and* the product of a blind mechanism, both spontaneous and regular. It seemed to combine the very qualities of necessity and freedom which transcendental idealism ascribed to humanity as the essence of *its* identity, but whose union remained paradoxically

---

[20] See Thomas McFarland, *Coleridge and the Pantheist Tradition* (Oxford: Clarendon Press, 1969), and Paul Hamilton, *Coleridge and German Philosophy* (London: Continuum, 2007).

unthinkable. For Schelling, 'Every plant is entirely what it should be; what is free therein is necessary, and what is necessary is free.' But man, on the other hand, is forever 'a broken fragment', because 'either his action is necessary, and then not free, or free, and then not necessary according to law'.[21] This was the antinomy that Heidegger repeatedly elicited in his studies of Schelling's *Philosophical Inquiries into the Nature of Human Freedom*: '(1) either system is retained, then freedom must be relinquished; or (2) freedom is retained, which means renunciation of system';[22] 'Freedom excludes the recourse to grounding. The system, however, demands the thoroughgoing connection of grounding.'[23] Moreover, for Schelling himself, even though the 'connection between the concept of freedom and a total world view will always remain the subject of an inevitable problem', not to resolve the problem leaves the concept of freedom ambiguous, and then philosophy in turn is left 'totally without value'.[24]

The turn to nature, then, deflects from the human subject, but only in order to open up the terms in which individuality, freedom and certainty can be thought – and this is crucial for the development of certain dynamic psychological ideas around the unconscious. As I will argue throughout the middle section of this book, the unconscious both designates a natural basis for the self, which resists the subject's own drive towards self-consciousness, *and* an a-conceptual domain through which individuality can be thought (which the subject therefore needs to preserve in some form). Turning from the subject to nature we have not left the terrain in which the self is to be theorised, but entered it. Thus Schelling's *Ideas* opens with the claim that, in examining the principles of nature, there is to be no question of 'converting the world into a play of concepts, or the mind within you into a dead mirror of things'.[25] Human identity is not to be yielded up to a dangerous scepticism about its foundations, nor is it to become a passive reflector of external forms. We are once again at the impasse familiar from Fichte's Introductions to the *Wissenschaftslehre* and *The Vocation of Man*. It is into this crisis in the theory of autonomy – epistemological, ontological and moral – that the theory of nature is to be inserted. But at the same time Schelling is forced to admit that, between the insupportable outside and inside, 'Nothing is left but an idea which floats midway between something and nothing.'[26] The turn to nature, then, aims to give an identity to this

---

[21] Schelling, *System*, 216.
[22] Martin Heidegger, *Schelling's Treatise on the Essence of Human Freedom*, trans. Joan Stambaugh (Athens, OH: Ohio University Press, 1985), 49.
[23] Ibid., 21.   [24] Schelling, *Human Freedom*, 9.
[25] Schelling, *Ideas*, 15.   [26] Ibid., 25.

middle, to this as yet vague idea on which, in turn, the nature of human identity will be constructed.

The direction that Schelling took in the *Ideas* was already implied in Kant's *Metaphysical Foundation of the Natural Sciences*. Here Kant posed the problem of knowledge of nature as follows: 'the word "nature" (because this word designates the derivation of the manifold belonging to the existence of things from their internal principle) necessitates a rational cognition of the coherence of things'.[27] For ideas to form chains of inferences and thus principles of rational coherence, nature must be capable of being thought in terms of mathematical laws. For this reason, the physical qualities of nature and the laws of physics were brought into the foreground of natural science. It was precisely this kind of 'enchained' system of coherence which Schelling was seeking to circumvent. But Kant had added that, because chemical laws remain merely empirical, 'they carry with themselves no consciousness of their necessity (are not apodeictically certain)'.[28] Thus so long as there is, 'for the chemical actions of matters on one another no concept which admits of being constructed', chemistry can become little more than a systematic *art*, or experimental doctrine.[29] Chemical phenomena suggest forms of relationship which, like freedom, fall outside the purview of the rational construction of necessity. More importantly, Kant linked chemistry in this respect with the empirical doctrine of the soul which 'must always remain yet even further removed than chemistry from the rank of what may be called a natural science proper'.[30] This correlation of chemistry with freedom is also glancingly picked up in *The Critique of Judgement* when, in 'The Dialectic of the Aesthetical Judgement', Kant ascribes the emergence of beauty in nature to nature's faculty of producing forms 'in its freedom ... according to chemical laws'.[31] Kant linked chemistry with the doctrine of the soul merely negatively, because of their joint inability to be schematised according to general rational laws. Schelling, in the *Ideas* and the ensuing manifestos of the *Naturphilosophie*, turned to chemistry and the dynamic phenomena of electricity and magnetism precisely in order to theorise the 'soul' of freedom.

I have noted already how Schelling's approach concentrates on a new kind of formal intuition of nature: not causal succession in time, but a principle of polar tension between modes of finitude and infinitude (or

---

[27] Immanuel Kant, *Metaphysical Foundations of Natural Science* [1786], in *Philosophy of Material Nature*, trans. James Ellington (Indianapolis, IN: Hackett, 1985), 3.
[28] Ibid., 4.   [29] Ibid., 7.   [30] Ibid., 8.
[31] Immanuel Kant, *Critique of Judgement*, trans. J. H. Bernard (New York: Hafner Press, 1951), 195.

the determined and the free). Schelling was drawing on Fichte's own accounts in the *Wissenschaftslehre* of the dialectic of self-relation in the subject of consciousness. Fichte suggested that the conditions of consciousness demand that the subject always relate itself to an object – hence the I's speculative construction of the objective world of nature with which it was faced. However, this relationship itself implied an infinite or unbounded quality in the subject which was able always to go 'beyond' the objectivity of nature, precisely in order to be conscious of it. According to Fichte, as the empirical I observes the world beyond it, there is always something within the I itself – its transcendental productivity – which has already provided the framework within which subject and object are related. This set of assumptions pervades Schelling's *Of the I* and the *System of Transcendental Idealism*: the real, the objective world, is the limitable (*Begrenzbare*) and also the 'found'; whereas the ideal, the subjective, is the illimitable, or the 'finder'. The Kantian 'thing in itself' is for Schelling 'nothing else but the shadow of the ideal activity, now over the boundary, which is thrown back to the I by intuition'.[32] That is to say, what the 'thing-in-itself' conceals is not something fundamentally external to the subject, but rather the previous and ulterior activity of the subject. It appears opaque or unknown only because the subject's own productivity is not yet representable in a form that can be re-appropriated by subjective consciousness.

Schelling took this idea of a dialectical relation between the finitude of the object and the infinitude of the subject and transposed it into nature as a general principle of nature's own productivity. Separated into its simplest elements, Schelling posits not an original relation between subject and object, but an original polarisation between a gravitational force and a 'light essence'.[33] While in the Newtonian paradigm attraction could be conceived as a ubiquitous law of nature, and therefore a unifying principle, for Schelling gravity was the more truly foundational concept. It represented the centripetal gathering of substance into a single inert mass, a primary but undifferentiated unity. Gravity serves, in *Naturphilosophie*, as the bond 'which binds all living things and unites the totality'; like the creator, 'its centre is everywhere and circumference nowhere'.[34] Against this, he posited light-essence [*Lichtwesen*], a hypothetical, as yet unknown, principle which was manifested in the phenomena of combustion and phosphorescence. Whatever its actual basis, its activity was associated with the disintegration of matter, and

---

[32] Schelling, *System*, 68. See also 54–6.
[33] F. W. J. Schelling, *On the World Soul: a Hypothesis of the Higher Physics, as an Explanation of the General Organism* [1798], in *Sämmtliche Werke*, part 1, vol. II, 369–70.
[34] Ibid., 364.

with motion, infinitude, and by implication spirit. Where gravity draws movement towards rest, light-essence sets all rest in motion.[35] Within this system of concepts, matter itself no longer appears as part of a fixed, inertly present object-world governed by the principle of sufficient reason. Rather, matter and the possibility of objectivity is generated out of the tension between these two original forces – gravity and light, contraction and expansion – with concrete presence emerging at the equilibrial point of their relation. This equilibrium, however, is inherently unstable. Whenever a form of objectivity develops in this theoretically middle space, it in turn creates new ratios within the general scheme of polar forces, and hence a more complex differentiation of the middle resulting in further and more complex forms of objectivity.

In Schelling's hands, then, the *Naturphilosophie* developed into an elaborate system of dialectics in which ways of uniting freedom and necessity, heteronomy and identity, were intellectually graded and grounded as modes of actuality. For instance, if gravity was an absolute force of contraction, trying to draw existence into a single inert point, the dynamic phenomena of electricity and magnetism represented a form of unity that contained contradiction within it – the polar oppositions of positive and negative forces: 'By virtue of gravity the body is in unity with all others; through magnetism it picks itself out and gathers itself together as a particular unity.' Magnetism is therefore the universal form of 'individual-being-in-itself'.[36] Chemical processes represent a further level of differentiation and spontaneity in the reactions of one substance upon another – such as the partial domination of light over gravity.

Not only the general forces and organic and inorganic levels of nature, but particular elements are described in terms of a formal counterpointing of degrees of identity and difference: every existing entity falls towards one end or the other on a scale of determination and freedom, or, by attaining a middle position, enables the emergence of a new synthesis, and the stabilisation of new forms of existence. For instance, Schelling conceived of carbon as an underlying unified ground within the realm of matter, while diamonds and nitrogen expressed, respectively, the poles of ordered structure and disintegrative force for carbon itself. What is essential is that the system is imagined not so much as a chain of beings, but a stratification of modes of existence in which the potential for relation and unity develops in complexity at each level. The different levels of nature do not themselves connect in a fully determined

---

[35] Ibid., 369–70.   [36] Schelling, *Ideas*, 128.

fashion – they cannot be conceived in terms of either a purely temporal or logical series – so much as revise and supplement each other. As Schelling noted, 'As soon as we enter the realm of organic nature, all mechanical linkage of cause and effect ceases for us.'[37] For this reason, he adapted the term *Potenzen* from the mathematical notion of potentiation, and used it to indicate the way in which phenomena might be raised to qualitatively higher levels and powers of integration.

The 'higher' levels here are reserved not for an absolute systematicity, but for the complexities of organisms, which introduce a further heightening of the synthesis between independence and relationship. In a formula strangely reminiscent of Fichte's calls for moral self-emancipation, 'Every organic product exists for itself; its being is dependent on no other being.'[38] The organic thus provides a new mediation of the concept of individuality, which is poised, as the idea of nature itself is, between forces of integration and disintegration, rationality and heteronomy. Ultimately consciousness itself is to be integrated into this evolving hierarchy of qualitative states. It too, going back to Fichte's insight, expresses a tension between infinitude and restriction which is necessary for subjectivity, and for the subject–object relation to emerge. At the pinnacle of Schelling's system is the ultimate synthesis of freedom and necessity in an organism that is not only living, but self-reflecting – that is, human individuality. Only such a self-reflecting consciousness would be able to reconstruct the complete system of nature out of which it had itself arisen.

What remains highly ambiguous in Schelling's exposition is whether the differentiated phenomena of nature are still meant as transcendental deductions in the Kantian manner – deductions that shed light not on nature itself, but on the kinds of ways reason is able to constitute the natural world mentally – or whether they are intended as an ontogenetic description of how nature has actually evolved, with human self-consciousness as a further development of the kinds of forces, oppositions and syntheses that are apparent at different levels of nature. Was Schelling concerned with the regulation and ordering of rational concepts of nature, or is the *Naturphilosophie* more concrete and metaphysical in its pretensions, hypothesising an evolutionary development in which stasis is successively ruptured and equilibrium overturned in the production of more and more complex forms of life? Arthur O. Lovejoy pointed out this ambiguity over the historical and ideal dimensions of Schelling's system, which appears partly to suggest an evolution

[37] Ibid., 30.   [38] Ibid., 30.

in time, and partly to resurrect the Neoplatonic 'scale of beings'.[39] Oskar Walzel likewise noted that 'In this sequence of stages Schelling wished expressly to trace a development'; however, Schelling did not explain 'whether this transition from the imperfect to the more perfect was also to be a historical fact and a temporal phenomenon'. This elicited Alexander Gode-von Aesch's comment that 'a development which is not necessarily a temporal phenomenon is either an absurdity or presupposes a very peculiar conception of time'.[40] Crucially, these equivocations go right back to the original arguments between Fichte and Schelling themselves. In 1800 Fichte objected that it was a logical error 'to assume that philosophical reconstruction of consciousness from its simple elements corresponds to some kind of natural history, as if the *logical* priority of the elements were also some kind of *temporal* priority'.[41]

It is not properly time itself which is at issue here, or not yet, but rather the foundation of freedom. If the system were manifestly evolutionary, or developmental in a simple linear sense, then humanity would be positioned once more as merely the result of nature's prior determination. It was precisely in order to escape from that sort of causal or logical chain that Schelling had forged a pathway out of Kant's mathesis of nature in pursuit of those forces – chemistry, contrariety, life – which could not be articulated along those lines. However, this resistance to determinate structures produces a paradoxical situation in which the ultimate nature of freedom remains suspended. Freedom awaits its complete ideological statement in the philosophy of nature, but the philosophy of nature in turn remains unfinished or equivocal, awaiting the final emergence of the principle of freedom in mankind. The arrival on the stage of history of a fully autonomous, self-reflecting individuality is not simply the final point in a sequence, it is the missing link which is to supply the as yet undiscovered principle through which the whole sequence can be finally understood. As a result there is a constant ambivalence in these works over where the system is going: whether the end will sanction the beginning or the beginning the end, or whether the whole is to be a timeless construct (these are questions which Hegel will return to in his Preface to *The Phenomenology of Spirit*). The first possibility

---

[39] Arthur O. Lovejoy, *The Great Chain of Being* [1936] (Cambridge, MA: Harvard University Press, 1964); Lecture XI deals particularly with Schelling and the question of temporalisation.

[40] Oskar Walzel, *Deutsche Romantik* (Leipzig: B. G. Teubner, 1908), cited in Alexander Gode-von Aesch, *Natural Science in German Romanticism* [1941] (New York: AMS Press, 1966), 76.

[41] Beiser, *German Idealism*, 495.

recurs constantly in Schelling's conception of philosophy: 'A system is completed when it is led back to its starting point.'[42] From a philosophical point of view, the final conclusions must square with the original premises. But at the same time the statement shows that the logical and philosophical development of ideas is being complicated by its entanglement in notions of historical development. What does it mean, in this context, for the system to comprehend its starting point, its historical rather than its conceptual origins? Can such a starting point be deduced and guaranteed within a set of philosophical premises? And if not, what kind of ideological structure can unfold the truth?

In the early 1800s the application of logical form to accounts of natural evolution reached an extreme formulation in Schelling's 'identity' philosophy. In *The System of the Whole of Philosophy and of Naturphilosophie* (1804) the very notion of development and differentiation as a real event was undercut by the idea of a permanent metaphysical basis beneath the supposed divisions made by consciousness. The underlying reality of nature, according to this view, is stable, absolute and undifferentiated, but the inherence of the absolute in limited, particular beings creates a parallax in the cognition of existence. Hence the familiar apparition of divisions into subject and object, self and nature. In the 1804 *System*, Schelling described the 'infinite real substance' (that which is beyond subjectivity and objectivity) as producing an absolute identity within particular things, but that these, by virtue of their own relativity, mediate the absolute with privation, lack, unreality.[43] Ironically, Schelling's philosophy here starts to approximate that of Spinoza, and indeed Fichte complained to Schelling already in 1801 that he was returning idealism to the very positions that had originally been rejected as dogmatism.[44]

These ambiguities over the shape and direction of the system noted by Walzel and Gode-von Aesch are then superficially a problem of 'temporality', but actually a symptom of Schelling's diverse priorities: to narrate the system of nature, to complete the system of philosophy, and to found the idea of freedom. From the standpoint of *freedom*, absolute stasis in the system – its completion – disavows freedom's ability to transcend any objective structural limitations. For this reason, Schelling

[42] Schelling, *System*, 232.
[43] Schelling, *System of the Whole of Philosophy and of Naturphilosophie in Particular* [1804], in *Sämmtliche Werke*, part 1, vol. VI, 141–587, 228–330.
[44] See, for instance, J. G. Fichte, 'Letter to Schelling', 15 October 1801, in Walter Schulz (ed.), *Fichte-Schelling Briefwechsel* (Frankfurt am Main: Suhrkamp Verlag, 1968), 142–3. For further aspects of this dispute, see Beiser, *German Idealism*, 504–5.

is keen to introduce notions of anteriority, development and potentiation. But from the standpoint of the *system*, nature's ability to evolve ever higher powers, ever more complex forms of freedom, introduces a condition of structural excess which Schelling struggles to recuperate within any foundational description of the whole. These structural anxieties come to a head with the representation of humanity itself, for it is human consciousness that lies inescapably at the crux of the system in which 'Nature should be Mind made visible'.[45] If one takes the *Naturphilosophie* in an evolutionary sense, then it is humanity that comes last: human consciousness is the ultimate achievement of whatever process has been occurring dialectically in nature. Insofar as this process has concerned the higher and higher synthesis of the principles of individuality and universality, freedom and order, humanity is to provide the apotheosis of that process. And yet, as we have seen, inherent in Schelling's break with Fichtean idealism is his recognition that human reason cannot (or cannot yet) articulate the principle on which it is founded. It is with human consciousness that, far from reaching its climactic manifestation, the search for *foundations* begins. It was after all nature, rather than rational consciousness, that was to provide the content for that elusive 'idea which floats midway between something and nothing'.[46]

This is the paradox haunting Schelling's *Naturphilosophie*: on the one hand, it purveys a vision of the human spirit as something that 'strives to make *itself* free, to disentangle itself from the fetters of Nature and her guardianship ... in order one day to return, as victor and by its own merit, to that position in which, unaware of itself, it spent the childhood of its reason'.[47] But at the same time, these texts initiate a radical curvature away from completion, away from a finally achieved philosophical statement. If they turn back to reflect on their origins, it is increasingly to be absorbed by the question of something necessarily obscure, something constitutively unconscious at the 'beginning' of the system. Most famously this occurs at the end of *The System of Transcendental Idealism* where Schelling, like Kant, concludes that philosophy must defer from reason to art in order to find an intuition of nature's creative process. Art now becomes paramount to the philosopher, 'precisely because it opens to him, as it were, the holiest of holies, where burns in eternal and original unity, as if in a single flame, that which in nature and history is rent asunder'.[48] Nature cannot reveal itself in a completed organon of

[45] Schelling, *Ideas*, 42.   [46] Ibid., 25.
[47] Ibid., 10.   [48] Schelling, *System*, 231.

philosophy, but remains 'a poem lying pent in a mysterious and wonderful script'.[49] The role of philosophy is to explicate scientifically why mind is held in such systematic tension with obscurity, and to lay out the wider symbolic function of art.

Schelling's 1803 revision of the *Ideas* also makes an explicit turn from consciousness towards obscurity. In the first edition of 1797 it had seemed that a complete science of nature was a plausible future goal, hence the sense of a preliminary sketch conveyed by the title, '*Ideas for ...*' a philosophy of nature. However, by the time of its re-edition with various new supplementary chapters, it seems the absolute basis of nature is *necessarily* removed from scientific or logical description, as an inaccessible depth which can only be obscurely divined. In a poetic revision to the Introduction, Schelling evokes the way in which 'The ideal world presses mightily towards the light, but is still held back by the fact that Nature has withdrawn as a mystery. The very secrets which the ideal harbours cannot truly become objective save in proclaiming the mystery of Nature.'[50] This is no longer simply an acknowledgement that the system or freedom have yet to emerge, and that further work is needed. The very way in which nature can be known is now held up to question, and the science of knowledge is exchanged for the mystery cult (much as Novalis had depicted it in his *The Novices of Sais*).[51] The goal of development is reached when 'all *finite* forms have been struck down', and mankind is forever united in a 'collective intuition'.[52]

The concept of development at which Schelling arrives in the early 1800s is a complex and ambivalent one – he finds himself bent on construing a relationship backwards into the mysterious depths of nature, at the same time as hypothesising an evolutionary leap into the future by human identity. There is pathos in his hesitation over whether it is growth, equilibration or return which adequately describes the transition between nature and consciousness, and in the way the project ultimately turns tail. We find not a nature transposed into consciousness, but a humanity whose 'essence' disappears back into nature. It is not simply that the system of nature cannot be finally conceived, but that Schelling, on the verge of completing his account of human subjectivity,

---

[49] Ibid., 232.   [50] Schelling, *Ideas*, 54–5.
[51] Novalis, *The Novices of Sais*, trans. Ralph Manheim (New York: Archipelago Books, 2005). See, for instance, 29: 'Within us there lies a mysterious force that tends in all directions, spreading from a centre hidden in infinite depth'; 31: 'they find beatitude in the contemplation of this living ornament hovering over the depths of night'; 41: 'The effort to fathom the giant mechanism is in itself a move towards the abyss, a beginning of madness.'
[52] Schelling, *Ideas*, 55.

is compelled to suspend or obscure that account. On this front one must counter the temptation, exhibited in recent interpretations of Schelling, simply to attribute the crises in his theory to the concrete difficulties of describing the beginnings and evolution of life.[53] To read the *Naturphilosophie* aright, one needs to recognise that the 'foundations' at issue are not simply the beginnings of nature, but also the metaphysical foundations of the concept of human identity whose fortunes have been twinned with, or sutured into, the natural-historical account.

There is a strange chiasmus here in which a theory of development (natural, historical) crosses paths with a quite different project which is to bury speculative metaphysical foundations within the obscurer regions of nature's past. If one bears this in mind, a very different reading of the 'failure' of the *Naturphilosophie* and its equivocations over time and development emerges. In this light, the failure of the project appears as the symptom of its own historical epoch. One finds reflected in it the full force of those anxieties about the foundations of human identity once philosophy has displaced religion, as well as the turning of the political tide from revolution to reaction, from the Fichtean radicalism of the 1790s to the remythologisation of power with which Schelling becomes associated in the post-Napoleonic era. One needs, in effect, to understand how the scientific vocabulary of dynamic and developmental forces was becoming inflected by more conservative tendencies, and by the need to preserve the metaphysical certainties of a social world, which was itself rapidly being left behind.

Confusing as this situation might appear, its general co-ordinates should be familiar from the discussion of Fichte. In the last chapter we saw that, though the overt emphasis of Fichte's project was to turn from theology towards a philosophy of human consciousness, the theory of the I at the same time aimed to preserve idealised notions of autonomy, self-identity and universality within a philosophical account of human being. The abstract concept of the will, rather than inaugurating an analysis of the fissures in moral and political practice, became a medium for the projection of obscure processes, 'hidden from mortal eyes', which could ground both the absolute self-determination of the individual and the harmonisation of all free wills. In the same way, in Schelling's *Naturphilosophie* nature indicates not only the evolved structure of the natural world as object of investigation, it is also the site of

---

[53] Andrew Bowie, for instance, considers at length Schelling's concern to identify the play of forces which 'makes life possible', or 'how life emerges', and reports on studies such as Marie-Luise Heuser-Kessler's on the 'productivity of nature' which connects Schelling's theories with those of Ilya Prigogine, in *Schelling and Modern European Philosophy*, 37–8.

a moral task: to ground the idea of freedom, the spiritual 'element' of man.[54] If individual freedom cannot be articulated on a purely philosophical basis, there is the temptation to sustain the idea on a pseudo-philosophical basis: to assume that freedom emerges out of an obscure, constitutive process operating in the unknown recesses of nature.

In *The System of Transcendental Idealism* Schelling characterises the conjunction of freedom and identity as an 'eternal unknown which, like the everlasting sun in the realm of spirits, conceals itself behind its own unclouded light'. Though never becoming an object, this conjunction, in a similar fashion to Fichte's will, 'impresses its identity upon all free actions, is simultaneously the same for all intelligences, the invisible root of which all intelligences are but powers'. It is at once 'the ground of lawfulness in freedom, and of freedom in the lawfulness of the object'.[55] Some ten years later, in the *Weltalter* texts of 1811–15, Schelling will describe the substance of freedom by simply asserting a primordial principle of life – *das Urlebendige* – in which identity and difference, productivity and eternal essence, are imagined to be always already resolved: 'Since there is nothing before or outside of this primordial life by which it might be determined, it can only develop (to the extent that it does develop) freely, purely from itself alone, out of its own drive and volition. It does not, for that matter, develop lawlessly; rather, development proceeds strictly according to law.'[56] Nature has again slipped outside the limits of thinking and now merely symbolises the ideal of freedom *and* lawfulness, holism *and* individuality, that philosophy could not systematise. The middle has been given a figurative body, but the operation of freedom is no more actualised than ever. One is left with a whole which may, or may not, develop; and if it did develop, would do so as a result of drive *and* volition.

Elsewhere Schelling reorients his attention around the 'beginning', and with it the contractive force of gravity, the 'dark bond which influences the kernel of things' and provides an imagined counterweight against the tendency towards dispersion in manifest existence.[57] Gravity takes on a value beyond its formal position in the original system (as that which, together with light, establishes the simplest form of polar tension in nature) and starts to become a metaphor for the ontological foundations of life as a whole. On the one hand, Schelling derives the origins of selfhood from it – it is that general force through

---

[54] See Schelling, *Ideas*, 10.   [55] Schelling, *System*, 209.
[56] Schelling, *Ages of the World*, 113.
[57] F. W. J. Schelling, *Von der Weltseele*, in K. F. A. Schelling (ed.), *Sämmtliche Werke*, I Abtheilung vols. I–X; II *Abtheilung* vols. I–IV (Stuttgart: Cotta, 1856–61), Abt. I, vol. II, 369.

which all entities seek to maintain themselves in their independence. On the other hand, it is also a general basis for the interactions of life as a whole: it couples entities together, 'not by an external cause (a pull), but through the universal pre-established harmony, whereby all is one and one is all'.[58] Consequently, nothing in the universe is 'oppressed, purely dependent or in subjection, for everything is in itself absolute, and hence also in the absolute'. The term 'absolute' here welds together the connotation of an unshakeable premise, an absolute starting point in the philosophy of existence, *and* the sense of the absolute autonomy of each self, conceived as freedom from any external subjection. The reorientation of the concept of gravity here, though appearing in the context of the scientific investigation of natural forces, has more in common with the poetical and ontological observations on gravity which Heidegger draws out of Rilke's poem 'The Force of Gravity' in his 1946 lecture '*Wozu Dichter*': 'The force of gravity named in this poem is the centre of all beings as a whole … It is the ground as the "medium" that holds one being to another in mediation and gathers everything in the play of venture.'[59] Just as for Schelling entities are both coupled together and maintained in their independence, so for Heidegger all entities are both inwardly bonded and outwardly freed in the 'play of venture'. I will return to consider the relation between Heidegger and Schelling later; here I want to point out merely that all of Schelling's speculative attempts to represent the structure of human individuality and social coherence, metaphysically, repeat Fichte's gesture in ascribing an obscure form of unity to the will. Indeed, in *The Vocation of Man* Fichte had already suggested that the supersensible law unites, contains and subsumes under itself all finite rational beings, just as 'the universal force of attraction holds all bodies and unites them with it and with each other'.[60]

This chapter has presented only the broadest outline of Schelling's *Naturphilosophie* as the preliminary for a much closer investigation of his work on the *Weltalter*, the *Ages of the World*, which will occupy us through the central chapters of this study. As well as providing a narrative link between Fichte's philosophy of the I and Schelling's developing interest in the unconscious past, I have traced the continued presence in post-Kantian philosophy of a metaphysics of individuality and freedom, and the attempt to give a foundational account of the liberal self. I have also wanted to show that, in making his philosophical

[58] Schelling, *Ideas*, 159.
[59] Martin Heidegger, 'What Are Poets For?', *Poetry, Language, Thought*, trans. Albert Hofstadter (New York: Harper & Row, 1975), 104–5.
[60] Fichte, *Vocation*, 105.

turn towards nature, Schelling picked up certain new structural idioms and motifs from the emerging dynamic and organic sciences but gave them connotations beyond their immediate scientific context. Though we began with a *system* of nature, we have ended with Schelling's general sense that the metaphysical basis of nature is ultimately concealed from conscious reflection, and that likewise the problem of how law and freedom interrelate must be referred to vaguer kinds of apprehension of a primordial and unfathomable power of life. But this is not the end point of Schelling's thinking. Rather it is where he leaves the bounds of *Naturphilosophie* to pursue other options.

It is in the *Ages of the World* texts of 1811–15 that Schelling pushes these obscure and recalcitrant questions about the origins of nature and subjectivity towards a speculative study of the experience of time and origins per se. Hence these works represent the point at which 'unconsciousness' and 'the past', rather than nature, become the key terms of Schelling's philosophy. It is here that the study of the unconscious properly begins. My investigation is split into three parts. The first, Chapter 3, focuses on Schelling's attempt to grapple with ontology at the most abstract level. It considers the formal problems involved in theorising the foundations of individual identity isolated from any other descriptive contexts (history, psychology, and so on). These problems, as has now repeatedly been anticipated, show two sides. On the one hand, there is Schelling's desire to connect individual identity to some absolute foundation, insofar as the self is to be grounded, and is to enjoy the sense of some relatively stable cosmos of values, in which a meaningful freedom can be developed. This need for a foundation is already a response to anxieties that individuals may lose their values and their bearings as inherited social patterns, political structures and religious and ethical codes are contested. For Fichte, there was the ever-present fear that life might become 'a mere game which comes from nowhere and goes nowhere'; for Schelling that, without the underpinning of some unified rational spirit, history will descend into a muddled drama.[61]

On the other hand, identity must also be detached from such hypothesised absolute foundations, insofar as the individual is plagued by the sense that its freedom, its existence as a self-developing entity in its own right, is denied if it is inserted too deterministically into such a static or pre-organised system. What the 'absolute' actually means here takes on many and shifting forms. Most simply, it stands for an achieved absolute certainty regarding the coherence of the world of which it gives an account, and the truth of the propositions regarding individual

---

[61] Fichte, *Vocation*, 71; Schelling, *System*, 210.

self-determination. But the nature and grounds of this certainty, even within Schelling's work, can be conceived in a number of ways – originally as reason, then as nature, and now most frequently as metaphysical 'grounds', as God, or as the necessary structure of time and reality.

Schelling's re-examination of absolutes and origins at first revolves around attempts to use such concepts in inverted forms, which rid them of their negative or ambivalent implications as regards freedom. Ultimately, it will lead Schelling to an explicit formulation of the unconscious. In Chapter 4, we will see how this principle of unconsciousness becomes absorbed into the wider discursive structures of the Romantic human sciences, where it is embedded in various accounts of temporality, history and the development of being. Chapter 5, in turn, will concentrate specifically on Schelling's ideas about the psyche, and trace the effects of the unconscious as a principle within Romantic psychology.

Part II

The Romantic unconscious

3 Divining the individual: towards a metaphysics of the unconscious

> One conceives the God outside of oneself with the God within oneself. One cannot know God except through a divine principle.[1]
>
> *C'est un 'dieu' (il est vrai, un dieu mortel).*[2]

By common agreement 1809, the year which saw the publication of Schelling's essay on *Human Freedom*, marks a point of no return in Schelling's intellectual development. It is his last major philosophical publication until the philosophy of mythology of the 1840s, and so brings to a close the phase of his youthful academic brilliance and inaugurates a new period of withdrawal and obscurity. It also marks the inception of a different kind of obscurity – it is the point at which Schelling's thought becomes overtly mystical, and thus for a long time it has defined the limit of a certain kind of philosophical interest in Schelling the idealist.

This change of direction in Schelling's work has been associated with a number of different factors. In the first place, and most broadly, it can be set in the context of a trend of 'dark' Romanticism affecting German literary and intellectual culture in the early nineteenth century, in which even idealism succumbs to a certain fascination with the gothic, the magical and the mysterious.[3] In terms of Schelling's own work, the shift follows his move to Bavaria and the Catholic South in 1806. Initially, this was as a member of the Academy of Sciences, but an oration delivered before the Academy in 1807 so impressed the Crown Prince Ludwig (in whose honour it had been given) that Schelling soon attained a relatively independent position as General Secretary of the newly founded Academy of Arts in Munich in 1808. The Munich circle brought Schelling into contact with a very different intellectual culture

---

[1] F. W. J. Schelling, from 'The Stuttgart Seminars', cited in F. W. J. Schelling, *The Ages of the World* [1815], trans. Jason M. Wirth (State University of New York: 2000), xxv.

[2] Alexandre Kojève, *Introduction à la lecture de Hegel* (Paris: Gallimard, 1947), 492.

[3] See, for instance, Thomas F. O'Meara, *Romantic Idealism and Roman Catholicism: Schelling and the Theologians* (South Bend, IN: University of Notre Dame, 1982), 79.

from that of Jena, an example being his close alliance with Franz von
Baader, the quasi-Catholic philosopher, superintendent of the Bavarian
mines and (from 1826) professor of theology at the University of
Munich, who twinned interests in *Naturphilosophie* and anthropology
with researches into Kabbalism. François Marquet suggests Schelling's
most consequential contact with mysticism happened during the first
years of his stay in Munich, while the distinguished Schelling scholar
and editor Horst Fuhrmans understood Munich as initiating a 'great
turn' in his thinking: 'Into the place of a Goethean world, filled with
divinities, shining with beauty, whose centre was a Nature penetrated
by Spirit, steps the abyssal world of Böhme reaching deep into the
irrational and the dynamics of Night-hood.'[4]

This 'irrationalist' intellectual constellation, viewed in the light of
Schelling's later role as apologist for Friedrich Wilhelm IV's regime in
the 1840s, as well as Baader's correspondence with De Maistre and
Lammenais in France, has also implicated the whole of Schelling's
post-Jena oeuvre in the context of European counter-Enlightenment
and reaction. For Georg Lukács Schelling was notoriously key to the
inauguration of the post-revolutionary 'destruction of reason'.[5] But it
would be wrong to read the assuredness of a much later triumph of the
German bourgeoisie into the period of work on the *Ages of the World*,
which fits so squarely into the era of disunity, soul-searching and political crisis between the Prussian defeat at Jena and the Napoleonic
finale of 1815. One can read Schelling's abstract theorisations of identity as partly an attempt to fill the vacuum over German political identity during the instabilities of the 1810s. A notebook for the year 1811
records Schelling's purchase of Sismondi's *Italian Republics* – a book
which celebrates the moment when inhabitants of the same country
became 'united by a single bond', and when the 'government belonged
to the people, not the people to the government'.[6] This period also saw
Schelling's short-lived attempt to found a magazine titled *Of Germans for
Germans*; but knowing who the 'Germans' were – within which boundaries and forming what kind of unity – was at this stage a far from easy

---

[4] Horst Fuhrmans, in Horst Fuhrmans (ed.), *F. W. J. Schelling, Briefe und Dokumente,
Band I 1775–1809* (Bonn: H. Bouvier, 1962), 356.
[5] The association with Baader marks the point at which 'aristocratism' begins again
to occupy a central place in epistemology, and with it the emergence of 'the pseudo-
historical, pseudo-dialectical philosophy of the restoration period', Georg Lukács, *The
Destruction of Reason* (London: The Merlin Press, 1980), 149.
[6] Jean Charles Léonard de Sismondi, *Italian Republics, or, the Origins, Progress and Fall of
Italian Freedom* (Paris: A. and W. Galignani, 1841), 2.

task. In 1806, the year of Schelling's move south, the formal dissolution of the ancient Reich took place. Bavaria itself supported Napoleon from within the Rhenish Confederation and by virtue of this alliance was in the process of acquiring various annexed lands, as well as gaining the status of a Kingdom. When, in 1813, Prussian reformers who had languished in exile in Moscow came to liberate *their* German fatherland under the wing of the advancing Russian army, Munich adopted a neutral policy and sought a treaty with Austria. The greater irrationalism and more pronounced mystical religiosity of the work, then, can equally be viewed as traumatic reactions to political turmoil: confidence in the self-generation of the 'system' in the minds of the freed middle class gives way to the intuition of the system's more violent and unruly basis in the struggle of absolute powers.

Finally, the greater emphasis in his writing on notions of longing and loss, along with an interest in spiritualistic beliefs, cannot be divorced from the various bereavements suffered by Schelling at this time, particularly the unexpected death of his wife Caroline in September 1809.[7] For Karl Jaspers, it was Caroline's death that drew Schelling away from the philosophy of existence into more theosophical concerns in which he 'tarries gladly with thoughts of the spirit-world and the conditions on the other side'.[8] Plitt records the desperate cycles of depression and withdrawal to the forest solitude of Hesseloh, which were repeated under the impetus of fresh setbacks – the death of his father in 1812, a public dispute with the philosopher Friedrich Jacobi in the same year, and further military humiliation by the French in 1813. All this fed into the broken rhythm of work on the *Ages of the World*, twice brought to near completion (1811 and 1813) and twice recalled from the printers,[9] and finds expression in the uneven, syncretic feel of the work which was finally published posthumously (in a version written in 1815) in the collected works edited by Schelling's son for Cotta from 1856 to 1861.

In some ways, the very eclecticism of these drafts, their speculative and open-ended construction, makes it easier to trace the tangled intersection of different philosophical and descriptive goals: the ongoing attempt to develop certainty through a metaphysics of the absolute;

[7] Caroline Böhmer Schelling (née Michaelis) was formerly married to August Wilhelm Schlegel, from whom she divorced in 1803. For an account of Schelling's developing affair with Caroline Schlegel, tied in to the break-up of the Jena Romantic circle, see Robert J. Richards, *The Romantic Conception of Life* (University of Chicago Press, 2002), 166–76.

[8] Karl Jaspers, *Schelling; Größe und Verhängnis* (Munich: R. Piper, 1955), 35.

[9] Plitt, *Aus Schellings Leben*, vol. II, *passim*.

the desire to outline a history of nature; and the concern to articulate a principle of individuality and of individual freedom. Though each of these raises the issue of foundations, they are essentially three different problems; however, Schelling was trying to integrate them, to weave the absolute and the individual, life and its emergence, necessity and freedom, together in a single ontology of existence. In the *Ages of the World* drafts we find Schelling searching for new patterns or metaphors through which to conceive of these interrelationships, and see him increasingly drawn towards a principle of the unconscious as a necessary starting-point.

The idea of unconscious 'beginnings' or the unconscious past seemed appropriate to Schelling as a way of approaching the dim and distant emergence of life, world and subjectivity. As the draft of 1813 speculates: 'the oldest formations of the earth bear such a foreign aspect that we are hardly in a position to form a concept of their time of origin or of the forces that were then at work'.[10] At the same time, this obscurity has quite a different role to play: as with the obscurity of Fichte's will, it allows Schelling to pin various notions of radical autonomy on the 'beginning' – autonomy of the individual, and of the life of the 'whole' – while avoiding the kinds of oscillation or fragmentation over concepts of freedom and necessity which had dogged previous forms of idealism. The point is still that the beginning of the individual, of all individuals, and the basis for their radical freedom, cannot be wholly transcribed into rational terms, cannot be made wholly explicit or subsumed under general principles such as the principle of sufficient reason: 'We are hardly in a position to form a concept ...'. But rather than abandoning philosophy, or advocating a religious leap of faith in other powers, Schelling starts to theorise obscurity or unconsciousness as necessary technical principles, and places unconsciousness at the heart of his account of the secular cosmos – of nature, life, history and the psyche. This assumption of obscurity and unaccountability starts to influence his philosophical descriptions of the nature and development of matter and preconscious life forms. Such aspects of resistance to conscious determination are integrated in turn with new accounts of the psychic foundations of selfhood and individuality which overturn the former transcendental accounts of consciousness and the I. The 'unreasonable' beginning of life, rather than the absolutely self-assured attempt at transcendental self-reflection, will now make a more convincing basis, a more realistic foundation, for the philosophical account of human existence.

[10] Schelling, *Ages*, 21.

Absolute beginnings

Idealism means to stand outside every causal nexus – and yet to be a cause of oneself.[11]

Eternity is precisely – to have the beginning in oneself – *causa sui*.[12]

One way to begin an examination of the *Ages of the World* is to focus on the way in which beginning itself becomes increasingly important to Schelling. I mean here not the beginning of the actual text (which thematises the importance of history for philosophy) but rather the way in which Schelling becomes preoccupied with conceptualising 'the beginning' and the problem of existential foundations in this period. 'Idealist thinking', wrote Habermas, 'gets caught up in a hermeneutic circle – the beginning of the system is systematically unthinkable. But Schelling looks for it.'[13] Schelling both shifts his notion of how one must begin, philosophically, and becomes caught up in the problem of searching for beginnings, of conceptualising anteriority – so much so that his projected analysis of the categories of time, which was to include 'present' and 'future', never escapes the gravitational pull of the past, the only section of the *Ages of the World* to be drafted in near complete form. As we shall see, that inquiry into origins, including his own, is crucial for the transcription of philosophical motifs into existential and even quasi-psychologistic ones.

This new concern with time is not the familiar problem of how to establish a notional starting point for a linear narrative of development. Schelling declares specifically that, when he speaks of time, he wishes to imply not merely the recursive problem of where one halts the backwards inference of a chain of events. Rather, his concern is how to theorise an origin or beginning structurally *outside* the system of objects and causes, that cannot fully be co-ordinated with it, and which instead of being subordinate to the system's own rational structure first makes that structure possible. In many ways the form of this question repeats the riddle with which Schelling and Fichte began: how to introduce freedom into the system of knowledge; how to theorise causality differently from a chain of cause and effect or line of temporal succession. For both philosophers, rationalist descriptions of the world threatened to insert the individual into 'an unbroken chain of appearances', thus

---

[11] Heidegger, *Schelling's Treatise*, 84.

[12] F. W. J. Schelling, *Philosophische Entwürfe und Tagebücher 1809–1813* (Hamburg: Felix Meiner, 1994), 103.

[13] Jürgen Habermas, *Theorie und Praxis* (Neuwied and Berlin: Luchterhand, 1963), 116.

annihilating its ontological independence.[14] Politically, too, Fichte wanted to liberate individuals from mechanistic views of government and society as an 'ingeniously constructed clock-work pressure machine, in which every single part will be continually compelled by the whole to serve the whole'.[15]

For exactly the same reasons, at the opening of the *Ages of the World*, Schelling refused to countenance an absolute contiguity in the temporal construction of experience: 'If the world were a chain of causes and effects that ran backwards and forwards to infinity, then there would in truth be neither past nor future.'[16] There could be no individual or independent grounds for action, and equally no chance for any radical transformation of human history or identity. Schelling instead wished to address the individual as someone able to 'separate himself from himself', who was able to break loose 'from everything that happens to him and actively oppose it', or to be 'conscious of having put something behind him'.[17] If the beginning of the system is systematically unthinkable, Schelling might then be looking for the beginning precisely because it *is* unthinkable. Deriving individuality from such a primal anti-systemic, or unconceptualisable basis might allow individuals to be, in some way, original to themselves.

Numerous commentators on Schelling have noted this desire to release the individual from the conditions of an absolute metaphysical identity. Heidegger observed in his seminar on Schelling's *Human Freedom* that 'what depends on God must come to stand as something independent', and further defined idealism itself as meaning 'to stand outside every causal nexus – and yet to be a cause of oneself'.[18] For Emil Fackenheim, Schelling 'had always been uneasy about the implications of the absolute system for human personality';[19] while Robert Brown describes the message emerging out of the essay on *Human Freedom* as being that 'True freedom is an unconditional power *alongside* the divine power'.[20] One might contrast this with G. H. Lewes' criticism of

[14] Fichte, *Vocation*, 10.
[15] J. G. Fichte, *Addresses to the German Nation*, ed. G. A. Kelly (New York and Evanston, IL: Harper & Row, 1968), 96. Compare Tocqueville's account of emergent individualism when he suggested that: 'Aristocracy links everybody, from peasant to king, in one long chain. Democracy breaks the chain and frees each link', *Democracy*, 508.
[16] Schelling, *Ages*, 120.   [17] Ibid., 120.
[18] Heidegger, *Schelling's Treatise*, 87, 84.
[19] Emil L. Fackenheim, *The God Within: Kant, Schelling, and Historicity*, ed. John Burbidge (University of Toronto, 1996), 95.
[20] Robert F. Brown, *The Later Philosophy of Schelling: the Influence of Boehme on the Works of 1809–1815* (Lewisburg, PA: Bucknell University Press, 1977), 120, my italics.

Schelling's earlier idealism that: 'Reason, inasmuch as it affirms God, cannot affirm anything else, and annihilates itself at the same time as an *individual* existence, as anything *out of* God.'[21] The *Ages of the World* begins to explore the reverse face of this proposition.

In order to resolve these ontological contradictions between individuality and the absolute (whether this latter is conceived as reason, God, nature or the I) Schelling will come to rely on a third, mediating space – beyond the cogito and the framing powers of reason, but within the ontological space of the individual. A psyche that emerges besides the 'I', as an alternative, more radical site of connection between the self and its metaphysical foundations, is not just the sign of a counter-Enlightenment return to the structures of religion – the transcendent language of soul – but an attempt to naturalise within the framework of psychology a site for thinking self-identity, for positing an identity *with oneself*. The challenge was to find in German metaphysics some equivalent for Rousseau's claim at the outset of his *Confessions*: 'I dare to believe that I am not made like any that exist. If I am worth no more, at least I am different.'[22] In Schelling's case, the subject must retain the minimal distance necessary to imagine its self-agency from an I that would resolve its identity into a common or universal quality. As Hegel argued: 'When we say "I", we mean, to be sure, an individual; but since everyone is "I", when we say "I", we only say something quite universal. The universality of the "I" enables it to abstract from everything, even from its life.' In an even more radical and un-Rousseauian formulation, the I for Hegel is 'the lightning which pierces through the natural soul and consumes its natural being'.[23] The challenge for Schelling will be, again, to reverse or resist this process of self-annihilation – to establish the constitutional importance of the self's existential and psychological individuality.

At the same time, Schelling was equally keen to retain the presentiment of an organised totality, which we saw emerging at the end of the previous chapter in the belief that 'one organism lies hidden deep in time and encompasses even the smallest of things'.[24] Schematised now in relation to temporality, rather than simply 'nature', Schelling required

[21] G. H. Lewes, *The History of Philosophy from Thales to Comte*, 2 vols. (London: Longmans, Green, 1880), vol. II, 584.

[22] Jean-Jacques Rousseau, *The Confessions, and Correspondence, including the Letters to Malesherbes*, ed. Kelly, Masters and Stillman (Hanover, NH: University Press of New England, 1995), 5.

[23] G. W. F. Hegel, *Philosophy of Mind*, trans. William Wallace and A. V. Miller (Oxford University Press, 1971), 11, 152.

[24] Schelling, *Ages*, 123.

that 'each great event, each deed rich in consequence, is determined to the day, the hour – indeed to the very moment – and that it does not come to light one instant earlier than is willed by the force that stops and regulates time'.[25] This is the initial paradox that Schelling faces in the *Ages of the World*: how can the absolute be preserved intact, to allow for notions of providence and harmonisation (without which the concept of freedom begins to self-destruct), and yet at the same time be displaced from existence? How can you have a foundation which stands prior to all else in creation, and at the same time disengage all entities from the influence of anything prior to their own self-determination? How can the absolute be real enough to found identity, but immaterial enough not to disturb the processes of individual self-authorisation? Schelling explored two very distinct kinds of answers to these questions, both of which returned to the site of classical Greek metaphysics.

One answer lies in Schelling's attempt, in the early nineteenth century, to redefine the absolute in increasingly Neoplatonic terms. A characteristic diary entry for April 1809 shows jotted reflections on contemporary politics interweaving with readings in classical and Renaissance ontology: 'In the morning leafed through Proclus and the works of Marsilio Ficino. Today the Austrian manifesto and the letter to the King will appear in the papers here. Evening began [Plato's] *Parmenides*.'[26] In 1802, Schelling had borrowed the persona of the Renaissance Neoplatonist Giordano Bruno as a mouthpiece for his changing views on *Naturphilosophie*, while letters to Carl Windischmann date his interest in Ficino's edition of Plotinus' work back to 1804.[27]

Critics have viewed this shift, from the seemingly materialist bent of the *Naturphilosophie* to the terrain of Renaissance magic and the obscure metaphysics of a pre-scientific era, as a regression. Sitting through the lectures of 1842, Burckhardt was so struck by Schelling's descent into 'genuine' Gnosticism, that he expected at any moment to see 'some monstrous Asiatic god on twelve legs' come waddling into the auditorium.[28] But at the same time such traditions allowed him to reorient the notion of the absolute he had inherited from Spinoza and from Fichte – to modify, qualify and ultimately invert it. In particular, Schelling became concerned with the Neoplatonic separation between the world of process and generation, and the divinity which is 'The Absolute of otherworldliness – self-sufficient, out of time', a being of

---

[25] Schelling, *Ages of the World*, 123.
[26] Schelling, *Philosophische Entwürfe*, 18.
[27] Werner Beierwaltes, *Platonismus und Idealismus*, 101–2.
[28] Jakob Burkhardt to Gottfried Kinkel, June 1842, in Xavier Tilliette (ed.), *Schelling im Spiegel Seiner Zeitgenossen* (Torino: Bottega d'Erasmo, 1974), 466.

'eternal, self-contained perfection'.[29] Plotinus, for instance, had argued that, 'Standing before all things, there must exist a Simplex, differing from all its sequel, self-gathered not interblended with the forms that rise from it', and that, 'If there were nothing outside all alliance and compromise, nothing authentically one, there would be no Source.'[30]

In some ways, this self-sufficient absolute seems little different from the Spinozan definition of substance which had plunged Fichte into such oscillations over the existence of self and other: 'That thing is called free which exists from the necessity of its nature alone, and is determined to act by itself alone.'[31] Plato, too, had argued in the *Phaedrus* that 'all that comes into being must derive its existence from a prime origin, but the prime origin itself from nothing; for if a prime origin were derived from anything, it would no longer be a prime origin'.[32] However, whereas Spinoza argued that nothing stands outside the absolute – thus there is ultimately room for only one self-subsisting agent – Neoplatonic ontology emphasised instead that the absolute could not be placed *inside* the world. Rather than standing at the head of an absolute chain of conditions, this was an origin which was transcendentally displaced from existence. It could not be directly connected with determinate being, and to this extent other entities were marginally released from the direct operation of necessity as represented in causal or mechanical systems. A notebook entry of Schelling's for 1813 stressed that, 'as a) every beginning (even eternal) contradicts the timelessness of the highest godhead, b) the actual being must always remain separate from eternal Possibility-to-be'.[33] Details of this transcendental conception (in the Platonic sense) found their way into the *Ages of the World*, where Schelling establishes that 'Man must be granted an essence outside and above the world', and suggests that 'where everything has come from can be nowhere else than where everything is still coming from ... and which was thus not only before time but is still in every moment constantly above time'.[34]

Although Žižek has argued that the split between transcendence and materiality in Schelling's thought (whereby 'God possesses his Being in advance' and creation 'involves an activity performed from a safe

[29] Lovejoy, *The Great Chain of Being*, 315.
[30] Plotinus, Ennead V, Tractate 4, 'How the Secondaries Rise from the First: and on the One', *The Enneads*, trans. Stephen MacKenna (Harmondsworth: Penguin, 1991), 387.
[31] Benedict de Spinoza, *The Ethics* (Harmondsworth: Penguin, 1996), 2.
[32] Plato, *Phaedrus*, trans. Walter Hamilton (Harmondsworth: Penguin, 1973), 49.
[33] Schelling, *Philosophische Entwürfe*, 96.
[34] Schelling, *Ages*, 114, 134.

distance'[35]) only emerges in the 1840s, this more theological absolute has a covert philosophical presence all along. In the 1807 Oration 'On the Relation Between the Plastic Arts and Nature', Schelling argued that 'Every single thing is preceded by an eternal conception schemed in the infinite understanding'.[36] The key point, however, is that this redescription of the absolute in Neoplatonic terms (its designs are relayed through eternal conceptions rather than a chain of conditioned causes) displaced the way the operation of necessity was understood; it shifted the absolute from a condition of *this* world into the realm of the ideal and the possible, and from mechanistic processes to more spectral ones.

This displacement of the absolute into another ontological domain was one avenue through which Schelling began to open up rifts between the basis of the self and the system, between the individual and its absolute ground. But he also drew on another metaphysical position, in some ways antithetical to the Neoplatonic one, which helped to implicate the absolute origin of things in a kind of non-being, and this was Aristotle's account of how form comes to inhere in matter. There was a certain aptness in this turn towards Aristotelian principles, for Aristotle himself made the same move in relation to his mentor, Plato, that Schelling performed in relation to Fichte. Each reacted against the transcendental leanings of their predecessors and each shifted their attention away from mathematics and logic, respectively, towards a practical interest in the empirical science of nature. Both thinkers, too, drew certain comparisons between the productive processes of art and nature. What Schelling took from Aristotelian metaphysics, however, was the radical distinction between form and matter whereby matter is defined as mere possibility – and thus absolutely indeterminate – while form is not itself generated but comes to supervene in the process of becoming as the manifestation of finality. In Book Theta of the *Metaphysics* Aristotle describes the emergence of form in material existence in terms of a shift from potentiality to actuality.[37] This account entails that entities come into existence as 'a mere craving for determination',[38] and are afterwards promoted to actuality, just as humans might self-consciously establish the terms of their own foundation at the end of a long process of development.

[35] Žižek, *The Indivisible Remainder*, 37.
[36] Schelling, *Plastic Arts*, 7.
[37] See particularly chapter 8 of Book Theta, J. L. Ackrill (ed.), *A New Aristotle Reader* (Oxford University Press, 1987), 329–33.
[38] Adorno, *Metaphysics*, 52.

From this doctrine of form and matter Schelling extracted two new implications fundamental for his project of freedom, and for the developing notion of the unconscious. One was that matter – the inferior and passive pole in the relationship with form – now, paradoxically, shares some measure of identity with the Neoplatonic source, insofar as it occupies a position of pure possibility in relation to the actual. Secondly, matter is now also implicated as an 'origin' because, within the framework of a metaphysics of becoming, identity arrives *after*, at the end of a process of generation. In the 1807 oration Schelling described how 'rough matter strives, as it were blindly, after regular shape, and unconsciously assumes pure stereometric forms'.[39] This figure of unconscious process was also transferred to descriptions of life in general. At the end of the Introduction to the 1813 *Ages of the World* Schelling described the origin of existence as being 'first with respect to development though last with respect to dignity'.[40] By 1815, in his philological *Treatise on The Deities of Samothrace*, he had sharpened the terms of this inversion maintaining that 'an absolutely first being ... must seem to itself as the most extreme poverty', and that, for all peoples who counted time by night, 'night is the most primordial of things' but it is 'a misrepresentation if one also regards this first being as the highest'.[41]

There are, then, two kinds of firsts, two origins, and in each version an absolute is posited, but at the same time displaced from its position of *absolute* priority. In the first, Neoplatonic case, this is because its existence is beyond process, an ideal, eternal entity, which is therefore devoid of tangible existence. In the second, more Aristotelian case, the absolute – as the formal truth of existence – does come to exist, but it arrives *after* the emergence of entities themselves, which must now, in some way, determine themselves *towards* identity. Initially, it appears that the problem which Schelling faces is how to integrate these two rather contradictory paradigms of validity and genesis in order to arrive at a coherent philosophy of existence. Some of these complexities had already emerged in Schelling's attempt to materialise the absolute as a history of nature. In the original terms of the *Naturphilosophie*: if the absolute is thought of as a world organism, or world soul, then the origin of that absolute is implicated in the origins of matter and thus in the process of becoming. It is for this reason that Arthur Lovejoy placed Schelling at the limit of his classic account of the *Great Chain of Being*, as

[39] Schelling, *Plastic Arts*, 7.   [40] Schelling, *Ages*, 119.
[41] F. W. J. Schelling, *Treatise on 'The Deities of Samothrace': A Translation and an Interpretation*, trans. Robert F. Brown (Missoula, MT: Scholars Press, 1977), 18.

a final Romanticised version of the Renaissance view of the cosmos as a densely interlinked but hierarchical whole which was now in the process of becoming temporalised rather than spatialised. In Schelling's work, 'The temporal order is, as it were, a projection, a spread-out image, of the Absolute Intelligence, and its concrete content consists of the succession of organisms and their states'.[42] As Lovejoy also pointed out, one of Schelling's most important acolytes, the embryologist Lorenz Oken, expressed such a scheme in his *Lehrbuch der Naturphilosophie* of 1810, which states that: 'The philosophy of nature is the science of the eternal transformation of God into the world'; as such 'it has the task of showing the phases of the world's evolution from primal nothingness'.[43] Note how the Platonic primal origin, which derives its existence *from nothing*, has itself entered into the temporal frame, and thus become a *primal nothingness*. Lovejoy comments that, like Schelling, Oken shows lingering traces of the Neoplatonic theory of emanation, but that at the same time 'this antecedent Absolute is described in the most unequivocally negative terms ... God = zero, or pure nothingness'.[44]

Though Lovejoy noted the negation, he did not seem to recognise the degree to which the desire to *invert* the relation between being and divinity may itself have provided a rationale for the temporalisation of hierarchy. In a striking passage from the earliest and incomplete drafts of the *Ages of the World*, Schelling makes the terms of this inversion of the Neoplatonic cosmos absolutely clear:

The systems which want to explain the origin of things by descent from above, necessarily arrive at the thought that the outflowings of the highest original power must finally lose themselves in a certain outermost extremity, where there was only, so to speak, a shadow of essence, the slightest leftover of reality ... This is the meaning of non-being for the Neoplatonists who no longer understood the truth in Plato. We, following the opposite direction, also maintain an outermost, beyond which there is nothing; but for us this is not the ultimate reach of an outward flow, but the first, from which everything begins, not pure lack or a reality almost wholly robbed of existence, but an active negation.[45]

What this passage brings out is that Schelling's inversion and temporalisation of the Neoplatonic scheme performs something of a double coup. On the one hand he materialises the notion of the absolute, preserving the idea of a certain kind of grounding structure to life, and embedding this in an account of the emergence of nature, a history

[42] Lovejoy, *The Great Chain of Being*, 318.
[43] Lorenz Oken, cited in Lovejoy, *The Great Chain of Being*, 320.
[44] Ibid., 320.
[45] F. W. J. Schelling, *Die Weltalter, Urfassungen*, ed. Manfred Schröter (Munich: Biederstein/Leibniz, 1946), 230.

of evolution. At the same time he has executed a profound reversal of the relations between God and human consciousness. The absolute has been made analogous to the individual by being implicated in the same condition of nothingness from which the individual is to emerge. As Schelling suggested most controversially in the *Deities of Samothrace*: 'In the concept of every beginning lies the concept of a lack',[46] and already in the *Human Freedom* essay: 'God is *Life*, and not merely being. All life has a *fate*, and is subject to suffering and becoming.'[47] Moreover, if the absolute is treated as if it were itself a thing of becoming, as if *its* original, unconditional possibility were akin to that craving for existence shared by all material things, then the lack of ontological security experienced by suffering individuals can in turn be read as the origins of their own self-founding (rather than merely evidence of their non-entity). In 1807 Schelling spoke of 'the miracle by which the finite should be elevated to the infinite, or by which humanity should be deified',[48] and in the *Ages of the World* the human soul is imagined as being 'drawn from the source of things and akin to it'; it thus has a 'co-knowledge of creation'.[49] Likewise for Oken, if the temporal origin of the system lies in the humble beginnings of life on earth, then knowledge of the system – the absolute consciousness of life's foundations – comes only with the emergence of mankind, which occupies the highest rung of the ladder of evolution. Thus Oken argued that God is 'a man representing God in one act of self-consciousness' and that 'Man is God wholly manifested'.[50]

Excursus on Schellingian ontology and French psychoanalysis

This seems a very arcane set of reference points for any post-Enlightenment philosophy of human identity. How is one to understand these strange narratives of genesis – part metaphysical, part histories of nature, part theogonic myth? Schelling appears to have taken the whole framework of post-Kantian idealism and shifted it into the territory of gnostic and Neoplatonic accounts of cosmic creation. Alongside his readings of Ficino and Bruno, Proclus and Plato, Schelling was in this period also

---

[46] Schelling, *The Deities of Samothrace*, 18.
[47] Cited in Lovejoy, *The Great Chain of Being*, 318.
[48] Schelling, *Plastic Arts*, 6.   [49] Schelling, *Ages*, 114.
[50] Lorenz Oken, *Lehrbuch der Naturphilosophie* [1810], trans. Alfred Tulk as *Elements of Physio-Philosophy* (London: Ray Society, 1847), 25.

beginning to draw on the work of Jakob Böhme and the mystical Pietist pastor Friedrich Oetinger. According to Irma Gleiss, the unconscious in Böhme has a 'radical genetic' bent, which 'brings it close to a phylogenetic concept, like those further developed by Schubert and Carus'.[51] Habermas has suggested that Schelling's two kinds of absolute, one Neoplatonic and transcendental, the other inverted and merged with matter, derive from mystical Kabbalism, which assumes the existence of a second god, Adamos Kadmos, to whom the original god consigns his creation.[52] However, Schelling's accounts should not be taken simply as mythical narratives of *real* events, which he has inserted into a gap in knowledge over the very beginning of the world (the equivalent of today's Big Bang theory). What Schelling was trying to locate was an *ontological* scheme that could accommodate the idea of a general self-determination of entities, or which would allow a certain originary point of freedom and self-motivation to be theorised at the heart of every life. By playing on these structural ambiguities in the notion of non-being – as both nothingness *and* origin, both absolute foundation *and* mere possibility – Schelling was establishing that the individual, though occupying a position of apparent nothingness in relation to the totality of things, could come to view itself as a substantial cause of its own identity. If, for instance, the construction of a cause can somehow succeed its own origin, then something can begin as nothing but later become the agent of itself.

This introduction of nothingness into the core of the 'system' of being has direct implications for the theorisation of individuality. This is borne out by the way such ontological concern with origins and points of non-being becomes a distinctive feature of later philosophies of existence. Most obviously, for Sartre, my consciousness must 'arise in the world as a *Not*' – a very similar assertion to Schelling's originary 'active negation'.[53] For Emmanuel Levinas, too, evanescence is 'the essential form of beginning' if the present is to be 'something that comes from itself', rather than something that 'would have received its existence from something preceding'.[54] Correspondingly – and here Levinas repeats the form of Schelling's dissatisfaction with totality – 'a notion

---

[51] Irma Gleiss, 'Der romantische Weg in die Tiefe', in Buchholz and Gödde, *Macht und Dynamik*, 109.

[52] Habermas, *Theorie und Praxis*, 125.

[53] Jean-Paul Sartre, *Being and Nothingness: an Essay on Phenomenological Ontology*, trans. Hazel E. Barnes (London: Routledge, 1993), 47.

[54] Emmanuel Levinas, *Time and the Other* (Pittsburgh, PA: Duquesne University Press, 1987), 53.

of being without nothingness' leaves 'no hole and permits no escape ... One is no longer master of anything'.[55]

All these examples fall outside the concerns of psychology. They are still, as in Schelling's own case, philosophical accounts of identity. However, one can already see how such structural demonstrations of selfhood will be transcribed into components of psycho-dynamic theory. One finds, for instance, a similar set of ontological assumptions in those psychoanalysts, mainly French, who have been influenced by readings of idealism that have come via existentialism. Jean Laplanche, who constructed a case history of mental illness in the poet Hölderlin (Schelling's youthful intellectual companion), diagnosed Hölderlin's madness in terms of a similar ontological antithesis between self and absolute. Quoting a line from 'The Poet's Vocation' – 'God's failure comes to (our) aid' – Laplanche comments: 'the absence of a defect, that's precisely what he is suffering from'.[56] That is, Hölderlin's concept of reality is ultimately too absolute and theological to allow a strong sense of individuality to emerge within it, much as Schelling's youthful apprehension of the transcendental I had driven the empirical I of the self towards extinction.[57]

Besides the dilemma of self and absolute, Schelling's attempt to reorient the causal understanding of temporality in the name of subjective freedom also finds its echo in French psychoanalysis. Laplanche and Pontalis remark of the Freudian concept of *Nachträglichkeit*, or deferred action, that 'The first thing the introduction of the notion does is to rule out the summary interpretation which reduces the psychoanalytic view of the subject's history to a linear determinism envisaging nothing but the action of the past upon the present'.[58] By the 1990s Laplanche had centralised the concept of *Nachträglichkeit* in his theoretical work on psychoanalysis, further counteracting the threat of determinism by asserting the 'implantation of [an] enigmatic message' within the historical passage traced between the individual's past and future.[59] However, it is in the work of Jacques Lacan that many of these Schellingian problems of displacing the individual from the absolute, or inverting the concept of causal determination, are most conspicuously repeated. Laplanche

[55] Levinas, *Time*, 50; Levinas is here considering the 'possibility of finding a meaning for existence through the possibility of suicide'.
[56] Jean Laplanche, *Hölderlin et la question du père* (Paris: Presses Universitaires de France, 1961), 131–2.
[57] See Chapter 2.
[58] Jean Laplanche and J.-B. Pontalis, *The Language of Psychoanalysis* (London: Karnac, 1988), 112.
[59] See Jean Laplanche, 'Notes on Afterwardsness', in *Seduction, Translation, Drives*, ed. Fletcher and Stanton (London: ICA, 1992), 222.

himself acknowledges Lacan's concern with *Nachträglichkeit* in the early 1950s, but this concern is indicative of Lacan's much broader interest in re-orienting notions of cause and history within the individual subject. Thus Lacan describes the mirror stage – that primordial moment in early Lacanian theory, whereby the child identifies itself as a unified being via an encounter with a specular image of itself – as 'a drama whose internal thrust is precipitated from insufficiency to anticipation', and which is experienced as 'a temporal dialectic that decisively projects the formation of the individual into history'.[60] 'True' beginnings, for Lacan, emerge at the end of a process of interpretive self-development, behind which lies a situation of original lack. The aim of analysis is likewise 'the advent of true speech and the realisation by the subject of his or her history in relation to his or her future'.[61] As Peter Dews has commented here, 'the actions of the subject cannot be seen as causally determined by his or her past'.[62] Lacan's Seminar II, given from 1954 to 1955, also repeats Schelling's assumption that individuality is founded on the basis of a fundamental non-entity – 'As soon as the subject himself comes to be, he owes it to a certain non-being on which he raises his being.'[63] In Seminar XI from 1964, he will again make clear that such original 'lack' is prior to the unity of the subject. However, an original void at the level of organisation and determinability may be precisely what is necessary for the subject to be conceived as *causa sui* – 'Cause is to be distinguished from that which is determinate in a chain, in other words the *law*.'[64]

The final chapter of this book will be devoted to a more thorough consideration of the relation between these Romantic and idealist assumptions about subjectivity, and those emerging with psychoanalysis. For the moment, one should note that these similarities between Schelling's concerns and those of Lacan and Laplanche are mediated partly through philosophers such as Heidegger, as well as the broad influence on a generation of French intellectuals of Koyré and Kojève's respective work on Hegel. Equally important is the fact that these twentieth-century thinkers were orienting philosophy and psychoanalysis around the

[60] Jacques Lacan, *Écrits: a Selection* (London: Routledge, 1985), 4.
[61] Jacques Lacan, 'The Function and Field of Speech and Language in Psychoanalysis', *Écrits*, 88. See also Lacan's comments on subjective history in the same article, 51–3.
[62] Peter Dews, *Logics of Disintegration* (London: Verso, 1987), 66.
[63] Jacques Lacan, *The Seminar of Jacques Lacan, Book II: The Ego in Freud's Theory and in the Technique of Psychoanalysis 1954–55*, Jacques-Alain Miller (ed.) (New York, W. W. Norton, 1991), 192.
[64] Jacques Lacan, *The Four Fundamental Concepts of Psychoanalysis* (Harmondsworth: Penguin, 1977), 22, 30.

same kinds of ontological queries which Schelling himself was posing: in what ways can the individual be its own cause? What is the relation between such causality and scientific knowledge? In what ways can these conditions be laid down in phenomenological or psychological description? In each of the cases cited above it is the subject's relation to the idea of self-constitution that is at stake – a question that, as we shall see, is foregrounded by later psycho-dynamic thinkers as diverse as Jung, Rank and Winnicott, and by contemporary post-Freudians from Adam Phillips to R. D. Hinshelwood.

The absolute who was not there ...

Yet, for all its descriptive advantages, it is not clear that this structural inversion of the absolute can be performed with philosophical impunity. In Aristotelian metaphysics there remains a certain ambiguity over the status of ideas and forms; they are to be embedded in things themselves but at the same time cannot be merged with the paradigm of genesis and becoming. Adorno referred to this duality, between the idea inhering in an existent and the idea 'which has being in itself', as Aristotle's 'two-pronged approach'.[65] With respect to accounts of genesis it gives rise to the paradoxical demand that form remain axiomatically prior to matter, even though it is manifested *after* it in terms of existence. According to David Ross, Aristotelian becoming 'cannot be explained by potentiality alone for nothing is promoted from potentiality to actuality without the agency of something actual'.[66] As Aristotle himself states: 'What is eternal is prior in nature to what is perishable; and nothing is eternal by virtue of potentiality.'[67] Thus a measure of logical transcendence is ascribed to form all the same, and this is implicit, of course, in the utter distinction between form and matter itself. Schelling, too, is caught between these same competing tendencies: between the devolution of the ideal – its incorporation into nature – and the need to reintroduce a transcendental ideality which retains a crucial formal distance from the conditions of the material world. 'Long before men created a system', asserted Schelling in the Stuttgart Seminars of 1809, 'there existed one in the cosmos – the true system cannot be created, *only uncovered as one inherent in itself*; in the divine understanding'.[68] As Schelling

---

[65] Adorno, *Metaphysics*, 44.
[66] David Ross, *Aristotle* (London: Routledge, 1995), 182–3.
[67] Ibid., 183.
[68] F. W. J. Schelling, 'The Stuttgart Seminars', in *Idealism and the Endgame of Theory: Three Essays by F. W. J. Schelling*, trans. Thomas Pfau (Albany, NY: State University of New York Press, 1994), 197. My italics.

realised, to make the absolute truly into nothing, at the same time as abandoning the Enlightenment structure of reason, or the apodicity of Fichte's transcendental I, would threaten the destruction of the system altogether, the collapse of identity per se, and with it the security of all self-governing individuals. This is why Schelling's inversion of the system is that much more radical than Oken's, for unlike Oken, Schelling grasped that one could not simply assume that the structural form of this temporalised system could survive such subversion of the absolute intact. This is the reason that Schelling wavers so much over the issue of origins in these drafts of the 1810s, reintroducing references to an ideal source for all entities, or a covert Leibnizian pre-harmonisation of creation, precisely at the moment when this divinity has supposedly been overcome.

There is a paradox, then, in Schelling's move away from idealism towards a more concrete concern with matter, life and history. Rather than moving wholeheartedly from metaphysical or transcendental foundations to evolutionary ones, he finds he has to preserve a certain parallax over the concept of origins, a certain doubling in the meaning of the primordial. The problem is not, as one might think, how to integrate these natural and transcendental paradigms, it is how to keep them apart. This is one point that Schelling makes absolutely explicit in the Stuttgart Seminars: 'by virtue of occupying the middle-ground between the non-being of nature and the absolute Being = God, man is *free* from both.'[69] Humanity, it seems, could not appear as self-determined were either of these descriptions of the basis of existence – matter or God – made absolute.

Schelling's quandary here was borne out in a curious exchange of letters which took place in the summer of 1810 between Schelling and an intellectual admirer, Eberhard Friedrich von Georgii, who was a bureaucrat in the employment of the Württemberg department of justice. Earlier that year Georgii had hosted a series of private lectures given by Schelling to a small circle of friends in Stuttgart, as a way of keeping his former intellectual associates up to date with the state of 'the system' since the publication of the essay on *Human Freedom*. It was also, as Plitt notes, intended to help Schelling recover his confidence after the shock of Caroline's death in September 1809.[70] The impact of this loss makes itself felt directly in the lectures, which are striking for the way in which they draw certain Swedenborgian notions of an after life into the parameters of idealist ontology. Schelling's attempt to construct a

[69] Schelling, 'Stuttgart Seminars', 225.
[70] Plitt, *Aus Schellings Leben*, vol. II, 90.

metaphysics of human identity converges at this point with a very personal demand to sustain the identity of the deceased.[71]

Georgii, however, came away from the seminar troubled by a particular logical objection which he could not lay to rest, and which drove at the very heart of Schelling's project. It was an issue which, as we shall see, came to dog the *Ages of the World* from its continually redrafted start to its postponed finish. The question concerned exactly that ambiguous relation (and non-relation) I have been examining, between transcendental divinity and nature: 'How can God have an inner ground within himself, which precedes him in terms of existence, [i.e. the primal origin of all things in nature] and yet God, at the same time, be the Prius of the ground, so that the ground also could not be, as such, if God did not exist in actuality?'[72] Here the paradox is posed in terms of a logical contradiction, but Georgii also states it as an ontological problem, referring to Schelling's suggestion that the absolute seems to need a material ground of nature within which to emerge: 'God is no *Ens a se*, because he seems to need another for his existence'; but if this other, continues Georgii, 'is in fact really also God all along, then one cannot still maintain the duality.'[73] Schelling's challenge was to demonstrate a meaningful sense in which the absolute can be *outside* itself, or embedded in the substance of *another* nature which resists it. Though this question may seem very distant from the domain of psychology, the working-out of the metaphysical basis of individual reality will prove decisive for Romantic commitments to an unconscious. What is partly at stake, already in this exchange with Georgii, is a theory of the necessary presence of resistance or repression as a fissure within identity.

The split between Neoplatonic and Aristotelian accounts of origins, between transcendental grounds and empirical or natural beginnings, helped Schelling towards a solution of the problem. His approach was to divide the notion of metaphysical foundation between two entities: A, *das Seyend* ('being' in its active verbal form) which is the ideal component of the divine; and B, *das Seyn* ('being' as abstract noun, or infinitive), which represents the material component, the natural basis of any phenomenal existence. He also refers to the material ground as fundament and support.[74] It is essentially a distinction between the *idea* of the

---

[71] See Friedemann Horn, *Schelling and Swedenborg: Mysticism and German Idealism* (West Chester, PA: Swedenborg Foundation, 1997) for an extended investigation of Swedenborg's influence on the thought of the Seminars.

[72] Schelling to Georgii, Stuttgart, 18 July, 1810, in Plitt, *Aus Schellings Leben*, vol. II, 218. Schelling's own letter to Georgii reproduces Georgii's main objections from his previous letter to Schelling.

[73] Ibid., 218.   [74] Ibid., 221.

absolute and its concrete existence, with the further complication that the ideal component here is metaphysically the active one (*Seyend*) but has no tangible existence, while the existing component carries with it a certain sense of passivity, or inertia: it merely is (*Seyn*). These are, in effect, Schelling's two absolutes: first of all, the Neoplatonic 'Absolute of otherworldliness – self-sufficient, out of time' (for which material *existence* is a mere possibility),[75] and, secondly, that God who originally 'becomes' and builds an existence out of primal nothingness, and is therefore 'possible' in another sense (that of a merely germinal potential life which 'precedes the active').[76] What is being proposed is something like a division, or doubling, between the 'spirit' and 'body' of the absolute, or between consciousness and its material base. Schelling will play with this bifocal vision of the absolute in order to construct a subtle ontological gap within which human freedom might appear, determined neither absolutely by a transcendentally designed system of being, nor by anterior temporal or material processes.

Schelling impressed upon Georgii the difference between the *principle* of God (termed *Ursache*) – that is, God as 'cause' persisting above and beyond any question of 'actual existence' – and, on the other hand, the deed whereby an actual world is created, which then provides a *material support* (*Grund*) for the divine as it exists in 'reality'. Actuality now has two very different registers, and neither is able on its own to support an absolute realm of consequences. 'Beginning' suffers a similar fate: when it comes to 'beginning', explains Schelling, 'The talk has never been of a ground [*Grund*] of God, but only of the ground of the actually existing God, that is, that which actively is [*Seienden*].'[77] The material world, B, is the ground only of that divinity which has material existence.

One can see here how Schelling's strategy of shifting backwards and forwards between two senses of real, and two notions of origin, started to break up the concept of the absolute between the different sites of its articulation (material basis and transcendent principle), leaving Georgii wondering exactly where he could grab hold of this amalgam of absolute and non-being, God and history. However, the strategy had its limitations. Schelling still needed to connect his two paradigms of actuality, otherwise he would be left with an absolute principle that simply may not exist, or may not come to be – not unlike the way Kant in the *Opus Posthumum* was faced with the problem that

[75] Lovejoy, *The Great Chain of Being*, 315.
[76] Schelling, *Ages*, 149.
[77] Schelling to Georgii 18 July 1810, Plitt, *Aus Schellings Leben*, vol. II, 220.

the metaphysical grounds of nature might be absolutely valid *in principle*, and yet even so might not actually be present in reality.[78] What if transcendental validity and existence were simply left to fall apart into two wholly separate phenomena?[79] What then of the possibility of combining human identity and human certainty? When pushed, Schelling assured Georgii that that which is 'in itself' (the absolute) is cause (*Ursache*) of the being in the ground, but this only returned the problem of how such causality could actually be thought. What Schelling lacked at this point was a way of identifying but at the same time barring or distancing the actions of the absolute within reality. He found himself caught by the insufficiencies of logical representation, which at most could shuffle his terms around between ever more complex degrees of possibility and actuality, or phases of the generation of the real. Thus Schelling explained to Georgii that 'God is *Seiende* already before all manifestation', but that this is 'according to his notion', and this notional agency was still not the same as *actual* agency.[80] Genetically, he assured Georgii, 'The Ideal god doesn't need a beginning as well', but then, in order to *manifest* himself – 'to reveal himself as the active-Being [*Seindes*]' – he does after all need to be embedded in some kind of resisting ground, though Schelling was obscure on the derivation of this need.[81] The gap through which human freedom was to be founded appeared as yet only as a point of prevarication within the unfolding of logical and causal relations, rather than an entirely new point of departure.

Schelling's attempts to find a more positive solution to the problem eddy through his notebooks of the period in ever more outlandish ways. The suggestion that 'There must be a possible that is not yet the actual actualisation, but at the same time not just the purely possible Ability-to-be ... the possible Actuality of God itself, in so far as it is not yet his real being' exemplifies the immense grammatical and semantic struggle Schelling underwent in trying to maintain the ideal of an absolute foundation for life, while trying to deny the full moral consequences of such a totalising anterior agency.[82] Likewise, on the generative front, Schelling's assertion that 'It begins itself – but in so doing, it only makes a start towards *possible* realisation, which must in turn be followed by a start of *real* realisation', uses the dimension of time merely to postpone

---

[78] See Beiser, *German Idealism*, 183.
[79] This is of course the problem generally faced by the neo-Kantian revival at the end of the nineteenth century. See Gillian Rose, *Hegel Contra Sociology* (London: Athlone, 1981), particularly 2–13.
[80] Plitt, *Aus Schellings Leben*, vol. II, 220.
[81] Ibid., 220.   [82] Schelling, *Philosophische Entwürfe*, 98.

the problem of authorship and being.[83] A further example in Schelling's *Notebook* of 1813 describes the divine will as the 'inexpressible', which is likened to a being in which everything still rests, which has not had occasion to express itself. When it speaks, however, 'three wills appear, which cannot operate at the same time'.[84] That is, the move from intention to act, from God's ideal being to created existence, is not negated, but neither can it be causally construed. Another *Notebook* entry considers the possibility of a rotation arising from 'now B swallowing A (positing internally) then A, B ... the one is Systole, the other Diastole'.[85]

The germinal absolute

Where Schelling was able to make more constructive advances in his work, however, was at the level of figurative expressions of the relationship between the absolute and nature. For the moment it is only here, in these speculative and metaphorical aspects of description, that he is able to evoke a different structural idea of foundation. For instance, Schelling frequently draws motifs from organic life in order to re-imagine the absolute as latent or germinal, and thus in some way withdrawn from presence. In the Stuttgart Seminars, 'God is in nature in His entirety, although in seedlike form'.[86] This notion is developed in turn through metaphors of states of arousal. In the *Ages of the World* Schelling compares the initial state of this divine wisdom in the world to a man who 'is sleeping, or dead, or enraptured', and to a child.[87] In the seminars the divine is 'slumbering' and needs to be 'awakened and cultivated'.[88] Other passages in the *Ages of the World* depict the move from non-existence to existence of the ideal in terms of 'longing' – 'a quiet longing producing itself in eternity without eternity helping or knowing', and in his response to Georgii he talks also of the 'arousal' of divinity in nature: 'A arouses A again in B'.[89]

Schelling was consciously drawing here on the language of Jakob Böhme, for whom the eternal will is 'desirous of the wonders of creation', as well as the Swabian pietist Friedrich Oetinger, who described god as 'an eternal desire [*Begierde*] to manifest himself'.[90] At yet another

---

[83] Ibid., 99. My italics.
[84] Ibid., 119.   [85] Ibid., 124.
[86] Schelling, 'Stuttgart Seminars', 212.
[87] Schelling, *Ages*, 164–5.
[88] Schelling, 'Stuttgart Seminars', 212.
[89] Schelling, *Ages*, 136; Plitt, *Aus Schellings Leben*, vol. II, 219.
[90] Friedrich Oetinger, *Biblisches und Emblematisches Wörterbuch* [1776], Dmitrij Tschizewskij and Ernst Benz (eds.) (Hildesheim: Georg Olms, 1969), 536. Some of Oetinger's entries for this work are cited by name in Schelling's notebooks for 1813.

point in the *Ages of the World* nature appears actively to pull 'that pur-
est spirit – what is objective of eternity – to itself', and as a result, all
the forces of the absolute 'assume passive qualities in comparison with
spirit as their higher, authentic subject, and they sink down, becoming
material for it'.[91] In other instances, in a strange conflation of heavenly
father and solar source, Schelling suggests that, after the existing God
(B) has been detached from the ideal one (A), this latter 'stays over B,
ie, both over Nature, and over the divine born in the womb of nature,
for as long as it takes to raise this wholly to its own level'.[92] There is a
mirroring here of Plotinus' description of the divine mind as 'a father
watching over the development of his child born imperfect in comparison with him',[93] but the image is also inverted in that, in this case, divinity falls ultimately to the child and it is the father who is implicated in
a relation of need – God 'proves itself as that which is Being according
to its nature, only by seeking to raise to itself that which relatively is not
[*das relativ Nichtseiende*], the B, so that it comes to resemble God, so
that it is divinised'.[94]

All of these figures, in different ways, implicate the absolute in nature
and nature in the absolute, and each finds a way of expressing an inversion in the notion of determinate agency. The absolute is there in some
form to connect idea and reality, origins and ends, and to help unite
identities and purposes, but its agency is not total, and its operation
cannot be thought of as a chain of conditions. Instead, the absolute
sinks down as something passive: it is either asleep, latent, distant, or
merely watchful. At the same time we have a new set of relational terms
which convey only the very faintest sense of external influence. We have
the development of nature as germination, awakening, arousal and
longing. These are not spurious creation myths, but attempts to figure
more complex and shifting modes of determinacy than Schelling had
been able to describe in logical terms, and on which one could ground
a different kind of ontological intuition.

There are a number of important observations that can be made
about these new metaphors of relationship. First of all, there is again
this strange equivocation over which entity is the truly active one. The
divine, the metaphysical foundation, needs to be awakened and cultivated as if it were a thing of nature; but equally, 'Matter is awakened

[91] Schelling, *Ages*, 148.
[92] Schelling, Letter to Georgii, 18 July 1810, in Plitt, *Aus Schellings Leben*, vol. II, 222.
[93] Plotinus, *The Enneads*, 350.
[94] Plitt, *Aus Schellings Leben*, 220. See also the 'Stuttgart Seminars', 207: 'All creation,
   then, involves a soliciting of the superior and properly divine within what had been
   excluded.'

to explicit life and properly animated only by the ideal or divine'.[95] Is it matter which craves the divine and draws the eternal towards it (much as humans, for Kant, generate regulative ideals), or is it the absolute which longs to exist?

Secondly, we can note the way in which Schelling's figures present a strange inversion of Hegel's narrative of master and slave in the *Phenomenology of Spirit*, published two years before Schelling delivered the Stuttgart Seminars. Both use foundational allegories to explore the emergence of a metaphysical division between existence and identity, and how this constitutes or is constituted within the particular conditions of human subjectivity. Both are also attempting to ground their particular philosophical co-ordinates in existential narratives rather than logic (or logic reformulated in existential terms) – hence the metaphysical division is enacted, for Hegel, in the animal world, for Schelling, in the general realm of natural entities. But something very different is unfolded in Schelling's account of the absolute compared with Hegel's. Rather than a struggle in which one party braves a trial by death in order to become lord of the other, here the victor has curiously withdrawn from the fight before its very inception. The absolute inflicts a kind of trial by death upon itself (that odd comparison of divine wisdom to a dead man) which allows a form of weakness to emerge in its stead (the father now watches quietly over the child). Power relations are operating in reverse – and this of course makes a strange kind of sense, because Schelling sets out with the intention of 'reversing' the metaphysical understanding of process, so that entities are no longer enchained by what precedes them. Slavery has been replaced by arousal. Correspondingly, the negative forces bearing on entities are no longer those of aggressive conflict; instead they must endure the negativity of uttermost origins – bare beginnings. The struggle is the struggle of each entity to solicit its being which exists only *in potentia*. 'Most people lack the requisite humility' to conceive of the beginning, wrote Schelling in the *Ages of the World*: 'they wish to begin everything straight away with the highest concepts and bypass the mute beginnings of all life.'[96]

Schelling's approach to the self-effacement of the absolute – an absolute which goes missing at the very point of agency – again bears a marked similarity to the theorisation of identity in a later existentialist context. His assertion, in the 1811 draft of the *Ages of the World*, that 'Everything can be communicated to the creature except one thing, to possess its being in and through itself', is mirrored in the account that Kierkegaard

95 Schelling, 'Stuttgart Seminars', 215.
96 Schelling, *Ages*, 148.

will give of an omnipotence which is also an absolute withdrawal.[97] As
Gillian Rose has described this Kierkegaardian proposition: 'No human
being can make another free: "omnipotence alone" can do so, "because
omnipotence is always taking itself back".'[98] From this perspective, the
only art of power which escapes implication in the corrupting influence
of self-love on the part of the giver, is that established in 'the idea of creation *ex nihilo* ... the creating of something out of nothing – a creature
which endures independently of its creator, and therefore does not persist by virtue of diminution of the creator's powers, nor by dependence
of the creature'.[99] Schelling's absolute that dies into matter, becomes
passive or watches from a position of non-existence, appears to be a
prime instance of such a withdrawal or involution of omnipotence, and
in the 1815 draft of the *Ages of the World* he will specifically link these
ideas to the concept of a creation '*ex nihilo*'.[100]

Once more, the transformation of concepts of dependency is at the
heart of what appears to be a series of texts about the evolution of
nature. This is true even of Schelling's most arcane speculations on
cosmic genesis. Thus Schelling argues that, 'This being [the nature
of the world] can't be posited from the eternal Possibility-to-be itself,
because then *it wouldn't be independent* of him';[101] and again: 'the eternal
Possibility to be [A] is necessarily differentiated from the real being [B].
Otherwise *it would be necessary* Being'.[102] At the opening of the *Ages of
the World*, Schelling suggests that 'Each era has always obscured its predecessor, so that it hardly betrays any sign of an origin',[103] and later on
he describes the creation of the world as a sudden act in which, 'when
the successor is posited, the predecessor is as well, although it remains
only as a predecessor'[104] – that is, there is mutual grounding but no
control by precedent because the relation is instantaneous. At another
point in the *Ages of the World* he again stresses that, 'We simply cannot
think about this in terms of becoming or beginning *out of some preceding
state of affairs*'; moreover, 'If one of the two wills were to precede, the
only one that could be posited at the beginning was the one that did not
will a beginning and that was overcome at that very moment.'[105] More
forcefully still, he suggests that to 'let someone accept subordination
as necessary, and hence as original' leaves them with nothing: 'What

---

[97] Schelling, *Die Weltalter, Urfassungen*, 52.
[98] Gillian Rose, *The Broken Middle* (Oxford: Blackwell, 1992), 86.
[99] Ibid., 87.
[100] Schelling, *The Ages of the World* [1815], 14.
[101] Schelling, *Philosophische Entwürfe*, 99. My italics.
[102] Ibid., 95. My italics.   [103] Schelling, *Ages*, 121.
[104] Ibid., 173.   [105] Ibid., 137, 176.

would he have? He would be finished.'[106] Schelling is, as it were, toying with Fichte's voluntaristic vocabulary, looking for ways in which will can be construed differently from determinacy, but as more than merely ideal, without allowing the vision of existence to become wholly indeterminable.[107]

The attempt at a benign transference of power from the point of origin to its aftermath, or from the absolute to the individual, remains problematic in whichever philosophical or descriptive form Schelling presents it. For Schelling remains unable, or unwilling, to state the connection between self and absolute, self and law, self and what is prior to it, yet still desires to make such relationships structurally explicit in a complex philosophical scheme. He wishes wholly to negate the connotation of dependency *and* yet maintain an original and foundational basis of truth – an 'absolute' – by which the identity of the self can be underpinned. Coleridge schematised Schelling's general dilemma succinctly and comically in a note written on the endpapers of his copy of *The System of Transcendental Idealism*, which he read first around 1813–15: 'Schelling finds the necessity of splitting not alone philosophy but the Philosopher – a sort of Kehama twy-personal at two several gates.' 'Kehama' here refers to Robert Southey's *Curse of Kehama* (1810) in which the hero 'storms the eight gates of Hell … by multiplying himself and appearing on all sides at once.'[108] Coleridge then sketched a representation of Schelling's system, which is reproduced in Figure 3.1: A represents a gate 'the Massive Door of which is barred on both sides: so that when he arrives at A from Bα he must return back, & go round by C to Bβ in order to reach the same point from that direction.'

What Coleridge recognised was that the attempt to have a foundation and in some way bar access to its presence can equally be represented as the attempt to be there prior to oneself; to be one's own foundation. In effect, this would be to arrive at a description of the self akin to that of the absolute – whether Plato's perception that 'all that comes into being must derive its existence from a prime origin, but the prime origin itself from nothing', or Spinoza's that 'That thing is called free

---

[106] Ibid., 180.

[107] Schopenhauer's *The World as Will and Representation*, trans. E. F. Payne, 2 vols. (New York: Dover, 1966) will of course make precisely this leap – inverting the claims of both consciousness *and* individuality by showing both to be the puppets of an anterior metaphysical will, moving the whole of nature blindly to its tune.

[108] Samuel Taylor Coleridge, *The Collected Works of Samuel Taylor Coleridge*, ed. H. J. Jackson and George Whalley, vol. XII, *Marginalia*, part 4 (Princeton University Press: 1998), 461.

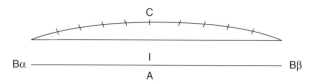

Figure 3.1 Coleridge's diagram of the logical form of Schelling's philosophy (from a note written on the endpapers of his copy of Schelling's *System of Transcendental Idealism*)

Source: The Collected Works of Samuel Taylor Coleridge, vol. XII, *Marginalia, Part 4: Pamphlets to Shakespeare*, ed. H. J. Jackson and George Whalley (Princeton, NJ: Princeton University Press, 1998), p. 461.

which exists from the necessity of its nature alone.'[109] Žižek has likewise observed that Schelling was trying to achieve a solution whereby 'the subject is somehow already here prior to his existence and then, by way of a free act, creates-posits himself, his own being.'[110] However, this attempt in fact only stores up for itself, in different forms, the very crises over identity which it seeks to overcome. It goes hand in hand with an acute problematisation of succession and precedent per se, and a suspension of or confusion over the account of agency. Schelling's various descriptions, however naive or labyrinthine, always stutter over the same dilemma: is what goes before actively able to sustain or prefigure its future development? Is identity sustained by an ascertainable form of recurrence? Or is the relation of self to origin obscure because it is in fact contingent and only subjectively imagined?

From within these hesitant, unhappy identifications and dis-identifications of God and nature, nature and origins, origins and nothingness, nothingness and the absolute, there proliferates an ever more restless and uncertain set of reflections on the obscure relations between the self and its antecedent natural or metaphysical grounds. In the midst of these, Georgii's question which Schelling so confidently dismissed in 1810 returns to haunt the working notes for the *Ages of the World* – 'In order to actualise himself, he must already have been [there].'[111] It is a

---

[109] Plato, *Phaedrus*, 49; Spinoza, *The Ethics*, 2. See also Nietzsche's later contention in *The Genealogy of Morals: an Attack* that the fruit of the process of human development is 'the sovereign individual, equal only to himself', in Friedrich Nietzsche, *The Birth of Tragedy and The Genealogy of Morals* (New York: Anchor Books/Doubleday, 1956), 191.

[110] Žižek, *The Indivisible Remainder*, 19.

[111] Schelling, *Philosophische Entwürfe*, 95.

neat statement of the paradox which Freud reformulates as the desire to be present at one's own birth, and which Fichte had anticipated in *The Vocation of Man*, where his protagonist, facing the possibility of his own production by a prior set of causes, admits: 'It would be the height of folly to suppose that I existed before I existed in order to bring myself into existence.'[112]

The alchemy of identity

Schelling could only resolve the metaphysical obstructions to a foundational account of the self by developing a principle of the unconscious. How Schelling finally comes to state the problem in this way and move the unconscious centre-stage – or perhaps, make it a foundational presence perpetually off-stage – will be demonstrated in the following sections. But I want first to look briefly at two other ways in which Schelling attempts to bridge the broken axes of his system: by insinuating either alchemical or spiritological processes at work in the whole. Both these sets of esoteric assumptions find a way round the proscribed law of succession or connection between the individual and the absolute, by intuiting quasi-magical forms of connection. The structure of these explanations is important, because it anticipates the kind of structure Schelling will want to introduce into the *psyche* as the condition of its autonomy and identity. However, in attributing alchemical and spiritological processes to the psyche, Schelling also anticipates a whole line of development in Romantic and dynamic psychology, from C. G. Carus and Justinus Kerner through to C. G. Jung, whose own psychiatric studies began in 1902 with the investigation of spirit-seeing and prophecy and culminated in the 1950s with extensive researches into alchemical procedures as a map of unconscious psychic processes.[113]

The principles which Schelling was struggling to construct at this point were no longer purely philosophical ones – certainly, we are getting further and further away from the premises of the original *Naturphilosophie*, let alone the deductions of transcendental idealism – nor are they properly materialist ones. We might think of them as pseudo-principles, in search of an empirical basis, through which Schelling was attempting to give concrete form to a set of specific metaphysical demands. These are the demands that entities possess the full measure

---

[112] Fichte, *Vocation*, 11.

[113] See C. G. Jung, 'On the Psychology and Pathology of So-Called Occult Phenomena' (1902), *CW*, vol. I, and *Mysterium Coniunctionis: An Inquiry into the Separation and Synthesis of Psychic Opposites in Alchemy*, *CW*, vol. XIV.

of autonomy, are capable of defining their own identities from a position of original indeterminacy, and yet are also in some way connected to an enigmatic causal power which harmonises the development of life as a whole. If this power can no longer be represented as a chain of conditions, it might be rendered instead as either a *sublime* force, brimming through nature but incapable of being fully objectified; or as an enigmatic principle, defying causal description, whereby the future already inheres in the past in an ideal *spectral* form. These two possibilities are also versions of those competing portraits of the absolute which Schelling drew from Aristotle and Neoplatonism, in which either the absolute exists but in a *blind, unconscious form*, or it is complete but *only as an idea*. In his alchemical and spiritological descriptions, however, Schelling was attempting to identify this elliptical condition of truth as an empirical phenomenon within existence.

Using the language of alchemy, Schelling suggests in the latter part of the *Ages of the World* that whoever has an eye practised in free consideration knows that 'things do not seem fully completed by what constitutes their existence in the strictest sense'. Instead, 'something else in and around them first grants them the full sparkle and shine of life'.[114] About this intangible 'essence', flowing and streaming through creation, Schelling asks: '[I]s this not just that inner spiritual matter which still lies concealed in all things of this world, only awaiting its liberation?'[115] He relates this intimation of inner being to the way in which metals have been regarded 'as individual sparks of light from this essence, glimmering in the darkness of matter', and to a universal instinct which has 'divined the presence of this essence in gold'.[116] In his notebooks Schelling names this materialised but latent form of spirit as *Tinktur*, a term with alchemical connotations derived from Böhme and Oetinger who used it to indicate the essence of divinity within beings.[117] In effect, Schelling has translated the concept of cosmic or natural integration, required to add certainty, security and providential harmony to the system of living beings, into a divine force, and then given this

---

[114] Schelling, *Ages*, 151.
[115] Ibid., 151.   [116] Ibid., 151.
[117] Schelling, *Philosophische Entwürfe*, 162. Compare Jakob Böhme on *Tinktur*: 'and in nature [it] bringeth forth the substantiality of the shining and glance, or brightness, which may be seen in gold, silver, and all glistering metals'; 'that is its lustre and light, wherein its *life* doth consist'. *The High and Deep Searching Out of the Threefold Life of Man, Through or According to the Three Principles*, trans. John Sparrow (London: J. M. Watkins, 1909, Kessinger reprint edition), 97–8. Compare also Jung on the signification of 'salt' in alchemical literature, *Mysterium Coniunctionis*, 240: it is 'the human soul imprisoned in the body as the *anima mundi* is in matter ... it is the tincture which "coagulates" all substances'.

force the form of an inscrutable material gleam within things. Freedom is engendered by liberating the essence which at present lies concealed within life. It is as if the problem of individuality and autonomy could be resolved by access to the potency of a particular substance. As Jung would conclude over a century later, alchemy was 'an individual undertaking on which the adept staked his whole soul for the transcendental purpose of producing a *unity*'.[118] What was at stake was not gold as such, but a new synthesis, both within the self, and between the self and the whole of creation.

Alongside this alchemical attempt to construe the relation between the universal and the individual, we could place other passages from the *Ages of the World* which demonstrate the unfolding of the absolute as an ideal agency – a form of prophecy or pre-vision. Reflecting on the origins of the world, Schelling suggested that the as yet only ideally existing God had an ideal preview of the whole of creation, directly before contracting into the nothingness of matter (this contraction being a further permutation of Schelling's notion of gravity as the most original force in nature). At that point, 'the Eternal saw for the first time, in the immediate ectype of its essence [that is, with the clarity of a wax seal] everything that will one day be in nature'.[119] This moment of pre-vision revealed not just everything in nature, but also 'the visions of future spirits whose creation was determined at the same time as that of natural things'.[120] This is essentially a theory of Platonic 'archetypes' and, as we shall see in Chapter 5, Schelling's mystical Platonism here is not quite as anachronistic as it seems. The circle of early nineteenth-century German nature philosophers reintroduced archetypes as an explanatory principle into the biological sciences in order to account for recurrency in nature in a non-mechanistic form.

But this theory also fulfilled another purpose; it was a way of introducing the eternal into reality in a *passive* form. Rather than controlling creation in a way that dominates individuality, the ideal archetypes representing the identity of future beings are in some way barely present, or present as the innermost possession of individuals themselves: hidden guides secreted in living matter which for that reason can be self-guiding. Any more explicit form of control would, like Kierkegaard's corrupting gift of being, immediately destroy the import of that which was given, subsuming it under the omnipotent agency of the giver. This passive form of the divine, as ideal or archetype rather

---

[118] Jung, *Mysterium Coniunctionis*, 554.
[119] Schelling, *Ages*, 155.   [120] Ibid., 155.

than as alchemical potency, is 'the material or matter for … the still future world of spirits'.[121] Whereas *Tinktur* ferried a concept of divine potency into the individualised nature of beings, here matter, though supposedly beginning from nothing and finding its form always *after* the event, illicitly contains some model of what it is to become. This 'spectral' materialisation of the absolute – conceived as a future state beyond the existential conflicts of material existence – is an identity carried forward from the origin of the world, but without the implication of prior control or determination: 'Spirit is not only the *final* unity of the opposite, A and B, but *the link from the original ground* (eternity) and the life built up below' – A and B here represent phases of reality dominated by the ideal and the material respectively.[122] Because we are now dealing in a spiritual medium which eludes objective causal presence, Schelling allows himself to reintroduce that proscribed term 'link' from the mechanistic philosophy, just as Fichte had allowed himself to conceive of a 'bond' between the individual and its absolute ground in his theory of the will, as long as it was an 'obscure bond'.

The secret birthplace of existence

The materialisation of the divine as unconscious substance, and the spirit-show that foresees the future, might be simply ignored as symptoms of Schelling's contact with theosophy in the Munich circle – the recently recovered texts of Böhme supplying the alchemical, Swedenborg the spiritological formulae. But at the same time these counter-Enlightenment terms of engagement with the absolute are there to overcome a specific structural flaw in the philosophy of individuality. Both enable the intuition of more absolute powers of certainty regarding the conditions of self-presence and self-determination; they supplement individuality with a sense of divine essence or pre-determination, but in

---

[121] Ibid., 155. Compare Jung's later interpretation of somnambulistic phenomena as a form of internal prophecy, Chapter 5 of this book, n. 40, and Shamdasani, 'From Geneva to Zürich: Jung and French Switzerland', *Journal of Analytical Psychology*, 43 (1998), 115–26, 119–20, which cites Théodore Flournoy's 1903 review of Jung's *On the Psychology and Pathology of so-called Occult Phenomena*: 'Jung thinks that … somnambulistic phenomena at the time of puberty (experiences of double consciousness, etc.) can have a teleological character: they express the transformations and neoformations of character, and represent the irruptions of the future personality.' For accounts of theories of evolution predicated on the 'somnambulistic' anticipation of archetypal forms in Bergson, Jung and early Deleuze, see Christian Kerslake, 'Insects and Incest: From Bergson and Jung to Deleuze', in *Multitudes: Revue Politique, Artistique, Philosophique*, 25 (22 October 2006) www.multitudes.samizdat. net/Insects-and-Incest-From-Bergson.

[122] Ibid., 147. My italics.

forms which at the same time do not quite impinge on the self's apprehension of its own freedom. Divinity and the absolute remain obscure or sublime intimations, certainly in comparison with the crushing force exerted by the principle of sufficient reason as elsewhere addressed by Fichte and Schelling.

Tellingly, these principles emerge at precisely those points in Schelling's argument where he is trying to materialise the incongruous ordering within his system, such that the end determines the beginning: humanity, or individuality, grounds itself. They are thus another manifestation of the logical problem parodied by Coleridge, in which Schelling installs an obstacle for the rational imagination of determinacy – the double-barred gate – which then must be illicitly circumvented in order to invoke an incremental manifestation or recognition of the absolute.

There is an undeniable pathos in the way Schelling's philosophical tools approach closer to figures of desire and premonition, the more he seeks to materialise the transcendent; and closer to the *supernatural*, the more he tries to *naturalise* the absolute in terms compatible with the individual experience of freedom. At such moments in his notebooks, Schelling's attempts to 'precede' himself descend into a web of marginal cross-references, penned linkages to earlier notes and then strikings-through of the same links (in some instances, all this is jotted, ironically, across the dates of his house calendar for 1813). At one of the most tortuous points, Schelling speculated: 'A3 [the highest potency of the spirit] is also brought to ecstasy through B [the material world] – to being outside itself – it is no longer a free realisation, and yet it creates – but where it creates, it creates blindly. NB. Don't forget, that it often wants to escape, but it can't leave B.'[123] Some pages earlier he also suggests that 'The will is inflamed through the aspect which shows it the future.'[124] Idealism at this point becomes palpably gothic, permeated with the language of imprisonment, arousal and escape. But such passages epitomise a further aspect of Schelling's philosophical style in the *Ages of the World*, which is that as he shifts from logical problems of precedence towards matters of anguish and erotic tension, the language becomes quasi-psychological.

On this front, the very pressure to have *already been there*, to be the founder of one's own existence, draws the metaphorical structures of the *Ages of the World* inevitably on from desire and towards the representation of procreation and birth itself. The introduction of such terms

---

[123] Schelling, *Philosophische Entwürfe*, 131.
[124] Ibid., 118.

can be ascribed to the general influence of the gnostic and the erotic on German Romantic thinking – described by M. H. Abrams as the 'myth of sexual division, opposition, and reconjunction which is at the centre of occult thought'.[125] One finds the same metaphorical conjunction in an essay by Franz von Baader of 1808, 'On the Analogy between the Knowledge-drive and the Procreative-drive', published in the *Yearbook of Medicine as Science*, co-edited by Schelling and Adalbert Marcus. Here Baader elaborates a general principle of yearning, coupling with the other, and productive expression operating between heaven and earth, man and wife, humanity and nature, the inner and the divine.[126] This is another example of *Naturphilosophie* searching for a non-mechanistic, non-logical language through which to think the principle processes of life and identity. But as these metaphors of arousal, desire and the emergence of life gravitate towards tropes of 'procreation', there emerges this complex double-coding in Schelling's work whereby the metaphysical stress on origins begins to be approached through the metaphor of birth itself. That is to say, human and mammalian 'birth' is yet another non-mechanistic metaphor filling in a gap in the knowledge of natural dynamic relationships of all kinds. It is not midwifery or foetal evolution that is being discussed, but metaphysical notions of origin and development, imagined through metaphors of birth processes.

At the same time, Schelling's attempt to redescribe the logic of nature was guided by the desire to posit individuals as self-founding. Hence it is entirely appropriate that his semantic and conceptual search curves back towards the terminology of human beginnings. The crisis over ontology and identity in general now hovers expressively as a riddle over the empirical birth of the individual. Metaphysical identity and physical origins appear to have become the same question – the 'question that gets raised in childhood but grows tiring in mature age: "where has everything come from?"', or again, 'Who can unveil the secret birthplace of existence?'[127] *Appear* to have become the same question because, though it seems that we are approaching the mystery of the genesis of the empirical individual, *its* human birth, we must remember that this is still an ontological allegory designed to figure the correct relation between foundations and being. One might protest that a philosophical account of the origins of individuality must begin with the event of

[125] M. H. Abrams, *Natural Supernaturalism: Tradition and Revolution in Romantic Literature* (New York: Norton, 1971), 169.

[126] Franz von Baader, 'On the Analogy between the Knowledge-drive and the Procreative-drive', in A. F. Marcus and F. W. J. Schelling (eds.), *Jahrbücher der Medicin als Wissenschaft*, vol. III, part 1 (Tübingen: J. G. Cotta, 1808), 113–24, 117.

[127] Schelling, *Ages*, 134, 136.

birth. However, Schelling is concerned not first and foremost with the life-history of the individual, but with its metaphysical grounding, its potential to be *causa sui*. What is at stake is not the production of the individualised body, but the metaphysical 'birth' of the possibility of individuality itself, which traditionally has played a subordinate role in metaphysical systems (subordinate to the task of describing the unity or totality of existence). However, once Schelling had reworked the theorisation of autonomy from a philosophy of selfhood, of the I, into a narrative of unknown grounds, secret sources and divined but effaced parentage, it was increasingly to become entwined with descriptions of the empirical self in distinctive and peculiar ways.

What, then, is the maternity and paternity of the individual? What is unveiled in the secret birthplace of existence? On the maternal front, Schelling proclaims that, 'Eternity is pregnant, cannot give birth, still awaits her midwife.'[128] The midwife will be nature, the point of origin for the *actual* existence of divinity, of the absolute; however, the gendering of eternity and nature as female is also designed to indicate their passivity in relation to the form of will that is produced: 'Unconscious longing is its [the will's] mother, but she only conceived it, it has produced itself';[129] and 'She [eternal nature] doesn't engender him, she only produces, eternally, in order that he can generate himself.'[130] A similar disqualification of feminine production is encoded in the 1809 essay on *Human Freedom*. Drawing on the Platonic notion of the dependence of life-forms on archetypes, such that the world's creatures are 'but the thoughts of the divine mind', Schelling is keen to point out that, even so, they necessarily have an independent life: 'thoughts are doubtless born in the soul; but a thought once born is an independent power which works on its own way'. This self-agency of the thought, acting as a metaphor for the creature's own independent spirit, 'grows so great in the human soul that it masters its own mother and prevails over her'.[131] The female ground (nature), though the point of origin for the real, becomes at the same time a vanishing or impoverished middle term between truth and the self-producing being – either because the feminine is considered as passive in relation to the male; or because nature is ultimately subordinate to the soul. The self has a mother, then, in the

[128] Schelling, *Philosophische Entwürfe*, 129.
[129] Schelling, *Ages*, 137.
[130] Schelling, *Philosophische Entwürfe*, 102. Compare Böhme, 'For there the flash desireth with great longing to have its *mother* for its food, and here is the true original of *life*', *The Threefold Life*, 49. The 'flash' is the spark of divinity within nature.
[131] Schelling, *Human Freedom*, 19–20.

natural body that supports the soul, but it is merely support – *conditio sine qua non.*

But it is not only the agency of the female which Schelling undermines in his biological metaphors. The agency of the father is also overturned, or reduced to the most basic and latent presence within matter. The dialectical scheme which moves from the divine ideal, A, to its positing in inverted form as material B, to the final emergence of original and independently existing divinity in the life of individuals, stymies the causal logic of production and the genetic agency of *logos*. There is 'something between [God's] unreality and reality that, however, is just ground'.[132] In the notebook for 1813, Schelling describes the highest potency of the divine within existence in Christological terms as the father that remains a constant influence and 'is ever drawn into material being, but, through the son, is always freed again'.[133] It is the son, not the parent, that is agent once more in these metaphors that attempt to displace causes with their effects. Even more strikingly, the first 1811 draft of the *Ages of the World* contains extended passages attempting to construe the relation of divine transcendence and divine incarnation – that is, the Father and Son of the Trinity – in reverse:

The Son is the reconciler, the liberator and redeemer of the Father, and if the paternal power was there before the Son, so it wasn't any the less present before the Father. Because the Father is only Father in the Son and through the Son. That is why the Son is also the cause of the Father's being, and it's here, chiefly, that the alchemical saying is valid: the son of the son, is the one that was the son's father.[134]

In Chapter 4 I will show how such a heterodox view of the incarnation was modelled on readings in Böhme and Meister Eckhart. What I want to stress here is that a metaphysical primal scene establishes the grounds of personal autonomy. A son produces its father, and a mother produces without engendering so that the son 'can generate himself', in just the same way as Schelling used the alternatives of ideal and material to complicate the question of prior agency in his letter to Georgii. On the one hand, human procreation stands in for the metaphysical notion of how identity is produced, displacing a model of determinate conditioning with a more elaborate set of relationships. The literal separation of child from mother and father at birth is used to figure the metaphysical separation of the individual from the absolute, and thus the constitution of the individual's autonomous ground.

---

[132] Schelling, *Philosophische Entwürfe*, 108.
[133] Ibid., 136.
[134] Schelling, *Die Weltalter, Urfassungen*, 59.

But then the metaphysical, conceived as the 'divine' origination of the individual, in turn displaces the model of procreation in reality. The individual does not derive from his or her human parents because, as idea or archetype, the individual is created via a secret bond with the metaphysical one, or source. This principle was already asserted in the *Human Freedom* essay: 'Man, even though born in time, is nonetheless a creature of creation's beginning (the centrum).'[135] The human embryo has, as it were, a navel string connected to the eternal: 'The act which determines man's life in time does not itself belong in time but in eternity ... Through it man's life extends to the beginning of creation.'[136] This chiasmus of divine birth and empirical origins functions exactly as that coming apart of God and nature, producing an ontological gap within which human freedom could be inserted: 'by virtue of occupying the middle-ground between the non-being of nature and the absolute Being = God, man is *free* from both'.[137] Just so, in this context, Schelling can assert that 'True beginning in the eternal comes only with self-genesis.'[138]

The descent of the unconscious

By using these metaphors of procreation – with distant fathers and passive mothers – Schelling establishes the right form of metaphysical foundation in the heart of the empirical description of individual beginnings. Absolute foundations are thus given a tangible foothold in descriptions of life in a way that advances beyond Fichte's rather vague and abstract concept of an 'obscure bond', linking the individual soul to the totality of creation. I will return to these metaphors from a different angle (not metaphysics, but psychology) in Chapter 5, which examines Schelling's assumptions about the individual psyche. There we will see that the scientific and philosophical study of the *empirical* soul of the individual takes on board these same ontological structures, allowing the self to affirm its individuality, its power of self-creation. This twinning of psychological with ontological problems will be carried forwards, through mid-century figures such as C. G. Carus, to psychoanalytic authors such as Rank and Jung, for whom 'Individuation, becoming a self, is not only a spiritual problem, it is the problem of all life.'[139] In many ways,

---

135 Schelling, *Human Freedom*, 63.
136 Ibid., 63–4.   137 Schelling, 'Stuttgart Seminars', 225.
138 Schelling, *Philosophische Entwürfe*, 102.
139 C. G. Jung, 'Individual Dream Symbolism in Relation to Alchemy', *The Collected Works of C. G. Jung*, vol. XII, *Psychology and Alchemy*, 2nd edn (Princeton, NJ: Princeton University Press, 1968), 124.

these prior Romantic symbologies of individuality, which drew so heavily on gnostic and Neoplatonic motifs of procreation, gave Jung confidence in over turning Freud's insistence on the purely sexual reference of Oedipal motifs in fantasy, dream and myth. Jung's main concern, by contrast, was to investigate, over and above its personal significance and biological function, the 'spiritual aspect' of such sexual motifs; for him, sexuality was an expression of the chthonic spirit, the 'other face of God'.[140]

Here, however, I want to introduce the most important point in our examination of Schelling. Schelling does not rest with this implied twinning of metaphysical procreation and individual birth. Fathers and midwives, longing and yielding, are ultimately figurative devices. What Schelling increasingly recognised was that it was the principle of ellipsis within such metaphorical devices that was key. Only some principled ellipsis within the description of relationships would allow the self to take shape on its own terms. The way in which Schelling will cement this idea is not, as Jung ultimately will, through the figure of sexual couplings (from anima and animus to alchemical *conjunctio*), but through the principle of unconsciousness. This principle was all along the goal of those drafts of the *Ages of the World* dealing with the emergence of 'The Past' (the only section to be written). In the last few pages of the 1813 text, the diverse registers of the philosophical narrative converge in a powerful finale in which, in an almost Faustian way, Schelling's pact with the absolute carries him down into the chthonic realm of the unconscious. This is all the more dramatic because unconsciousness is invoked not just in one respect, but as a set of necessary conditions pertaining to *all* points of ontological reference – the absolute itself, the act of creation, and the individual. The whole city of life – its foundations, transactions and inhabitants – is consigned to the abyss; not as a punishment, though, but as an imperative for freedom.

First of all, as the divinity or the absolute 'gets posited through revelation at the beginning', as it externalises itself in some notional first moment of time from an original position of pure possibility and ideality, it 'renders itself amenable to overcoming'.[141] The eternal thus 'leads the force of the highest consciousness into *unconsciousness* and sacrifices it to externality so that there might be life and actuality'.[142] Secondly, not only the absolute, but the act which establishes the relation between the absolute and the individual life, must also become unconscious: 'That primordial deed which makes a man genuinely himself precedes

---

[140] See Carl Jung, *Memories, Dreams, Reflections* (London: Fontana Press, 1995), 192.
[141] Schelling, *Ages*, 181.   [142] Ibid., 181. My italics.

all individual actions; but immediately after it is put into exuber-
ant freedom, this deed sinks into *the night of unconsciousness*'.[143] This
notion of 'deed' echoes Fichte's formulation of the I as an act, rather
than a fact. However, the deed occurs once 'and then immediately
sinks back into the unfathomable depths'.[144] Likewise the will posited
behind such an act 'must immediately sink into *unconsciousness*'. Once
'led into unconsciousness' this will 'does not know its own relation'.[145]
Unconsciousness beats relentlessly across Schelling's successive sen-
tences here as he labours to drive the principle home. Lastly, insofar as this repression of anteriority is successful, the beginning (from
the point of view of individual life-forms) becomes a point of absolute
obscurity, a nothingness, which stands behind life as its source. Thus
unconsciousness now stands for the outermost limit of remembrance
and of the subjective reconstruction of origins. The deed 'can never
again be brought before consciousness. For man to know of this deed,
consciousness itself would have to return to nothing'. Correspondingly,
by 'sinking into *unconsciousness*' the will 'is actually already acting as
past – namely, for us'.[146]

All roads lead to the unconscious. It gathers the various strands of
Schelling's metaphysical project into a complex triadic injunction: the
privation of the absolute; a crisis of transition; and a bar on remembering which would otherwise destroy the horizon of individual identity.
These points of reference now centralise the role of obscurity and forgetting in Schelling's understanding of ontology as the only possible
resolution. This is not about the death of god. The complex stage management of these final pages, in which characters are whisked away and
curtains fall, has more to do with the deity's theatrical displacement
and concealment within matter and the soul, rather than its ultimate
negation. This assertion of an unconscious past has been implicit, as
an ideological need, since Fichte. It came more obviously to the fore in
Schelling's pursuit of a system of nature – in the apprehension of nature's
resistance to mind and a new valorisation of its mysterious and powerful depths. Here, in the *Ages of the World*, Schelling's interest passes
from the examination of beginnings, to non-being and finally to unconsciousness itself. In this triad of obscured foundation, forgotten will
and deed, and oblivious individuality, the significant points of Fichte's
transcendental philosophy of the I are thoroughly transcribed under the
aegis of a principle of the unconscious. Schelling here explicitly affirms
the functional need for a bar on the representation of identity within

[143] Ibid., 181. My italics.   [144] Ibid., 181.
[145] Ibid., 181–2. My italics.   [146] Ibid., 181–2.

the philosophy of freedom. This bar sustains an account of an absolute agency set over and above the determinations of rational consciousness, and in turn prevents the individual from being subsumed under the absolute by establishing its foundation precisely as an obscure conceptual vacancy – the unconscious beginning.

With the turn to the unconscious we have reached the limit of this investigation of Schelling's ideological manoeuvring at the level of metaphysics. It is also the point where the individual is *divined* – both elicited from the absolute, and divinised, insofar as nothing now appears to intervene between the self and its own grounds, except for a certain condition of obscurity. But, as suggested at the start of the chapter, Schelling's analysis of unconscious beginnings in the *Ages of the World* sheds light on much broader transformations within the Romantic human sciences. If the final point of Schelling's speculation here is that the beginning *must not be thought*, the implications of this principle were at the same time beginning to be mapped out in various new apprehensions of historicity within life. For experience to be historical, argues Schelling, there must be aspects of the past that simply *cannot be remembered*. Seen from this point of view, the self now constructs its identity back towards an unknown historical ground, retracing 'the long path of developments from the present back into the deepest night of the past'.[147] The move from a metaphysics of nature to concepts of history, development and repression, represents the point at which the implications of Schelling's work touch the broader currents of nineteenth–century thought. It is via the concept of the inaccessible past that certain less formal or metaphysical apprehensions of the unconscious will be carried over into theories of individual existence. The unconscious is more than just a veil drawn over the system of nature. It heralds the development of a new ideological culture, one that resists or overturns eighteenth-century paradigms of systematicity, and for which truth and necessity emerge in relation to the foundational independence of the person. Moreover, the idea of the true nature of that person is increasingly submerged in the depths of its obscure history and psychology.

[147] Ibid., 114.

4 The historical unconscious: the psyche in the Romantic human sciences

We will now enter the way of times ...[1]

[T]he true in history is not in the present ...[2]

The last chapter concentrated on Schelling the metaphysician. It explored the way in which he wrestled with notions of the system, of 'wholeness' and the 'absolute', in an attempt to make them permeable or even subservient to ideas of selfhood, individuality and freedom. Ultimately, in order to secure these terms of freedom and self-development, he shifted decisively away from idealist apprehensions of objectivity and casual connection, towards a paradigm in which the 'absolute' was necessarily and foundationally displaced from presence (though somehow also operative within it) being either latent within the world or obscurely beyond it. This move effectively establishes an idealism of the unconscious. But in the *Ages of the World*, the latent and the beyond are also both modes of the book's explicit subject, time: latency as the past or as the future still to arrive. The opening of the text itself attempts to make a new start in metaphysics by revealing it to be a mode of historical inquiry: 'Why ... has it been impossible until now that philosophy – which is history with respect to its name and content [that is, 'history' from Greek ιστορια, knowing by inquiry] – be history with respect to its form as well?'[3]

If Schelling's interest in the genesis of life proved to have ulterior motives, so his concern with the past and history is not historical in the usual sense of the term. Schelling was not interested in gathering historical information about either the progress of civilisation or the organic differences between civilisations and epochs, and though his later philosophy of the 1840s centred on a structural investigation of

[1] Schelling, *Ages*, 180.
[2] C. A. Eschenmayer, *Einleitung in Natur und Geschichte*, cited in Joseph L. Esposito, *Schelling's Idealism and Philosophy of Nature* (London: Associated University Press, 1977), 142.
[3] Schelling, *Ages*, 114.

classical and pre-classical mythology, its motive, as we shall see, was not strictly historiographical. Indeed, the psychiatrist and existentialist philosopher Karl Jaspers, in his major study of Schelling, gave a shortlist of methodological implications of the term 'history' which were absent from Schelling's work. These include 'historical knowing of the world' and 'the possibility that something that becomes historically lost, can become present again'.[4]

The first thing to note about Schelling's turn to the historical is that history cannot be assimilated to reason, or to a simple sequential narrative: 'Science is history, but was not able to be so as long as it was intended as a mere succession or development of one's own ideas.'[5] Historical thinking for Schelling implies a necessary revision of notions of order, connection and meaning per se. The past is a primordial threshold at which reason's account-giving peters out. Of the geological formations which testify to the chaotic nature of the early history of the world, Schelling notes that 'We find the greatest part of them collapsed in ruins, witness to a savage devastation.'[6] The suggestion here is of something both catastrophic and enigmatic which renders the primeval past unaccountable. If 'a great work of the ancient world stands before us as an incomprehensible whole until we find traces of its manner of growth and gradual development', how much more must this be the case in relation to the earth's own prehistory: 'What entirely different intricacies and folds must take place here.'[7] In considering origins, reason must be prepared to step down from both habitual and logical modes of self-certainty and make way for the intuition of quite other forms of process. Later in the century, these 'different intricacies' will take shape as greatly extended notions of process in time, for instance in the work of Lyell and Darwin. Here, they testify simply to something *other* than reason, something as yet inconceivable.

Secondly, just as there was a primordial split in the models of *Naturphilosophie* between gravity and light, so Schelling now apprehends a decisive split in *time* between presence and the past. The new emphasis on the historical past opens up a perpetually obscured foundation beyond the horizon of existence. In the opening of his 1827 lectures on the 'System of the Ages of the World', Schelling indicated that his object would be a nature 'before which material explanations fall silent' and a history which is 'wrapped in mist'.[8] Here he repeats an observation made by another nature philosopher, Carl August Eschenmayer,

---

[4] Jaspers, *Schelling*, 337.   [5] Schelling, *Ages*, 113.   [6] Ibid., 121.   [7] Ibid., 121.
[8] Schelling, *System der Weltalter: Münchener Vorlesung 1827/28 in einer Nachschrift von Ernst von Lasaulx* (Frankfurt am Main: Vittorio Klosterman, 1998), 4–5.

in his *Introduction to Nature and History* of 1806: 'The true in nature is not in the actual, and the true in history is not in the present.'[9] Note how far the depiction of truth has now drifted from Fichte's positing of deeds and acts within the I. For Schelling, this perpetual polarisation of time into the present and a historical unconscious is simply a temporalised version of that fundamental displacement of the absolute made necessary by the philosophy of freedom. Indeed, from those final paragraphs of the *Ages of the World* cited in the last chapter, we can see that for Schelling it is not *time* that induces forgetting; rather, it is the structural inception of forgetting and repression itself which constitutes the categorial dimensions of time. The night of unconsciousness, the unfathomable depths, provoke the emergence of the past as a category distinct from the present, and these obscure depths in turn depend on the foundational self-withdrawing of the absolute: 'Even in the primordial essence itself something had to be posited as a past before the present time became possible, and ... it is precisely this past that is borne by the present creation, and that still remains fundamentally concealed.'[10] One might add that, as this obscure past is identified with the absolute itself, so history can be said to conceal a ground which is unavailable to consciousness but is fundamentally involved in sustaining the world of appearances.

Hegel's idea of a dialectical movement within the frame of history – of spirit advancing its contradictions and syntheses – is inverted by Schelling to give the form of an unrevealed and 'remaindered' absolute, a hidden basis to human life which merges in turn with the motif of a 'primordial nature'. History, as the obscure and primeval past, is here more akin to 'nature' than its opposite, and is approached through metaphors of inaccessibility (*Verschloßenheit*), concealment (*Verborgenheit*) and secrecy (*Geheimnis*). Ιστορια, implying that which needs to be sought, thus becomes the principle through which Schelling hypostasises the past precisely as the 'unknown'. In the *Ages of the World*, this past is perpetually working against the possibility of manifestation – it is 'a dynamic hiding away [*Verschloßenheit*], an active striving backwards into the depths [*Tiefe*], into concealment [*Verborgenheit*]' – which brings this notion into proximity with Freud's later theorisation of a dynamic unconscious.[11] Truth defers to the one organism that 'lies hidden deep [*tief verborgen*] in time', and the 'secret [*geheime*] birthplace of existence'.[12] In 1805, in a letter to Voss setting out the plans for his own

[9] Eschenmayer in Esposito, *Schelling's Idealism*, 142.
[10] Schelling, *Ages*, 122.
[11] Ibid., 143.   [12] Ibid., 123, 136.

philosophical project, Hegel warned of the kind of false philosophy of the 'secret' that had been growing up in Jena for which, 'as well as that which was attainable through genuine efforts, there was in addition a wholly hidden [*versteckte*] knowledge, a locked secret [*verschloßenes Geheimnis*] that was the preserve of members of the caste'.[13] It is hard not to find Schelling's work, and his pervasive influence on the wider circle of nature philosophers, implicated here.

Likewise, in the 1830s, it was Schelling's conception of history that emerged as one of the main targets of post-Hegelian critique. Wishing to reclaim the religious motif of revelation for a more anthropocentric idealism, Ludwig Feuerbach proposed 'recollection' as 'the principle, the foundation, and the possibility of history', arguing that 'Time only lifts the veil in the temple of Isis; its total activity consists in unveiling'.[14] For Feuerbach, humanity was to reclaim its own past as part of its project of Enlightenment. But in one of the original fascicles for the *Ages of the World*, Schelling, perhaps drawing on Schiller's 'The Veiled Image of Sais', used this image of Isis to emphasise precisely the *veiling* of truth: '"I am what then was, what is, and what shall be; no mortal has lifted [*aufgehoben*] my veil." Thus once upon a time, according to some old narratives, from under the veil of the image of Isis, spoke the intimated primal essence in the temple of Saïs to the wanderer.'[15] Schelling here makes the object of the philosophy of history equivalent to the veiled image of the goddess. Tellingly, Marx in 1843 urged Feuerbach to contribute a polemic against Schelling to the first issue of the *Franco-German Yearbooks*, characterising Feuerbach as 'Schelling in reverse'. Marx attempted to persuade Feuerbach that he was nominated by 'Nature and History' themselves to engage with Schelling, and their struggle would be 'the struggle of the imagination of philosophy with philosophy itself'.[16]

There is a third point arising out of Schelling's preoccupation with a historical unconscious. If history seems once more to resemble a religious mystery, what is at stake is not so much the specific historical content to be concealed or revealed – for instance, the nature of lost or prehistorical

---

[13] Schelling, *Briefe und Dokumente*, vol. I, 501.
[14] Ludwig Feuerbach, *Thoughts on Death and Immortality* (Berkeley, CA: University of California Press, 1980), 128, 138.
[15] Schelling, 'Frühestes Conceptblatt. Gedanke der Weltalter', in *Die Weltalter, Urfassungen*, 187. Friedrich Schiller, 'Das Verschleierte Bild zu Sais', in Julius Petersen and Friedrich Beissner (eds.), *Schillers Werke Nationalausgabe*, vol. I (Weimar: Hermann Böhlaus Nachfolger, 1943), 245–56.
[16] Marx to Feuerbach, 3 October 1843, in Karl Marx and Frederick Engels, *Collected Works*, vol. III (London: Lawrence & Wishart, 1975), 350–1.

cultures.[17] Rather, it is the principle itself: that there is a constant and hidden basis to reality from which alternative and speculative accounts of the self can be derived. Alongside this sense of historical depth, Schelling was keen to develop intimations of secret relationships between the psyche and the unconscious past, on to which he could transfer the burden of self-authentication. This new axis of mediation between identity and origins falls at an oblique angle to the structures of the I, of rational intelligence, and the world of objective presence developed in earlier phases of idealism. The paean to history at the opening of the *Ages of the World* contains a poetic invocation of man's essence, through which he is able to 'retrace the long path of developments from the present back into the deepest night of the past'.[18] The suggestion here is not of a historical consciousness per se, but of a secret or counter-rational connection with the past which eludes, supplements or perhaps overturns the rational theorisation of development. Note how the direction of agency (from present to past) runs counter to the expected development of causal succession, and how the path itself leads from consciousness back to obscurity, not the other way round. Schelling continues:

Man often sees himself transported into such wonderful relations and inner connections through precisely this innermost essence, such as when he encounters a moment in the present as one long past ... Accordingly the unfathomable, prehistoric age rests in this essence; although it faithfully protects the treasures of the wholly past.[19]

An essence latent within the psyche, rather than the faculty of the conscious I, mediates the relationship with the past here; and, as with the alchemical and spiritological formulae touched on in the previous chapter, it allows for *wonderful* relations and *inner* connections – moments of déjà vu, moments in which past and present switch places. Crucially, these are moments whose causal interconnections cannot be construed logically or dependently. Just as humanity's metaphysical birth was to link it aporetically to the origin of creation and to the eternal, so here this innermost essence anamorphically *contains* the prehistoric age, the foundation. It is important to notice the switch whereby the obscurely displaced 'primal essence' comes to be intuited within the individual

---

[17] Compare Bachofen's more particular study of Mother Right: 'We will see a strange world unfold before our eyes ... This world contradicts our notions of a civilized culture. However, we must judge this primordial world, its conceptions, and customs by its own fundamental law', Johann Jakob Bachofen, *An English Translation of Bachofen's Mutterrecht (Mother Right) (1861), A Study of the Religious and Juridicial Aspects of Gynecocracy in the Ancient World, vol. I: 'Lycia', 'Crete' and 'Athens'*, abr. and trans. David Partenheimer (Lewiston, Queenston and Lampeter: Edwin Mellen, 2007), 1.

[18] Schelling, *Ages*, 114.   [19] Ibid., 114.

itself. It is as if the transformation of the absolute into an unconscious past allows the self to locate the absolute within itself, within its own unconscious past. The I may consciously seek the past of eternity, suggests Schelling enigmatically in the *Ages of the World*, but eternity is 'what your "I" was before it found itself'.[20]

These points provide us with a very basic outline of the way Schelling moulds connotations of the 'historical' around the structure of the unconscious. But there remains much more to be said about the way in which history, psychology and the unconscious become intimately allied with each other in Romantic research into human existence. Ultimately, my purpose here is to explore how these ideas start to shape the contours of Romantic theories of psychic life, but before concentrating more specifically on Romantic psychological theory in Chapter 5, I want to show that Schelling's structural assertion of the unconscious past integrates with a much wider set of contemporary attempts to figure psychic selfhood through intuitions of the historical. Indeed, Schelling's shift of interest from metaphysics and cosmogony to the historical structure of an unconscious exemplifies how such ideas will become involved in nineteenth-century ideology more generally.

Schelling will pursue this covert source of identity in history in a number of different ways. One such project emerges from his theory of a historical process of repression, outlined in his later lectures on the 'Philosophy of Revelation'. Another facet is represented by Schelling's increasing fascination with the tradition of German religious mysticism, gradually being uncovered by Romantic medievalists, and which oriented the identity of the self around the notion of an abyss in the divine, which Schelling could equate with his earlier concept of gravity, and now with the past. A third concerns the growth of a particular dynamic discourse of transitions and crises within the Romantic science of existence – particularly as expressions of 'higher development' or states of emergence. The unconscious in psychiatry and psychology must be set in the context of these wider identifications of unconsciousness in the human sciences, all of which seek to preserve the idea of individual self-determination and to manifest obscure relations running between the self and its 'inner' foundations. The rest of this chapter will outline each of these developments of the unconscious in turn. But I will begin with a simpler narrative of the unconscious past, which again weaves freedom, foundation and psyche together, and that is the speculations concerning human prehistory that Schelling pursued in an exchange of letters with his former student, G. H. Schubert. This association

[20] Ibid., 138.

with Schubert, who might be described variously as a nature philosopher, educationalist and theorist of the psyche, brings to the fore certain aspects of Schelling's *Ages of the World* which might otherwise pass unnoticed. As Horst Fuhrmans noted, 'whoever tries to understand Schelling's turn of 1808–9 won't be able to pass Schubert by'.[21]

The land that time forgot

Gotthilf Heinrich von Schubert is one of those figures who, in the backlash against the mystical and speculative elements of the *Naturphilosophie* in the second half of the nineteenth century, has almost entirely faded from view. His 1814 work on *The Symbolism of Dreams* was cited by Freud in the *Interpretation of Dreams* as representative of an intellectual period 'now behind us', in which 'philosophy and not the exact sciences' dominated the mind,[22] though Ellenberger singled out this work along with Schubert's 1830 *History of the Soul* for their striking anticipations of modern psychodynamic ideas.[23] Like Schelling the son of a priest, Schubert switched from being a student of theology to medicine, coming to Jena in 1801 and completing his medical degree there in 1803. This brought him into contact with Schelling who, now at the height of his powers, was lecturing on his systems of idealism and on the philosophy of nature and art. Schubert's autobiography describes how students from many different countries and disciplines (including medicine, theology and law) flocked to hear Schelling on the *Naturphilosophie*: 'The powerful content that lay in his speech seemed like a bound Prometheus, and the task of the inquiring mind was to loose its bonds and to take the unquenched fire out of his hand.'[24] Later in the same work he commented that Schelling 'became more to me than a teacher; he became a fatherly friend, a saviour in time of need, a founder of my earthly happiness.'[25]

After qualifying and working for some time as a doctor, Schubert moved to Dresden in 1806 where he completed the two parts of his work *Intimations of a General History of Life*,[26] before Schelling found him a position as Rector of the School of Sciences in Nurnberg, where Hegel was Rector of the Humanities. Schubert's *Intimations* had a

---

[21] Fuhrmans in Schelling, *Briefe und Dokumente*, vol. III, 599.
[22] Freud, *The Interpretation of Dreams*, 54.
[23] Ellenberger, *Discovery of the Unconscious*, 205–6.
[24] Gotthilf Schubert, *Der Erwerb aus einem vergangenes und die Erwartungen von einem zukünftigen Leben: eine Selbstbiographie*, vol. I (Erlangen: J. J. Palm and Ernst Enke, 1854), 388.
[25] Ibid., 392.
[26] Gotthilf Schubert, *Ahndungen einer allgemeinen Geschichte des Lebens*, 2 vols. (Leipzig: Reclam, 1806–1821).

substantial impact on the Romantic science of nature in Germany as well as on Schelling himself.[27] Even more important for their exchanges in this period was Schubert's next work, *Views of the Nightside of Natural Science*, which developed out of a series of informal public lectures in Dresden and was published there in 1808.[28] This volume, whose topics included animal magnetism and dreams (the 'nightside' of the title indicating both obscure processes and a certain gothic fascination with the supernatural) became something of a Romantic bestseller, influencing E. T. A. Hoffmann, amongst others, to become interested in contemporary accounts of psychopathology. As with the *Ages of the World*, one of Schubert's key concerns in this work was the significance of the past as a lost or suppressed epoch. In fact, if one examines their correspondence between 1807 and 1809, it becomes clear that Schelling's turn to the 'ages' of the world was not just an eccentric departure from philosophical idealism, but equally a relocation of his work in relation to trends that were developing within Romantic anthropology. In a letter of April 1808, Schubert described how the themes of his lectures on the nightside of nature and the history of man had developed: 'I began with the dark primal history of man', moving on to 'oracles, human sacrifice and other remains of the old paganism in the new, and finally the intimation of a whole epoch [*Weltalter*], before the true appearance of Christianity'.[29] At this time Schubert was beginning to propound an ingenious theory regarding the significance of the ancient mystery religions. Whereas emerging nineteenth-century scholarship saw in these religions the corrupt traces of primitive rituals associated with the yearly agricultural cycle, for Schubert the relationship was precisely the opposite: the mysteries contained a garbled memory of a transition from a lost 'primal epoch'. This epoch had reached its apex and then passed dialectically into a new, higher phase of culture, and it was the drama of this prehistorical revolution which the mysteries dimly recollected, and which had then wrongly been associated by later times with a representation of the death and rebirth of crops.[30]

In a letter in November 1808, Schubert conveyed further ideas which he was in the process of formulating as a sequel to *Intimations*. Whereas *Intimations* had been mainly concerned with the description of epochs of organic life, this new volume would deal with investigations concerning the age of the world, bringing the history of the

---

[27] Schelling, *Briefe und Dokumente*, vol. III, 159.
[28] Gotthilf Schubert, *Ansichten von der Nachtseite der Naturwissenschaft* [*Views of the Nightside of Natural Science*] (Darmstadt: Wissenschaftliche Buchgesellschaft, 1967).
[29] Letter to Schelling, April 1808, Schelling, *Briefe und Dokumente*, vol. III, 493.
[30] Schubert, *Views of the Nightside*, 83.

world into relation with the sagas of ancient peoples and with Biblical chronology.[31] Soon after, in January 1809, Schubert wrote excitedly to Schelling about a novel he wanted to write: 'The whole first half of this work dwells in the dark, wondersome element of the dim and distant past', and concerns the embryonic stirring of another world. The same letter related the topic of the novel to Schubert's new theories about a lost primordial science concerning which he added: 'the whole is buried [*verborgen*]'.[32] Schelling replied asking for Schubert's comments on his *Human Freedom* essay, published later in 1809, and whether 'what I say of the period of the Golden Age and concerning the appearance of Christianity chimes with your Dresden lectures'.[33] Later in 1815, in a public lecture to the Bavarian Academy of Sciences on the 'Deities of Samothrace', Schelling distinctly echoed Schubert's previous speculations, asking: 'What if already in Greek mythology ... there emerged the remains of a knowledge, indeed even a scientific system, which goes far beyond the circle drawn by the oldest revelation known through scriptural evidences.' A footnote to the published version adds that such a 'primordial system might represent the common source of all religious doctrines and representations'.[34]

A number of things strike one concerning this primordial past with its lost science intuited by both Schelling and Schubert. First of all, how easily this combination of fascination with, but secrecy over, a lost primordial epoch fits the ontological structure which formed Schelling's recurrent theoretical object in the *Ages of the World*: that of consciousness set against unconsciousness, apparent subjectivity against a veiled and absolute ground. The past contains a sublime organic truth of which we have always already been unconscious, and the threshold that separates the historical present from the past mirrors a similar threshold between the conscious and the unconscious within the self.

There are further factors, however, which link the psyche more concretely to this historically buried past. One is that this forgotten legacy was thought by Schubert to concern 'the wonderful and inexplicable harmony between our own nature and the whole external world'.[35] That is, the past is a repository for precisely that relation of self to freedom which philosophy could not rationally construct in the present. In addition, Schubert speculated that the way in which knowledge of this harmony had been conveyed in ancient times was itself a demonstration of

---

[31] Letter to Schelling, November 1808, *Briefe und Dokumente*, vol. III, 553.
[32] Ibid., 584.
[33] Letter to Schubert, 28 April 1809. Ibid., 599.
[34] Schelling, *Sämmtliche Werke*, vol. VIII, 362, fn. 90.
[35] Letter to Schelling, mid December 1807, *Briefe und Dokumente*, vol. III, 477.

the 'true' relation between the soul and knowledge. Egyptian priests retained only the fragments of an old natural wisdom, but this wisdom was not intended to be 'conveyed as a science – not taught or learned'.[36] Instead, 'the old revelations of nature had to reach the understanding through the soul of the student itself, as enthusiasm (*Begeisterung*)'.[37] The ultimate content of the mysteries was conveyed to the faculty of imagination (*Phantasie*) and the inner sense 'was inflamed more through a general impression of the whole' – the contrast being with rational analysis and piecemeal exposition.[38] There is an interesting echo here of Fichte's attempt to liberate the freedom of thought and invoke a form of transcendental self-apprehension in the I. At the opening of Chapter 1, we saw how Fichte and the young Schelling pitted idealist philosophy against the dead or enslaving systems of philosophical 'dogmatism'. Here the attempt to liberate the self from the 'dead body of a science' assumes access to an augmented mode of knowing, a special dilation of the self which takes place in the proto-Dionysian 'enthusiasm and divine drunkenness of the spirit [*Gemuth*]'.[39] It is interesting to note that similar terms recur in Schubert's autobiographical recollections of Schelling's charismatic ability to convey the Fichtean concept of intellectual intuition – 'through which our spirit grasps the infinite primordial ground [*Urgrund*] of all being and becoming' – in his turn of the century lectures in Jena.[40] Only a few years on from the bewilderment and confusion described by Henrik Steffens, an attendee of Fichte's own lectures on 'self-intuition', the same idea has been spiritualised and Romanticised. Both the message and the style of delivery now concern forms of revelation which transcend analytical comprehension.

Theories about prehistory and about the nature of the psyche are here mutually supporting each other in order to subvert the notion of reason and consciousness as arbiters of human truth claims. The relationship between the two kinds of 'unconscious' are not merely analogical (the psyche has an unconscious, just as history has an unconscious). Rather, the mysterious portion of each term grounds the alternative foundational claims of the other. On the one hand, history suggests the existence of a lost and unconscious past, within which Schelling and Schubert posit a forgotten science, one in which knowledge and truth were harmonised through the psyche, rather than by reason. On the other hand, by turning to the psyche they resist identifying the sources of the self with the I, or with intellectual knowledge or social relationships. Delving into

---

[36] Schubert, *Views of the Nightside*, 84.
[37] Ibid., 85.   [38] Ibid., 85.
[39] Ibid., 85.   [40] Schubert, *Der Erwerb*, vol. I, 391–2.

the psyche allows them to intimate a different kind of origin for the self, and this sets them on the trail of a buried and more absolute past underlying the present. With respect to the psychic pole in this relationship, Schubert told Schelling in a letter of December 1807 that he had taken twenty works on oracles out of the Dresden library and was exploring 'animal magnetism, the world of dreams and intimations', as well as the gift of prophecy, both in recent times and in paganism.[41] 'Intimations' was of course already the title of Schubert's work on the origins of nature; of its sequel, concerning the transition from the primordial to the realm of human history, Schubert commented that 'the whole [is] to be prophetic'.[42] The overlap between some of these ideas and developments in contemporary Romantic psychology (which again look forward to the work of Jung) will be explored in the following chapter. For the moment we can observe that many of these suggestions found an echo in Schelling's reformulations of scientific understanding as 'history'. While Schubert argued that 'what with us is science, in those oldest times was more the revelation of a higher spirit',[43] Schelling in *Human Freedom*, written the following year, evoked the age of the sovereign gods and heroes in which 'wisdom came to men only from the depths, the power of oracles issuing from the earth guided and formed their lives'.[44]

These obscure processes linking the soul internally with the past also supplied Schelling with an assault on the Hegelian notion of dialectic as 'external' mediation. We have already touched on Schelling's idea that man is granted an innermost essence which 'faithfully protects the treasures of the wholly past'.[45] At the opening of the *Ages of the World*, Schelling further characterises this essence as mute by nature: it must be awakened by another, younger being – the conscious self – which turns 'to that inner oracle, the only witness from a time before the world'.[46] The two essences, the one emerging from its secret slumber, the other ignorant but seeking the truth, are yoked together in a 'doubling of ourselves'.[47] In the Hegelian dialectic, the attempts of the individual to understand the universal as a scheme, property or feeling within itself, are constantly subverted by the demonstration that any internalised universal is already the product of an activity in relation to an external world. In wanting to abstract itself from the whole in

[41] *Briefe und Dokumente*, vol. III, 477.
[42] Letter to Schelling, November 1808. Ibid., 554.
[43] Schubert, *Views of the Nightside*, 50.
[44] Schelling, *Human Freedom*, 56.
[45] Schelling, *Ages*, 114.
[46] Ibid., 114.   [47] Ibid., 115.

order to comprehend it, the self is always thrust on towards a renewed recognition of its suppressed social relatedness. For Schelling, however, dialectic signifies a purely internal and 'silent dialogue': 'this inner art of conversation, is the authentic secret of the philosopher from which the outer art (which for this reason is called "dialectic") is only a replica and, if it has become bare form [that is, dead science], is only empty appearance and shadow.'[48]

The relations evoked may still be between the self and something far grander, more absolute, which lies beyond it – a 'witness from a time before the world' – yet knowledge originates at the same time 'from inside by a thoroughly peculiar process'.[49] The agency in this relationship comes through the self's obscure recollection of origins, through its own peculiar qualities. The reference here is partly to Platonic anamnesis, in accord with Schelling's increased interest in Platonic archetypes. However, the whole notion of transcendent archetypes has creatively collided with Schelling's attempt to find ways of narrating the autonomous logic of the individual. The search for knowledge now throws its emphasis not on to the demonstration of an eternal truth or the existence of universals, but on to the incomplete, enigmatic and self-constitutive process of the search itself. The ontologically 'primordial' and 'antecedent' are passive and latent, and this allows the individual seeking its own origin to be supposed as the active agent in its own self-understanding. That which will come to authorise each person's identity is assumed to be already lodged within the self, as its hidden soul or essence, its witness from a time before the world, or its link to creation's *centrum*. The self is not a creation of its societal context, but of the submerged ground which conditions all subjects and does so in a way that sustains the particularity of each.

The abyss of origins

The second area into which Schelling extends his thinking on the unconscious is not strictly speaking historical, though it is concerned with origins, pastness and the primordial 'non-being' of the absolute. It relates to his increasing interest in a tradition of German religious mysticism which was being unearthed and re-read by his Romantic associates. This is the tradition of negative theology stemming from the doctrine of Meister Eckhart in the early fourteenth century, particularly Eckhart's

---

[48] Ibid., 115.   [49] Ibid., 115.

understanding of the relation between an absolute but unknown ground of existence and the 'true self', with unconsciousness as a form of mediation between the two. From the fourteenth to the seventeenth centuries, Eckhart's ideas were gradually constellated into a set of motifs that remained central for a certain apprehension of 'soul' in later German thought. I include this tradition here both because Schelling found within it a corroboration of his own theory of unconsciousness, and because out of this ontology of the divine there emerges yet another approach to the psyche and the condition of its self-experience which centres on its suppressed and absolute past.

What amounts to a republic of mystical letters operated through the Munich circle, and via Schubert, who, based not too far away in Nurnberg, had access to the thriving antiquarian book trade there. In 1809 Schelling wrote to Schubert asking him to look out for the 1715 Quarto edition of Jakob Böhme's works, explaining that he had given his own copy to Franz von Baader.[50] At the beginning of 1811, within the timescale of the first draft of the *Ages of the World*, Schelling enquired whether Schubert had managed to get hold of the *Cherubinic Wanderer* by the baroque mystic Angelus Silesius (Johannes Scheffler). The book was intended for Baader, who had a borrowed copy belonging to the influential theologian Johann Michael Sailer. Schelling described the book as one of his own favourites.[51] Later in the same month he asked Schubert for works by Johannes Tauler, this time for himself, asserting that 'these writings are almost as important for the study of our language, as for mysticism'.[52] Out of this circle of nature philosophers, who were collectively becoming interested in these alternative and anti-rationalist traditions of thought, it was Baader who was most instrumental in the recovery of the German mystical tradition for the nineteenth century. It was he who brought Meister Eckhart to Hegel's notice in 1823, and who then spent the 1830s working on his own editions of Eckhart and Böhme. These figures, particularly Tauler (1300–61), Böhme (1575–1624) and Scheffler (1624–77), form something of a tradition of mystical inwardness in German thought. They drew on Eckhart's late thirteenth-century teachings which directed the self's attention to the 'innermost core, the deepest ground of the

---

[50] Schelling, *Briefe und Dokumente*, vol. III, 611. This copy itself had previously been a present from another correspondent and *Naturphilosoph*, Carl Windischmann, in 1804; Schelling had already acquired the earlier 1682 edition of the works of Böhme in Jena.

[51] Schelling to Schubert, 4 April 1811. Plitt, *Aus Schellings Leben*, vol. II, 252.

[52] Schelling to Schubert, 25 April 1811. Plitt, *Aus Schellings Leben*, vol. II, 252–3.

soul',[53] in a far more radical manner than the Lutheranism that succeeded it, at the same time as attempting to centre religious life not in the institution but in the individual.[54] Eckhart and Tauler were part of the newly founded Dominican order and their emphasis on psychic life was Augustinian, but they belonged to that apophatic strand of the tradition which stressed the negative aspects of divine contemplation – the unsayable and the unknowable.

It was in his ministry to the Beguines – the antinomian and enthusiastic movement amongst lay women in Western Europe in the fourteenth century – that Eckhart developed his peculiar use of vernacular German, along with a set of terms clustered around the notions of wilderness and abyss. As with the abyss of unconsciousness which closes the *Ages of the World*, 'wilderness' and 'abyss' in this tradition are multifaceted principles. They allude to the primordial nature of God and to the self's original condition, as well as to 'the locus of the soul's encounter with God', and 'the self's detachment from contingent reality'.[55] According to Eckhart the soul has a 'ground' (*Grunt*) in which the 'union of the person with god is consummated',[56] but as in Schelling's work, this ground is itself impenetrably obscure. For Eckhart, all three persons of the Trinity flow out of this deeper ground which he terms the Godhead and describes through 'the correlative terms of abyss, nothingness and darkness'.[57]

The negative ground, experienced by the soul as a loss of identity, was a symbol of the divine (whose foundational depths and origins lay beyond the descriptions of reason). But it was also the sign of the self's spiritual autonomy from both physical and social determination. Thus, as in Schelling, one of the features of this supervening power of 'obscurity' was the degree to which it allowed for the figurative suspension and even imaginative reversal of the concepts of determinacy and dependence. This loss of self turns remarkably into a gain, and wilderness provides a form of locatedness. These are not merely paradoxical expressions. Rather, by undermining the notions of objectivity and determination, Eckhart was able to figure an aporetic or original

---

[53] Sermon 44, 'Feast of the Nativity of John the Baptist II', in Johannes Tauler, *Sermons*, trans. Maria Shrady (New York: Paulist Press, 1985), 146.

[54] R. W. Southern, *Western Society and the Church in the Middle Ages* (Harmondsworth: Penguin, 1979), 302.

[55] Paul A. Dietrich, 'The Wilderness of God in Hadewijch II and Meister Eckhart and His Circle', in Bernard McGinn (ed.), *Meister Eckhart and the Beguine Mystics* (New York: Continuum, 1994), 40.

[56] August Langen, *Der Wortschatz des Deutschen Pietismus* (Tübingen: Max Niemeyer, 1968), 161.

[57] Dietrich, 'The Wilderness of God', 32.

cause within the self. For Eckhart, as for Schelling, the abyss of origins functioned as a way of resisting ideological reflection of the system of hierarchical dependency organised within feudalism: 'While I yet stood in my first cause, I had no God and was my own cause.'[58] Likewise, it is through its own peculiar 'spark' of reason that the soul accomplishes a unification with the absolute in which 'God's ground is my ground, and my ground is God's ground'.[59]

This exploration of the 'groundless ground', which implicates identity in the form of non-identity, was extended in the work of Johannes Tauler, a disciple of Eckhart's in the early fourteenth century. Detachment, abandonment and union constantly resurface as themes in Tauler's sermons.[60] In Sermon 44, for instance, he described how 'the abyss of the soul belongs to the divine abyss' in a way that accords with both Schubert's and Schelling's notion of the internal, primordial oracle: 'As it is said: "Deep calls on Deep". And if we are carefully attentive, this ground sheds light upon our faculties, drawing and leading the higher and lower ones back to their source and their origin.'[61] The 'origin' of the soul is traced not back through a line of determination, but runs enigmatically into the interior of the person, where the axes of identity, selfhood and absolute meet. This figure of the abyss as the origin of the soul resurfaced in the work of the sixteenth-century religious poet Angelus Silesius (Johannes Scheffler), the third in that triad of mystical writers which so galvanised Schelling's interest at the time of his move to Munich. His work the *Cherubinic Wanderer* presents a succession of enigmatic couplets on selfhood and the negative, one of which Schelling introduced into the 1815 draft of the *Ages of the World* precisely as an expression of the inverted ontological relation between being and nothingness: 'The gentle Godhead is nothing and beyond nothing.'[62] Schelling observes that most people aspire to be a subject because they have never felt the freedom of the negative, whereas the highest itself, the Godhead, resists objectification: it is nothing (no-thing) 'in the way that pure freedom is nothing'.[63]

---

[58] Cited in Richard Woods, 'Women and Men in the Development of Late Medieval Mysticism', in McGinn (ed.), *Meister Eckhart*, 157.

[59] John D. Caputo, *The Mystical Elements in Heidegger's Thought* (New York: Fordham University Press, 1986), 110.

[60] See Stephen Fanning, *Mystics of the Christian Tradition* (London: Routledge, 2001), 105.

[61] Tauler, *Sermons*, 148.

[62] Schelling, *The Ages of the World* [1815], 24.

[63] Ibid., 24.

It was this triple function of the abyss and the unconscious – as a figure of the self's inalienable detachment from the world of objects; the inversion of the absolute as a source of total determination; and a source for the foundation of freedom – which made the German mystical tradition particularly useful for Schelling's attempts to both ground the self *and* release it from the conceptual closure of the system. One readily sees how the terms of this triadic relation could be mapped over the principle of unconsciousness defined at the end of the *Ages of the World*. Even when Schelling's interest in the unconscious appears to lead him towards the most mystical and anachronistic terrain, his focus is invariably on some solution to the theoretical description of individuality and autonomy. Here, as elsewhere, Schelling's tendencies can reveal an unexpectedly 'modern' orientation. Max Weber found that Tauler and the mystics, with their absorption of the divine by the soul, paradoxically upheld 'the psychological foundations for a rational ethics' which Luther then undermined.[64] Heidegger, too, observes of Schelling's notion of the 'eternal past' that remains in God as his ground, that this 'is only the continuation of an attitude of thinking which begins with Meister Eckhart and is uniquely developed in Jakob Böhme'.[65] But for Heidegger it is precisely here that 'the whole boldness of Schelling's thinking comes into play'. These are not the 'vacuous play thoughts of a manic hermit'; Schelling 'is no "mystic"'; rather he is attempting to 'bring this being, the ground in God, "humanly closer to us"'.[66] Lezsek Kolakowski likewise cites Silesius as a source for the transmission of 'The dialectic of God's self-limitation and the idea of the non-self-identity of man's Being' into nineteenth-century German thought, and again identifies this reversal in the absolute with a corresponding valorisation of the self: 'Only in me can God find his double; only in me does God become something.'[67]

There is a second point to be made here which concerns not just the self, but the valorisation of the *psychic*. This is the profound inversion whereby the foundational justifications of selfhood in this tradition shift their terms from those of logic and intellect (so important to medieval scholastic traditions) to metaphors drawn from the language of psychical and emotional states themselves. Not only does the notion of a determining absolute give way to the idea of the soul as, in some sense, self-caused, but the affects, uncertainties and intimations

---

[64] Max Weber, *The Protestant Ethic and the Spirit of Capitalism* (London: Unwin University Books, 1930), 86.
[65] Heidegger, *Schelling's Treatise*, 117.   [66] Ibid., 117.
[67] Lezsek Kolakowski, *Main Currents of Marxism*, 3 vols. (Oxford University Press, 1978), vol. I, 37.

of the person start to represent absolute processes and relations. With Eckhart, argues Paul Dietrich, the ground and darkness that are initially an apophatic statement about the divine nature are 'interwoven with anthropological claims about the nature of the soul'.[68] One dimension of this development of psychological language can be traced back to the cross-fertilisation between religious mysticism and courtly love lyric in the thirteenth century in which 'the soul's relation to God was that of the noble lady in the Minne-ideology'.[69] The language of love and rapture, along with that of wilderness, spread through the writings of the Beguine movement and so into the terms of Eckhart's vocabulary as a distant extension of that courtly literature. We have seen how longing entered into Schelling's metaphysical descriptions in the *Ages of the World* via the influence of Böhme – for instance, the 'arousal' of the divine in matter, and eternity's 'longing to come to itself, to find and savour itself'.[70] In a psychoanalytic context, Jacques Lacan reanimated this same conjunction of courtly love and negative theology in developing his own late concepts of psychic identity and non-identity. In Seminar XX,[71] Lacan developed his concept of *jouissance* – a category which resists universal identification – with reference to both Angelus Silesius and the Beguine Hadewijch d'Anvers.[72] Likewise Jung was drawn towards an investigation of the work of Meister Eckhart, and in particular the way in which he was able to 'rise to a purely psychological and relativistic conception of God'.[73]

In a similar fashion, Schelling was led, via the psychological and emotional emphases of negative theology, to identify his own theory, not just with the ontology of non-being, but also with the terms of *psychic* unconsciousness. Already in the mystical tradition one finds this conflation of metaphysical and psychical states, of different conditions of *Unbewußtsein* (both 'unknowing' and 'unconsciousness'). Both are twinned in Eckhart's suggestion that, 'This then is God's desire – that God should reduce himself to nothing in the soul so that the soul may lose herself.'[74] Schelling makes similar links between the terms of theology, ontology and psychology in his 1827 lectures on the '*System of*

---

[68] Dietrich, 'The Wilderness of God', 37.

[69] Friedrich Heer, *The Intellectual History of Europe* (London: Weidenfeld & Nicolson, 1966), vol. I, 172–9.

[70] Schelling, *Ages*, 136.

[71] Jacques Lacan, 'God and the *Jouissance* of T̶h̶e̶ Woman' from 'Seminar XX', *Encore*, trans. in Juliet Mitchell and Jacqueline Rose (eds.), *Feminine Sexuality, Jacques Lacan and the École Freudienne* (Basingstoke and London: Macmillan, 1982), 139.

[72] Ibid., 147.

[73] C. G. Jung, *Psychological Types, Collected Works*, vol. VI (Princeton, NJ: Princeton University Press, 1971), 242.

[74] Fanning, *Mystics of the Christian Tradition*, 103.

the Ages of the World'. In lecture 24, for instance, he reformulates the distinction between the transcendental existence of an absolute *in principle*, and its reduced or inverted existence in actuality, in Eckhartian terms. God is present, but not present to himself, and this is described as a condition of *Ohnmächtigkeit*, which translates literally as powerlessness but means a state of unconsciousness: 'That unconsciousness of himself is essential to him [*ist ihm wesentlich*]; this belongs to the original concept of God.'[75] In the following lecture he talks of this 'selfless' condition of God as also the 'magic of God' and relates this notion specifically to the work of Tauler.[76]

The important point here is that '*Ohnmächtigkeit*' properly connotes unconsciousness not as a lack of knowledge, but as a specifically psychical state – a fit, or loss of consciousness associated, for instance, with a faint. It is another word that, like desire, touches on the formulae of medieval courtly literature – its states of swooning and ravishing – but is now transcribed into a mystical discourse of the relation between the soul and God. Schelling's use of this language, as we shall see in the next chapter, also points to his interest in psychiatric phenomena. Indeed, Schelling's 1827 lecture series encourages precisely these kinds of connections between ontology, theology and psychiatry. In a lecture the week previous to that mentioning Tauler, Schelling expressed his interest in animal magnetism and the fashionable theories of the mesmerists. Just as the principle of an unconscious absolute shifts the burden of foundation towards the self, towards self-foundation, so the language of unconsciousness allows for subtle interplay between an ontological and a psychical condition. Unconsciousness (ontologically) helps to beget the idea of the autonomous or self-originating individual, and the individual thus generated develops its own sense of psychic self-apprehension around the idea of *its* unconscious basis (ontological *and* psychological). This unconscious is carried in turn into the emerging constructions of Romantic psychology.

Uncanny foundations

An antecedent and a horror ...[77]

The third organisation of unconsciousness to be explored is explicitly historical, but in a far more technical and developed sense than Schelling's earlier forays into the romance of prehistory. It emerges

[75] Schelling, *System der Weltalter*, 106.
[76] Ibid., 109.
[77] H. P. Lovecraft, 'The Case of Charles Dexter Ward', in *At the Mountains of Madness* (London: HarperCollins, 1999), 156.

most clearly in Schelling's later 'positive' philosophy of revelation and his lectures on the history of mythology. The idea of an unconscious here is also somewhat more threatening and gloomy than that science of a lost oracular knowledge with which he was engaged in the first two decades of the nineteenth century. The triple face of the unconscious at the end of the *Ages of the World* – as an excess of the absolute over reason; as a crisis of transition; and as a bar on remembrance which would otherwise destroy the horizon of individual identity – centralised the role of obscurity and forgetting in Schelling's ontology. Consequently, its removal was associated with a certain threatened destruction of the self's identity. One way in which this threat was expressed was through the notion of concealed foundations – a veiled omnipotence – which sometimes permeates the present with intimations of a submerged horror. In the 1811 draft of the *Ages of the World* humanity learns that its 'peaceful dwelling place is built on the hearth of a primeval fire'. This past remains 'hidden [*verborgen*] in the ground' but 'the same principle carries and holds us in its ineffectiveness which would consume and destroy us in its effectiveness'.[78] Linked with this passage is a mystical lyrical fragment titled 'The Springtime' which is undated but generally associated with this same period of early work on the *Ages of the World*, particularly following the death of Caroline. Here Schelling speculated that one day 'even this solid construction of the world' will be transfigured into spirit. Then everything which has been imported into the 'true inner, purely through the power of external repression [*Zurückdrängung*]', will be consumed by 'the divine fire, which now rests locked within her'.[79]

This withdrawn presence, which holds the present in tension with its unconscious past and necessitates a certain active forgetting on the part of the subject, still expresses at long range the basic idea of the *Naturphilosophie*: that all formal presence exists not in a state of inertia but is the product of opposing forces of contraction and expansion. There would be no physical reality if the absolute had not first of all contracted its power – its divine fire – to allow for the milder dynamic presence of nature. Thirty years later, however, in a greatly transfigured form, one finds this same intimation of a primal and powerful but repressed ground entering into Schelling's more concrete science of the stages of primal history and human development. This is the period of his lectures in Berlin attended by Kierkegaard, Burkhardt and Engels and given in a climate of reaction and political repression – the

---

[78] Schelling, *Die Weltalter, Urfassungen*, 13.
[79] Ibid., 275.

uneasy ferment leading up to the revolutions of 1848. The language of repression [*Zurückdrängung*] and pent-up danger filters through into troubled political descriptions in Schelling's notebooks of the 1840s. An anguished private note of 1848 observes: 'In the evening, the worst news from all sides!! What, since decades, has been held under precariously enough, is suddenly breaking out everywhere. Today insurrectionary pamphlets were found in Berlin.'[80]

What I want to trace here, however, is the link between ideas of historical repression and repression in the psyche. In these later lectures the obscure negations which Schelling had found it necessary to perform upon the concept of the absolute in the *Ages of the World* were historicised in a more literal fashion. Whereas the earlier texts had concerned themselves more abstractly with the possibility of introducing crisis, pastness and unconsciousness into the metaphysical absolute, the later philosophy assumes these ontological dimensions to have occurred as events in prehistory. The unconscious is part of the actual structure of history – formed by processes of primal division and repression within culture – and the task is to track the imprints of such crises in the earliest records of human life. That primordial rift in which the absolute sank into unconsciousness was not just a principle of ontology, but a real occurrence whose trace Schelling discerned in Greek mythology, much as Schubert had intimated the traces of a primal lost epoch in the classical mystery cults. For Schelling, the Homeric epics were the residue of a still ineffable crisis, pre-dating historical narrative itself, which produced a diremption between the world of Olympus and the dark abyss of Hades.[81] Hades is not only the negative portion of this early separation of powers within existence, which leaves its imprint on mythology; it also represents a historical rift in the ontology of the human subject, and the opening up of a dialectic between that which is present, and that which is withdrawn from presence. That is to say, the split in the mythological cosmos (the earliest tool of human self-representation) is yet another transposition of that loss of identity in the absolute which allows the objective world to emerge. However, Schelling approaches these opposed qualities of the absolute not as mere constructs of the philosopher, but as historically transmitted features of human narrative.

[80] F. W. J. Schelling, *Das Tagebuch 1848*, ed. Hans Jörg Sandkühler (Hamburg: Felix Meiner, 1990), 48.
[81] F. W. J. Schelling, *Philosophie der Mythologie* [1842], in *Sämmtliche Schriften*, Abt. 2, vol. II, 648.

Schelling's metaphysics of the past, then, fed into a current of nine-teenth-century philology concerned with the history of the formation of mythic consciousness. But from the point of view of Schelling's developing interest in the psyche, what is interesting is first of all the nature of what is repressed into the past, and, secondly, the way in which this past is clandestinely retained *within the self*. What was over-come, in Schelling's account of primal development in myth, were the more timeless and self-negating world views which preceded historical consciousness, and which Schelling associated with oriental religion. These religions were identified with more archaic layers of culture, and particularly with a primitive experience of chaos and destruction. In 1815 Schelling had begun to try to connect his metaphysical description of the past with speculative philological research around the ancient deities of Samothrace. But even earlier than this, in the abandoned first draft of the *Ages of the World*, he found a corollary of a primal principle of unconsciousness in classical reports of the drunken riot of the Dionysiac cult, as well as in the dances associated with the near-Eastern goddess Cybele. Just as Schelling represented the past of matter as a primal chaos and craving, so here the past of humanity contains a wild tumult, riven by centripetal and centrifugal forces, symbolised in that 'terrifying display of primitive ritual custom, to wit, insensate, frenzied dancing, which accompanied the terrifying procession of the mother of all things'.[82] In the later 'Philosophy of Mythology' lectures, Schelling described this older mythological layer as presenting 'a graver, more serious' version of madness, but in Homeric times the destructive centripetal force gets 'covered up by polytheism and hidden within it'.[83] In Homeric times this madness is considered by Schelling to be more muted and thus the experience of it in myth is 'lighter, even enticing.'[84]

Schelling's history of prehistory is partly concerned with the overcom-ing of a foundational madness (within which no identities can emerge) by forms of culture that thrust the destructive aspects of experience deep inside, binding them somehow in the unconscious, and allowing more formal experience of selfhood to emerge. At the same time, he argues that religious cults are displaced by more objectifiable forms of religious experience, by plastic and dramatic art. Here he in effect anticipates the duality which Nietzsche will explore in *The Birth of Tragedy* between Dionysian chaos and the gentler Apollonian principle

---

[82] Schelling, *Die Weltalter, Urfassungen*, 42–3. Compare Novalis, *The Novices of Sais*, 41, on how the effort to fathom the mechanism of nature, which is 'a terrible mill of death', is in itself 'a move towards the abyss, a beginning of madness'.
[83] Schelling, *Philosophie der Mythologie*, 648.
[84] Ibid., 645.

that allows for the stabilisation of plastic representation, eventually at
the expense of tragedy and natural vigour. Nietzsche, too, suggests an
original historical transition in which an epoch of Titanic struggle is
buried and obscured by the artificial majesty of Homer's Olympus.[85] As
Walter Kaufmann noted, Nietzsche's distinction between Apollonian
and Dionysian 'could already be found in Schelling's *Philosophie der
Offenbarung*', and he suggested Jacob Burkhardt, who had been present
at the original lectures, as a possible intellectual mediator.[86] Ellenberger
traces a separate line of influence from philology and the science of myth
running up to Nietzsche and Freud through the Swiss anthropologist
of primitive culture, Johannes Bachofen.[87] Citing Adrien Turel's work
Bachofen-Freud, he suggests that it was Bachofen who, in his theory of
the forgotten stages of history preceding patriarchal culture, had originally formulated the idea of repression and reaction formation, as well
as a notion of 'a limit beyond which the memory of the individual or
of mankind cannot reach', which requires the further reaches of history to be reconstructed through the interpretation of myth. It seems
likely, however, that behind Bachofen's work lie these key lectures of
Schelling's from the 1840s which were already explicit about the epoch
of the mother goddess, the hatred directed at the repressed past, and
the imposing thresholds of unconsciousness which became foundational for the ensuing re-orderings of the Homeric cosmos.[88]

In terms of later developments in depth psychology, this same set of
assumptions will emerge most obviously in Jung's interest in the figure of Dionysus as an emblem of unconscious and archetypal forces,
which led him to engage with Bachofen's work and more extensively
with Nietzsche.[89] However, these same ideas also found their way into
Freudian psychoanalysis. For it is precisely in the lecture on Homer
from which I have been quoting that Schelling formulates the idea of
the *Unheimlich*, the 'uncanny', which was to engage Freud's attention at
the end of the First World War. Schelling argues that Homer achieved
the overthrow of the principle of the past 'and put it back within the
"inner", that is the secret, the mystery', and it was only after burying

[85] Nietzsche, *The Birth of Tragedy* in *The Birth of Tragedy and the Genealogy of Morals*, see
particularly sections III and IV.
[86] Walter Kaufmann, *Nietzsche; Philosopher, Psychologist, Antichrist* (New York: Vintage,
1968), 125.
[87] Ellenberger, *Discovery*, 222–3.
[88] Ellenberger cites Engels and Bakunin as two more figures who took up Bachofen's
ideas, but both of these, as already noted, had also attended Schelling's original lectures in the 1840s.
[89] See C. J. Jung, *Collected Works of C. G. Jung, Seminar Papers*, vol. II, 2 parts, *Nietzsche's
Zarathustra: Notes of the Seminar Given in 1934–9* (London: Routledge, 1994).

this principle of the older religion internally – 'the dark and darkening power of this uncanny [*unheimlichen*] principle' – that the Homeric era could cultivate its purely poetic history of the gods. Here Schelling added in brackets the further explanation: 'Uncanny [*unheimlich*] is what one calls everything that should have stayed secret, hidden, latent [*im Geheimniß, im Verborgenen, in der Latenz*] but has come to the fore.'[90]

This 'put it back within the "inner"' is a curious formulation, on the one hand redolent of the notion of the 'secret', or the 'inner chamber' of the mystery cults, and hence of Schelling and Schubert's suggestion of a primordial lost science of the soul. But on the other hand it suggests dialectical processes within the psyche itself – the internalisation within human subjects of the self-negating aspect of the older religions. The pre-Homeric horror is now buried within the past of the *psyche*, and so in some form continuously present within it, rather than merely left behind in the cultural-historical past. One of the implications is that the experience of madness and destruction is not entirely culturally superseded, but remains latent within human subjectivity – a primeval layer in the development of consciousness, and thus in some sense its underlying basis. It is also noticeable that Schelling's concept of the uncanny occupies that same transitional space as the bar on remembrance which we saw was central to the grounding of free existence in the *Ages of the World*. As such, 'unconsciousness' once more transforms the idea of foundation from an attribute of the absolute (in this case the ground of human history per se) into a psychical quality of the individual. The individual's self-apprehension involves a principle of necessary blindness in relation to its own ground. A return of the uncanny past would both represent the resurfacing of that older epoch of being, and threaten the dissolution of the grounds of individuality, hence the horror which attaches to it.

Freud found this very phrase of Schelling's, concerning the uncanny past suppressed in the Homeric epoch, while leafing through his copy of Sanders' *Wörterbuch der Deutschen Sprache*, which he used to pin down the meaning of 'unheimlich' for his essay on 'The "Uncanny"' published in 1919.[91] Freud, in fact, makes exactly the same point as Schelling, contrasting the uncanny with Homer's 'jovial world of Gods', which suggests that he may have looked up the source context of the quotation in Schelling's lectures.[92] Curiously, a second phrase quoted by Freud,

---

[90] Schelling, *Philosophie der Mythologie*, 649.
[91] Sigmund Freud, 'The "Uncanny"', *SE*, vol. XVII, 224.
[92] Ibid, 250.

this time concerning the connotations of *heimelig* meaning the familiar, comes from Schubert: 'The warm room and the *heimelig* afternoon.'[93] In *Views of the Nightside* Schubert suggested that the future, 'This highest and most spiritual possession of human beings, doesn't appear to be wholly at home [*einheimlich*].'[94] Freud was thus traversing ideas which had their provenance earlier in the century, but without recognising or investigating the psychological contexts of these earlier theories of the unconscious and historical repression. Even so, his own terms were slipping inadvertently into the traces of concepts developed by Schelling.

Further evidence of the transmission of this principle of repressed historical contents from Schelling's anthropological work to psychoanalysis emerges in *Totem and Taboo*. Here, citing Wilhelm Wundt's *Völker Psychologie*, Freud suggests that it is 'a general law of mythology that a stage which has been passed, for the very reason that it has been overcome and driven under by a superior stage, persists in an inferior form alongside the later one, so that the objects of its veneration turn into objects of horror'.[95]

This was exactly Schelling's position in his 'Philosophy of Mythology' of the 1840s – with this difference, that Schelling's uncanny ground, placed outside the structure of present consciousness, is not first and foremost an issue for individual *psychology*, but derives from his philosophical attempts to locate the historical inception of the ontological possibility of individual identity. At the same time Schelling's formal interest in the unconscious repeatedly slips beyond the bounds of an overtly philosophical ontology, into an emerging nineteenth-century science of human culture and development (via Schubert and Bachofen, for instance) where it starts to condition presuppositions for a later psychoanalytic science.

The fires of transfiguration

I have traced Schelling's elaboration of the philosophical structure of the unconscious through three separate regions in the Romantic human sciences. First of all, there was his attempt to surmise a lost science stemming from a buried epoch of history; secondly, the religious ontology of a divine abyss, newly recovered by work on German medieval spiritual traditions; thirdly, a theory of historical repression developed

---

[93] Ibid., 223.
[94] Schubert, *Views of the Nightside*, 320.
[95] Sigmund Freud, *Totem and Taboo: Some Points of Agreement between the Mental Lives of Savages and Neurotics*, SE (1913), vol. XIII, 25.

as part of his theory of myth. The fourth facet of the unconscious I want to trace involves yet another way of construing the self's aporetic foundation, this time implicating not the lost, the mystical or the uncanny, but much subtler gaps emerging in Romantic descriptions of natural and historical process. I have concentrated so far on the topological configuration whereby the unconscious is that portion of reality which is structurally excluded from presence – that which takes place in the abyss, or is repressed as the past. But for all its displacement, Schelling also hesitantly theorises an active role for the absolute, just as Freud and Jung later will for the unconscious. It is a hidden organism, but it still controls and determines 'each deed rich in consequence ... to the day, the hour', and as such it can be identified with obscure processes of development in existence itself, with thresholds and transitions in nature and history, from lower into higher states, and from latency to futurity.[96] In this active mode, the absolute is not completely withdrawn. Rather, it is the divine operating in mysteriously clandestine ways within the material and organic world – what Schelling sometimes refers to quasi-alchemically as 'the flash of light concealed in the hard stone'.[97]

This dynamic facet of the absolute runs back to some of the earliest ideas in the *Naturphilosophie*, but it is not those older systems of nature which concern us here so much as the way in which certain of their descriptive figures of latency, futurity and emergence were taken up as important metaphors within a wider Romantic science of life. In 1827, for instance, at the same time as Schelling was delivering his revised 'System of the Ages of the World' in Munich, Friedrich Schlegel gave a series of lectures on the 'Philosophy of Life' in Vienna, in which he suggested that 'in the natural world every object consists of living forces, and ... properly nothing is rigid and dead, but all replete with hidden [*verbognem*] life ... Beneath the vast tombstone of the visible world there slumbers a soul, not wholly alien, but more than half akin to our own.'[98]

Hiddenness is here a condition not just of the past, but of life in general, and it mediates the emergence of futurity in life. Thus Schelling, Schlegel, Schubert, Baader and others attach the unconscious to manifestations of identity which exceed objective presence but continually forge their way through it, mysteriously transfiguring and developing it. The unconscious grounds what is essentially an alternative Romantic

[96] Schelling, *Ages*, 123.
[97] Schelling, *Plastic Arts*, 12.
[98] Friedrich Schlegel, *The Philosophy of Life, and Philosophy of Language*, trans. Rev. A. J. W. Morrison (London: Bohn, 1847), 86.

account of objectivity – one which subverts the philosophy of mechanism with concepts of life, change and self-creation. The identities of things exceed objectification, not so much by recourse to Kantian arguments regarding 'things-in-themselves' which fall outside the categories of the understanding, but because of that which has still to emerge – because of the way temporality and 'higher development' are latent within nature. Thus Schelling suggested in the *Ages of the World* that, 'in even the most corporeal of things there lies a point of transfiguration'.[99] Likewise in the earlier *Human Freedom* essay he referred to man's will as the 'seed' of God, 'present as yet only in the depths'.[100] Schubert's *Views of the Nightside* also aimed to show 'the connection of a present existence with a higher one in the future, and how the embryo of the new and future life gradually unfolds in the middle of the present one'.[101] In a letter to Schelling of 1808 he explained how the 'deep lying kernel of the future system' can be felt in moments of passivity, just as 'the embryo first makes itself felt with hearty movements when the mother rests'.[102]

As with the past, this higher or future state indicates more than simply a further unfolding of historical events. Futurity is not conceived as a development of the world as it already exists. Rather, it indicates that transformation which will reveal the apotheosis of freedom and unity, and towards which nature, history and spirit equally tend. As a consequence, in the passages just quoted, nature, temporality and spiritual or psychic force are to some extent interchangeable terms. Each stands for a state of dynamic emergence which can be represented equally by the embryo, the kernel, the seed or the idea (in contrast to the stasis or determinability of the objects of reason) – and each indicates an alternative dimension of truth concealed within presence, where potential is waiting to be unfolded. Schlegel's slumbering 'alien' soul could equally be included in this series of metaphors. Schubert and Schelling characteristically take a metaphor from one paradigm of presence (whether nature, history, or psyche) and insert it in another, as the symbol of its *alien* future. This lends to the idea of development a sense of discontinuous or oppositional dimensions: something at variance with the present emerges from concealment and dynamically alters the conditions of existence. Thus *futurity* is a *seed* or kernel; *nature*'s depths are a slumbering *soul*; and the *spirit* is impregnated with the archetypes of the *future*. The identification of the soul with the historical and the

---

[99] Schelling, *Ages*, 151.   [100] Schelling, *Human Freedom*, 38.
[101] Schubert, *Views of the Nightside*, 3.
[102] Letter to Schelling, 29 April 1808, *Briefe und Dokumente*, vol. III, 495.

natural appears to ground the language of being in material conditions. But by switching between these terms Schelling and Schubert elaborate dimensions of selfhood that are paradoxically counterposed to presence and unavailable for objectification.[103]

There is a second way in which identity exceeds objectification. The transition between seemingly incompatible states introduces a certain violence into the continuity of process itself – whether this is a violence done to the concept of reason (and reason's attempts to conceptualise process), or the violence evoked by material metaphors of the overflowing, bursting, or lightning flash of presence. Thus unconscious history may indicate an obscure or buried foundation through which the self can imagine an alternative and superior synthesis of identity, but equally historicity (*Geschichtlichkeit*) indicates for Schelling a dynamic process of separation and individualisation in which unconsciousness is implicated as a kind of violence or disruption at the points of change or contact with other beings. The unconscious enables moments of flickering disconnection within a system of imagined universal connectivity.[104] In the terms of the *Ages of the World*, historicity is the point at which a self 'puts something behind it', creates a rift in its identity and establishes a past. In nature, too, the seed is that which promises futurity; but whatever brings a higher unity must also be radically different from the present. Hence the arrival of new identity cannot be expressed in an orderly sequence but entails a sudden violent and unconscious breakthrough.

Writing to Schelling in 1808 on transitions in both nature and history, Schubert hypothesised that 'everywhere death came out of the love and flowering of life, because precisely in this moment, the seed of the new, higher existence is generated' which 'destroys the old husk'.[105] In *Views of the Nightside*, Schubert generalises this relation between crisis, death and the emergence of higher states and extends it to moments of heightened perception or rapture: 'From the phenomenon of electricity,

---

[103] For a fuller discussion of the aporetic logic of these descriptions, and of some of the material in this section of the chapter, see ffytche, 'F. W. J. Schelling and G. H. Schubert: Psychology in Search of Psyches', *Romantic Psyche and Psychoanalysis* issue, *Romantic Circles Praxis Series* (December 2008), www.rc.umd.edu/praxis/psychoanalysis/ffytche/ffytche.html.

[104] Though the terms are different, the logic of the description is not unlike Friedrich Schlegel's development of notions of irony, incomprehensibility and the indefinite, in 'On Incomprehensibility' and *Lucinde* respectively. See Friedrich Schlegel, *Friedrich Schlegel's Lucinde and the Fragments*, trans. Peter Firchow (Minneapolis: University of Minnesota Press, 1971), 118–21, 259–71. The perpetual interaction of the definite and the indefinite ensures that every individual should be 'unique and new, a true image of supreme, indivisible individuality', ibid., 120.

[105] Letter to Schelling, 29 April 1808, *Briefe und Dokumente*, vol. III, 493.

and even deeper than this, right up to the organic union of the sexes, we see the burning element in nature appearing at the highest points of existence and interaction, aroused by the highest activity of life'.[106] This incandescent point of union causes 'a momentary annihilation of the organic life', and this is why for many organisms 'the moment of copulation falls together with death'.[107] Whatever absolute principle is guiding processes of development in the material world, it is doing so in such a way that entities are at the same time uniquely and violently isolated from each other. Nothing can simply be thought of as inserted into a kind of mechanical whole.

Finally, the psyche itself is both the dimension through which the self is attached to the unfathomable foundations of the unconscious, and a field of illumination through which (as later for Jung) the self intimates that which is higher and that which is emerging. This intimation of futurity is no longer made through the apprehension of a system, or the deduction of causal sequence, but by a sudden insight, the grasping of an archetype, or a flash of recognition whereby, as Schelling puts it in the *Ages of the World*, man 'sees himself transported into such wonderful relations and inner connections'.[108] This language of prophecy and illumination, as we will see in greater detail in the following chapter, is closely bound to observations of pathological phenomena in Romantic psychiatry. In the present context we can observe that Schelling relates this flash of insight to the 'combustible element of the soul', that same empirical principle which Schubert inferred was active at points of transformation and rapture in natural organisms. This hidden fire 'becomes free at the highest moments of experience' and 'breaks out of the depth of the inner essence, granting a view deep into the inner'.[109] The insight flashes out where objective presence is momentarily disturbed and indicates a release of that divine spirit which has been pent up within nature's materiality.

There is a strange conjunction here of Meister Eckhart's depiction of wisdom in the soul as a spark (*Funke*), Schelling's natural philosophical investigations into processes of combustion, and the Stoic theory of divine law inhering in the world as fire. In a late addition to the *Ideas* concerning a 'New View of the Combustion Process', Schelling gives an account of how the ancients worshipped the universal substance in the image of fire: 'In this they left us a hint that fire is nothing other

---

[106] Schubert, *Views of the Nightside*, 358.
[107] Ibid., 358–9.   [108] Schelling, *Ages*, 114.
[109] Schelling, *Briefe und Dokumente*, vol. III, 495.

than the pure substance breaking through in corporeality, or a third dimension.'[110] Schelling's *Ideas* was probably the source for Schubert's investigation of a flammable material pent up in the body. This excessive fire also recalls Schelling's theory of the primeval hearth underlying man's peaceful dwelling place, which may one day tear through the world, restoring it to the purity of its spiritual essence.

A number of observations can be made about the way in which Schelling and Schubert in the early 1800s characterise objects and organic bodies as subject to crisis, or intimate missing dimensions of existence within them. One is that, with the divine fire, the flash of insight in the soul or the transfiguration wrought by futurity, one finds a set of religious metaphors which are only very crudely tied in to these more secular and scientific narratives of development. It is always possible to find points at which the idealist subtext of sublime or supersensible grounds points literally outwards and upwards to a redemptive state beyond the framework of mundane existence – for instance, Schelling's suggestion that the solid world 'will one day dissolve itself into the spiritual', or Schubert's that the bound wings of the psyche will one day be released, allowing the 'freed one' to return 'cheerfully to the old homeland'.[111] Such formulations indicate narratives of spiritual transcendence which hearken back towards Christian eschatology, or to the pagan and gnostic motifs beyond it. As Xavier Tilliette has argued, the ecstatic dimensions of Schelling's later 'philosophy of man' are 'through and through God's business'.[112]

On the other hand, if one concentrates simply on the logic whereby these figures of futurity, emergence and unconsciousness rupture the conceptualisation of objective presence, what stands out once more is a tentative realignment of those older spiritual discourses with the new impetus to give a philosophical representation of autonomy. That is to say, these ubiquitous Romantic metaphors of uncanny or incandescent processes represent another way of claiming the foundation of identity through figures of non-identity. In the elusive, circular game played with presence, there is always a missing portion of experience (whether time within nature; divinity in the psyche; or the idea in time) which twists the assumed present into a topology of un-presence. Likewise, in Schubert's connection of a present with a higher future, or Schelling's man transported into such wonderful 'inner connections', there is a

---

[110] Schelling, *Ideas*, 65.   [111] Schubert, *Views of the Nightside*, 320–1.
[112] Xavier Tilliette, 'Die "Höhere Geschichte"', in Ludwig Hasler (ed.), *Schelling, Seine Beduetung für eine Philosophie der Natur und der Geschichte* (Stuttgart: Frommann-Holzboog, 1981), 193–204, 202.

suggestion of more perfected states of identity waiting to unfold.[113] Above all, this lurking principle of autonomy is registered in the way such inscrutable dimensions of embodiment free the notion of grounds from conceptual representation. Instead of a causal relation, the self intimates its own ground as an unassigned force that potentiates it, as a form of severance that detaches it from the moribund whole of the system, or as an enigmatic vision that identifies its own latent and ideal essence. It is via this triad of excessive terms that Schelling is able to return the possibility of self-founded identity to the site of the individualised being.

It is instructive here to consider once more the way in which Schelling and Hegel diverge in their descriptions of the actualisation of the absolute – particularly as it was in those first few years of the nineteenth century, just prior to Schelling's work on the *Ages of the World*, that the radical contrast in their positions began to emerge. Both held that the manifestation of the absolute was necessarily polar or contradictory, but for Hegel this crisis in manifestation is essentially an intersubjective phenomenon. In the founding conflict between master and slave or the mature tension between individual and state, the dialectic between universal and particular produces a disequilibrium in self-consciousness, which is itself always and at root involved in wider human totalities. Hegel argues that the ideal of self-recognition is ultimately stabilised within conditions of social practice and cultures of belief. It is here, at the societal level, that the absolute spirit which might reconcile truth and freedom, individual and universal, strives to emerge, as a culture struggles to realise it. However, the individual cannot secure its autonomy without recognising that such autonomy must always also be socially mediated – be authorised or conditioned at higher, wider or anterior levels than the merely individual. Schelling's turn to the materialisations and discontinuities expressed in figures of nature, history and psyche reverses this position. First of all, the missing conjunction of truth and freedom is not a symptom of social existence (for instance, the disjunction in ethos between different classes). Instead it results from the original structural withdrawal of an absolute ground beyond present existence, to become the past, the depth of nature, or the buried truth of the psyche. Whereas in Hegel identity comes into conflict with itself, and this induces a corresponding shift in the self-apprehension of the person, Schelling approaches this negative moment of identity via the 'unconscious'. Identity is in tension with itself because a portion of identity is concealed.

[113] Schelling, *Ages*, 114.

Secondly, even though this unconscious aspect may be experienced as a crisis in identity, this crisis also preserves apprehensions of the self's 'deeper' unity or essence from fragmentation, reductive object-ification or other forms of socially mediated alienation. Furthermore, this internalised and dissociated foundation of identity is explored not against the backdrop of social interactions, but as a kind of mysterious potential, anterior to cultural history and housed within the self. Freedom (as Jung will later explore in very similar terms) is something that organisms conceal within themselves – either as an enigmatic feature of their self-development, or as a mysterious and precious quality, hidden beyond the bounds of their conscious I. Freedom is always there, and can be engaged through the right kind of withdrawal into inner existential process. Ironically, it is Hegel, the idealist, who undermines the certainty of ideas as they are initially or immediately grasped, while Schelling (who appears to subvert the logic of the ideal by subordinating it to the realms of nature and history) actually preserves the ideal of the inalienable origin of the self, as well as its higher, or emergent, transfiguration into unity. He does this by preserving a notional 'essence' of identity apart from the possibility of its conscious articulation – whether as inner truth, or crisis, or fire. Hence his overriding interest in the crises, or absent dimensions, of presence.

Supplement on the political inversions of Romantic ontology

From the outset of this book I have emphasised that the unconscious emerges in conjunction with a general concern for the nature and possibility of autonomy – and that this question, in turn, is loosely allied to the development of liberal identity and the conditions of modern individualism as a whole. But my main task has been to depict the evolution of conceptions of the absolute grounds of identity towards forms in which individuality itself could be thought, and to show how this evolution became bound to a theory of the 'unconscious'. I have been able to introduce only the most intermittent remarks on the relation of this figuring of autonomy to the contemporaneous political fortunes of freedom, individuality and social unity. The prime aim has been to investigate how the intellectual figuring of individual human existence became interconnected with the terms of an empirical science of the individual mind, the psyche.

However, Schelling's positing of violent and secret grounds of identity prompts certain observations about the instability of such foundational discourses of the individual, once they are inserted into social and political culture. We have seen how crisis itself can become the sign of an identity counter-claimed against apparent unities and orders, intellectual and social, which render the self in too circumscribed and dependent a fashion. This discourse of crisis and transfiguration persists in twentieth-century aesthetics, philosophy and political critique. Although Walter Benjamin's work is often characterised as riven between transcendental and materialist tendencies, Messianism and historical dialectics, it is not common to link him to a Schellingian rhetoric of the sublime and singular potentiation of identity. However, Benjamin's concern with the non-identical in history, and with relations to truth manifested in 'crisis', 'danger', 'destruction', 'catastrophe' and 'shock', at least raises the question of theoretical and thematic parallels between this aspect of their work. Both address the intersection between a quasi-theological theory of truth and concepts of history. In his notes for the *Passagen-Werk*, Benjamin recognised that his interest in the origin (*Ursprung*) 'is a rigorous and decisive transposition of this basic Goethean concept from the domain of nature to that of history',[114] which seems to repeat Schelling's own trajectory from *Naturphilosophie* to the inquiries into historical time in *Ages of the World*. Both authors were likewise attracted by the discontinuous relations between the ideal and the manifest, and between truth and the system. In *The Origin of the German Trauerspiel*, Benjamin cites Creuzer's characterisation of the Romantic symbol under the following headings – 'The momentary, the total, the inscrutability of its origin, the necessary'.[115] His interest is drawn particularly by the quality of the momentary, in which truth is manifested 'like the sudden appearance of a ghost, or a flash of lightning ... a force which seizes hold of our entire being'.[116] However, Benjamin cites this Romantic definition of the symbol in order to contrast it with the character of meaning in allegory. Rather than momentarily transfiguring nature 'in the light of redemption', allegorical meaning for Benjamin is staged within human history, in which it suffers a perpetual decline and corruption of identity. The ultimate allegorical image of meaning in history is a death's head.[117]

This passage from nature to history is rather different from Schelling's, even though it is mediated by Creuzer whose *Symbolik*,

---

[114] Walter Benjamin, notes for Konvolut N, 'On the Theory of Knowledge, Theory of Progress', *The Arcades Project* (Cambridge, MA: Belknap/Harvard University Press, 1999), 462.

[115] Friedrich Creuzer, *Symbolik und Mythologie der alten Völker*, cited in Walter Benjamin, *The Origin of German Tragic Drama* (London: Verso, 1985), 163.

[116] Benjamin, *The Origin of German Tragic Drama*, 163.

[117] Ibid., 166.

originally appearing in four volumes between 1810 and 1812, evidently influenced Schelling's own move into philological researches on myth after 1815. But neither Schelling nor Benjamin can be located so easily. Schelling depicts history at times in language remarkably close to Benjamin's own – for instance, in the 'Stuttgart Seminars', 'history is most appropriately understood as a tragedy that is staged on a stage of mourning for which the world provides merely the floor, whereas the agents, i.e., actors, come from an entirely different world'.[118] On the other hand, Benjamin imagines redemption in terms very close to Schelling's. In a very early essay on the 'Life of Students' Benjamin describes the 'historical task' as being to disclose the 'immanent state of perfection and make it absolute, to make it visible and dominant in the present'.[119] This condition 'cannot be captured in terms of the pragmatic description of details (the history of institutions, customs, and so on); in fact it eludes them'.[120] For Benjamin the students themselves are a likeness of the highest metaphysical state of history, and this fact 'casts light on a crisis [Krisis] that hitherto has lain buried in the nature of things'.[121] Through a singular, rather than reasoned, form of understanding, 'everyone will succeed in liberating the future from its deformed existence in the womb of the present'.[122] Thus, like Schelling, Benjamin imagines the non-rational syntheses of truth and freedom in terms of concealment, crisis and futurity, which are in turn naturalised through metaphors of gestation and childbirth.

Benjamin would soon move away from this notion of a history that literally germinates futurity, but that invocation of a radical crisis which ruptures the alienated continuity of history remains a constant theoretical and figurative presence in his work. Even though in the *Trauerspiel* work Benjamin appears to distance himself from Creuzer's description of truth as a ghost, or flash of lightning, these metaphors remain significant for him. In his late notes on the theory of knowledge, Benjamin conceives the project of rendering history in terms of a 'dialectical image' which will function as a 'lightning flash': 'What has been is to be held fast – as an image flashing up in the now of its recognisability'.[123] Benjamin's 'Theses on the Philosophy of History' likewise addresses historical materialism insofar as it retains 'that image of the past which unexpectedly appears to a man singled out by history

[118] Schelling, 'Stuttgart Seminars', 240.
[119] Walter Benjamin, 'The Life of Students', in Walter Benjamin, *Selected Writings, vol. I: 1913–1926* (Cambridge, MA: Belknap/Harvard University Press, 1996), 37.
[120] Ibid., 37.   [121] Ibid., 37.   [122] Ibid., 46.
[123] Benjamin, *Arcades Project*, 473.

at a moment of danger', and invokes the historical materialist as one 'man enough to blast open the continuum of history'.[124]

As with Schelling, these moments of crisis relate to a kind of redemption of the particular that endorses precisely its individuality, its resistance to incorporation by the concept. Moments of recognition are achieved not through sequences of intelligible propositions, but rather as 'image' or 'fire'. The same motifs emerge in Benjamin's work on surrealism, a movement which has itself been characterised as 'the collective experience of individualism'.[125] The 'profane illumination' which Benjamin identifies in Louis Aragon's *Paysan de Paris* is a momentary transfiguration of perception – its dreamlike potentiation of the everyday 'loosens individuality like a bad tooth' in the structure of the world.[126] One could add here that, if Aragon's mythical transformations of Paris supply some of the inspiration for the monumental structure of Benjamin's own incomplete *Passagen-Werk*, Aragon himself had been reading Schelling during the summer of 1924, just prior to writing the latter half of *Paysan de Paris*, 'A Feeling for Nature at the Buttes-Chaumont'. It was under Schelling's influence that Aragon arrived at the notion that the mechanism of thought was analogous to the genesis of myth. According to Jacqueline Chéniex-Gendron, 'Aragon replaces Schelling's Absolute with the Unconscious.'[127]

A second example of the afterlife of this Schellingian discourse of crisis, futurity and sublime individuality occurs in a rather different current of modern criticism. Jacques Derrida, in *Spectres of Marx*, contrasts Marx's invocation of an 'ontology of presence as actual reality' with a more radical and deconstructive questioning of knowledge. Such questioning is manifested as 'seismic events' that come from the future: 'they are given from out of the unstable, chaotic, and dis-located ground of the times', a disjointed time 'without which there would be neither history, nor event, nor promise of justice'.[128] In the same text Derrida cites the 'uncanny' (with reference to both Freud and Heidegger) as that which 'makes possible fundamental projects or trajectories', but does

---

[124] Walter Benjamin, 'Theses on the Philosophy of History', in Walter Benjamin, *Illuminations*, ed. Hannah Arendt (New York: Schocken, 1968), 255, 262.

[125] André Masson, quoted in Michael Richardson and Krysztof Fijałkoski (eds.), *Surrealism Against the Current* (London: Pluto, 2001), 205.

[126] Benjamin, 'Surrealism: the Last Snapshot of the European Intelligentsia', *Selected Writings*, vol. *II: 1927–1934* (Cambridge, MA: Harvard University Press, 1999), 208–9.

[127] Jacqueline Chéniex-Gendron, *Surrealism* (New York: Columbia University Press, 1990), 105.

[128] Jacques Derrida, *Spectres of Marx: The State of the Debt, the Work of Mourning, and the New International* (London: Routledge, 1994), 170.

so 'while destabilizing permanently, and in a more or less subterranean fashion, the order of conceptual distinctions that are put to work'.[129]

Derrida had of course read Benjamin closely, and invokes him in this text, but the reference to Heidegger is equally pertinent, for we have already found Heidegger engaging with Schelling's work, for example, in his comments on the 'force of gravity' as 'the centre of all beings as a whole', and in his interest in the 'eternal past' of God in the German mystical tradition.[130] In *An Introduction to Metaphysics* (1935), Heidegger suggested that the fundamental question of metaphysics – the question concerning Being – has more and more 'proved to be a hidden ground of our historical being-there. This it remains even, and particularly, when self-satisfied and busy with all manner of things, we move about over this ground as over a flimsily covered abyss [*Abgrund*]'.[131] This 'abyssal' ground of Being is often connected by Heidegger to the notion of the 'uncanny' (*Das Unheimliche*). A crucial passage in *An Introduction to Metaphysics*, and much of the second half of Heidegger's 1942 seminar series on Hölderlin's 'The Ister', is given over to a discussion of the uncanny as it emerges in Sophocles' *Antigone*, and in particular its evocation within the choral ode which begins: 'Manifold is the uncanny, yet nothing/ more uncanny looms or stirs beyond the human being.'[132] Heidegger links the German word '*unheimlich*' to the Greek terms το δεινοτατον, and δεινον, which he finds to be the fundamental word of Greek tragedy in general, and transliterates as the 'terrible', 'the powerful' and the 'uncanny', or 'the strangest of the strange'.[133]

Just as for Schelling the undisclosable axis of the absolute (the true ground of freedom) is associated with the most powerful, obscure or destructive forces, now repressed in the past, in mysterious historical reserve, so in these texts from Heidegger and Derrida an undisclosed ground unites with the sense of imminent 'crisis' to provoke the question of Being, or the promise of justice. In each case projections of identity are allied to the pathological (this anticipates some of the arguments to be made in the following chapter, concerning the integration of the unconscious with Romantic psychiatry). For Heidegger and Derrida,

---

[129] Ibid., 174.
[130] See Chapter 2, and this chapter.
[131] Martin Heidegger, *An Introduction to Metaphysics* (New Haven, CT: Yale University Press, 1959), 93.
[132] In Heidegger's own translation, 'Vielfältig das Unheimliche, nichts doch/ über den menschen hinaus Unheimlicheres ragend sich regt', Martin Heidegger, *Hölderlin's Hymn 'The Ister'* (Bloomington: Indiana University Press, 1996), 66–7. Heidegger here makes a specific point of replacing Hölderlin's use of the word 'Ungeheuer' (extraordinary) in his own translation of the same lines, with 'das Unheimliche'.
[133] Heidegger, *An Introduction to Metaphysics*, 149–51.

as for Schelling, it is ironically a chronic *instability* in objects which testifies to their sublime grounding within a larger missing whole. But this generates a very unstable ontological position. There is a danger that, when the principle of non-equivalence necessary to establish an ontology of singular identity is drafted into large-scale representations of human activity on the plane of nature and history, it can become the hostage of a dangerous political appeal made to mythic communities and irreducible freedoms. Amplified into a general opposition to reason, representation or social institution as modes of grounding the self within a social context, this principle of non-equivalence can undermine legitimating unities of any kind, and become a tool in violent forms of political organisation. There are perils where the ground sought for freedom beyond logic is one that identifies with primordial disaster, or with 'the fearful, the powerful and the inhabitual'.[134]

Gillian Rose, in a commentary on Derrida's *Of Spirit* (a work which itself investigates the rhetorical structure of Heidegger's seminars on Schelling), has made the same point and warned of the danger that Derrida's 'expiation of the singular' is connected with the 'ontologising of "Violence as Revelation"'.[135] For Benjamin, too, the desire to release the singular from its bondage to the concept drew him into an alliance with the work of the Catholic conservative Carl Schmitt and his theorisation of the 'state of exception'. Within Schmitt's political ontology, the 'state of exception' indicates the point at which a sovereign responds to a crisis in the operation of the state by suspending the law and deciding on its own authority. Samuel Weber has referred to it as 'a pure act, somewhat akin to the act of creation except that what it does is not so much to create as to interrupt and to suspend',[136] while for Derrida it represents 'the moment when the justification of law hovers in the void or over the abyss'.[137] The idea of the 'pure' political act, detached from the normal conditions of legitimacy, resonates here both with Schelling's discussion of creation *ex nihilo* (the absolute that emerges into actuality from nothingness) and Tauler's abyss of God. However, as events unfolded in Weimar Germany, Schmitt was to use this concept to justify Nazi dictatorship. Benjamin's editors in the 1950s felt

[134] Heidegger's characterisation of *das Unheimliche*/ το δεινον in *Hölderlin's Hymn 'The Ister'*, 64.
[135] Gillian Rose, 'Of Derrida's Spirit', in David Wood (ed.), *Of Derrida, Heidegger and Spirit* (Evanston, IL: Northwestern University Press, 1993), 56.
[136] Samuel Weber, 'Taking Exception to Decision: Walter Benjamin and Carl Schmitt', *Diacritics*, 22, 3–4 (Fall–Winter 1992), 5–18, 10.
[137] Jacques Derrida, *Force de loi: Le 'Fondement mystique de l'autorité'* (Paris: Galilée, 1994), 89; cited in Horst Bredekamp, 'From Walter Benjamin to Carl Schmitt, via Thomas Hobbes', *Critical Inquiry*, 25, 2 (Winter 1999), 247–66, 265.

this association to be so compromising in retrospect that his reference to Schmitt in the *Trauerspiel* study was removed and a letter to Schmitt was withheld from the published correspondence.

In a rather different political connection, Jason M. Wirth describes the political implications of Schelling's emphasis on *Umsturz* (overthrow) in the inaugural Berlin lectures of 1841, 'suggesting a *coup d'état* or a *Putsch*'. For Wirth, 'This coup reverses the priority of reason and makes it beholden to the superiority of that which, considered in itself, can have no positive content and can result in no completed principle. It opens reason to its Other.'[138] Opening reason to its 'Other' might be construed, within contemporary theory, as a positive allegory of the opening up of the political imagination of the oppressor to its repressed political ground. It is notable that, in the aftermath of the Second World War, Schelling's grave, enigmatic and suffering model of history – as opposed to Hegel's seemingly triumphalist apology for the Prussian State (as his philosophy was then commonly interpreted) – seemed the less historically tainted position. For Karl Jaspers, 'Schelling learned what it means to encounter the force of history in a world that is falling apart, to see it and then to try and get one's bearings, half-desiring, half-suffering.'[139] Likewise Jung suggested that Hegel's identification of reason with spirit 'led to Nietzsche's superman and hence to the catastrophe that bears the name of Germany'; however, the forces 'compensating this calamitous development personified themselves partly in the later Schelling, partly in Schopenhauer and Carus'.[140] Even so, the attempt to centre identity on the notion of unconscious agency remains inherently unstable. There is nothing to prevent the appeal to 'otherness' coinciding with political acts of repression that reserve the right to give *no* reasons. This ambivalence in the rhetoric of a sublime ground – which appears both as crisis *and* as redemption, the space of the possible *and* the space of denial – has enabled it to underwrite both the iconographies of hope, belonging to the victims of history, and the intellectual insignia of violence, projected by the would-be victors. This perhaps explains the uncanny position of Heidegger himself in late twentieth-century theory, as he unwittingly exposes the convergence of both possibilities in the same vocabulary.

---

[138] Wirth, 'Introduction' to Schelling, *The Ages of the World* [1815], xvi.
[139] Jaspers, *Schelling*, 337.
[140] C. G. Jung, 'The Spirit of Psychology', in Joseph Campbell (ed.), *Spirit and Nature: Papers from the Eranos Yearbooks*, vol. I (London: Routledge & Kegan Paul, 1955), 381–2. The phrase about Germany was removed from the revised text, published as 'On the Nature of the Psyche', in *The Collected Works of C. G. Jung*, vol. VIII: *The Structure and Dynamics of the Psyche* (Princeton University Press, 1972).

In this respect, Heidegger's frequent reiteration of Nietzsche's phrase – 'God is dead'[141] – in no way shields him from the charge of intimating alternative dimensions of unity and totality, in which freedom finds its 'true ground' or 'essence', even if this essence is posited, as with Schelling, through the discourse of history, nature and the abyss of origins. One can read Heidegger's avowal of the flimsily covered abyss, or the dark ground of history (which again appears in his 1936 lectures on Schelling: 'a *ground* which remains in the *dark* for us up until today'[142]) as an attempt to resist the language of domination through an appeal to the irreducible indeterminacy of Being. Or one can read it back into the context of Heidegger's 1933 Rectoral address on 'The Self-Assertion of the German University' in which the same terms are implicated in propaganda for the 'inner truth' of National Socialism. In this speech, Heidegger once more drew on Greek tragedy to make the point that 'all knowledge of things remains beforehand at the mercy of overpowering fate and fails before it', and when 'the entire might of the concealedness of what is' first rises up, 'what is reveals itself in its unfathomable inalterability and confers its truth on knowledge'.[143] The system of knowledge here, much as in Schelling, stands on the shoulders of something much more unknowable and dangerous, which is concealed in the origin, and has the power to overturn the more superficial layers of 'truth' built over it. This relation to violent foundation concerns not just knowledge, but the grounds of social unity itself. The spiritual world of a *Volk* is not its cultural superstructure, but comes from the violent and unthinkable depths: 'it is the power that comes from preserving at the most profound level the forces that are rooted in the soil and blood of a Volk, the power to arouse most inwardly and to shake most extensively the Volk's existence'.[144]

As in the discourses of Romantic anthropology, violence appears in Heidegger's philosophy as both a crisis in identity, and the sign of another, non-identical medium from which a freer and truer identity of self and whole will emerge. 'The placing of one's existence in the most acute danger in the midst of overpowering Being'[145] enables a return to and a return of the 'essence' and the 'origin'. Because of its structural exclusion from the framework of reason, the abyss of origins is both projected as a ground that was always there, *and* as the

[141] Heidegger, *Schelling's Treatise*, 50.
[142] Ibid., 32.
[143] Martin Heidegger, 'The Self-Assertion of the University', in Richard Wolin (ed.), *The Heidegger Controversy* (Cambridge, MA: MIT Press: 1993), 31.
[144] Heidegger, 'The Self-Assertion of the University', 33–4.
[145] Ibid., 35–6.

vacant site for aggrandising projections of the possible conjunction of 'freedom', 'identity' and 'unity'. Relation to the essence entails obeying 'what the beginning of our spiritual-historical existence decreed in the distant past';[146] but the beginning, as ever, is an empty space that allows for the retrospective insertion of new laws. Thus German students, through the new Student Law, 'place themselves under the law of their essence and thereby delimit this essence for the very first time'.[147] Decreed 'in the distant past', yet delimited 'for the very first time' – this is precisely the paradox that Schelling explored in relation to the emergence of higher identity and its original grounds (and curiously also replicates the structure of Laplanche's 'afterwardsness').[148] The basis of determination is emphatically stated but also ambiguously, imaginatively adrift here. Heidegger adds that, 'To give law to oneself is the highest freedom', while 'leading' means 'the strength to go alone', and yet this questioning arising out of crisis is 'pervaded with a sense of community'.[149] In a similar fashion, in the Schelling seminar of 1936, Heidegger presents German idealism as 'truly recognising the *general nature* of freedom as independence and self-determination in the *law of one's own* being.'[150]

Through the simultaneous assumption and repression of a meta-principle, the subject's imagination of the sources of his or her authority, freedom and constitution can always be notionally oriented towards a ground but never tested against it. The political emotions of the individual are aroused, and the individual encouraged to imagine the ground of his or her autonomy and certainty at the very points where this exceeds the individual's capacity to construe it intellectually. At the same time, the very absence of this ground, which appears only through intellectual lacunae and disturbances in the frame of the apparent world, is taken as direct evidence of its *excessive* nature, and thus its withdrawn but latent power to overrule the world as it is in the present. In this way, an imaginary and spiritually recuperative dialogue with authority, identity and community, via the 'unknown', is set up in such a way that it is vulnerable to political uses which are, ironically, knowing, selective and violent. For this reason, Lukács in *The Destruction of Reason* aimed to present a line of development 'running from Schelling to Hitler', via figures such as Nietzsche, Spengler and Heidegger.[151]

---

[146] Ibid., 36.   [147] Ibid., 34.
[148] See Chapter 3.
[149] Heidegger, 'The Self-Assertion of the University', 34.
[150] Heidegger, *Schelling's Treatise*, 91. My italics.
[151] Lukács, *The Destruction of Reason*, 12.

Habermas provided a crucial critique of both the sources and implications of these discourses of origins, forgetting and dark grounds. In
his review of Heidegger's *An Introduction to Metaphysics*, published in
1953, he chides Heidegger's assertions concerning a progressive 'for-
getfulness of Being' in Western philosophy: 'Heidegger does not take
into account the fact that the specific formulation of his questions is
by no means original but has its origins in that peculiarly German
way of thinking that goes back, via Schelling, Hölderlin and Hegel, to
Böhme.'[152] More importantly, the 'unconsciousness', so necessary to
an ontology of the individual, is in danger, in this political context, of
becoming a zero which throws all attempts at ethical arbitration awry.
Habermas asks: 'can the planned murder of millions of human beings,
which we all know about today, also be made understandable in terms
of the history of Being as a fateful going astray?', and adds, 'Is it not the
foremost duty of thoughtful people to clarify the accountable deeds of
the past and keep the knowledge of them awake?'[153]

---

[152] Jürgen Habermas, 'Martin Heidegger: On the Publication of the Lectures of 1935',
in Wolin (ed.), *The Heidegger Controversy*, 194.
[153] Ibid., 197.

5   Post-idealism and the Romantic psyche

Pathologies of the idea

I have looked at four very different currents of late German Romantic thought – speculations about primordial history; the rediscovery of negative theology; a science of myth and revelation; and theories concerned with transfigurative states of development. Together, they show the breadth of Schelling's conceptual turn to the unconscious, and the forms in which this unconscious could be identified in cultural and historical theory. Each of these discourses, as well as centring the self in relation to an unconscious past, also constructs that foundational relation *through* the psyche. The psychic bonds linking the individual to its unconscious past are of various kinds. They appear in one case as a magical or oracular relation to truth; in another as a loss of consciousness that paradoxically founds the self; in yet another as an inner madness which the self seeks to escape; and lastly as a crisis in self-experience which produces a view into the 'inner'. These discourses are not entirely separate, and are always capable of evoking each other. Schelling's Munich lectures of 1827–28 on the 'System of the Ages of the World' characteristically skip from one trope to another, circling around a principle of unconsciousness which is constantly surmised, rather than directly, psychologically, investigated.

The intimations of the psyche here are never fully integrated by Schelling into a complete theory of psychic life, and the vocabulary through which he constructs the psyche as a medium of the self is constantly shifting.[1] What remains constant, however, is that the psychic opens up aspects of self-experience which are more directly involved (than normal consciousness) in the 'essence' or foundation of the person as individual. From these co-ordinates, as we have seen, there developed a remarkable series of psychoanalytic notions *avant la lettre* – the

---

[1] For further details of these vocabularies of the psyche, see ffytche, 'F. W. J. Schelling and G. H. Schubert'.

178

unconscious, repression, forgetting, the self's duality and historicity, an uncanny relation to the past, and the potentiation of the self. It now remains to examine how these various strategies for describing and conceptualising the individuality of the self and its unconscious grounds were integrated with the field of Romantic psychiatry and psychology itself. It is here that the philosophy of the I completes its conversion into a psychology of the unconscious; at the same time these terms of 'crisis' and 'concealed grounds', dual identities and obscure origins, begin to function concretely within a new, Romantic science of the soul.

The interpenetration of this Romanticised version of idealism with psychology and psychiatry was facilitated in a number of ways. Nature philosophers such as Schubert, Baader and Eschenmayer were first of all drawing on psychiatric and psychopathological material to flesh out their more general descriptions of the psyche. At the same time, Romantic psychiatrists, such as J. C. A. Heinroth, would increasingly orient their notion of health and sickness in the mind around notions of a person's spiritual autonomy and potential for creative self-transformation. Heinroth's *Textbook of Disturbances of Mental Life*, published in 1818, exemplifies this psychiatric focus on 'individuality' as itself something subject to illness. This trend towards treating the 'self' and the psyche, rather than simply 'nerves' or 'reason', is already clearly present in the work of J. C. Reil, for whom the task of psychiatry was to restore the balance of personality.[2]

A milestone in German Romantic psychiatry was the publication in 1803 of Reil's *Rhapsodies on the Application of Psychic Methods of Cure to Disorders of the Mind*, which contained one of the first systematic outlines of psychotherapy. Reil's impact is comparable to that of Philippe Pinel in France, in terms of reorienting the treatment of the insane from incarceration towards moral therapeutics. However, unlike Pinel, Reil's theory of the mind came to centre on idealist assumptions, such as the involvement of will and consciousness in constituting the divisions of self and reality, and the theoretical construction of types of madness as modes of loss of freedom of the will. As Robert J. Richards notes in a work on Romantic theories of life, 'Quite clearly [Reil] had

---

[2] The new concern of the Romantics with the nature of the psyche 'brought psychiatry to the threshold of modern concepts and techniques', Franz Alexander and Sheldon T. Selesnick, *The History of Psychiatry*, 135. For accounts of psychoanalysis in relation to Romantic medicine and psychiatry, see also Iago Galdston, 'Freud and Romantic Medicine', *Bulletin of the History of Medicine*, 30 (1956), 489–507; David Beres, 'Psychoanalysis, Science and Romanticism', in Max Schur (ed.), *Drives, Affects, Behavior: Essays in Honor of Marie Bonaparte*, vol. II (New York: International Universities Press, 1965), 397–417; and Ellenberger, *Discovery*, 77–83, 199–223.

been reading Schelling, whose Romantic idealism ... fundamentally reoriented Reil's understanding of the root causes of mental illness.'[3]

There was an interesting criss-crossing of influences between philosophers, psychologists, psychiatrists and physicians in this period, as disciplinary boundaries over the 'science of the soul' had anyway yet to emerge. Reil's work, along with Schubert's *Views of the Nightside* and the earlier *Magazine for Empirical Psychology* edited by Karl Philipp Moritz,[4] provided the main source of details concerning the phenomena of magnetism and somnambulism for German Romantics, idealists and *Naturphilosophen* alike (many of Schubert's cases are taken directly from Reil's work). But, as we have also seen, Schelling's idealism, in attempting to frame the autonomy of the individual, had been led to develop its own concern with pathological manifestations of experience. We see evidence of this in Schelling and Schubert's interest in violent transfigurations within the organic realm, and of the intersection of material crisis with psychological insight. That same absorption in pathology is evident in Schubert's suggestion, in the final chapters of *Views of the Nightside*, that the as-yet unborn powers of a future existence become visible above all, 'as a sickly or unconscious [*ohnmächtig*] condition in the present'.[5] That term, *Ohnmacht*, resonates in turn with Schelling's theorisation of the involution of the absolute and the original state of the soul discussed in Chapter 4. Luigi Pareyson has made a study of the abundance of metaphors in Schelling's later work pertaining to particular kinds of incapacitation: rapture, stupefaction, vertigo, paralysis, mutism and blindness, and Xavier Tilliette has developed this point to suggest that Schelling's later philosophy of freedom emerges precisely 'when reason loses its feet and finds itself struck with mutism and vertigo'.[6] In a different fashion, Odo Marquard has pointed out Schelling's increased interest in medical literature after 1800, suggesting that, 'When history is grasped in terms of "nature" then the difficulties of history have to be formulated as difficulties of nature – as illnesses.'[7]

This idea of the interrelationship between illness and the dialectic of subjective identity had a wide currency in both German Romantic and idealist thought. Jean Hippolyte noted of Hegel's *Realphilosophie* of the early 1800s that 'the universal is manifested to the living being

[3] Richards, *The Romantic Conception*, 263.
[4] For details of Moritz's magazine, see Bell, *The German Tradition of Psychology*, 94–7.
[5] Schubert, *Views of the Nightside*, 301.
[6] Xavier Tilliette, 'Une philosophie en deux', in Jean-François Courtine and Jean-François Marquet (eds.), *Le Dernier Schelling* (Paris: J. Vrin, 1994), 63. Tilliette cites Luigi Pareyson, 'Lo stupore della ragione in Schelling', *Romanticismo, Esistenzialismo, Ontologia della libertà* (Milan: U. Mursia, 1979), 137–80.
[7] Marquard, *Transzendentaler Idealismsus*, 170.

inside himself in such a way that man is posed as the "sick animal"'.[8] A similar fascination with the precarious relationship between the transformations of identity in *Bildung* and in madness likewise permeated early-nineteenth-century German literature. We have seen this as an ironic apprehension in the writings of Jean Paul, but for the Romantic Achim von Arnim writing in 1812, it was clear that 'The contradiction ... is only present in sickly circumstances' – the 'contradiction' becoming, in this late phase of German idealism, the motor of spiritual and historical transformation and the sign of active freedom.[9] Such ideas become woven into Schelling's later work on myth, where it is spiritual crises, occurring in the historical foundation of human consciousness, that give rise to the original separation of humanity into peoples and nations: 'new sicknesses appearing in powerful forms appear as parallel symptoms of great spiritual emancipations'.[10] Polytheism was, from this perspective, a 'profound shock', a 'cision that was hurled into the homogenous humanity'.[11]

To understand how such relationships between idealism and psychiatry became culturally cemented, one has to look at the impact of theories of mesmerism and animal magnetism in Germany at this time. Their influence came in successive waves, at first gaining only a tentative foothold but gradually acting as a point of convergence for various theoretical needs. Already in the 1780s, as Mesmer was pursuing his career in Paris, Eberhard Gmelin, a doctor based in Heilbronn, was working on a six-volume work on magnetism published in 1787.[12] However, this speedy reception of Mesmer's insights in Germany was counterbalanced by the negative verdict on its merits by the enquiry set up by the Parisian scientific establishment in 1785, which included the opinion of such eminent figures as Lavoisier, Franklin and Guillotin. The enthusiastic elaboration of a more spiritualist dimension to the theory also jeopardised its credibility in Germany.[13] Thus Johann Kaspar Lavater, based in Bremen, was more impressed by the Marquis de Puységur's experiments with somnambulism and clairvoyance, and repeated such

[8] Jean Hyppolite, *Genesis and Structure of Hegel's Phenomenology of Spirit* (Evanston, IL: Northwestern University Press, 1974), 251.
[9] Cited in Werner Leibbrand, *Die Spekulative Medizin der Romantik* (Hamburg: Claassen, 1956), 174.
[10] F. W. J. Schelling, *Historical-critical Introduction to the Philosophy of Mythology* (Albany, NY: State University of New York Press, 2007), 73.
[11] Ibid., 76.
[12] Eberhard Gmelin, *Ueber den Thierischen Magnetismus* (Tübingen, 1787), followed by *Neue Untersuchungen über den Thierischen Magnetismus* (Tübingen, 1789).
[13] See Robert Darnton, *Mesmerism and the End of Enlightenment in France* (New York: Schocken, 1970), 62.

investigations in Germany as early as 1785.[14] But it was just this kind of expansion of mesmerism in occult or supernatural directions that early on made it an object of mockery in cosmopolitan circles. Gmelin even remarked that he had considered calling his magnum opus 'Essays on the Forces of Human Nature', so as to avoid the troublesome associations that had since arisen with magnetism and mesmerism.[15]

As the eighteenth century drew to a close, however, animal magnetism increased its hold on mainstream medical and scientific theory. This was partly due to the influence, on medical practitioners associated with the *Naturphilosophie*, of Galvani's experimentation with muscle response and electricity (reproduced in Germany by Alexander von Humboldt and the Romantic physicist Joachim Ritter) and of Thomas Brown's physiological theory of irritability. Both Brown and Galvani's explorations of the life of the body chimed, potentially, with Mesmer's own concept of invisible polar forces. Mesmer's ninth proposition, at the end of his *Mémoire sur la découverte du magnétisme animal* from 1779, had been that humans, like magnets, contained 'different and opposed poles, which can be communicated, changed, disrupted or reinforced'.[16] This polar notion, in turn, was well-suited to combine with the preference for 'dialectical' explanations of phenomena which permeated the culture of both idealism and *Naturphilosophie*. Schelling, as we saw earlier in the context of the *Ideas*, had his own reasons for thinking of magnetism as the universal form of 'being-in-itself': it was that force whereby the body 'picks itself out and gathers itself together as a particular unity'.[17] By the early nineteenth century, *Naturphilosophie* and theories of animal magnetism were being closely interwoven. Thus the doctor Friedrich Hufeland claimed that, when magnetised, iron receives a soul and becomes actively alive. For Hufeland magnetism made apparent 'the simple splitting of unity into contradiction, the first awakening of opposed forces', and as such represented 'the first creative act of nature'.[18] Not only was Mesmer's theory being integrated with Schelling's developmental philosophy of nature, but this theoretical amalgam had now acquired its own adherents in medicine.

Another sign of this intermingling of magnetic and philosophical theory emerges in a letter written by Hegel to Schelling on 1 May 1807. This letter famously announces the completion of the *Phenomenology of Spirit* the night before the battle of Jena, but also goes on to report

---

[14] Justinus Kerner, *Franz Anton Mesmer, aus Schwaben, Entdecker des thierischen Magnetismus* (Frankfurt am Main: J Rütter, 1856), 94, and Leibbrand, *Spekulative Medizin*, 176.

[15] Kerner, *Mesmer*, 98.   [16] Leibbrand, *Spekulative Medizin*, 180.

[17] Schelling, *Ideas*, 128.   [18] Leibbrand, *Spekulative Medizin*, 175.

Hegel's interest in J. W. Ritter's theory of 'siderism'. According to Hegel, siderism proposed that a large-scale equivalent of magnetic forces affects both matter and spirit, and through this connection the spirit 'descends to the so-called inorganic, and articulates a magical unification and co-feeling of higher and lower natures'.[19] In the years leading up to the *Ages of the World*, Schubert and Schelling were also forming their own interpretations of the mesmerist literature. In *Views of the Nightside*, Schubert began to speculate that 'sensitive and sickly people of the other sex, especially those suffering from incurable nervous illnesses', were 'most suitable to be magnetised' – this is because their identity was already that much closer to points of internal transfiguration.[20] For the same reason, Schubert believed that people who were mad or were dying gained special powers of insight which put them in touch with nature's release of futurity (a phenomenon later to be investigated by C. G. Jung). They were the ones most likely to diagnose the signs of death in strangers,[21] and by a reverse inference, magnetism had power over incurable diseases, because it causes a 'little death'.[22]

That interest in violent thresholds, touched on in the last chapter, connects here with specific therapeutic suggestions and merges with the application of magnetic theory in medicine. But Jason M. Wirth has also suggested that Schelling's occasional use of the term *Krisis*, to describe the ontological 'fall' and passage into existence of the absolute, was a sign that he was incorporating Mesmer's studies into his own metaphysic: for Mesmer, crisis was a state 'intermediate between wakefulness and perfect sleep'.[23] *Krisis* provides another equivalent of *Ohnmächtigkeit*, that term emerging in negative theology which, as we have seen, was associated with a psychic state of unconsciousness. Even more strikingly, in the Stuttgart Seminars of 1808, Schelling borrowed another mesmerist term when he alluded to the *rapport* that the soul establishes with God: 'no human being can exist without this rapport'.[24] Elsewhere we have seen Schelling describe the inner essence of the soul as a repressed fire, but here he speaks of it as a 'madness', anticipating the 'graver madness' of the late lectures on mythology. Rather than clairvoyance releasing a combustible element in the soul which 'breaks out of the depths of the inner essence', Schelling here suggests 'the highest state of clairvoyance is that of madness', and that, outside the

---

[19] G. W. F. Hegel, *Hegel: The Letters*, ed. Clark Butler and Christiane Seiler (Bloomington: Indiana University Press, 1984), 79–80.
[20] Schubert, *Views of the Nightside*, 331.
[21] Ibid., 351.   [22] Ibid., 357.
[23] Editorial footnote in Schelling, *The Ages of the World* [1815], 142.
[24] Schelling, 'Stuttgart Seminars', 232.

rapport with God (in which God takes up the position of magnetiser in relation to the unconscious soul), such madness is the 'most profound essence of the human spirit'.[25]

As this brief outline shows, philosophy and metaphysics on the one hand, and Romantic magnetisers, physicians and psychologists on the other, were finding support in each other's assumptions concerning the nature of the soul. Nature philosophers supplied a philosophical grounding for more empirical studies of the psyche, and also ways of reformulating notions of presence, process and self-development in terms of polarities, or the tension between conscious and unconscious aspects of the self. Such notions of process meshed quite easily with some of Mesmer's ideas. As early as 1811, Schelling's disciple Lorenz Oken was corresponding with Mesmer, who coincidentally had himself been reading Reil's psychiatric work. Mesmer suggested to Oken in a letter at the end of that year that people were generally discontented with the ever-increasing confusion and lack of objectives in the field of medicine. 'Now by the discovery of a previously unknown natural force, as being that which constitutes the real principle of life, it has been proved that an entire transformation is rendered possible.'[26] Mesmer suggested that Reil should come to him in Switzerland to receive the outlines of a course on mesmerism which could be introduced into the Prussian state. Reil, in turn, had already felt the need for a rapprochement between psychiatry and philosophy. He corresponded with Schelling in 1808, seeking help in the project of grounding a theory of the soul: 'What is lacking is a presentation of the soul in itself, or in its primordial state, without which psychiatry can never receive even the faintest sketch of a scientific treatment.'[27] As we have seen, much of Schelling's work of this period was concerned precisely with such primordial states of being.

The philosophers of nature had much to offer Romantic psychology and psychiatry. But the new studies of psychopathological phenomena previewed in Reil and Schubert's work, and now increasingly marshalled and interpreted in theoretical and medical journals, also supplied the philosophers with empirical evidence for Schelling's philosophical stress on the agency of the unconscious within existence. As Henri Ellenberger observed, 'whereas the French were seeking extra lucid *somnambules* as auxiliary subjects for medical practice, the Germans

---

[25] Ibid., 238, 232.
[26] Mesmer to Oken, 22 December 1811, Alexander Ecker, *Lorenz Oken: a Biographical Sketch*, trans. Alfred Tulk (London: Kegan Paul Trench, 1883), 134.
[27] Schelling, *Briefe und Dokumente*, vol. III, 510.

utilised them in an audacious attempt at experimental metaphysics'.[28] That is to say, the French were exploring the way in which patients in trance states could give insights into the nature of their own illness; but the Germans were more keen to corroborate the insights of idealism, to map out the transcendental structures of the self.

This meshing of the new psychiatric material emerging from magnetist and mesmerist experimentation with the metaphysical conjectures of the *Naturphilosophie* achieved something of an apotheosis in German cultural life around the time that Schelling was working on the *Ages of the World*. It was then that in 1812, more than thirty-five years after the Berlin Academy had originally dismissed his ideas, the Prussian government made an attempt to return Mesmer to Germany. Mesmer, now eighty and only three years away from his death, was too weary to travel to Berlin, so the Prussians contented themselves with sending a royal commissioner to receive instruction from him on the growing field of magnetic and somnambulistic investigations in Germany. The Germans were also eager to claim Mesmer as one of their own. For Justinus Kerner, author of the famous study of Friederike Hauffe, the seeress of Prevorst, Mesmer was *Franz Anton Mesmer, of Swabia, discover of Animal Magnetism*. Schelling, in his Munich lectures on the 'System of the Ages of the World', likewise claimed Mesmer as a symbol of Southern Germany's intellectual vitality, and as an inspiration for the new university. According to Schelling it was the South, whose intellectual currents were more in tune with nature, that had early responded to the potential of Mesmer's theory, while journals in the Prussian capital, now dominated by their stultifying Hegelian orientation towards 'the concept', had vilified the movement as 'the secret machinations of the Jesuits'.[29] In any case, the enquiry sent to Switzerland resulted in the founding of two chairs of mesmerism in the universities of Berlin and Bonn in 1816, and this same year saw a boom in publications, including an *Essay on the Apparent Magic of Animal Magnetism* by Schelling's former disciple C. A. Eschenmayer, now Professor of medicine and philosophy at Tübingen, and Joseph Weber's *Animal Magnetism, or the Mystery of Human Life, Explained through Dynamic-Psychic Forces*. Franz Baader's own *On Ecstasy, or the Rapturous Nature of Magnetic Sleep-talking* followed in 1817, along with the founding of an influential journal, *The Archive for Animal Magnetism*, published by Eschenmayer in conjunction with the doctors D. G. Kieser and Friedrich Nasse. Unsurprisingly, the boom in

---

[28] Ellenberger, *Discovery*, 78.   [29] Schelling, *System der Weltalter*, 84.

psychological interest in animal magnetism and uncanny experiences had its impact on literature as well. The year 1817 saw the publication of the first volume of E. T. A. Hoffmann's *Nachtstücke* containing the stories 'The Sandman', 'The Sanctus', and others exploring various aspects of psychopathology and the occult.

The philosopher and the psyche

Schelling's contact with psychopathology took place through a number of different routes. His direct involvement with medical science had its origins in a period of leave from Jena in 1800, which he spent in Bamberg, making the acquaintance of the doctor and psychiatrist Adalbert Marcus.[30] At that time Schelling was mainly interested in pursuing connections between idealism and the Brownian theory of irritability on which Marcus based his practice. In 1806 the two joined forces to edit the *Jahrbücher der Medicin als Wissenschaft*, a journal devoted to the interactions of medicine, psychology and the new philosophy, copies of which were annotated by Coleridge in England. In the first issue, Schelling called medicine the 'crown and the flower of natural science, as man is of the world',[31] and articles in the first couple of years included Marcus on the use of iron in medicine, and Schelling's brother, the physician Karl Schelling, on animal magnetism and on the theory of the soul. Insofar as these studies intrude on the *Ages of the World*, Schelling links this world of therapy with the foundational, unconscious centring of the soul upon itself. Schelling speculates, for instance, on gradations of mesmeric sleep in which, at the deepest level, man is 'completely cut off from the sensuous world and entirely removed to a spiritual realm'.[32] Schelling's son added an explanatory note to the draft at this point suggesting that 'Disease is only possible to the extent that all forces and organs of life are subjugated to a common exponent, whereby the individual is sacrificed to the whole.' According to Schelling himself, mesmeric sleep presents the possibility of a healing state in which 'the individual force, temporarily freed from the chain of the whole, gains time to re-establish itself in its integrity and

---

[30] For Schelling's contact with Romantic medicine in particular, see Werner E. Gerabek, *Friedrich Wilhelm Joseph Schelling und die Medizin der Romantik* (Frankfurt am Main: Peter Lang, 1995), and Nelly Tsouyopoulos, 'Der Streit zwischen Friedrich Wilhelm Joseph Schelling und Andreas Röschlaub über die Grundlagen der Medizin', *Medizinhistorisches Journal*, vol. XIII (1978), 229–46.

[31] A. F. Marcus and F. W. J. Schelling (eds.), *Jahrbücher der Medicin als Wissenschaft* (Tübingen: Cotta, 1806), vol. I, 1, v.

[32] Schelling, *Ages*, 159.

originality'.[33] Schelling's pursuit of an ontological framework through which to conceive of the individual's independence and freedom is here mingling with the notion of therapeutic isolation of the self's more absolute and universal grounds, as well as speculation on psychological and physiological processes in the body.[34] For Schelling, normal sleep likewise releases the person from an outer force and 'a freely willed sympathy takes the place of an externally determined unity'. He related this procedure to states induced by animal magnetism in which: 'the power seems actually given to one man to transcend that outer potency and return another man to the free inner relations of life, so that he appears dead externally, while internally a steady and free connection of all forces emerges from the lowest up to the highest'.[35]

There are some intriguing intersections here between notions of psychic health and ontological representations of individuality and autonomy. Mesmeric trances, sleep and even death are all being used to figure a state of absolute disconnection from the world – the emergence of an autonomous world of psyche, as it were – and this is in turn described as a freedom, a 'free connection', or as the self's integrity and originality. These psychic states of unconsciousness are, in a literal and technical way, stepping in to organise that state of metaphysical unconsciousness through which Schelling theorised the foundation of individuality itself. We can see, too, a connection with Schelling's notion that the soul is held ontologically in a *rapport* with God. Except in this case the magnetiser's *rapport* returns the soul to its condition of 'free relation', and as such, in a new way, stands in for that generous act of omnipotence whereby life is founded in the individual precisely through an act of detachment and withdrawal on the part of the absolute. In mesmeric sleep it is the soul, not the absolute, which is detached and involuted. However, Schelling foregrounds the same sense of a magical relation through non-relation, and a beneficent exercise of power that releases rather than binds the individual. Conversely, for Schelling, it seems that disease is in some way consonant with that original object of idealist critique – that ceding of the self to the notion of a fully interconnected or causally enchained world.

This association between Schelling and Marcus in Bamberg bore another offshoot in the writings of E. T. A. Hoffmann. In 1808,

---

[33] Ibid., 160.

[34] The French surrealists, influenced by psychoanalysis but also by trends in Romanticism and German idealism, would later investigate sleep, trance and dream states along similar lines. See, for instance, André Breton, *Communicating Vessels* (Lincoln: University of Nebraska Press, 1990).

[35] Schelling, *Ages*, 158.

Hoffmann took up the position of *Kapellmeister* at the theatre in Bamberg, where Marcus was coincidentally a patron, and it was through Marcus that Hoffmann developed an interest in contemporary parapsychology. A diary entry for December 1812 records Hoffmann's consternation on the afternoon on which he 'saw a somnambulist for the first time in the hospital'.[36] In the same year Hoffmann, despite having little interest in philosophy, began to acquaint himself with Schelling's ideas concerning nature. A local wine merchant called Kunz granted the writer access to his library, which included copies of Schelling's revised *Ideas* and his *On the World Soul*. Hoffmann's diary entries make reference to reading both Schelling and Novalis from Kunz's library in 1812.[37] This was the period when Hoffmann's writing became more seriously concerned with the possibility of darker, more magical aspects of existence. In 1813, shortly before moving on to Dresden (where Schubert had previously lectured on the nightside of nature), Hoffmann signed a contract with Kunz to publish his *Fantasiestücke*. He wrote to Kunz from Dresden that summer telling him that he was working on an idea for a tale, 'The Magnetiser', that would deal with the 'nightside' of the topic, which had not yet received a proper, poetic treatment.[38] A week later, Hoffmann implored Kunz to send him a copy of Schubert's *Views of the Nightside*. The book was delivered to Hoffmann in August and he reported back that he was hungry for anything written by the brilliant Schubert, and that he admired the latter's description of 'the intimations of somnambulists'.[39] Hoffmann's praise in turn opened doors for Schubert, for it was Kunz who published Schubert's *Symbolism of Dreams* in 1814, later read by Freud in preparation for his *Interpretation of Dreams*.

Schelling's growing fascination with psychic disorders merged inevitably with the increasing professional interest in Germany in the possibility of parapsychological experience. In a letter of 1807, Marcus thanked Schelling for making some important observations about the possible connections between magnetism and dowsing, and reported back about a farmer's wife, newly admitted to the Bamberg hospital, whose occult powers were becoming a local sensation.[40] The philosopher also became caught up in the fad for pendulum swinging as a form

---

[36] E. T. A. Hoffmann, *Tagebücher*, ed. Hans von Müller and Friedrich Schnapp (Munich: Winkler, 1971), 186.

[37] Ibid, 150.

[38] Letter to Kunz, 20 July 1813, *E.T.A. Hoffmann Briefwechsel, Erster Band von Königsberg bis Leipzig 1794–1814*, ed. Hans von Müller and Friedrich Schnapp (Munich: Winkler, 1967), 400.

[39] Ibid., 409.

[40] Schelling, *Briefe und Dokumente*, vol. III, 429–30.

of divination, and Ellenberger lists Schelling, along with Schubert, Baader and Eschenmayer, amongst those who paid visits to the celebrated somnambulistic seeress, Friedericke Hauffe, who was taken into care by Justinus Kerner in his asylum in Weinsberg, Württemberg, in the late 1820s.[41] In this context, the investigations of *Naturphilosophie* merge with a set of mystical expectations concerning undisclosed spiritual truths which may be intimated in dreams and magnetic trances. In a letter of December 1808, Schelling thanked Schubert for sending him a copy of *Views of the Nightside* and reported back about his own researches on medicine and clairvoyance. He was convinced, for instance, that Joan of Arc had been a clairvoyant and went on to suggest, in terms that would later be repeated by Jung, that clairvoyance represented a 'foretaste of our future being'.[42] Just as Schubert had been interested in a lost primordial science, on account of its access to special intuitive forms of knowledge, so for Schelling the reports of somnambulists were important for what they revealed about possible future forms of existence, and the transition of the world from its current material basis towards its spiritual essence.[43]

Why did this interest in parapsychology achieve such an active hold over this generation of German philosophers and scientists? For Karl Jaspers it was Caroline's death that drew Schelling away from his philosophical and existential focus into more supernatural concerns, but there are broader developments that need to be taken into account. One is the sheer weight of recorded details of instances of prophecy or clairvoyance achieved in somnambulistic or magnetic trances emerging out of Germany's rural hinterlands, and now being gathered into journals such as Friedrich Nasse's *Journal for Doctors of the Psyche (with particular consideration of magnetism)* (1818–22), and *Journal of Anthropology* (1823–26); Eschenmayer and Kieser's *Archive for Animal Magnetism* (1817–24, which continued as *Sphinx* in the mid 1820s); and Justinus Kerner's *Leaves from Prevorst* (1830–39) which continued as *Magikon* (subtitled 'Archive for Observations of the Spirit World and of Magnetic and Magical Life', 1840–53). The cumulative impact of such researches left their mark on the study of psychology in Germany right into the mid century and beyond, despite the backlash against *Naturphilosophie* led by Hermann Helmholtz and Emil du Bois-Reymond. Speculations

---

[41] Ellenberger, *Discovery*, 81.
[42] Schelling, *Briefe und Dokumente*, vol. III, 571. Compare Jung, 'On the Psychology of So-called Occult Phenomena', 79, 'It is therefore conceivable that the phenomena of double consciousness are simply new character formations, or attempts of the future personality to break through ...Here I am thinking especially of Joan of Arc'.
[43] Ibid., 571.

on spiritual or occult phenomena survived particularly in the work of those philosophers and scientists who were still predisposed, one way or another, to credit the soul with teleological, prophetic or spiritual functions. Gustav Fechner, for instance, whose 'psycho-physics' helped lay down the empirical basis for a future scientific psychology (including the early work of Freud), at the same time developed a complex account of spiritual life which ambiguously straddles the world of the paranormal. In his 1836 work, *The Little Book of Life After Death* (reissued with an introduction by William James in 1904), Fechner observed that 'Man does not often know from whence his thoughts come to him: he is seized with a longing, a foreboding or a joy, which he is quite unable to account for … These are the visitations of spirits, which think and act in him from another centre than his own'.[44] In terms similar to those suggested by Schelling and Schubert thirty years earlier, Fechner describes the influence of such spirits as more manifest in 'abnormal conditions (clairvoyance or mental disorder)' when people only passively receive 'what flows into us from them'.[45] At the end of the century, such studies, which attempted to draw reports of the paranormal into the sphere of scientific psychology, received new impetus via figures such as Theodor Flournoy and C. G. Jung.[46]

The accumulated evidence for parapsychological phenomena, as it was then viewed, also impressed itself on thinkers with a more sceptical bent such as Schopenhauer, whose 'Essay on Spirit Seeing' published in 1851 refers to 'the extremely marvellous and positively incredible feature of somnambulistic clairvoyance, difficult to believe until it was corroborated by the consistency of hundreds of cases of the most trustworthy evidence'.[47] The facts simply had to be accounted for. Justinus Kerner, who perhaps did most to pursue this occult line of investigation, published his *Tales of Contemporary Possession* in 1835, and as late as the 1850s was corresponding with Prince Adalbert of Bavaria who was keen to get news of relations between Greece and Turkey from somnambulistic sources.[48]

---

[44] Gustav Fechner, *Little Book of Life After Death* (New York: Pantheon Books, 1943), 38.

[45] Ibid., 38.

[46] See Theodor Flournoy, *From India to the Planet Mars*, ed. Sonu Shamdasani (Princeton, NJ: Princeton University Press, 1994) and C. G. Jung, 'On the Psychology and Pathology of So-Called Occult Phenomena'.

[47] Arthur Schopenhauer, 'Essay on Spirit Seeing and Everything Connected Therewith', in *Parerga and Paralipomena*, trans. E. F. J. Payne, vol. I (Oxford University Press, 1974), 263.

[48] Franz Pocci (ed.) *Justinus Kerner und sein Münchener Freundeskreis: eine Sammlung von Briefen* (Leipzig: Insel, 1928), 155.

Gaps in the science of life

Interest in such occult, transcendental or magical attributes of the psyche fitted neatly into other aspects of Schelling's investigations of the unconscious. In relation to a science of the primordial past, we saw Schelling and Schubert discussing the role of the ancient oracles and the possibility of a knowledge conveyed in states of ecstatic possession. We also saw that prophetic revelations of a higher identity might come at critical moments in organic existence, hence their keen interest in predictions actually made in pathological states of mind. However, those thinkers who remained attached to specific spiritological theories – either deriving from Swedenborg, or Romantic reinterpretations of gnostic or Christian beliefs – must be distinguished from those for whom the other 'realms' of insight, the beyond that the psyche tapped into, were the obscure dimensions of organic nature or history itself. A useful comparison can be made here with Eschenmayer, who began within the sphere of *Naturphilosophie* and, like Schelling, became increasingly interested in magnetism under the influence of Mesmer, Reil and Schubert. In his *Attempt to Explain the Apparent Magic of Magnetism through Physiological and Psychical Laws* of 1816, Eschenmayer appeared to follow Schelling and Schubert closely in his elaboration of the soul's 'double nature', its possession of a 'day and a night side', reflected in the distinction between consciousness and magnetic sleep.[49] By 1835, however, he was attempting to integrate Schelling's dialectical physics with Christian eschatology and angelology. In *Reflections on Possession and Magic*, he suggested that because force and matter are inversely related, the bodies of demons are without mass, but therefore gifted with immense power. This power is only visible to those who are in thrall to the kingdom of non-nature, just as the 'light-bodies' of guardian angels are visible to somnambulists who have attained the positive extreme of the world of revelation.[50] Eschenmayer's cosmos, with its competing magnetic and angelic forces, is constructed on a middle ground, somewhere between Christianity and *Naturphilosophie*, and draws equally on Schelling's *Ideas* and contemporary reports of somnambulistic visions.

---

[49] C. A. Eschenmayer, *Versuch die scheinbare Magie des thierischen Magnetismus aus physiologischen und psychischen Gesetzen zu erklären* (Vienna: Haas'schen Buchhandlung, 1816), 49.

[50] C. A. Eschenmayer, *Über Besessenseyn und Zauber*, published in Justinus Kerner, *Geschichten Besessener neuerer Zeit. Beobachtungen aus dem Gebiete kako-dämonisch-magnetischer Erscheinungen* (Karlsruhe: G. Braun, 1835).

By comparison, and despite his interest in the functional possibility of clairvoyance, Schelling is little concerned with the content of such visions, nor with maintaining an orthodox religious view of the cosmos. He was more interested in the way in which such acts of super-sensible insight and foresight might structurally confirm the existence of unconscious historical and ontological processes – and therefore confirm the enigmatic grounds on which the notion of freedom could be founded. Ellenberger suggests that Schelling saw in magnetic somnambulism 'a means for establishing a connection between man and the World Soul'.[51] But Schelling's 'world soul' was itself a conceptual stand-in for the 'absolute', or whatever power or process enabled the organic world to produce and reproduce its forms. These as yet obscure processes seemed to require the inference of a kind of organising intelligence which was not in any way objectively apparent. Thus because Schelling's idealism already supposed some kind of ideal presence or process holding nature together, it was predisposed to endow nature with invisible interior aspects and superior prophetic capacities. Hence the willingness to credit somnambulistic reports which, however outlandish, gave some kind of empirical support for this assumed power behind the scenes.

It was the epistemological conundrum surrounding the appearance of teleological organisation in nature as a whole, then, which seemed to encourage this projection of mind on to nature, or at least an ideal purpose and supra-rational or supersensible forces within it. How could one understand a system as complex as that of nature, which was capable of generating stable living forms, but which could not be reduced to any rational description of its processes? This question revisits Kant's careful statement in the *Critique of Judgement* of the *subjective* need to suppose the existence of an intelligent original Being in order to account for the apparent purposefulness of nature – 'which can be thought according to no other principle than that of a designing causality of a highest cause'.[52] This *idealist*, rather than merely occult, case for conceding the existence of parapsychological phenomena exerted a considerable sway over the philosophy of nature throughout the nineteenth century. Schopenhauer's 'Essay on Spirit Seeing' made a specifically Kantian case for assuming such obscure reaches of the soul, though, like Schelling, he transgressed the limits Kant placed on merely supposing such a supersensible organism as a regulative ideal. 'A clairvoyance to which are revealed the hidden, the absent, the remote, and even that

---

[51] Ellenberger, *Discovery*, 159.   [52] Kant, *Critique of Judgement*, 247.

which still slumbers in the womb of the future', loses its incomprehensibility, argued Schopenhauer, if one accepted the Kantian position that the structure of the world is itself a product of subjective consciousness.[53] If the thing-in-itself – 'that which alone is the truly real in all phenomena' – is free from the subject's imposition of temporal and spatial form, and if it thus 'knows no distinction between near and remote, between present, past, and future', then such distinctions might not apply to the unconscious essence of the person.[54] Animal magnetism, second sight, 'dreaming the real' and spirit seeing all indicate, for Schopenhauer, 'a nexus of entities that rests on an order of things entirely different from [objective] nature', and in which changes 'are brought about in a way quite different from that of physical causality with the continuous chain of its links'.[55] The same set of assumptions return in Jung's later work, and reading Schopenhauer (and particularly his reworking of Kant's assumptions) helped Jung to recognise the epistemological gaps in contemporary positivist constructions of psychology.[56]

There was a second conundrum which encouraged nature philosophers in their investigation of the ideal and unconscious dimensions of existence, and this was the issue not of collective coherence, but of where individual life itself comes from: how the embryo is formed within the mother, how it happens that bodies grow and repeat certain complex forms, yet appear to be able to shape themselves by purely immanent or internal means. In the 1815 draft of the *Ages of the World*, Schelling matched his query over the 'secret birthplace of existence' with a more empirical question concerning bodies: 'What happens with the initial formation of the foetus?' He answered himself that, 'everything that occurs around us is, if you will, a constant alchemy'.[57] Birth took its place alongside clairvoyance as an enigmatic attractor for various Romantic and *Naturphilosophische* speculations on the sources of life, for the good reason that biological processes of gestation and birth were still little understood in this period. Reproduction and embryology were consequently laden with metaphysical suppositions, such that for some philosophers and psychologists they epitomised the divine or inscrutable axis of the self's origin. Moreover, within the idealist notion of the 'Idea', the process of thinking and the process of being born had already come to reflect each other. We saw in Chapter 2 that Schelling, like Goethe, had become interested in a theory of archetypes

---

[53] Schopenhauer, 'Essay on Spirit Seeing', 263.
[54] Ibid., 264.   [55] Ibid., 265.
[56] For details of Schopenhauer's influence on Jung, see Shamdasani, *Jung*, 197–200.
[57] Schelling, *The Ages of the World* [1815], 63.

early on in the nineteenth century; the 1807 Oration on 'The Relation between the Plastic Arts and Nature' described the 'idea' as 'the only living power in nature – all else is beingless and empty shadow'.[58] In *Ages of the World*, nature's productivity depends on patterns laid down by secret archetypes: 'These archetypes still stream out from the innermost part of creative nature, just as fresh and alive as they were before time.'[59] Thus while human beings give birth to ideas, ideas themselves give birth to living organisms. 'No entity to this day can be created without the repeated production of its archetype.'[60]

What appeared in an earlier chapter as a purely metaphysical issue, a problem for ontology which sent Schelling back to reconsider the interconnection of truth and existence in Platonic and Aristotelian philosophy, returns here as an empirical issue in Romantic theories of biology. The classical theory of archetypes had partly been reactivated in biology by the seeming absurdities imposed by a strict adherence to mechanical models. This had led to the theory of pre-formationism and *emboîtement* defended by Charles Bonnet in France at the end of the eighteenth century, and still influential in Schelling's day. On the other hand, the popular counter-argument that introduced a simple *Bildungstrieb* or life force governing organic matter, seemed to many, including Schelling, to be itself too supernatural and to add nothing structurally to the enquiry into living processes.[61] In contrast to both of these solutions, the assumption of the agency of an invisible *Urtyp* or *Urbild* (archetype, or archetypal image) which supplied the formative principle behind each new generation of entities, seemed to the nature philosophers to be the lesser of three evils. Invisible relation to an archetype explained how the individual appeared to develop independently of any obvious chain of determination, and yet at the same time could repeat a general pattern. Such an *Urbild* could, in Aristotelian fashion, be insinuated directly into the living organism itself, although idealists argued that archetypes had their ultimate foundation in an absolute mind. Schelling published his brother Karl Schelling's 'Principles for a Future Theory of the Soul' in the *Jahrbücher der Medicin als Wissenschaft*, an article that concerns itself with the functional inter-relation between living organisms, the absolute organism of the whole, and the highest principle of the 'idea'.[62]

---

[58] Schelling, *Plastic Arts*, 11.
[59] Schelling, *Ages*, 161.   [60] Ibid., 162.
[61] See Stefan Goldmann, 'Von der "Lebenskraft" zum "Unbewussten"; Stationen eines Konzeptwandels der Anthropologie', in Buchholz and Gödde, *Macht und Dynamik*.
[62] Karl Schelling, 'Grundsätze zu einer Künftigen Seelenlehre', *Jahrbücher der Medicin als Wissenschaft*, vol. II, 2 (Tübingen: Cotta, 1807), 190–224.

The question of the archetypal origins of individual entities was also energetically pursued at a biological level by Lorenz Oken and Karl von Baer, both credited with being founders of modern embryology. In 1830 Oken demonstrated the cellular origins of tissue and bone, and von Baer discovered the mammalian egg in 1827. According to Oken, 'The ovum is the entire animal in idea, or in design, but not yet in structure.'[63]

The key point is that the epistemological gap within philosophical and scientific concepts of nature – which required that determinist or mechanical processes be supplemented with idealist or spiritological solutions, making use of archetypes and futurity operating through an unconscious – at the same time preserved an ideological space for moral and ontological projections about the foundations of 'individuality'. It is exactly these suppositions of alchemy and prophecy, active in Romantic biological description, that Schelling tended towards when attempting to invert metaphysical notions of structure, so that foundations could both be there but only come to light *after* the assumption of identity by the individual. In Chapter 3 the sense of life's potentiation *towards* foundation found expression, on the one hand, in terms of a sublime sparkle or gleam of vitality which Schelling linked to the Böhmeian term, *Tinktur*. On the other hand, Schelling hypothesised a divine and ideal previewing of nature's ectypes by the absolute, which knowledge was then buried unconsciously within nature. We now see that these two counter-rational functions which Schelling attributes to the unconscious (a special kind of substance, and a special kind of causal-temporal structure) helped to create a guiding thread for the post-idealist scientific understanding of nature. They are the two forms which help sustain a belief in nature's profound intelligibility, in the face of its structural incomprehensibility.

However, this incomprehension of nature itself, as I have wanted to show throughout this book, has a moral and ontological role to play. It is only by virtue of such a gap in knowledge that Schelling could sustain, at one and the same time, the notion of absolute foundations *and* conceptualise the freedom of individual emergence and self-determination. One sees this in the *Ages of the World* in Schelling's regard for the individual who is able to break loose 'from everything that happens

---

[63] Lorenz Oken, *The Elements of Physiophilosophy*, trans. Alfred Tulk (London: Ray Society, 1847). 483. As Elizabeth Gasking has noted, 'The Romantics themselves might have had little effect on biology, but the philosophers of the period' – and here she mentions Fichte, Schelling and Hegel – 'had a profound effect on the science'. *Investigations into Generation 1651–1828* (London: Hutchinson, 1967), 149.

to him and actively oppose it', while adhering to the presentiment that 'one organism lies hidden deep in time and encompasses even the smallest of things'.[64] This itself repeats the paradox which occupied Schelling at the end of the *System of Transcendental Idealism*, when the philosopher finds himself confronted by the contradictory concepts of an absolute intelligence, common to all subjects, and a freely determining subjectivity which cannot consist in 'conformity to law'.[65] The only way Schelling can assimilate these is to hypothesise an 'eternal unknown' which is 'at once the ground of lawfulness in freedom, and of freedom in the lawfulness of the object'.[66] We are returned once more to Fichte's obscure formulation of the will which attempts to hold individuality, universality and freedom together in a single medium of connection. But it is in this *naturalised* and *historicised* version of Schelling's that the presentiment will live on in the nineteenth century. Indeed, it is this very paragraph from the *System of Transcendental Idealism* that Eduard von Hartmann singled out for special praise in his Introductory remarks to the *Philosophy of the Unconscious* of 1868, commenting on the 'purity and depth' with which Schelling 'had seized the notion of the unconscious'.[67]

The ontological structure of nature, then, must remain awkwardly uncoupled – its connectives addressed now in terms of a blindly productive divine spark of life in matter, now in terms of a buried image which is only revealed *after* the event. In each case, the world of life 'never [becomes] an object'.[68] There is a remarkable concurrence here between the life sciences, struggling to find structural metaphors to fill real epistemological gaps, and the philosophers of individuality who, for their part, were searching for an irreducible gap in the systems of science into which they could project their unimaginable syntheses of freedom and determination. This convergence on the mysterious portions of life and soul allowed scientists with an idealist bent to find support for their attempted completion of a science of existence, and the philosophers of freedom to give their idealisations of the self a basis in nature. If these claims that nature is governed by a prophetic structure appear to hover between parapsychological assertions and a metaphorical framework for the study of organic life processes, what also kept such claims in this particular form (tied to principles of obscurity and unconsciousness) was the attempt to construe a plausible science of individuality

---

[64] Schelling, *Ages*, 123.
[65] Schelling, *System*, 208.   [66] Ibid., 209.
[67] Hartmann, *Philosophy of the Unconscious*, 25.
[68] Schelling, *System*, 209.

itself – to tie the metaphysics of individual origins, and the empirical organic development of bodies, together.[69] It is precisely towards such gaps in the theory of knowledge that the assumption of individuality had to gravitate: 'There always remains a residual obscurity' within the striving for clarity over life, argued Schelling in the Stuttgart Seminars, just as later Freud will acknowledge a limit to all dream interpretation, 'beneath which lies the Unknown'.[70]

C. G. Carus and the future of the Romantic psyche

The psychologists and anthropologists emerging from Schelling's circle of influence continue to define the psyche with reference to these two liminal forms of manifestation: the psyche as an obscure developmental energy, or as the medium through which unconscious archetypes are symbolised. For this reason, it is instructive to examine how the theoretical understanding of psychic life and unconsciousness was carried forwards and codified in the work of mid-century figures such as C. G. Carus, to whom Ellenberger attributes 'the first attempt to give a complete and objective theory on unconscious psychological life'.[71] Pursuing an early interest in both medicine and the science of nature, Carus emerged with a doctorate from the university of Leipzig in 1811 and moved to Dresden, where he took up a position as Professor of Gynaecology and director of the university obstetrical clinic in 1814 (he was later to become court physician to the King of Saxony). At this time, Hoffmann was moving to Dresden, Schubert had left and was working on the symbolism of dreams, and Schelling was in the process of redrafting the *Ages of the World*. As well as being a proficient landscape painter in the Romantic mould of Caspar David Friedrich (also based in Dresden), Carus explored the interface between life and unconsciousness in a series of works from *Lectures on Psychology* (1831) to *Psyche: on the Development of the Soul* (1846), *On Magnetism* (1857) and *Nature and Idea* (1861). Though not directly a pupil of Schelling's, Carus

---

[69] It is telling that a rift emerged in the field of embryology itself around the issue of system versus individuality and particularity – that is to say, at the applied end of these speculations on life, the irresolvable oscillation over freedom and determinism still makes itself felt. The split was between Oken, whose account of ontogeny centred on the repetition of the adult forms of lower species (life organised through the order of the past) and von Baer, for whom the history of the development of the individual was the history of its increasing individuality. See Stephen Jay Gould, *Ontogeny and Phylogeny* (Boston, MA: Harvard University Press: 1977), 7.

[70] Schelling, 'Stuttgart Seminars', 207; S. Freud, *The Interpretation of Dreams*, trans. Joyce Crick (Oxford University Press, 1999), 341.

[71] Ellenberger, *Discovery*, 207.

acknowledged him, along with Kant, as one of the two major influences on his development. Schelling was in fact an influence both on Carus the painter and Carus the physiological researcher – with respect to both aesthetics and natural science, Schelling's *Naturphilosophie* awakened in him 'the specific thought of a world soul', and the conviction that life formed a 'single, infinite, organic whole'.[72]

Ironically, Carus saw himself as diverging from Schelling because the philosopher was associated in his mind with that early goal of the *Naturphilosophie*, of bringing nature to completion in a conscious theoretical system. In contrast, Carus asserted that the key to an understanding of the conscious life of the soul 'lies in the sphere of the unconscious' and as such the route to a genuine psychology 'can only be found there'.[73] But of course, it is precisely here that he follows in Schelling's footsteps, and Carus' theories of the 1840s, as we shall see, very much repeat the pattern of assumptions made in the *Ages of the World*. First of all, like Schelling in the middle period of his work, Carus eschewed the attempt to grasp the whole of nature as a 'system'; instead he devoted his attention to the more temporalised question of origins. He sought a genetic method which set out 'to really begin with the beginning', with the 'first obscure, vague, uncertain movements of the spirit in our interior'.[74] He also recognised a principle which 'guides the world mass in its pathways', and which was both divine and obscure.[75] In line with Schelling's development of new structural figures, Carus conceived empirical existence in terms of ideal and material facets, neither of which could be represented as systems or objects. On the one hand, he described the principle that generates the development of the body from embryo to maturity as an unconscious, productive force – an ever-flowing spring or 'unconscious radiation'.[76] On the other hand, he claimed that this development is the work of the 'divine' in the form of 'the idea or the primordial image' which provides the primary basis of individual life.[77] These are essentially the same two versions of that unconscious principle which Schelling intimated throughout the *Ages of the World* – sometimes as a sublime power, sometimes as a secret foreknowledge. As with Schelling, Carus conceives the psyche in such a way that, rather than oscillating between a world of objects and a world

[72] C. G. Carus, *Denkwürdigkeiten aus Europa* (Hamburg: Schröder, 1963), 77, 37.
[73] Carus, *Psyche*, 12.
[74] C. G. Carus in his 'Lectures on Psychology' held Winter 1829–30 in Dresden, cited in Jutta Müller-Tamm, *Kunst als Gipfel der Wissenschaft: Ästhetische und Wissenschaftliche Weltaneignung bei Carl Gustav Carus* (Berlin: Walter de Gruyter, 1995), 64.
[75] Carus, *Denkwürdigkeiten*, 155.
[76] Carus, *Psyche*, 15.   [77] Ibid., 8.

of purposes in the self, he writes in terms of a single principle of unconscious life, the formative axis equally of the body's development and the soul's identity, both of which elude full structural representation.

The enigmatic form of psychical representation connects once more with the way individuality is conceived. For Carus, 'if we want to find the *primary cause* for our individuality' we must 'go back into the history of the idea of our being'.[78] As in the *Ages of the World*, the return to the beginning and the tracing of development can no longer be construed as a simple causal relation from past to present. Instead, the temporal structure of individuals can only be conveyed as a set of winding ellipses over connection, through which subjects are able to return on themselves and to ascribe to themselves the obscurity of an origin through which they are *causa sui*. Carus argued that all living entities 'contain something hidden which refers back to something past, something that has been before, and which yet suggests further development, something in the future'.[79] Schelling and Schubert had sought to give subjective identity some kind of material form, but this was approached through dimensions of latency, possibility and unconsciousness. So for Carus, the relation between past and future indicates powers 'of remembrance and foresight' which 'assert themselves in the region of unconscious life'.[80] In a compound statement which beautifully asserts a determinism in nature, but also an unconscious core to such processes, Carus argues that 'This force, innate in the divine principle of the soul, *absolutely dominates and pervades* matter' – however, it creates 'while still completely absorbed in itself, as if dreaming, or thinking in shapes, because it cannot yet think in concepts'.[81] The model subverts any connotation of dependency and mirrors exactly Schelling's absolute in a state of *Ohnmächtigkeit*: it dominates matter, and yet appears not as a ruthless enchainment of consequences, but as a form of dreaming, as a withdrawal, a lack of intent or control.

Given this passive condition of the absolute, it remains for entities to claim their identities for themselves. Such notions of a 'dreaming power' provoke connections once more with magnetism and somnambulism. The empiricist who analyses development with the greatest microscopic precision, Carus suggests, will necessarily be led to concede the magic of nature when he observes the effects of magnetism on the 'intimating or self-clairvoyant power of the unconscious in the deeps of our soul, or on

---

[78] Ibid., 14.
[79] Ibid., 22. Compare Freud's similar observation in 'Creative Writers and Day-Dreaming', *SE*, vol. IX, 148.
[80] Carus, *Psyche*, 23.   [81] Ibid., 29. My italics.

the sympathetic effects of certain outer events in the sickly conditions of the organism'.[82] Again, as with Schelling, this crediting of animal magnetism and clairvoyance is embedded within a much wider theoretical assertion about a nature whose operations do not reflect consciousness, and whose determining structures – the structures of the unconscious itself – escape being bound by the 'chains of determination' so central to eighteenth-century materialist and rationalist assumptions.

The final point here is that, although the impulse behind Carus' research was medical, psychological and scientific, the assumptions he makes about unconscious structures and processes are equally the site of a moral identification of freedom. In Schelling we might say that the relationship was reversed: it was the pursuit of an ontology that would allow for self-determination that led him to theorise the unconscious and to co-ordinate this idea with his previous work on nature and his new speculations on the historical. But if Schelling laboured to convert idealism into a form in which it could generate a foundational science of the individual, the structures he developed and the principle of unconsciousness, once incorporated into a model of the psyche, laid the basis for an empirical science of the autonomous person. As with Schelling, the unconscious for Carus takes on a kind of axiological priority. It always supervenes on the system of knowledge: 'a perfect understanding of nature through scientific means is impossible, and a gap must always remain'; 'the realm of the wondrous, the magical, will never be completely superseded'.[83] Carus is even led to repeat the uncanny threat that Schelling lodges at the end of the *Ages of the World* – 'woe to the explorer who now no longer feels any horror before this originally deeply-veiled Isis'.[84] Into the obscurity of this gap in knowledge, and in the representation of nature, Carus inserted the same assumptions about individual autonomy: the psyche, whether conceived as life force or soul, 'must always and in all of its forms be self-moving, not moved by outside factors'. It must 'be something individual', and contain 'the *primary cause* for our individuality'.[85] In his most explicit formulation, the unconscious is in itself 'precisely our ownmost [*eigenste*] and most genuine nature'.[86] This is so even though 'our unconscious life is affected by all humanity, by the life of the earth and by the universe, for it is definitely an integral part of that totality';[87] even though, 'In the unconscious, the general existence of the world continues to flow on

[82] Carus, *Denkwürdigkeiten*, 161.
[83] Carus, *Psyche*, 11; Carus, *Denkwürdigkeiten*, 152.
[84] Carus, *Denkwürdigkeiten*, 157.
[85] Carus, *Psyche*, 6, 14.   [86] Carus, *Denkwürdigkeiten*, 153.
[87] Carus, *Psyche*, 63.

without interruption; all the threads linking the individual to the whole remain unbroken.'[88] Exactly as in Schelling's work, the unconscious allows for the simultaneous assumption of autonomous individuality and of a complex and organised totality.

The psyche, for both authors, is not merely an intermediary between corporeality and mind. It is more essentially a mediator between determination and freedom – between the ethical and psychological need to think of oneself as securely founded, but also as self-creating and free. Seemingly, the psyche has been given an empirical form, and yet this is an empiricism in which structural laws perform odd twists of direction or become necessarily unconscious at key moments. What keeps the psyche in place is this need to conceive of the self as *causa sui*, and this wrests all the representation of interconnection out of joint. This way of apprehending the integrity of the individual relates back to that earliest proposition of the 'Oldest System Programme of German Idealism' – 'The first Idea is naturally the notion of *my self* as an absolutely free being'[89] – and to Schelling's question: 'what is the perfection of a thing? Nought else but the creative life in it – its power of asserting its own individuality.'[90] It also links to the theory of liberalism, to Mill's interest in 'individuality of power' and 'the inward forces which make [human nature] a living thing',[91] as much as to Tocqueville's individuals who 'form the habit of thinking of themselves in isolation and imagine that their whole destiny is in their hands'.[92] Finally, it is present in more modern apprehensions of individuality, whether as Taylor's ethics of authenticity, Lukes' 'autonomy, privacy and self-development', or Lacan's necessary 'delusional discourse' affirming man's 'irreducible autonomy as an individual, as individual existence'.[93]

With the foundation of the self through the unconscious, everything apparently falls into place. The individual is once more able to be at home within itself, paradoxically through the *unheimliche* aspects of its own psyche, which is out of place in relation to a world of discrete and conditioned objects. In the chapter on metaphysics we saw how the search for an ontology which could ground the individual without effacing it led Schelling towards a principle of unconsciousness and the self-effacement of the absolute itself. Since then we have seen how this unconscious was itself insinuated into theoretical descriptions of history and nature – as the past, as the secret, as the obscure origin. Now we

---

[88] Ibid., 62.   [89] Bowie, *Aesthetics and Subjectivity*, 265.
[90] Schelling, *Plastic Arts*, 4.
[91] Mill, 'Liberalism', 186, 188.
[92] Tocqueville, *Democracy*, 508.
[93] Lukes, *Individualism*, 125; Lacan, *Psychoses*, 133.

find that these same principles mediate the structure of the psyche. It is the unconscious foundations of the psyche (unconscious with respect to its beginning, and unconscious with respect to its nature) that allow for an account of the self to emerge in which the person can accommodate the notion of its 'secret birthplace', its *own* existence. 'Secret birthplace' was the very term we saw Schelling pressing earlier as a metaphysical issue – looking for the beginning, as Habermas suggested, for somewhere to take root. With the elaboration of the psyche, we find that this requisite principle of secrecy is able to merge itself into the phenomenon of forgetting – the unrecollected past that the self trails behind it, as its history. Schelling's lectures on modern philosophy of 1827 express this shift very clearly:

> Admittedly now, as the I becomes an *individual* I ... having arrived, then, at the "I am", with which its individual life begins, it does not remember the path any more which it has covered so far, for since consciousness only arrives at the end of this path, it must have travelled this road to consciousness itself unconsciously and without knowing it.[94]

Amnesia, here, appears casually as a contingent feature of development, a by-product of the journey undergone from the past to the present of the individual. But we know that the order of justification is in fact the reverse. Schelling has laboured to centre identity on that obscure origin, precisely so that the self can grasp itself as an individual, so that it can begin itself: '*Ich beginne*', commences one of the earliest sets of notes for the *Ages of the World*.[95] As the I becomes an *individual*, it *must* dissemble the logic of its own existence.

This form of self-grasping, grounded in the unconscious dimensions of identity, pervades a certain kind of post-Romantic form of self-description, which is intent on establishing and preserving the credentials of individuality. The person now accounts for himself or herself *from the beginning*, but it is precisely at the beginning that narratives meet with a certain inalienable obscurity, at the furthermost horizon of self-recollection. G. H. Schubert, contemplating this anterior darkness in his autobiography – whose very title, *The Gleanings of a Former, the Anticipations of a Future Life*, reflects the characteristic ellipsis in his thought around the 'present' – writes of 'the buried [*verborgene*] beginning' as well as 'the mysterious [*geheimnisvollen*] beginning of human life'.[96] For Schubert, the apparent 'has everywhere emerged

---

[94] Schelling, *On the History of Modern Philosophy* (Cambridge University Press, 1994), 110.

[95] Schelling, *Urfassungen*, 187.   [96] Schubert, *Der Erwerb*, vol. I, 21.

from a non-apparent, the visible course of life from an invisible beginning, and as the beginning of our life emerges from the darkness, so it runs off again at the end into the darkness of a world that does not appear to the senses'.[97]

The empirical mysteries of birth and the ontological mystery of being *causa sui* here shade imperceptibly into each other – and both are merged with a more generic language of oblivion, of unconscious pasts. We have met this *verborgene* content before as a general condition of Schubert's understanding of both history and the psyche; but here these temporal and internal displacements are focused specifically on his own enigmatic origins as a person. Such generalised wonder about the origins of life seems uncontroversial in the context of a nineteenth-century autobiographical account. Why shouldn't the self apprehend the anterior contexts of its life only vaguely or obscurely? However, the problem of the person's existence and the memory of its practical beginnings are, as we have seen, interlinked with the conceptual problem of granting significant life to 'individuality' itself – the problem of representing or legitimating the 'singular' within the order of knowledge. Such accounts are equally identifications of the autonomous self. In this light, the gravitation of terms towards unconsciousness is structurally important.

To glance for a moment at transcendentalism in America, another key site in the transmission of German idealism, Romanticism and *Naturphilosophie* in the middle of the nineteenth century, it is interesting to compare some of Emerson's statements on the soul with Schelling's, not the least because Emerson possessed a manuscript of James Elliott Cabot's unpublished translation of Schelling's essay on *Human Freedom* in the mid 1840s.[98] For Emerson, writing in 1845, 'The philosophy we want is one of fluxions and mobility ... Any angular dogmatic theory would be rent to chips & splinters in this storm of many elements.' Rather than the system, 'The form of man, the soul of man must be the type of our scheme.'[99] The soul itself is the basis from which the philosopher anchors the enigmatic structure of identity. And how should one think this structure? '[A]ll philosophy begins from Nox & Chaos, the Ground or Abyss which Schelling so celebrates. And in every man we require a bit of night, of chaos, of

---

[97] Ibid., 21.

[98] Ralph Waldo Emerson, *The Journals and Miscellaneous Notebooks of Ralph Waldo Emerson*, Ralph H. Orth and Alfred R. Ferguson (eds.) vol. IX 1843–47 (Cambridge, MA: Harvard University Press, 1971), 101.

[99] Ibid., 222–3.

Abgrund, as the spring of a watch turns best on a diamond.'[100] The 'abyss' of structure now substitutes for the perfection of mechanism in this post-eighteenth-century world.

The same attraction to origins and unconsciousness as the basis for an ontology of human being will lead the philosophers of German existentialism to revalue Schelling's contribution to philosophy in the twentieth century. We have already seen how Heidegger acknowledges a debt to Schelling, but for Karl Jaspers, too, Schelling provided a model in that he 'forces us to release ourselves from the quotidian commonplaces, demands to penetrate through the finite to the infinite'.[101] This release from the quotidian is a condition opened up by the philosophy of history itself – 'Engrossment in the specifically historical brings the enigma [*Geheimnis*] of the unique to more lucid consciousness'[102] – but it is also the specific goal of Jaspers' philosophy of existence, which aims to redeem the ontological fortunes of men who 'could be themselves' but instead woke up in the pitiless atmosphere of modernity 'in which every individual was sacrificed as individual' and in which there reigned a 'universal interchangeability of everything and everyone, where no one seemed to exist any longer as himself'.[103] Jaspers will weave a new ontology of the individual into his apprehension of the historical basis of life precisely by representing the latter as infinitely elusive: 'Our consciousness is borne by the unconscious' which is 'endlessly ambiguous in its implications.'[104] As Richard F. Grabau comments in his Preface to Jaspers' *Philosophy of Existence*, 'Jaspers comes to the realisation that both the thinker and reality are more than what can be known about them in objective terms.'[105] The search for origins thus enjoins a double task of historical- and self-realisation: 'to catch sight of reality at its origin and to grasp it through the way in which I, in thought, deal with myself – in inner action'.[106] At the same time, as with Schelling and Carus, the notion of the obscure origin connects one to a higher whole. It 'imports the satisfactions of affinity in the midst of the alien, and of the community of the human running through all peoples'.[107]

---

[100] Ibid., 222.   [101] Karl Jaspers, *Schelling*, 342.
[102] Karl Jaspers, *The Origin and Goal of History* (New Haven, CT: Yale University Press, 1953), 267.
[103] Karl Jaspers, *The Philosophy of Existence* (Philadelphia, PA: University of Pennsylvania Press, 1971), 4.
[104] Jaspers, *Schelling*, 274.
[105] Jaspers, *The Philosophy of Existence*, xiv.
[106] Jaspers, Ibid., 3.   [107] Jaspers, *Origin*, 269–70.

Breaks in the chain of life: from reproduction to deconstruction

I have traced the intellectual futures of Schelling's principle of the unconscious as an obscurity or vagueness about origins, which paradoxically allows for claims about the autonomy of the individual to emerge. However, there is another way of reviewing the distance travelled from the Fichtean I to the Schellingian unconscious, and this concerns the transformation wrought upon the simple figure of the chain. The metaphor of the chain has provided its own link through these shifting contexts in which individuality is asserted against the apprehension of structure. In *The Vocation of Man*, Fichte found that 'an unbroken chain of appearances' annihilated the possibility of freedom in the self.[108] For Tocqueville, 'Aristocracy links everybody, from peasant to king, in one long chain', but democracy 'breaks the chain and frees each link'.[109] In a psychotherapeutic context, Schelling argued that states of unconsciousness free the individual 'from the chain of the whole' re-establishing it in its 'integrity and originality'.[110] Likewise, Schopenhauer finds in animal magnetism an indication of an order of things entirely different from 'physical causality with the continuous chain of its links',[111] while Carus suggests that the unconscious allows 'all the threads linking the individual to the whole' to remain 'unbroken'.[112]

If the self, for Schelling, finds its *own* origin by being released from a chain of events, then the inception of the unconscious, the birth of the individual, can also be figured in this way – not just as an obscure horizon of recollection, but equally as a literal *disconnection* in the order of reality. We have seen a hint of this approach in Schubert's representation of copulation as a moment of rupture, even of death, for some organisms. It is at the point where the individual is conceived (both literally and mentally) that the chain of life must be represented as broken. Schubert articulates this moment as a point of incandescence, a point at which the material world is transfigured into the psychic, but for Schelling the same moment is portrayed as a literal gap in occurrence. In human reproduction, it seems, the very question of connection and disconnection, enchainment and freedom, is acted out in an elaborate

[108] Fichte, *Vocation*, 10.   [109] Tocqueville, *Democracy*, 508.
[110] Ibid., 160.
[111] Schopenhauer, 'Essay on Spirit Seeing', 265.
[112] Carus, *Psyche*, 62.

existential masque. In the *Ages of the World*, the 'sudden and momentary suspension of that external exponent' in copulation releases a feeling of bliss in the individual.[113] At the same time, 'There is a disruption
of all forces, a relaxation of all links, and being is posited outside itself.
It is as if the external link had momentarily been abolished.'[114] In the
exact moment that one self couples with another to produce a new individual, the bonds sustaining subjectivity in its rational form are felt to
collapse. It is the break that Schelling emphasises, not the bond – 'connect I must but I cannot connect with another being' as Fichte had
originally asserted.

Elsewhere on the same page Schelling represents the birth of the
individual in an aporetic figure of enchainment itself, working his own
transformation on the eighteenth-century models of *Verkettung* and
Verknüpfung: 'It is as if a guiding connection and a chain of mutually independent elements were established whereby the first element
becomes capable of effecting the last, just as the father undeniably
begets [*einzeugt*] the character and disposition of the child.'[115] For once,
the father undeniably begets the disposition of the child; and yet his
influence is a 'guiding connection' operating via a chain of 'mutually
independent elements'. Can there be such a thing? However, as he
develops the thought, Schelling gives increasing emphasis to the breaks
in the chain – the states of detachment. In a passage, ingenious for
the way in which it combines and resolves different levels of reference
(metaphysical, temporal and genetic) in a single figure of relationship,
Schelling asserts that:

Every act of generation occurring in nature marks a return to a moment of the
past, a moment that is allowed for an instant to enter the present time as an
alienated (re)appearance. For, since time commences absolutely in each living thing, and since at the beginning of each life time is connected to eternity
anew, then an eternity must immediately precede each life.[116]

Here the notional line of paternity gives way to both an absolute spacing – the intervention of eternity itself – and the notion of a return. We
are reminded of Schelling's remark, 'we simply cannot think about this
in terms of becoming or beginning *out of some preceding state of affairs*'.[117]
Schubert, at times, reaches a similar insight by drawing on the motif
of a series of magnets in which the negative pole of one magnet stands
in relation to the positive pole of the next in the series – a form of connection that includes the inversion of powers between one term and the

---

[113] Schelling, *Ages*, 162.   [114] Ibid., 162.
[115] Ibid., 162.   [116] Ibid., 162.   [117] Ibid., 137.

next;[118] likewise Schelling depicts natural history as 'the series in which each term obscures its predecessor'.[119]

We have encountered this point before, but from a different angle. At the end of Chapter 3 on Schelling's metaphysics we found that he explored figures of generative process and allegories of procreation in order to reconceive the philosophical representation of a metaphysical cause. The dialectical passage of divinity from father (absolute) to mother (nature) – where the mother is made to stand for a point of non-being, or passivity – broke up the notion of a single line of determination and helped detach the concept of individuality from its foundation in the absolute. Here, however, the relations are somewhat reversed: Schelling represents the empirical process of human reproduction itself via the trope of broken chains of logic. Again, as with the metaphors of obscurity, these tropes appear in more recent philosophical contexts, amongst thinkers working between deconstruction and post-Heideggerian philosophy. Jean-Luc Nancy, for example, uses a similar strategy to represent freedom and structure in *The Experience of Freedom*, writing of 'the passage or transfer of existence' as a 'spacing of time', and a time which is opened 'onto a free space at the heart of which freedom can exist'.[120] He likewise posits an existence which 'affirms and abandons itself in a single gesture', and an 'origin removed from every logic of origin'.[121] Later in the same work, Nancy avoids characterising the phenomenon of freedom as either 'individual or collective' by theorising instead a foundational 'partitioning of origin' within the ontology of human identity whereby 'singularities space apart and space their being-in-common'. He further describes this as 'an entire link of unlinking, a fabric without weave or weaver'.[122] In an article co-written with Philippe Lacoue-Labarthe, 'The Unconscious is Destructured like an Affect', Nancy also writes of that which in Freud resists 'a logic of the identity-of-subject' and which leads to '"dissociation": the identificatory tie of an untying in which identity withdraws'.[123] Interestingly, 'dissociation', the term used by Pierre Janet to describe a nervous weakness in the mind, leading to the separation of aspects of the mental life

---

[118] Schubert, *Views of the Nightside*, 322.

[119] Schelling, *Ages*, 121.

[120] Jean-Luc Nancy, *The Experience of Freedom* (Stanford, CA: Stanford University Press, 1993), 18–19.

[121] Nancy, *Experience*, 10, 13.

[122] Ibid, 74. See also Howard Caygill, 'The Shared World – Philosophy, Violence, Freedom', in Darren Sheppard, Simon Sparks, Colin Thomas (eds.), *On Jean-Luc Nancy* (London: Routledge, 1997).

[123] Philippe Lacoue-Labarthe and Jean-Luc Nancy, 'The Unconscious is Destructured like an Affect', *Stanford Literary Review*, 6, 2 (Fall 1989), 192.

of a person, is here reclaimed as an ontological figure, one central to the theorisation of autonomy. The authors further describe how their own work on psychoanalysis has been drawn to the difficulties of this 'sociality', and its ontologico-political implication, which is more 'originary' than any 'primitive sociality'.[124]

One is already close here to those figures which Derrida will extract from Freud as the centrepiece of an ontology which supposedly resists ontological formulation. Freud alludes in the *Interpretation of Dreams* to that limit point of interpretation – the impenetrable navel of the dream – as 'the place of a *tie*, a knot-scar that keeps the memory of a cut and even of a severed thread at birth'.[125] Derrida wonders here 'how the cut can tie a knot or, inversely, how the link can be interruption of itself',[126] and suggests that analysis itself represents an act of 'tying and untying' the link.[127] As with Schelling, the metaphysics of identity, the constitution of knowledge, and the literal birth of the person, are folded into a single figure which seeks to establish the aporetic 'grounds' of the individual as an oxymoronic broken tie or disconnected chain.

At one point in his discussion of the Freudian unconscious in Seminar XI, Lacan asks if 'the *one*' is anterior to 'discontinuity', and ventures: 'I do not think so', for he has learned that the need for a 'closed one' is 'a mirage to which is attached the reference to the enveloping psyche, a sort of double of the organism in which this false unity is thought to reside'.[128] Instead, discontinuity 'is the essential form in which the unconscious first appears to us as a phenomenon', a 'discontinuity, in which something is manifested as a vacillation'.[129] Referring back to Schelling's own origination of an unconscious principle, one could argue that the opaque detachment of a psychic interior (the obscure representative of the essence of the self) and the broken chain which also represents the self's point of origin (the interruption of a network of relations) are both involved in the *same* attempt to release individuality from the restraints of structure, while endowing the self with a kind of grounding objectivity, law or cause. The aporia which Schelling sought to introduce into the notion of connectedness, and the enigmatic position occupied by the origin of the self in autobiographical recollection, reflect and relate to each other as a crisis in self-representation – but Schelling managed to incorporate both of these into psychical accounts

---

[124] Ibid., 192.
[125] Jacques Derrida, *Resistances of Psychoanalysis* (Stanford, CA: Stanford University Press, 1998), 11.
[126] Ibid., 12.   [127] Ibid., 11.
[128] Jacques Lacan, *The Four Fundamental Concepts*, 26.
[129] Ibid., 25.

of selfhood, whether as a phenomenology of obscurity and forgetting, or as a structural ellipsis in the very nature of the psyche. This is not to say, of course, that Schelling was the *only* person initiating such discourses of the 'obscure' or unconscious self in this period of late Romanticism in Germany, but he was the only one who had explained the theoretical reasons for such descriptions, and who argued that such descriptions were structurally necessary, in a way that could be philosophically underpinned. Both these kinds of discourses – that of ontological disconnection, and that of obscurity and oblivion – are played out in that founding moment of unconsciousness at the end of the *Ages of the World*, and both indicate the future importance of Schelling's insights here with respect to modern theories of the individual.

Coda: from the psyche to the psychoanalytic

These brief glimpses of different kinds of returns of the unconscious demonstrate the way in which it is continually bound into the theorisation of individuality and autonomy in modernity (whether this is in Carus, Emerson, Jaspers, Lacan or Nancy). They are included here as a way of consolidating a sense of one of its key ideological functions. It is through the unconscious that aspects of psychology, or the theory of the soul (the inner self), converge with issues in ontology – the autonomy of the self, its freedom of self-development, its individuality. These snapshots of future theory are not in themselves intended to map out the history of the unconscious. As suggested in the Introduction, the unconscious takes on many forms throughout the nineteenth century – in philosophy, psychiatry and neurology, aesthetics, theories of history, metaphysics, religion and theosophy. Many different strands of its influence, its adoption and redescription, particularly in the latter half of the century, would have to be pieced together in order to provide such a history. If one were to attempt to track the concept forwards in German intellectual life from the time of Schelling, Schopenhauer and Herbart, then the most significant intermediaries, before one reaches the reformulation of the concept in modern psychology, would be first of all Carus in the 1840s, and then von Hartmann and Nietzsche in the last decades of the century, of whom only the first two could be said to explore the concept in a systematic way. Von Hartmann aimed explicitly to synthesise the theories of Schelling, Schopenhauer and Carus, and to connect them with Darwin and Haeckel's work on evolution. However, the final part of this book will focus not on the further reaches of Schelling's influence in the nineteenth century and beyond. Instead I want to examine how the particular constellation of problems we have been tracing in his work relates to the emergence of specifically psychoanalytic ideas in the work of Freud. I am interested not so much in 'lines of influence', but in the ideological function of the concept of the unconscious, and the issues it raises concerning individuality and autonomy.

Here a certain amount of caution must be exercised. An unconscious that is structurally wedded to the conscious; the ontological tension between remembrance and forgetting; a principle of repression; the enigma surrounding the birth of the individual; a conflictual tension in the absolute, drawing on a gendered dualism of paternal spirit and maternal ground; desire as a motor for change; the development of the self through states of crisis and transfiguration; the concern with origins and the trauma of the past; the attempt to understand the truth of the self through the experience of dreaming and magnetic sleep: all these are present in the *Ages of the World*, and all of them figure in early psychoanalytic theory in the twentieth century, and yet one could not call the *Ages of the World* a 'psychoanalytic' text. First of all, because Schelling, despite his avowed interest in medicine and contemporary psychiatric literature, is primarily a philosopher and not a psychologist. But, secondly, because an approach to subjective identity that centres on individual development and psychology is precisely not self-evident for him. As much as individuality and the knowledge of one's freedom is constantly invoked, the labour of the *Ages of the World* is to transfigure metaphysical structures so that they can somehow become internalised – so that a person can carry the grounds of their identity (as *philosophically* conceived) within themselves, as *their* basis, *their* origin or repressed past: 'to have the beginning in oneself'.[130] But the means towards this internalisation of foundations is not self-evident, nor can Schelling simply assume that people exist de facto as individuals, with their own autonomous identities and psychologies. For Schelling, that possibility can only be accomplished by performing some kind of perspectival negation on the absolute itself. The 'unconscious' would become, by the end of the nineteenth century, one of the tools through which that idea of individuality was asserted. But at the time at which Schelling was writing, the modern and liberal idea of the individual was still in its nascent stage.

In contrast, then, to the concern of psychoanalysis with the traumatic constituents of individual identity, Schelling was faced with the difficulty of introducing trauma into the reigning concepts of the absolute and the universal. Trauma, imported into such transcendental

---

[130] Schelling, *Philosophische Entwürfe*, 103.

principles of order, would allow the non-universal agent to speak as if it were secretly, and absolutely, its own agent. It was the means necessary to conceive of the independence of the individual who had been as yet only fraily constituted in the shadow of metaphysical cosmologies. Within the worlds theorised by Spinoza and Leibniz, which had exerted such dominion over the German imagination, all power was imaginatively devolved to a single central point – whether this was the unique and singular substance of God,[131] or a God which is alone 'the primary Unity, or original simple substance, from which all monads, created and derived, are produced'.[132]

Schelling's solution attempted both to hold on to the notion of a meaningful, or intelligently guided totality, and wholly inverted the relations between knowledge and individuality, paving the way for the foundational assertions of existentialism. In fact, in a double *coup*, Schelling was already toying with the way in which the aporias of individual existence (its origins, its unconsciousness) could come to ground the philosophical description of the nature of connection. Knowledge, and the representation of determinism through which the whole is conceived in the older forms of philosophical rationalism, is superseded by the idea of an unconscious foundation of life, buried within the realm of the actual. At the same time, the individual learns to pose the question of its essential freedom *and* groundedness towards the horizon of its own unconscious basis. It is no surprise then that existentialism and poststructuralism have continually crossed paths and solicited each other's support on the ground of the 'unconscious', nor that they should have provided a constant accompaniment to this investigation of unconsciousness in Schelling. Each shares a motivation against the system and towards individuality; each tries to find an aporetic philosophical form with which to express the ontology of the individual; and key figures for each tradition (Jaspers, Heidegger, Žižek) have consciously read and returned to the work of Schelling himself.

In contrast to Foucault, I would argue that the 'shadow' cast by man does not emerge simply out of the epistemological transition from 'knowledge' to 'man' as object of representation;[133] rather man and the unconscious emerge as a condition of re-imagining the independence of the individual in relation to both structures of knowledge and structures of social dependency. The conditions for articulating this freedom are

---

[131] Spinoza, corollary 2 of Proposition 14, *The Ethics*, 10.
[132] Leibniz, *Monadology*, in *Philosophical Writings*, 186.
[133] See discussion in the Introduction to this book and Foucault, *The Order of Things*, 326.

gradually integrated – naturalised, almost – within the empirical and theoretical description of the psyche in the nineteenth century. At the same time as metaphysics has been drawn towards the individual by denying the priority of certain concepts of integration in knowledge, a particular field of empirical research into individual existence has come to meet the shadow of metaphysics half way.

The new logic which demanded the introduction of obscurity, instability and prophecy into concepts of identity, in order to ground individual freedom, drew to itself the pathological, the enigmatic and the unconscious elements within contemporary psychiatric accounts. Hence Schelling's attraction to unconsciousness and to crisis, Carus' to an unconscious which is the key to an understanding of the conscious life of the soul and 'which will never be completely superseded',[134] Nancy's to a 'there is' which is 'no longer an affidavit, but a seizure',[135] and Derrida's to 'the secret of my inconsolable nostalgia' attached to the word '*résistance*' and which itself 'resists analysis'.[136]

The most peculiar inference concerning the psyche in this context is the way in which the supposed empirical and structural features of the psyche itself – its topological division; the structural weight given to the unconscious; the role of trauma in generating the concept of an unconscious agency; and the foundational appearance of trauma in narratives of individual development – emerge, on the one hand, from the psychoanalytic observations of Freud's consulting room, and the piecing together of ideas from the work of Charcot, Breuer, Meynert, Bernheim and others. But on the other hand they reveal themselves to have longer historical and philosophical pedigrees, and to have developed, to some extent, out of the structural requirements of an ontology capable of representing the independence of individuals.

In Schelling, the pathology of consciousness in relation to the psyche, and the 'metaphysical' pathology of the concept of individuality, are woven into a single issue. But they need not be. There is no inherent reason why a metaphysics of 'human existence' should draw on precisely these features, emerging from the investigations of Romantic psychiatry. But the basic and oft-repeated criticism that writers in the period were simply attracted by the fantastic and the miraculous gives us nowhere near an adequate account of the problems Schelling was pursuing; nor is it anywhere close to acknowledging the centrality of the implications he drew concerning an 'unconscious' for accounts of individual identity in modernity.

---

[134] Carus, *Denkwürdigkeiten*, 152.
[135] Nancy, *Experience*, 13.   [136] Derrida, *Resistances*, 2.

In all of this, however, I have been keen to implicate the work of Freud himself only peripherally – not the least in order to avoid letting an account of psychoanalysis slide too easily into Romantic, existential or deconstructive appropriations of the psyche and the unconscious. Though Frederick de Wolfe Bolman, in a footnote in his translation of the 1815 draft of the *Weltalter*, suggests that 'Throughout *The Ages of the World* Schelling's interpretations of psychic crisis, the unconscious basis of consciousness … the feelings of fear, vexation and dread … unavoidably remind one of the work of Sigmund Freud';[137] and though Ellenberger presents Freudian psychoanalysis as 'a late offshoot of Romanticism',[138] there are good reasons for not equating Freud's approach prima facie with a resistance to determinative structure or the search for an ontology of the individual (whatever Freud's debt to Romantic thought and Romantic science). To take just one representative comment on Freud's achievement from within the psychoanalytic tradition itself, Harry Guntrip maintains that 'Psychoanalysis began with a defective realization of the importance of the concept "Person", owing to the cultural era of its origin.' Freud's approach to the id 'completely destroys the unique and responsible individuality of the person. It reflects the materialistic determinism of the nineteenth- and early twentieth-century science.'[139]

Although it will become clear that, from its inception onwards, psychoanalysis has both been surrounded by and invested with the power of these previous discourses of the psyche, the unconscious and the individual, I want to take Freud's foundational narrative of the psyche on its own terms, to trace his own apprehensions of structure and cause in the science of the individual mind, and to see where his own negotiation of the relationship between individuality and knowledge, identity and unconsciousness leads. By exploring the boundaries of such ideas within Freud's own account we may gain a much clearer sense of whether or not, and in what ways, the psychoanalytic unconscious relates to the framework of Schelling's own investigations into the principles of identity, or shapes itself in response to a similar demand to think freedom and individuality.

---

[137] Schelling, *The Ages of the World*, trans. Frederick de Wolfe Bolman, Jr. (New York: Columbia University Press, 1942), 165–6.
[138] Ellenberger, *Discovery*, 657.
[139] Harry Guntrip, *Psychoanalytic Theory, Therapy and the Self* (London: Karnak, 2001), 105.

Part III

The psychoanalytic unconscious

6   Freud: the *Geist* in the machine

The barriers suddenly lifted, the veils dropped, and everything became transparent ... Everything seemed to fall into place, the cogs meshed, I had the impression that the thing now really was a machine that shortly would function on its own.[1]

[Y]ears afterwards, they create the repetition in their dreams, but in their dreams they leave out the hands that held them, so that now they hover and fall freely.[2]

---

[1] Sigmund Freud, Letter to Fliess, 20 October 1895, in Masson (ed.), *The Complete Correspondence*, 146.

[2] Sigmund Freud, *The Interpretation of Dreams*, trans. Joyce Crick (Oxford University Press, 1999), 209. Throughout this and the next chapter, all references to *The Interpretation of Dreams* will be from this new translation unless otherwise stated. There are two reasons for this choice, one is that Crick has returned to this text not as a psychoanalyst but as a Germanist, and has paid particular attention to restoring 'the literary and cultural resonances of Freud's German' (xli), as opposed to James Strachey's tendency to medicalise much of Freud's colloquial terminology for an English scientific audience in *The Standard Edition* of Freud's work. I have wanted to use Crick's version, therefore, as a way of maintaining continuity with some of the terms used by Fichte, Schelling and others. Most importantly, this affects choices such as rendering 'Ich' as 'I', rather than 'ego'. For a useful summary of the history of opposition to Strachey's linguistic choices in *The Standard Edition* see Mark Solms, 'Controversies in Freud Translation', *Psychoanalysis and History*, 1, 1 (1998), 28–44. The second reason is that the Oxford University Press translation is based on the original edition of *The Interpretation of Dreams* from 1899 (given as 1900). This core text went through many re-editions in which important emendations and additions were made. As Strachey notes in his Introduction to *The Standard Edition* translation (based on the 1930 German edition), 'new material sometimes implied a knowledge of modifications in Freud's views dating from times long subsequent to the period at which the book was originally written', *The Interpretation of Dreams, SE*, vol. IV (1900): *The Interpretation of Dreams (First Part)*, xii. For my purposes, the coherence of the work is at issue, and the ability to pursue a cross-section of Freud's understanding of the unconscious and the psyche at this crucial juncture is more important than maintaining consistency with contemporary psychoanalytic usage. For this reason, and even though newly inserted paragraphs and footnotes are dated by Strachey, I have also found it simpler to resort to the Crick. Where I have found it necessary to quote from *The Standard Edition* instead, I have rendered this as 'Freud, *The Interpretation of Dreams [SE]*'.

The last three chapters have shown how a particular set of ideas con-
stellate around Schelling's project of grounding the identity of the individual. His drift away from the terms of an absolute idealism, in search
of concepts with which to underpin the autonomous nature of the self,
led him to forge a new philosophical vocabulary centring on the psyche,
the unconscious, a tension over the past and forgetting, and the enigma
of (ontological) birth. If an omnipotent God or an absolute structure
of reason threatened to make the individual into a posterior effect of a
prior set of determining causes, the unconscious indicated to Romantic
philosophers, psychologists and anthropologists 'precisely our ownmost
and most genuine nature'.[3] What does it mean, then, when these terms
from the post-idealist philosophy of freedom re-emerge in the project of
psychoanalysis? Do they still function in the same way? Not only does
psychoanalysis stake out its own ground for a science of the soul, but
Freud undoubtedly also centred his account of the person on a similar
constellation of terms: the unconscious, the past and a traumatic relation to origins. Ellenberger suggests that Freudian psychoanalysis is
in any case 'a late offshoot of Romanticism',[4] while for Odo Marquard
'psychoanalysis is a disenchanted Romantic *Naturphilosophie*, that's why
it thinks in the manner of this *Naturphilosophie*'.[5] In order to understand
the hold psychoanalysis gained over the human sciences in the first half
of the twentieth century, should we be setting it not in the context of
the 1900s, but in the much wider frame of problems emerging already
in the 1800s? What would psychoanalysis look like viewed from this
perspective?

Alternatively one could argue that looking backwards may give us
'background' histories of the significance of such notions – the unconscious, the trauma of individuality – before they become established as
psychoanalytic ones. But in psychoanalysis they are given new functions and new points of reference and we may usefully draw a line in
the history of the topic dividing the 1890s from the 1810s. Far from
having any power to elucidate the psychoanalytic theory of the psyche,
the relationship is now reversed and idealist forebears are more likely
to crop up as case studies in neurosis. Ronald Britton, former president
of the British Psychoanalytical Association, relates the case of Miss A,
who 'was imprisoned in a subjective monistic world exactly like that

[3] Carus, 'Über Lebensmagnetismus', 153.
[4] Ellenberger, *The Discovery of the Unconscious*, 657.
[5] Marquard, *Transzendentaler Idealismus*, 163. See also Michael Worbs argument, cited
in Luprecht, 'What People Call Pessimism', 61, that Freud 'came to medicine via
Naturphilosophie, attracted by the influence of Schelling's philosophy on the essay 'Die
Natur', often attributed to Goethe'.

envisaged by such philosophers as Schelling, in his "Transcendental Idealism"'.[6] Not only has Schelling's complex labour to introduce tension and freedom into absolute notions of system been reduced to a caricature of the kinds of position he eventually found untenable, but all sense of Schelling's connection with the development of the unconscious itself has been effaced. Such retranscriptions of the relationship between philosophy and psychoanalysis are not a late twentieth-century development; they go back to the early years of the movement. Alfred von Winterstein, in the second issue of *Imago*, noted that 'every consistently developed idealism leads to a solipsism, to which even nonpsychoanalysts have to ascribe a pathological character. Despite the importance of his ideas, an idealist system such as Fichte's lies on this path'.[7]

One feature of Freud's work that indicates the historical relationships here are rather more complex than either of these alternatives suggests is the way in which Schelling and the *Naturphilosophie* crop up as ambivalent points of reference in some of Freud's major texts. On the one hand, Freud frequently cites the prior *Naturphilosophie* as that which was philosophical or speculative and had to be discarded for a scientific psychoanalysis to emerge. Thus Freud mentions 'the high value accorded to the dream-life by many schools of philosophy, for example, by Schelling's followers', and sees in this 'a distinct echo of the undisputed divinity accorded to dreams in antiquity'.[8] His 1901 article 'On Dreams' makes the same point, referring to Schubert's theory that 'dreams are a liberation of the spirit from the power of external nature, and a freeing of the soul from the bonds of the senses'.[9]

On the other hand, the concept of the psyche which emerged from the confluence of magnetism and idealism, Romanticism and *Naturphilosophie*, had a bearing not only on the reaffirmation of religious concepts of supernature, but also on the construction of more secular anthropologies which addressed the functional autonomy of the person and the nature of individual freedom – and this aspect has a more modern tenor. Jung, for instance, in his review of Freud's 'On Dreams', distinguishes between theories of dreams as divine revelations

---

[6] Ronald Britton, *Belief and Imagination: Explorations in Psychoanalysis* (London: Routledge, 1998), 138–9.

[7] Alfred von Winterstein, 'Psychoanalytische Anmerkungen zur Geschichte der Philosophie', *Imago: Zeitschrift für die Anwendung der Psychoanalyse auf die Geisteswissenschaften*, vol. II, 1913 (Nendeln: Kraus reprint 1969), 175–237, 216–17.

[8] Freud, *The Interpretation of Dreams*, 8.

[9] Sigmund Freud, 'On Dreams', *SE*, vol. V (1900–1901): *The Interpretation of Dreams (Second Part) and On Dreams*, 629–86.

and Schubert's work, in which the emphasis is on a soul that 'produces dreams independently'.[10] Something of this nuance, that allies the idea of the soul's 'independence' with the theoretical object of psychoanalysis – the autonomous structures of the psyche – can be detected within Freud's remarks too. Schelling and the *Naturphilosophie* crop up as points of reference where the question of the soul itself (rather than the divine) is at stake. A notion of 'soul' is ostensibly a primitive anachronism, but also a concept that cannot so easily be parted with, that must in some sense be retained by psychoanalysis against the grain of contemporary positivism. At the opening of *The Interpretation of Dreams* Freud refers to the prior epoch of nature philosophy as one in which 'philosophy, and not the exact sciences dominated the mind'.[11] But at the same time he takes issue with the way contemporary psychiatry steels itself against the return of Romantic notions: 'anything possibly showing that the life of the psyche [*Seelenlebens*] might be independent of demonstrable organic changes, or could act spontaneously, fills the psychiatrist of today with alarm, as if to acknowledge this would inevitably mean a return to the days of Natural Philosophy and the metaphysics of the soul'.[12] This professional mistrust has demanded that the psyche 'should make no movement that might reveal that it possesses a competence of its own', but in fact this attitude 'implies a lack of trust in the causal chain extending between the body and the psyche'.[13]

Who does Freud side with here? It seems, ultimately, with the question of causal determinism; and yet the argument is also made in the name of a psyche possessing 'a competence of its own'. More explicitly, in *Totem and Taboo*, after noting two aspects of animism in primitive societies – that it populates the world with spirits and regards these as the cause of natural phenomena – Freud suggests that: 'A third, and perhaps the most important article of this primitive "philosophy of nature" strikes us as less strange, since ... we ourselves are not very far removed from this third belief. For primitive peoples believe that human individuals are inhabited by similar spirits.'[14] James Strachey, editor of the *Standard Edition* of Freud's work, comments that with 'philosophy of nature' Freud indicates '"*Naturphilosophie*", the pantheistic philosophy of Schelling'.[15]

[10] C. G. Jung, 'Sigmund Freud: "On Dreams"', in *Collected Works*, vol. XVIII: *The Symbolic Life: Miscellaneous Writings* (Princeton University Press, 1980), 361.
[11] Freud, *The Interpretation of Dreams*, 54.
[12] Ibid., 37.   [13] Ibid., 38.
[14] Sigmund Freud, *Totem and Taboo* (1913) SE, vol. 13 (1913–1914): *Totem and Taboo and Other Works*, vii–162, 76.
[15] Ibid., 76.

Jung, in argument with the more positivist exponents of psychology associated with Wilhelm Wundt, the founder of academic experimental psychology in Germany, also placed Freud with the nature philosophers. While Wundt attempted to limit the significance of the unconscious to 'dimly' aware states of consciousness, Jung stressed that Freud's theory, like Schelling and Schubert's, posits a 'double consciousness'.[16] Wundt's position, according to Jung, 'implies a clear rejection of the unconscious as a psychological hypothesis'; moreover, 'Wundt thinks that the idea of a double consciousness, and hence of a "superconscious" and "subconscious" in Fechner's sense, is a survival from the psychological mysticism of the Schelling school.'[17] In his autobiography, *Memories, Dreams, Reflections*, Jung likewise portrayed Freud as having 'demonstrated empirically the presence of an unconscious psyche which had hitherto existed only as a philosophical postulate, in particular in the philosophies of C. G. Carus and Eduard von Hartmann'[18]– thus presenting psychoanalysis as the empirical verification of that more Romantic and ontological version of psychology. Freud's own suggestion that dream interpretation 'is capable of providing us with information about the structure of our psychical apparatus which till now we have sought in vain from philosophy',[19] can be read in a similar manner – as improving upon the prior philosophical psychology, rather than asking entirely different questions. Freud may distance himself from Romantic dream interpretation itself, but not entirely from its theory of the soul.

I want to focus this question of Freud's relation to the ontological theory of the unconscious in a closer study of *The Interpretation of Dreams* – the 'founding text of psychoanalysis',[20] Freud's 'major' and 'most original work'[21] and the work in which psychoanalysis 'emerged before the world as something new'.[22] The dream book holds a special position in these discussions because its topic more easily assimilates it to that earlier Romantic context; and yet, it is also the work in which Freud gives one of his most sustained accounts of a scientific model of the psyche. The question I am putting is not merely one of historical transmission. One can trace with little difficulty the points of contact

---

[16] Jung, 'The Spirit of Psychology', 375.
[17] Ibid., 376.   [18] Jung, *Memories*, 193.
[19] Freud, *Interpretation of Dreams*, 114.
[20] John Forrester, *Dispatches from the Freud Wars: Psychoanalysis and Its Passions* (Cambridge, MA: Harvard University Press, 1997), 140.
[21] Ernest Jones, *The Life and Work of Sigmund Freud*, 3 vols. (New York: Basic Books, 1953), vol. 1, 350.
[22] Sigmund Freud, 'A Short Account of Psychoanalysis' (1924), *SE*, vol. XIX *(1923–1925): The Ego and the Id and Other Works*, 189–210, 191.

between Freud and the *Naturphilosophie* to which he had anyway been attracted in his youth[23] – not only through intermediary figures in psychology and philosophy (Fechner's psycho-physics, and von Hartmann's philosophy of the unconscious, for instance), but also in literature (E. T. A. Hoffmann) and cultural history. When we hear Schellingian overtones in these opening lines of Jakob Burkhardt's *History of Greek Culture* – 'All beginnings are lost in obscurity, including those of a race or people'[24] – we should not forget that Burkhardt attended Schelling's lectures on the philosophy of revelation in the 1840s. It is this book that Freud was avidly reading in 1899, just prior to the publication of *The Interpretation of Dreams*, and which, as he reported to Fliess, provided unexpected parallels with his psychoanalytic findings.[25]

But this kind of investigation on its own would miss the point. The question I want to address is not how might Freud have inherited these ideas, but 'What role do they play in his work?', and for this it makes no difference whether Freud was consciously aware or not of these prior connections. To what extent does the defence of autonomy and individuality, which I have traced as a driving force within the work of philosophers and psychologists of the unconscious such as Schelling and Carus, attach itself to Freud's account of unconscious psychic life? Does Freud, merely by isolating a science of the psyche, by attempting to give a final structure to the internal life of the person, inevitably resurrect the same ambiguities and oscillations over rational justification which, as we have seen in the previous chapters, prompted the elaboration of unconscious foundations in the first place? Is *The Interpretation of Dreams* beyond this prior context in which Romantic and idealist metaphysics vie on the ground of the 'unconscious' to imagine the basis for human autonomy? Or is it still very much entangled in it and in the fall-out from eighteenth-century antinomies in the secular science of freedom? Perhaps the very attempt at cleansing the unconscious of its Romantic connotations sets psychoanalysis up for a return of the intellectual repressed?

That psychoanalysis, from its earliest phase as a movement, was capable of reactivating Romantic ideals of individual freedom and self-development is evident from the writings of practitioners such as Otto Rank and C. G. Jung. For Rank, the human being is, in the ideal case, 'creator of himself, his own personality' and psychoanalysis traces the 'conflictual separation of the individual from the mass, undertaken and

---

[23] Jones, *The Life and Work of Sigmund Freud*, vol. I, 43.
[24] Jakob Burkhardt, *History of Greek Culture* (London: Constable, 1964), 3.
[25] See Masson (ed.), *The Complete Letters of Sigmund Freud to Wilhelm Fliess*, 342, where he reports also his 'predilection for the prehistoric in all its human forms'.

continued at every step of development into the new'. Rank designates this as 'the never completed birth of individuality'.[26] But it is to Jung's work that I want to turn for a moment in order to catch a glimpse of how a complex and conflicted set of questions about the self might emerge from the framework of the original psychoanalytic project.

We have seen that, immediately after the Second World War, Jung championed Schelling along with Carus as part of a redemptive counterweight to the ravages of modern technocracy – 'the catastrophe that bears the name of Germany'.[27] In fact, Schelling has a presence in Jung's earliest writings, alongside Kant, Schopenhauer and von Hartmann, as part of the German philosophical tradition which Jung was attempting to integrate, already in the late 1890s, with references to Darwin, Wundt and the new psychology.[28] Moreover, in a key post-Freudian text such as 'Archetypes of the Collective Unconscious', we find numerous parallels to ideas that had already been emphasised in Schelling and Carus' work. Beyond the obvious concern with an 'unconscious' forming the greater and more potent part of the life of the self, Jung describes the soul as being linked to a wider totality of nature, and he foregrounds the archetype as a 'primordial idea'.[29] The soul is described as a principle of movement and connected with classical notions of divine fire,[30] while the processes of the soul are viewed as a dialectic (Jung terms this 'enantiodrama'),[31] which may confront the individual with crisis points (a 'moment of collapse' or 'involuntary death').[32] Such crises may also become the source of compensatory, therapeutic knowledge, a window on to future possibilities in life.[33] As suggested intermittently in previous chapters, Jung's use of alchemical and gnostic templates for notions of psychic process parallel Schelling's own returns to Böhme, Ficino and Neoplatonic and Christian mystical traditions; both Jung and Schelling also twin these with examples drawn from Romantic or late nineteenth-century psychiatry (somnambulistic visions, split personalities, and so on) to found alternative descriptions of the self. Jung's work on the unconscious, both pre- and post-Freud, consciously feeds off that prior tradition of nature philosophy and Romantic psychology.[34]

---

[26] Rank, *Truth and Reality*, 11.

[27] C. G. Jung, 'The Spirit of Psychology', 382.

[28] See, for instance, C. G. Jung, *The Zofingia Lectures*, 71.

[29] C. G. Jung, 'Archetypes of the Collective Unconscious', in *The Collected Works of C. G. Jung*, vol. IX, part I: *The Archetypes and the Collective Unconscious*, trans. R. F. C. Hull (London: Routledge, 1968), 20, 32–3.

[30] Ibid., 26, 33.   [31] Ibid., 38–40.

[32] Ibid., 32.   [33] Ibid., 21.

[34] For more on Jung's relation to Romanticism, including to the work of Schelling and Schubert, see Sonu Shamdasani, *Jung and the Making of Modern Psychology*,

What is most striking, however, in terms of the arguments I am putting forward here, is the way in which Jung is driven throughout his work on the unconscious by a concern with what makes a person 'individual', how to become an individual, or how the individual 'becomes what he always was'.[35] In the mystical text 'Seven Sermons to the Dead', written during a period of mental crisis in 1916, which he referred to as a confrontation with his own unconscious, Jung makes the observation, familiar from Schopenhauer, that 'the natural striving of the creature goeth towards distinctiveness, fighteth against primeval, perilous sameness. This is called the PRINCIPIUM INDIVIDUATIONIS. This principle is the essence of the creature'.[36] In the early 1950s he would restate this as: 'Individuation, becoming a self … is the problem of all life'.[37]

The problem of 'becoming a self' is more than just a problem of ethical self-direction, socialisation or mental developmental. Individuation in Jung, which is throughout a precarious process (and a select one), straddles very complex intellectual ground – there is a deep-running uncertainty over what the basis of an 'authentic' and autonomous self might be or mean. In particular there is an ambiguity over how to locate or dislocate the individual from a wider or more absolute whole. The ego, or 'I', and a universalising rational consciousness, are displaced by Jung, as in Schelling's work of the 1810s, in favour of a deeper, more primordial and psychic basis of the person. However, this unconscious basis points in a number of different and contradictory directions. Without attempting to rank these in any way, it points first of all to the soul's immersion in nature as a whole. Through the door of the unconscious, the 'soul of everything begins';[38] archetypes manifest the influence of 'inborn and universally present formal elements';[39] the psyche is 'anything *but* an incapsulated personal system'.[40] Secondly, and perhaps

---

109–10, 171–5. Richard Noll has also suggested that after 1916, Jung's psychological theory, with its concepts of unity, graduated stages of development, polarity and archetype 'is a twentieth-century regression or degeneration to nineteenth-century *Naturphilosophen*'. Richard Noll, *The Jung Cult: Origins of a Charismatic Movement* (London: Fontana Press, 1996), 272.

[35] Jung, 'Archetypes of the Collective Unconscious', 4.
[36] C. G. Jung, 'Seven Sermons to the Dead', in Robert A. Segal (ed.), *The Gnostic Jung* (Princeton University Press, 1992), 181–93, 183.
[37] C. G. Jung, 'Individual Dream Symbolism in Relation to Alchemy', 124.
[38] Jung, 'Archetypes of the Collective Unconscious', 21–2.
[39] C. G. Jung, 'The Concept of the Collective Unconscious', in *The Archetypes and the Collective Unconscious*, 44.
[40] Jung, 'Archetypes of the Collective Unconscious', 21.

only partly distinguishable from such notions of the 'universal', individuation means 'the better and more complete fulfilment of the collective qualities of the human being', that is, the unconscious relates to the collective history of human life.[41] But, thirdly, individuation 'is the process by which beings are formed and differentiated; in particular, it is the development of the psychological *individual* as a being distinct from the general, collective psychology'.[42] In an earlier article from 1934, individuation means 'becoming an "in-dividual"', where individuality embraces 'our innermost, last and comparable uniqueness'[43] – this last phrase resonating with Carus' 'ownmost grounds'.

It is of great interest to see Jung probing these competing sites of identity, familiar from Schelling, within the obscure terrain of the unconscious. The unconscious contains a personal unconscious (Jung's term for the Freudian unconscious, with its collection of repressed contents from the history of the personal life) and a collective unconscious, or a 'collective and universal' mental function,[44] along with the moral drive to individualise or 'individuate' the self. Andrew Samuels and others have pointed out the inherent paradox that 'the person becomes conscious in what respects he or she is both a unique human being and, at the same time, no more than a common man or woman'.[45] As with Schelling and Fichte, notional dynamic or developmental tendencies, through which a person is linked both to the 'whole' and uniquely to him- or her-'self', are internalised and assumed to operate mysteriously at the heart of the unconscious constitution of the person. Instead of a perpetual indecision or oscillation over self and absolute, I and another, self-constitution or prior determination, what obtains are 'unconscious' processes which, as in Schelling, cannot be determinately or causally represented in conventional scientific ways. Ultimately they will be descriptively developed and resolved through a therapy modelled on the alchemical process of sublimation. For Jung, 'the entire alchemical procedure for uniting the opposites ... could just as well represent the individuation process for a single individual'.[46]

---

[41] Jung, 'The Relations Between the Ego and the Unconscious', in *The Collected Works of C. G. Jung*, vol. VII: *Two Essays on Analytical Psychology*, 2nd edn (Princeton University Press, 1966), 121–241, 173–4.

[42] C. G. Jung, 'Psychological Types', in *The Collected Works of C. G. Jung*, vol. VI: *Psychological Types* (Princeton University Press, 1971), 448.

[43] C. G. Jung, 'The Relations Between the Ego and the Unconscious', 173.

[44] C. G. Jung, 'The Structure of the Unconscious', in *The Collected Works of C. G. Jung*, vol. VII (1916), 269–304, 275.

[45] Entry on 'Individuation', in Andrew Samuels, Bani Shorter and Fred Plaut (eds.), *A Critical Dictionary of Jungian Analysis* (London: Routledge, 2003), 76.

[46] C. G. Jung, '*Mysterium Coniunctionis*', 555.

Where Jung does attempt to formalise the question of individual development, and the relation between collective and individual aspects of the self, in more conventional terms, he often reopens a set of relational paradoxes. Thus 'repression of the collective psyche was absolutely necessary for the development of the personality, since collective psychology and the personal psychology exclude one another'.[47] But we learn at the same time that 'the personal grows out of the collective psyche', and they are therefore hard to distinguish.[48] Furthermore, the collective turns out to be constituted by 'everything that is universally understood, universally said and done', and looked at in this way, much of what appears to be 'so-called individual psychology is really collective'.[49] Somewhere along the line the problem of describing how the collective generates the individual, in processual terms, has given way to the logical problem of defining individuality itself. One suspects that certain questions regarding the basis for the individual's ultimate self-creation, or self-meaning, have been deflected into the unconscious because they cannot be attributed to the self in any other way.

For all its seeming abstraction from the protocols of everyday life, the notion of self-creation in the unconscious is closely tied to the development of external social conditions. This is amply borne out by Jung's more political writing, for instance on 'The Plight of the Individual in Modern Society'. Here Jung sets the stage for the difficult drama of self-knowledge in terms very similar to Fichte and Schelling's work of the 1790s. What is at issue, first of all, is a form of scientific knowledge whose framework of suppositions crushes or denies the possibility of individuality. For Schelling, this meant the prevalence of mechanistic and causal explanation; for Jung it is the generalising and statistical bent of 'scientific rationalism', which 'robs the individual of his foundations and his dignity'.[50] Scientific education is based 'on statistical truths and abstract knowledge and therefore imparts an unrealistic, rational picture of the world, in which the individual, as a merely marginal phenomenon, plays no role. The individual, however, as an irrational datum, is the true and authentic carrier of reality.'[51]

This epistemological crisis is again attached to a socio-political one. Where for Fichte and Schelling it concerned the difficult emergence of an autonomous bourgeois self, against the background of feudal religious and political structures, now it is the crisis of the same bourgeois

---

[47] Jung, 'The Structure of the Unconscious', 277.
[48] Ibid., 279.   [49] Ibid., 279.
[50] C. G. Jung, *The Undiscovered Self* (London: Routledge, 2002), 10.
[51] Ibid., 7.

individual in relation to mass society and the state. 'The mass crushes out the insight and reflection that are still possible with the individual';[52] the individual is 'increasingly deprived of the moral decision as to how he should live his own life'.[53] Modern science is itself to blame for mass mentality – it 'displaces the individual in favour of anonymous units that pile up into mass formations' and supplies us with 'the abstract idea of the state as the principle of political reality'.[54] Jung, who is concerned instead with that which lays the foundation 'for the freedom and autonomy of the individual',[55] is obliged, as Schelling ultimately was, to 'turn a blind eye to scientific knowledge',[56] in order to characterise the individual not as 'a recurrent unit but as something unique and singular'.[57]

It is interesting to note that Jung's conclusions draw him right back to the terrain of metaphysics and religion, with which Schelling was uneasily half-allied in his preservation of the 'absolute' as the unconscious and repressed basis of the self. The individual 'will never find the real justification for his existence, and his own spiritual and moral autonomy' except in 'an extra-mundane principle capable of relativizing the overpowering influence of external factors'. The individual who is not anchored in God 'can offer no resistance on his own resources to the physical and moral blandishments of the world'.[58]

The unconscious here – Jung's 'undiscovered self' – quite apart from the role it plays in psychological investigations into psychosis, dreams, word associations, emotional conflict, and repressed and archetypal material in the mind, provides an alternative theoretical ground through which to mediate the integration of ideas of self and whole, collectivity and individuality, and counters the sense of the arbitrariness or insignificance of personal experience with the idea of its deeper psychic foundation. It mediates these terms in such a way that the person can have its unique ground *and* be linked into a meaningful whole. It also retains an element of obscurity or mystery, such that the nature of this connection cannot be told, cannot be generalised or made a function of external processes or causation by 'others', and yet is still proposed as something 'objective', more than imagined. 'Our psyche ... remains an insoluble puzzle and an incomprehensible wonder, an object of perplexity – a feature it shares with all Nature's secrets.'[59]

The point I want to bring out is that what began as psychoanalysis, as the investigation of forms of pathology within mental life, here sets itself

[52] Ibid., 2.   [53] Ibid., 8.   [54] Ibid., 8.
[55] Ibid., 18.   [56] Ibid., 6.
[57] Ibid., 5–6.   [58] Ibid., 16.   [59] Ibid., 32.

a much larger moral and existential task: the problem of how to become 'a self', or to reveal 'truer' or more autonomous layers of the self, as opposed to simply layers of a 'psychical' process. Jung, Rank and others drew on such connotations of the unconscious established within earlier Romantic theories of the psyche, while Ludwig Binswanger sought to establish a new form of existential analysis in the 1930s, based on a fusion of Freud with Heidegger.[60] Jung and Rank split off from the main psychoanalytic movement in 1914 and 1926 respectively, and one might argue that it was precisely against such psychologies, with their concern for the creative development of the individual – or that of Adler, for whom resistance to the negative experience of individuality was the root of all neurosis – that the specifically Freudian tradition defined itself as one less interested in salvaging the ontology of the individual. However, some of these concerns, particularly the desire to theorise individual freedom, or to broach the question of what it means to be a 'self', have ultimately filtered back into the Freudian tradition itself. In the work of D. W. Winnicott, for instance, one finds a reorientation of psychoanalysis around the idea of the autonomy or authenticity of the person. He wanted his patients to be 'both intelligible and hidden' and wrote of 'an incommunicado element' at the centre of each person which 'is sacred and most worthy of preservation'.[61] Winnicott incorporated a Romantic and proto-liberal interest in the creativity and the authenticity of the self, whose health is characterised by 'spontaneity' and 'intuition' – 'it is only in being creative that the individual discovers the self'.[62] Moreover, the hope that the individual can come together as a unit, 'as an expression of I AM, I am alive, I am myself', is one of the aims of psychotherapy.[63] As Adam Phillips notes, Winnicott's writing has roots in the English Romanticism of Wordsworth and Coleridge and bears comparison with Emerson as well as drawing in influences from existentialist philosophy, all three of which sources bear the imprint of Schelling's influence.[64] Neville Symington has equally argued that 'freedom is at the core of [W. R.] Bion's thinking': anxiety is the 'inner threat to my personhood', while 'freedom lies in a person's activity of thinking his own thoughts', an activity which itself depends on capacities evolving in the unconscious strata of the personality.[65]

---

[60] See Ludwig Binswanger, *Being-in-the-World: Selected Papers of Ludwig Binswanger*, trans. Jacob Needleman (New York and Evanston, IL: Harper & Row, 1968).

[61] Adam Phillips, *Winnicott* (London: Fontana, 1988), 14, and D. W. Winnicott, 'Communicating and Not Communicating', cited in Phillips, *Winnicott*, 3.

[62] D. W. Winnicott, *Playing and Reality* (London and New York: Routledge, 1991), 54.

[63] Ibid., 56.   [64] Phillips, *Winnicott*, 15, 11.

[65] N. Symington, 'The Possibility of Human Freedom and its Transmission (With Particular Reference to the Thought of Bion)', *International Journal of Psycho-Analysis*, 71 (1990), 95–106, 95–99.

However, despite these contexts which surround and develop Freud's work in this way, it is clear from a perusal of *The Interpretation of Dreams* that Freud himself does not purposefully orient his study around posing or answering ethical or philosophical questions about individuality, and it is this core Freudian context that I specifically want to examine. It is true that in the opening chapter, Freud resurrects various aspects of the Romantic theory of the self. He quotes G. H. Schubert and notes the Romantic interest in the splitting of the personality in dreams – how 'our own knowledge is divided between two people, with the alien figure correcting our own ego'[66] – just as Schelling had written about 'this doubling of ourselves, this secret intercourse between the two essences, one questioning and one answering'.[67] He includes a remark by Novalis that 'the dream is a defence against the ordinary regularity of life, a recreation for the fettered fantasy',[68] which reflects the idealist attempt to imagine the liberty of the individual. And just as Schelling had taken sleep as a cipher for the soul's autonomy – in sleep 'a freely willed sympathy takes the place of an externally determined unity'[69] – so Freud builds on Burdach's comment that in sleep, 'the psyche isolates itself from the external world and draws back from the periphery'.[70] But one cannot argue that Freud's work is primarily concerned with a theory of the self, the paradox of 'individuation', or the need to recover a 'true self', and the final pages of the book contain a very measured disclaimer over the ethical significance of his insights into mental functioning: 'My thoughts have not pursued the problem of dreams under this aspect.'[71]

Even so, Freud's dream-book is thoroughly implicated in questions of autonomy and individuality, which are present in at least a three- or fourfold way. One could begin by distinguishing between two particular and conflicting meanings of the term. On the one hand, there is the way in which scientific description aims to clarify the function of the psyche as an 'autonomous system', in the sense of Freud's letter to Fliess of 20 October 1895: 'I had the impression that the thing now really was a machine that shortly would function on its own.'[72] But Freud's book is also concerned with autonomy in another, more sociological or existential sense, for instance, as represented in notions of willfulness and egotism – the personal drive towards autonomy. This is evidently different

[66] Freud, *The Interpretation of Dreams*, 77.
[67] Schelling, *Ages of the World*, 115.
[68] Freud, *The Interpretation of Dreams*, 69.
[69] Schelling, *Ages of the World*, 158.
[70] Freud, *The Interpretation of Dreams*, 46.
[71] Ibid., 411.
[72] Freud to Fliess, 20 October 1895, Masson (ed.), *The Complete Correspondence*, 146.

from the descriptive problem of isolating autonomous functional features within the mind. However, it becomes clear as one tries to piece the features of Freud's dream book together that these two questions are in fact confusingly involved with each other. The whole function of the autonomous 'machine' is geared towards processing desire and the consequences of its obstruction; likewise the key topographical structures of the psyche are mapped with reference to the child's earliest experiences of the conflict between autonomy and necessity, and pleasure and reality. In yet a third way, the book implicitly raises questions about the nature of 'individual identity', and whether the unconscious fragments this identity, or in fact sustains it at a deeper level. Fourthly, there is Freud's interest in dreams that dramatise a conflict between son and father. Such dream portrayals of tussles over independence (whether recollected or fantasied) seem to be of paramount importance in the life of the unconscious and form part of its interior symbolic language. All of these aspects of the investigation raise issues of autonomy and independence. These are themes which, due to their evolving structural significance in the book become central both to Freud's interpretation of dreams and his wider theory of the psyche.

However, this is where the peculiar problems begin. There is no doubt that, as a therapeutic practice, psychoanalysis was intended to strengthen the powers of independence in the individual. Although Freud's remarks on what constitutes psychical health are actually few and far between, where male patients are concerned he invariably raises the issue of overcoming dependency, submissiveness or passivity – by implication, the normal individual is able handle his own affairs, according to the demands of 'reality'. In the case history of the Wolf-man, the child at one period, under the influence of a male authority figure (his German tutor), 'got free from his passive attitudes, and found himself for the time being on fairly normal lines'.[73] In 1924, Freud argued that in neurosis 'a piece of reality is avoided by a sort of flight' but 'normal' or 'healthy' behaviour 'leads to work being carried out on the external world'.[74] Where the problems enter in with this vision of independence is at the theoretical level, at the level of representation, and the modelling of psychic coherence and causality. It is here that the need for a functional description of the psyche collides awkwardly with an unconscious which is determinate but descriptively elusive; this collision has

---

[73] Sigmund Freud, *From the History of an Infantile Neurosis*, SE, vol. XVII (1918), 1–124, 69.

[74] Sigmund Freud, 'The Loss of Reality in Neurosis and Psychosis', SE, vol. XIX *(1923–1925): The Ego and the Id and Other Works*, 181–8, 185.

in turn provoked various competing possibilities for understanding dimensions of individuality, will and freedom, in Freud's work. It is this question, of how the problem of autonomy inhabits the innermost structures of Freud's technical description of the psyche, that I want to pursue in the following sections. I will deal in turn with the language of thought associations, with wishing, and then in Chapter 7 with the father–son relation.

Entangled in determinism

Freud tried to explain the whole person in causal terms, and individuality per se; but individual means meta-causal, transcending causality.[75]

The Interpretation of Dreams contains some of Freud's most speculative thinking through of the problem of consistency and connectedness as it affects the psychic life of the person, second only to the full-scale revision of the earlier system in 1922 in *Beyond the Pleasure Principle*. It is also a text which has given rise to quite different accounts of what psychoanalysis intends concerning selfhood and freedom. In the following sections I will argue that, behind the difficulty Freud has in defining a set of consistent laws through which to determine the acknowledged inconsistencies of human behaviour, lies an *unacknowledged* inconsistency over how the individual is to be situated both in relation to knowledge of its own determinism, and in relation to authority per se. This inconsistency is intimately connected with the ambivalent appeal to the self in liberal modernity, with which this book began: to be both explicable and inexplicable, determinable and indeterminable.

One of the most obvious jumping-off points for such an investigation is the very language of determinism itself. There is a familiar perception of Freud that, throughout his career, he had recourse to the assumption of an absolute determinism in mental life. One of the contexts given for this is Freud's university training in the Institute of Physiology under Ernst Brücke. According to Jones, Freud was deeply imbued with the principles of causality of the Helmholtz school,[76] and in various passing statements in *The Interpretation of Dreams* Freud asserts that psychologists 'underestimate the factor of determination in matters of the psyche' or 'have dispensed with the stability of the psyche's interconnected structure much too soon'.[77]

[75] Otto Rank, *Psychology of the Soul: a Study of the Origin, Conceptual Evolution, and Nature of the Soul* [1930] (Baltimore, OH: Johns Hopkins University Press, 1998), 123.
[76] Jones, *Sigmund Freud*, vol. I, 245.
[77] Freud, *The Interpretation of Dreams*, 334.

There is a subtle relationship between these kinds of assumption of determinism and the language Freud uses to describe thoughts – as interconnected lines (*Linien*), threads (*Faden*), chains (*Verkettungen*) and trains (*Züge*).[78] Freud partly inherits this descriptive language from the British associationist tradition of David Hartley, James Mill and J. S. Mill, which was absorbed by later nineteenth-century academic psychology in Germany; likewise the assumption that ideas and sensations, though they may appear to be unique or isolated events, in fact 'enter into connections and associations' and form something of a network.[79] Associationist psychology had taken on many modifications in the nineteenth century which distanced it from the more 'mechanical' descriptions of mental life found in works by James Mill or William Godwin in the eighteenth century. In particular, J. S. Mill had thought through the problems associationism posed for theories of self-consciousness and moral freedom and attempted to counteract some of the negative implications concerning automatism in the person. In the metaphysical debate concerning the influence of liberty or necessity in the moral life of humans, Mill still adhered to a strict determinism, supposing that the theory of free will had been admitted only because the alternative had been 'deemed inconsistent with every one's instinctive consciousness, as well as humiliating the pride and even degrading the moral nature of man'.[80] And yet, like Fichte, he personally recoiled under the weight of the doctrine of necessity – 'I felt as if I was scientifically proved to be the helpless slave of antecedent circumstances'[81] – and he came to cultivate instead the notion of 'inward forces which make [human nature] a living thing',[82] and a sense of spontaneity dependent on not consciously regarding one's own actions.

Moreover, in contrast to his father James Mill's emphasis on the mechanical operation of the laws of association, Mill foregrounded the possibility of a 'chemical' model in which 'genuinely novel outcomes' may occur.[83] Where James Mill had assumed a general spatial and temporal contiguity in associations, J. S. Mill raised the difficulty of tracing the causal sequences involved in determining a psychological

[78] J. Laplanche and J.-B. Pontalis, *The Language of Psychoanalysis*, 41.
[79] Freud, *The Interpretation of Dreams*, 39.
[80] J. S. Mill, *Collected Works of John Stuart Mill*, vol. VIII, *A System of Logic Ratiocinative and Inductive, Books IV–VI* (University of Toronto Press, 1974), 836.
[81] J. S. Mill, *Autobiography* (Oxford University Press, 1971), 101.
[82] J. S. Mill, 'On Liberty', 188.
[83] See Richards, *Mental Machinery*, 341.

event.[84] The lengthy *An Examination of Sir William Hamilton's Philosophy* – J. S. Mill's attack on the main representative of idealist influence from Germany – admitted further contradictions into the theory of mental life which appear to parallel some of Schelling's arguments. If the mind is a *series* of feelings, for instance, how can it 'be aware of itself as past and future'? Either 'the Mind, or Ego, is something different from any series of feelings', argues Mill, or one must accept the paradox that 'something which *ex hypothesi* is but a series of feelings, can be aware of itself as a series'.[85] On a related front, Mill acknowledged the obscurity which, for any individual, veils the original moments in which associations were forged, such that one could retain the feeling, but 'forget the reason on which it is grounded'.[86]

So even here, within a strand of philosophical psychology from the empiricist tradition, whose determinist leanings contrast most sharply with the psychological theories of German Romanticism and German idealism, one finds the question of unconsciousness being introduced, albeit incidentally, as an issue for the science of the person. It was, in the end, not such a long step from Mill's modification of the more determinist assumptions of associationism to his acute moral interest in Wordsworth's 'Ode: Intimations of Immortality from Recollections of Early Childhood', with its 'shadowy recollections', its 'thoughts that lie too deep', its 'vanishings' and its 'sleep and a forgetting' at birth,[87] which imitates on English terrain the kind of principled unconsciousness so important for Schelling and Schubert. Intriguingly, this material brings us back directly to Freud who translated Mill's essay on Grote's *Plato* in 1880 while still a medical student at the University of Vienna. Later in life Freud remarked that while engaged in that work he had been 'greatly impressed by Plato's theory of reminiscence' and had 'given it a great deal of thought'.[88] Mill, in explaining Plato's theory of reminiscence, quotes Wordsworth's Ode, making the point that the poem is erroneously called Platonic because it actually demonstrates the opposite movement to Plato's theory – not recollection, but 'a sleep and a forgetting'; or as Freud renders this in German: '*bei Wordsworth*

---

[84] Ibid., 342.

[85] J. S. Mill, *The Collected Works of John Stuart Mill*, vol. IX: *An Examination of Sir William Hamilton's Philosophy* (University of Toronto Press, 1979), 194.

[86] Ibid., 463.

[87] William Wordsworth, 'Ode: Intimations of Immortality from Recollections of Early Childhood', *Wordsworth's Poetical Works*, ed. E. de Selincourt and H. Darbishire, vol. IV (Oxford University Press, 1947), 279–85.

[88] Jones, *Sigmund Freud*, vol. I, 56.

ist unser Leben hienieden "ein Schlaf und ein Vergessen", bei Plato ist es ein Sich-Erinnern'.[89] It is intriguing to speculate that this metaphysical foregrounding of forgetting, much as Schelling requires in the *Weltalter*, should come to Freud not via German Romanticism but from Mill's account of Plato.

At any rate, in the associationist model of psychological description which Freud adopts, there is no definite sense of the psyche as a 'machine', or a 'strict chain of necessity'; Freud endorses the language of interconnectedness, but without pressing the issue of causality in a deterministic fashion – at least at this level of description. In fact, throughout *The Interpretation of Dreams*, accounts of 'wide-ranging' associations or their 'multiple convergence' complicates the paradigm of sequences of thought and evokes more the kind of intricate nerve structures whose connections Freud sought to isolate in his histological research in the 1880s.[90] In dreams, each element 'enters by way of multiple connections deeper and deeper into the maze of the dream thoughts'.[91] Sequence becomes sometimes insoluble in ways that recall Schelling's subversion of the problem of precedence: 'are all the dream thoughts present side by side, or will they follow one after the other, or are there simultaneous trains of thought formed from different centres, which then converge?'[92]

Such considerations are in many ways still 'technical' ones within the theory of thought association, and as such give no indication, one way or the other, of a general attachment to individual autonomy or 'freedom of the will'. And yet, Freud's deterministic inferences do constantly press towards grander statements concerning 'apparent freedom' and nothing being left 'to arbitrary choice' in the psyche. In 1895 he argued that, 'as soon as one has uncovered the hidden motives ... there remains nothing in the connection between the thoughts of hysterics that is enigmatical or lawless',[93] while in *The Interpretation of Dreams* Freud

---

[89] J. S. Mill, *Gesammelte Werke*, ed. Theodor Gomperz, vol. XII: *Ueber Frauenemancipation. Plato. Arbeiterfrage. Socialismus*, trans. Sigmund Freud (Leipzig: Fues, 1880), 88.

[90] See Jones, *Sigmund Freud*, vol. I, 204, and also Freud's translation of a passage from Ewald Hering's lecture 'On Memory' from 1870: 'Who could hope to disentangle the fabric of our inner life with its thousandfold complexities ... Chains such as these of unconscious material nerve-processes, which end in a link accompanied by a conscious perception, have been described as "unconscious trains of ideas"', quoted by Strachey in 'Appendix A' to 'The Unconscious', *SE*, vol. XIV, *On the History of the Psycho-Analytic Movement, Papers on Metapsychology and Other Works*, 205.

[91] Freud, *The Interpretation of Dreams*, 215.

[92] Ibid., 214.

[93] Josef Breuer and Sigmund Freud, *Studies on Hysteria*, in *SE*, vol. II (1893–95), 294.

repeatedly refers to the psyche as an 'apparatus' (*seelischen Apparats*) and 'instrument' (*Seeleninstruments*).[94]

Ernest Jones was keen to present such moments as evidence of a more extensive scientific *Weltanschauung*: all Freud's research into the workings of the mind, we are told, 'is entirely based on a belief in a regular chain of mental events' and was imbued with a disbelief in the notion of 'spontaneous or uncaused acts'.[95] Besides the influence of Brücke and the Helmholtz school (for whom 'No forces other than the common physical and chemical ones are active in the organism')[96] Jones also traces Freud's adherence to deterministic models to his other early mentor, the professor of psychiatry Theodor Meynert, and beyond this to the important influence of J. F. Herbart in German psychology. Herbart had in 1824 protested against Romantic trends in psychology, in particular 'this false doctrine of a free will that has raised its head in recent years'.[97] Herbart was himself a student of Fichte's at Jena in the mid 1790s, and his criticism was here levelled against the rising tide of post-idealism and *Naturphilosophie*. Such a genealogy would then place Freud in a specific tradition that takes on board the concept of the unconscious, but resists using it to ground any extraneous sense of the individual's absolute autonomy or original self-creation. Rather, it suggests the operation of an intelligible and necessary law in precisely those moments where rational continuity appears to break down. In 1924 Freud was prepared to list 'the thorough-going meaningfulness and determinism of even the apparently most obscure and arbitrary mental phenomena' as one of the constitutive elements of the theory of neuroses.[98]

Read in this light, the many points throughout *The Interpretation of Dreams* in which Freud admits the urge to find 'connections', to 'fill the gaps', do start to impinge on the conceptualisation of personal autonomy. In fact, they provide a perfect instance of how the drive towards a complete functional description of the psyche – autonomy at the level of systemic isolation – provoked various anxieties over autonomy in the second, existential sense, that is the theorisation of freedom or independence within the person. In a debate over psychic determinism in an early issue of the psychoanalytic journal *Imago*, Sandor Ferenczi hailed the supreme advance of psychoanalysis as being 'precisely the possibility it opens up

[94] Freud, *The Interpretation of Dreams*, 332.
[95] Jones, *Sigmund Freud*, vol. I, 365–6.
[96] A statement by Emil Du Bois-Reymond, quoted in Bernfeld, 'Freud's Earliest Theories', 348.
[97] Jones, *Sigmund Freud*, vol. I, 366.
[98] Sigmund Freud, 'A Short Account of Psychoanalysis', in *SE*, vol. XIX, 197.

for establishing the same thoroughgoing regularity and determinism in the experience of the soul, that can be established throughout the physical domain'.[99] But it was precisely such a vision of the 'soul' that other collaborators found offensive. Eric Fromm compared Freud's view of man as an automaton to La Mettrie's eighteenth-century *l'homme machine*.[100] Bruno Bettelheim, on the other hand, argued that the reductively scientific interpretation of Freud was a misreading based on the translation of his work into the Anglo-American context. For Bettelheim, Freud was interested not in a 'science' of mental life but in the 'soul' or 'psyche', and in an unconscious which itself eludes scientific description. Freud's unconscious – like Wordsworth's 'thoughts that lie too deep' or Carus' 'ownmost and most genuine nature' – is 'deeply hidden' and 'intangible' but also 'what makes us human'.[101] Bettelheim likewise stressed the more Romantic idea of 'a spontaneous sympathy of our unconscious with that of others', and suggested that psychology in Freud's Vienna was not a natural science but a 'science of the spirit', 'deeply rooted in German idealist philosophy'.[102] One sees a familiar debate emerging here amongst Freud's associates over the 'soul' of psychoanalysis, over regularity and freedom, and what it is that makes us truly 'human'. Indeed, it seems to mirror the conflict between 'dogmatism' and 'idealism' that Fichte dramatised one hundred years earlier in *The Vocation of Man*.

The navel of the dream

The dimension of thought associations, and whether they are absolutely determined or not, is one example of a way in which *The Interpretation of Dreams* has attracted a controversy over 'autonomy' which bears some resemblance to the quandaries raised for Fichte and Schelling by a science of the 'I'. Characteristically, the presence of determinist strategies has drawn attention to those points in the text where the causal description appears to break down or exceed Freud's descriptive capacities.

---

[99] Sandor Ferenczi, 'Philosophie und Psychoanalyse (Bemerkungen zu einem Aufsatze des H. Professors Dr. James S. Putnam), in *Imago, Zeitschrift für die Anwendung der Psychoanalyse auf den Geisteswissenschaften*, vol. I, 1912 (Nendeln Liechtenstein: Kraus reprint, 1969), 519–26, 523.

[100] Eric Fromm, 'Freud's Model of Man and its Social Determinants', in *The Crisis of Psychoanalysis: Essays on Freud, Marx and Social Psychology* (New York: Henry Holt, 1969), 45.

[101] Bruno Bettelheim, *Freud and Man's Soul* (London: Hogarth Press, 1983), 77–8. Compare also Winnicott's incommunicado element at the heart of the person which is 'sacred and most worthy of preservation', D. W. Winnicott, 'Communicating and Not Communicating', in *The Maturational Processes and the Facilitating Environment: Studies in the Theory of Emotional Development* (London: Hogarth Press, 1965), 187.

[102] Bettelheim, *Freud and Man's Soul*, 5, 41.

Such instances have marked the point of entry for a number of different appropriations of Freud, all of which are concerned to raise an existential question over human being as that which resists systematic narration. The 'primal scene' for such attempts to locate the breakdown of Freud's determinist model is the metaphor of the navel of the dream, which is now one of the main tourist attractions of the dream book itself. It occurs twice in the text, once in a footnote to the dream of 'Irma's Injection' – the foundational dream of *The Interpretation of Dreams* – in which Freud concedes that 'Every dream has at least one place where it is unfathomable, the navel, as it were, by which it is connected to the unknown',[103] and once more in chapter VII 'The Psychology of the Dream-Processes'. Here Freud expands:

The best-interpreted dreams often have a passage that has to be left in the dark, because we notice in the course of interpretation that a knot of dream-thoughts shows itself just there, refusing to be unraveled, but also making no further contribution to the dream content. This is the dream's navel, and the place beneath which lies the Unknown.[104]

These moments in the text have attracted a number of commentaries, all of which are keen to amplify the notion of an ineluctable obscurity destabilising the psychoanalytic enterprise as a whole. Most famously Derrida cultivates the idea of 'resistance' to analysis in Freud – a point where analysis is 'destined to obscurity' and where Enlightenment progressivism has to reckon 'with a portion of darkness'.[105] Derrida presses the implication of hidden meaning beyond a provisional limit on interpretation and towards 'a night, an absolute unknown'. The navel of the dream is 'impenetrable, unfathomable, unanalyzable',[106] it portrays the very defeat of knowledge, the sphinx lording it over Oedipus, much as for Schelling knowledge succumbs before the veiled image of Isis. Some of Derrida's analysis here derives from Samuel Weber, for whom the navel of the dream indicates that 'there is no Archimedean or transcendental point' from which a definitive interpretation of the dream can be made.[107] The very forces which instigate the dream also 'render its results uncertain, incalculable, and impossible to verify (or to falsify) definitively'.[108] Elizabeth Bronfen suggests that Freud purposefully designates a detail within his 'integrative narrative' which 'resiliently

---

[103] Freud, *The Interpretation of Dreams*, 88.
[104] Ibid., 341.
[105] Jacques Derrida, *Resistances of Psychoanalysis*, 16.
[106] Ibid., 11.
[107] Samuel Weber, 'The Meaning of the Thallus', in *The Legend of Freud* (Stanford, CA: Stanford University Press: 2000), 112.
[108] Ibid., 112.

undermines the entire project of analysis';[109] for Susan Budd, 'the most important part of the dream will always be too deep for us to capture it, because we can never know the unconscious'.[110]

A further feature of the way this navel has been interpreted is that it is taken to imply the conceptual birth of a human subject that is dislocated from a series of determinable occurrences or the logic of external authority. For Bettelheim the core of the psyche was intangible and 'essentially human', for Winnicott the centre of the person is sacred and incommunicable. Just so, these counter-readings of Freud assert a link between limit points in the interpretation of psychic life and the birth of the human individual. Lacan suggested that, in analysing the Irma dream, Freud proceeded 'as an occultist might', trying to find 'the secret designation of the point where as a matter of fact the solution to the mystery of the subject and the world lies'.[111] For Bronfen the navel symbolises 'the making of an independent human being'[112] and a dream therefore 'relates to the *unknown* in the act of interpretation, just as the child relates to the prenatal maternal body at the moment of birth'.[113] For Weber the navel connotes a 'reassuring sense of continuity, generation, and originality'.[114] Derrida is more careful not to affirm anything concerning an inner identity of the self, though he does emphasise the 'originary' function of the unknown. It seems the very warding-off of causal determination cannot help but imply a space for freedom, or creative possibility, just as Kant's bar on representing the thing-in-itself became the royal road for the Romantic unconscious and its association with inner self-creation.

However, there are problems with resolving the issue at this point and in this way, not the least being that it appears to sell Freud's thinking short. A number of things must be taken into consideration. In the first place, dreams are not necessarily consonant with the heart of psychic life – as well as devoting itself to the elucidation of dreaming, *The Interpretation of Dreams* is also a first sketch or showcase for a number of different hypotheses about mental life, including the Oedipus complex, revised theories of hysteria and anxiety, the theory of the unconscious, and the dynamic model of the psyche. Dreams provide a useful

[109] Elizabeth Bronfen, *The Knotted Subject: Hysteria and Its Discontents* (Princeton, NJ: Princeton University Press, 1998), 64.
[110] S. Budd, 'The Shark Behind the Sofa: the Psychoanalytic Theory of Dreams', *History Workshop Journal*, 48 (Autumn 1999), 142.
[111] Lacan, *The Seminar: Book II*, 170.
[112] Bronfen, *The Knotted Subject*, 3.
[113] Ibid., 64.
[114] Weber, 'The Meaning of the Thallus', 113.

window onto such mental mechanisms, but are not necessarily to be identified with our 'ownmost nature', nor even, fully, with the unconscious. As Freud will point out, 'the place of dreams in the interconnected life of the psyche is yet to be located'.[115] To base a Freudian theory of individuality on the process of dream interpretation, then, does not fully engage with some of the book's more complex implications concerning identity and autonomy. This move also tacitly assimilates *the unconscious* – as a complex theoretical object with specific laws and processes – to a point of *unconsciousness* in dream interpretation, to the merely obscure or unfathomable. Again, there is a simplification of Freud's position here. In addition, one must allow for a completely different factor giving rise to moments of discontinuity within the text, which is Freud's caution over revealing the personal details of his own dream analyses. Ilse Grubrich-Simitis writes of the 'holes torn in the emerging textual tissue' for this reason.[116] In the 'Dream of the Three Fates', Freud must refrain from explaining fully a neglected part of a dream 'as the personal sacrifices it would demand are too great'.[117] On the basis of all these objections it seems premature to argue outright from these limit points in dream interpretation that the unconscious is intended to remain intellectually unresolved, or that, as in Schelling's emphatic decree at the end of the *Weltalter*, it *must be so* for an individual self-consciousness to emerge. This is not an argument Freud makes concerning psychic life.

But an even more important objection can be raised which has to do with the quite different grounds on which Freud will explain the 'heart' of psychic life, and which takes us beyond the paradigm of chains of association, whether complete or incomplete. Most of the commentators quoted above note that, in the longer account of the navel of the dream, in the chapter on 'The Psychology of the Dream Processes', Freud makes the further revelation that 'the dream-thoughts we come upon as we interpret cannot in general but remain without closure, spinning out on all sides into the web-like fabric of our thoughts', and that it is here, 'out of a denser patch in this tissue' that the dream-wish 'arises like a mushroom from its mycelium'.[118] There has been much discussion over whether the phallic nature of Freud's metaphor here encodes something about the sexual nature of the dream wish, or

---

[115] Freud, *The Interpretation of Dreams*, 347.
[116] Ilse Grubrich-Simitis, 'How Freud Wrote and Revised *The Interpretation of Dreams*: Conflicts Around the Subjective Origins of the Book of the Century', *Psychoanalysis and History*, 4, 2 (Summer 2002), 114.
[117] Freud, *The Interpretation of Dreams*, 159.
[118] Ibid., 341.

whether the web and the mycelium complicate the very centralising model of phallic symbolisation itself.[119] However, what none seem to acknowledge is that this mysterious point of entry for the wish marks the place where Freud prepares to shift his theoretical paradigm, enabling a decisive distinction between the dream thoughts spinning out in the preconscious – the terrain to which the logic of associationism itself is bound – and that which touches on the unconscious proper, with its dynamic resistance and repressed contents. It is at this point that Freud raises the possibility that the unconscious may manifest *another* kind of process entirely from the ideas of rational connection held by consciousness. The language of interconnected chains of association is not the one through which Freud aims to constitute an overall sense of the psyche as an apparatus, or the ultimate significance of dreams. Instead, it is Freud's analysis of the 'wish' that comes to dominate the book's theoretical core and is the source of his most dramatic revelations. It is the wish which will provide the motive for and the meaning of dreams, and which locates their function in the interconnected life of the psyche: 'The dream is the (disguised) fulfillment of a (suppressed, repressed) wish.'[120] The investigation of dreams comes to turn so significantly on the theory of the wish partly because the wish is able to reveal wider aspects of psychic causality. It bridges the passage to the unconscious system (topographically), and it is here that Freud will further pursue the issue of continuity and determinism in the person. But it also acts as a bridge to the infantile life of the child (historically). It thus mediates past and present, and conscious and unconscious sources of identity and behaviour. As Freud will later put it, the 'past, present and future are strung together, as it were, on the thread of the wish that runs through them'.[121]

What are wishes for?

One of the first points to be made about the shift from the terrain of the preconscious to that of the wish and the unconscious is that Freud does not abandon the framework of scientific determinism at this point; indeed, he addresses it all the more avidly. The wish, for Freud, still conforms to the functional principles of a psychic apparatus, though we have slipped through into a different kind of paradigm construed in terms of unpleasure, energy and the defence against stimuli. At the same time,

[119] See Weber, 'The Meaning of the Thallus'.
[120] Freud, *The Interpretation of Dreams*, 124.
[121] Freud, 'Creative Writers and Day-Dreaming', *SE*, vol. IX, *Jensen's 'Gradiva' and Other Works* (1906–8), 148.

the language of associationism is exchanged for the language of energetics. Thus memory is described in terms of 'gradations of conductive resistance in the transmission of excitations',[122] while the wish is 'a current in an apparatus, issuing from unpleasure'[123] and wish-fulfilment is 'the fundamental motive power of the machine'.[124] At times Freud seems to have achieved a remarkable integration of *Naturphilosophie* and the Helmholtz school, taking up the Romantic concern with polarities and tensions and grounding them in a positive discourse of energetics, such as in his description of a 'continuous current' by day which at night comes to an end, 'flowing back in the reverse direction' indicating the psyche's 'withdrawal from the external world'.[125]

A much more complicated situation arises here over the question of 'autonomy'. On an immediate front, the very object, the wish, appears to bring us up against individual desire. It connects in principle with notions of volition, but also with the deflection or inflection of intentions: a wish, we might argue, is the sign of an unfulfilled or compromised act.[126] But Freud subverts the conventional understanding of wishing in quite striking ways. In the first place, the wish acts as a hinge between a psychological or intentional account of desire and another more functional one. As Paul Ricoeur noted, the task of accounting for the mechanisms of the dream work 'requires combining two universes of discourse, the discourse of meaning and the discourse of force. To say that the dream is the *fulfillment* of a *repressed* wish is to put together two notions which belong to different orders'.[127] This duality threatens a certain dislocation within the discourse of psychoanalytic theory, and Chapter VII of *The Interpretation of Dreams* is in some ways the point at which Freud aims to co-ordinate his scientific account of mental life. Thus the wish is also defined as a psychic impulse which seeks to re-cathect the mnemic image deposited as a trace by a previous experience of satisfaction. Much of this terminology, as Strachey noted, derives from Freud's 1895 attempt to describe psychical processes in scientifically quantifiable terms – as quantities of excitation subject to a general principle of inertia.[128] This is, then, another of those points at which the

[122] Ibid., 352.   [123] Ibid., 394.
[124] Jones, *Sigmund Freud*, vol. I, 390.
[125] Freud, *The Interpretation of Dreams*, 356.
[126] Wittgenstein describes the wish, along with belief and opinion, as something 'unsatisfied', Ludwig Wittgenstein, *Philosophical Investigations* (Oxford: Basil Blackwell, 1989), 129.
[127] Paul Ricoeur, *Freud and Philosophy: an Essay on Interpretation* (New Haven, CT: Yale University Press, 1970), 92.
[128] 'It is no exaggeration to say that much of the seventh chapter of *The Interpretation of Dreams* ... has only become fully intelligible since the publication of the "Project"',

psychological implications of autonomy (as willed motivation) are made to coincide with the conception of an autonomous machine, which in turn threatens to eviscerate notions of freedom and spontaneity from the model of psychic life.

Furthermore, Freud subverts the ordinary understanding of wish by his concentration on unconscious wishes and even consciously not-wanted wishes. Rather than the wish as something 'unsatisfied', we have a wish that 'can be satisfied, even though the man who has it isn't'.[129] This disturbs and alters our sense of what the wish implies for the person, and makes it hard to correlate 'wishing' with, for instance, Fichte and Schelling's notions of unconscious willing as laying the basis for the emergence of conscious and moral life. Is this a theory which puts desire into central position? Is the person causally determined? How do we even conceive of individuality now? When Freud, in his *Introductory Lectures*, asks 'No doubt a wish fulfillment must bring pleasure; but the question then arises "To whom?"', the patness of his response, 'To the person who has the wish, of course', seems insufficient.[130] Some of these problems arise from our need to rethink the conventional understanding of wishing in unanticipated ways, but there are new problems, internal to Freud's account, which disturb both the structural description of wishing and its intended reference. One obstacle to causal representation is the fact that the theory of the unconscious wish bridges phenomena occurring within quite different timescales or objective scenes of action. These disparities become most pronounced in the final technical chapter in which Freud attempts to schematise them within a series of functional diagrams of the psyche as 'a composite instrument'.[131]

To give a brief explanation of the components in Freud's third model reproduced here,[132] the diagram represents first of all a sequential passage (from left to right) from an initial Perception (Pcpt.) to a motor response at the other end of the diagram (see Figure 6.1). The scheme thus has a direction, and temporality of occurrence (the present), and is modelled on the paradigm of the reflex arc. Secondly, the diagram distinguishes between the direct passage from perception to response (the reflex arc), and a secondary passage from stimulus/perception to the record of perception in memory – these are represented by the memory

Sigmund Freud, *The Interpretation of Dreams (First Part)*, in *The Standard Edition*, vol. IV (London: Hogarth Press), xv.
129 Richard Wollheim, *Freud* (London: HarperCollins, 1991), 68.
130 Sigmund Freud, *Introductory Lectures on Psychoanalysis*, in *SE*, vol. XV, 215–16.
131 Freud, *The Interpretation of Dreams*, 350.
132 My account follows the description given in Freud, *The Interpretation of Dreams*, 353–5.

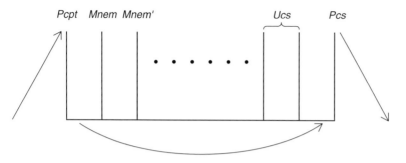

Figure 6.1 Freud's third model

traces labelled 'Mnem' and 'Mnem''. This distinction opens up new descriptive axes within the system – those of depth, and preservation over time. But both of these features are complicated by a third distinction, which is that between the preconscious, which is allied with the conscious ego and 'holds the key to our voluntary motor actions',[133] and the unconscious which represents the earliest or primary layers of memory traces; it is from here that we have been told the wish arises. The preconscious/unconscious distinction involves us in further relational features (that of displacement and resistance within the memory system), but more significantly it opens the model, which was initially oriented around a reflex arc in the present, to issues of deep historical layering and phylogenetic development. From this perspective, the distinction between the unconscious and preconscious is also one between primary and secondary levels of memory traces, and between different operational systems and different principles of thinking. All this before one has even begun to correlate the terminology of the functional system with more conventional psychological descriptions of wishing, memory and perception.

In the *New Introductory Lectures* Freud will admit that, 'We cannot do justice to the characteristics of the mind by linear outlines like those in a drawing.'[134] It soon becomes apparent that such schematisations of 'systems in a constant spatial orientation to each other' are incapable of containing and organising the disparate facets of psychical identity they are meant to clarify.[135] How, then, are we to determine the issue of

---

[133] Freud, *Interpretation of Dreams*, 353.
[134] Freud, *SE*, vol. XXII, 79.
[135] Freud, *The Intepretation of Dreams*, 350. Freud admits the dream diagram presents a task for which his expository skills 'are scarcely equal', namely, to 'express the

'sequence' or influence in a system which, under one aspect, deals with the discharge of energy in the present on the model of a reflex arc (the human machine), and under another straddles the history of the individual and the complex psychological relation between its present and past experiences, and in yet a third way introduces the phenomenon of unconscious resistance? These ideas are not necessarily incompatible. The problem is whether the relations between the different structural orientations of the system can be sufficiently described, let alone understood. What, we may ask, *is* the key topographical orientation in the psyche? That between input and output, the flow from high to low stimulus in the system? That between surface and depth as one moves from the preconscious to the unconscious? Or that of historical influence, as one moves from the primary to the secondary – 'as a consequence of this belated entry of the secondary processes, the heart of our being, made of the unconscious wishful impulses, cannot be comprehended or inhibited by the preconscious'?[136] This confusion over causal relationship is replicated in Freud's indecision over the topographical location and direction of the wish which leads him eventually to concede a range of wishes and orientations, capable of originating from all points in the conscious, preconscious and unconscious psyche.[137]

We are on far more complex descriptive ground here than the 'chains' of mental association. A preliminary attempt to insert the wish into the schematism of the psyche is left causally indeterminate, and this indeterminacy in turn prevents our complete understanding of the meaning of wishing. If the wish causes the dream, and *is* its meaning, can we understand, for instance, exactly what this cause implies in the self-experience of the person? The issue is of some concern, because the wish is so obviously related to the issue of identity and volition, as the dream had not been. Is the bridging presence of the wish, which links past, present and future, evidence of a broader coherence in the person – 'the person who has the wish' – which ultimately helps to consolidate a sense of the self? Or of a determinism which implies something more machinic? Or do the discontinuities in Freud's conception of the system restore a sense of the hidden and intangible contours of selfhood – much as Bettelheim had suggested? As we have seen, the very

---

simultaneity of such complicated interrelationships in terms of linear sequence'. (*The Interpretation of Dreams*, 385.) Ricoeur described Freud's earlier 'Scientific Project' as a 'demonstration by way of the absurd that the content exceeds the frame' (Ricoeur, *Freud and Philosophy*, 73).

[136] Freud, *The Interpretation of Dreams*, 398.
[137] 'We may now ask where the wish realized in the dream comes from', ibid., 360.

complexity of psychic determinism is liable to attract inferences concerning an inner autonomy of the person which eludes rational construction. This gives rise to a situation in which the operational laws of the psyche are to transfix the development of the wish and the will in their most obscure redoubts, but the very structural complexities introduced into that account continue to make room for something that (wishfully) eludes causal identification. This uncertain resolution of the role of the wish is all the more problematic for Freud's suggestion that the unconscious wishful impulses, which 'cannot be comprehended or inhibited by the preconscious', are also 'the heart of our being',[138] conjuring up again all the hidden, intangible or incommunicable 'cores' of the person in modern theories of individuality.

It is significant that these instabilities in the attempt to position the wish within the causal structure of the psyche are again matched by broader disputes over its existential implications, particularly over whether such wishes provide the main obstruction to, or the preserve of, the individual's hope for autonomy. Let me clarify the problem by pointing out a paradox in Freud's description of the wish quite separate from the obstacles to formal representation. Freud uses the wish, first of all, to indicate a form of automatic continuity in experience, which occurs despite any notion of conscious desire. In 'The Aetiology of Hysteria' he had noted that, 'with hysterical patients it is as if all their old experiences – to which they have already reacted so often and, moreover, so violently – had retained their effective power'.[139] Likewise in *The Interpretation of Dreams*, 'impressions from our earliest childhood (the prehistorical period up to about the end of our third year) demand reproduction *for their own sake*', perhaps even 'regardless of content'.[140] Unconscious repetition establishes a form of continuity in the person – perhaps the oldest and most powerful continuity in identity per se: 'These wishes of our Unconscious, ever stirring, never dying – Immortal, one might say.'[141] But this powerful continuity is at the same time less an instance of the integrity of selfhood, and more like an automatic function in which elements of past experiences are contingently and idiosyncratically caught up in the life of the person or carried along by default. Freud's description of his nephew John's appearance in a dream, as a 'revenant' whose nature is 'ineradicably fixed in my unconscious memory',[142] suggests unconscious recollection

---

[138] Ibid., 398.
[139] Freud, 'The Aetiology of Hysteria', in *SE*, vol. III, 218.
[140] Freud, *The Interpretation of Dreams*, 189.
[141] Ibid., 362–3. [142] Ibid., 271.

as a process involving the inert repetition of a past which is increasingly, uncannily disconnected from conscious developments in the present.

Yet – and here is the real twist – whereas Freud's earlier work on hysteria had foregrounded the unconscious mental recollection of traumatic instances of sexual seduction in childhood, the wish that is so inorganically bequeathed to the person in *The Interpretation of Dreams* is so often a wish that preserves an image of willfulness itself, a cipher of the person's selfhood: 'since the dream's only objective is wish-fulfilment it can be completely egotistical'.[143] From this point of view, the continuity of the wish represents not a continuity *in spite of* the autonomy of the person, but *of that* autonomy, or its exaggerated core. It allows for the notional 'origin' of personal identity to persist in terms of an original self-love or self-concern ('children love themselves first', Freud will later say)[144] – against the grain of the social fashioning of selfhood. We can see here how the shift in this chapter from Jung's concern with 'individuation' towards Freud's more technical investigation of determinism in the psyche, here shifts back towards the problem of being an individual.

These paradoxes in relation to the wish can be brought out more clearly by comparing Freud's views with Winnicott's, both on the after-life of the infantile wish, and the continuity of the adult with the child. The Winnicottian individual is encouraged to gather the sense of himself as an expression of 'I am alive, I am myself', and of 'a self he was born with as potential'.[145] A healthy individual maintains a continuity throughout its life, and '*survival* of the true self is associated with authenticity'.[146] Trauma implies that a baby has experienced 'a break in life's continuity', a deprivation of 'the root which could provide continuity with the personal beginning'.[147] In an important sense, here, continuity with the child represents the continuity of individuality *per se*, and as such allows for the very possibility of conceiving freedom and autonomy within the individual. Continuity with the child establishes that the person is a certain kind of autonomous entity, in the first place, because such continuity testifies to a coherence within the self of its very own. The self coheres not just as a body in space but as a lived experience in time (a similar point of view had been adopted by Bergson in his influential descriptions of memory and *durée* earlier in the century). But, secondly, and more importantly, because the child

[143] Ibid., 99.   [144] Freud, *Introductory Lectures*, 204.

[145] Winnicott, *Playing and Reality*, 56; Phillips, *Winnicott*, 7.

[146] Eric Rayner, *The Independent Mind in British Pyschoanalysis* (London: Free Association Books, 1990), 117, 81.

[147] Winnicott, *Playing and Reality*, 115.

indicates an original and uncompromised *urge for autonomy* – as Freud put it: the urge to remain 'gloriously unfettered'.[148] Winnicott suggests, for instance, that bed-wetting can be an effective expression of the child's 'protest against strict management, sticking up for the rights of the individual so to speak'.[149] In this case, the symptom is not an illness, 'rather it is a sign that the child still hopes to keep the individuality which has been in some way threatened'.[150] Thus when Freud remarks that, 'to our surprise, we find the child, with its impulses, living on in the dream',[151] surely this is something affirmative?[152] If the wish threads past, present and future together, and the indispensible part of a dream is a childhood wish, then might not childhood in Wordsworthian fashion bind the life together – and bind life precisely through an art which is not completely rationalised, which, as in Kant's formulation of aesthetics, includes a healthy dose of spontaneity as an integral principle?

Yet according to Freud's own account, continuity with the child is what must *not* be established, because that would undermine a different kind of demand concerning adult identity – that it should evidence an intelligible and conscious coherence *against* the world of the child. Freud's illustration of the activation of childhood wishes in adulthood centres very much on the question of an overblown selfishness or egotism. The dream of 'Count Thun' reveals 'the issue of a ludicrous megalomania long since suppressed in my waking life';[153] the dream of the 'dissection of his own torso' conceals a 'grossly selfish train of thought' which comes from a 'forbidden infantile source';[154] and yet another dream of his friend 'Otto with Basedow's disease', fulfils 'one of my immortal childhood wishes, my rage for greatness' which is now 'unconscious and suppressed'.[155] Dreams preserve the 'absolutely self-centred' nature of the child's psyche. Rather than 'sticking up for the rights of the individual' (which for Winnicott might provide the underpinnings of a life which values and sustains its own autonomy) these instances of selfishness are subversive or obscene and so discontinuous with the

---

[148] Freud, *The Interpretation of Dreams*, 116.

[149] D. W. Winnicott, 'What Do We Mean by a Normal Child?', in *The Child and the Family: First Relationships* (London: Tavistock, 1957), 103.

[150] Ibid., 103.

[151] Freud, *The Interpretation of Dreams*, 147.

[152] See also Jacqueline Rose's suggestion that when Freud argues that no wish will make itself felt in a dream 'unless an unconscious infantile wish has attached itself to it', it is not clear 'whether Freud means a childhood wish (a wish of childhood), or – as seems far more to be the case – the wish to be a child', Jacqueline Rose, *On Not Being Able to Sleep: Psychoanalysis and the Modern World* (London: Chatto & Windus, 2003), 115.

[153] Freud, *The Interpretation of Dreams*, 166.

[154] Ibid., 316.   [155] Ibid., 365.

conscious self. To make the child truly the ground of the adult would be to bind one's days each to each in natural impiety. What appeared earlier as a structural difficulty over where to place the action of the wish within Freud's topographical model of the psyche, is now compounded by a disturbance in the way self-identity should be thought at the level both of unconscious self-recollection and theories of development.

One way out of the contradiction is to concede that Freud's position is coherent in itself and it is only the comparison with Winnicott which alerts us to instabilities in the connotations of the infantile wish. And yet there are inconsistencies within Freud's own account of leaving childish egotism behind. There seem to be two kinds of discoveries at stake concerning wishes emerging from earliest infancy, and the forms of identification running backwards and forwards between adult and child. On the one hand, Freud associates the 'obscenity' of childhood with a certain ambitiousness – a rage for greatness, a ludicrous megalomania. But at other moments the repressed infantile wishes which resurface in adult dreams indicate the return of more directly sexual, and certainly corporeal experiences. Amongst such childhood sources of dream wishes Freud mentions 'the need for nourishment going back to the mother's breast', the child's delight in urination and faeces, and masturbation, which is in turn connected with hallucinatory regression.[156] How do these features of wishing fit together? Is Freud making a single point about childhood?

The first set of examples centre on feelings of mastery and autonomy, the second express a particular kind of relation to the body – orality, anality, for instance – which may be connected with feelings of superiority, but equally may express dependence. One set emphasises the self's situation in a power struggle amongst other selves, the other the development of sexual or libidinal drives. At first glance we are on familiar territory here, for one can easily suggest that these two forms of the infantile wish correspond to the two facets of Oedipal relations: the desire for gratification attached to the mother, and hostile competition with the father. Viewed in terms of the wider stratagem of *The Interpretation of Dreams*, as a window on to the nascent theory of psychoanalysis, the wish emerges once more as a pivotal concept, this time between the subject of dream interpretation and the theories of the Oedipus complex. From this point of view, the resolution of the theory of the wish depends ultimately on the degree to which Freud was prepared to centralise the theory of the Oedipus complex within the

---

[156] Ibid., 180, 307, 356.

general account of dream life at this stage. One answer would be to suppose that the egoistic representations of childhood wishes are sanitised or incomplete versions of Freud's more directly sexual examples. They would represent those wish examples that Freud felt himself most able to air publicly. It is here, where the wish meets infancy, one might continue, that the many different parts of Freud's psychological project *should* converge: the dream's 'command of childhood material which falls through the gaps in our conscious power of recollection'[157] links with the theory of the unconscious wish, and this in turn with the theory of sexuality ('the factor to which I attribute the greatest significance in the origin of the nervous afflictions').[158] If Freud cannot make these links explicit, so the argument would go, it is out of discretion. Didier Anzieu, for instance, reconstructs a missing sense behind the reference to the navel in the Irma dream – 'a visible sign of man's origin in his mother's body'[159] – by pointing out that Freud uses not the expected word, *Unbekannten*, to designate the 'unknown', but *Unerkannten*, which recalls the biblical expression '*ein Weib erkennen* (to know a woman)'. Though Anzieu acknowledges that the overall meaning of the note is unclear, he suggests that if Freud 'had used plain language' the note would run: 'the woman we dream of is the woman to whom we were once connected by the umbilical cord, and who remains "unknowable" by us in the biblical sense'.[160] The implication is then that the dream of 'Irma's Injection' holds such an important place in the book – the first specimen analysis, and the dream that confirmed to Freud the theory of wishes – not just because it reveals *a* wish, but because behind it Freud already intimates the key role to be played by infantile sexual material.

By the time of the *Introductory Lectures* Freud will claim more straightforwardly that dreams are instigated by 'actively evil and extravagantly sexual wishes' and that 'from the very first children have a copious sexual life'.[161] Whatever Freud is saying about the relationship between individuality, unconscious wishes and the rage for greatness, then, is ultimately to be resolved within the sexual theory as part of the Oedipus complex. Aspects of autonomy are framed within a critique of childish egotism, which is itself closely allied to the developmental structure of the sexual instincts. Indeed, in the 1914 paper 'On Narcissism', the ego itself will be more closely linked to an original erotic condition – the

---

[157] Freud, *The Interpretation of Dreams*, 16.
[158] Ibid., 93.
[159] Didier Anzieu, *Freud's Self-Analysis*, 154.
[160] Ibid., 154.   [161] Freud, *The Introductory Lectures*, 201, 208.

psychic life of the self begins with a libidinal attachment to one's own body, expressed via hallucinations of gratification.

But this hypothetical answer will not do for a number of reasons. First of all, we must remember that even if Freud was already making connections between dream wishes, infancy and sexuality, the theory of infantile sexuality was not yet fully evolved in Freud's mind. One could not state exactly what it was that Freud was certain about concerning infantile sexuality.[162] What Freud says concerning the Oedipus complex is itself very fragilely stated. It is the experience of *psychoneurotics*, that perhaps magnifies 'what goes on less clearly and intensely in the inner life of most children';[163] equally it is the 'theory of the *psychoneuroses*' that maintains 'with absolute certainty that only wishful impulses from infancy that are sexual in nature and have been subject to repression ... are capable of revival in later periods of development.'[164] That is, Freud finally leaves it as 'an open question whether sexual and infantile factors should also be required for the theory of dreams', admitting that 'I leave the theory unfinished at this point, for I have already taken a step beyond what can be demonstrated by assuming that dream-wishes always originate in the unconscious'.[165] In a footnote Freud adds that the fact that he has not 'dealt exhaustively with the part played by sexual ideas in dreams' has a particular reason which is *not* that he regards 'sexual life as a shameful thing' but that he would 'have to become deeply involved in the still unsolved problems of perversion and bisexuality'.[166] It is this awareness that he has not been able to complete the schema of the apparatus within which dream-wishes are ultimately to make sense that will send Freud retreating towards a humbler fall-back position in the final chapter of the book. As Freud conveyed to Fliess rather despondently in June 1899, 'The whole matter again resolves itself for me into a commonplace. Invariably the dream seeks to fulfill *one* wish that has assumed various forms. It is the wish to sleep!'[167]

The different strands of the theory cannot, then, be so easily resolved into a single structure, and for this reason we cannot so entirely master the ambiguities over selfhood and egotism, affirmative and pathological individuality, at least not by conscripting them within the more familiar patterns of sexual repression. A further observation on this

---

[162] 'Two other characterizations of the dream-wish – that it is infantile, and that it is generally (though not always) sexual – are intimately connected with this thesis, but at the time that Freud was writing *The Interpretation of Dreams*, he was not yet in a position to establish the connections', Wollheim, *Freud*, 73.

[163] Freud, *The Interpretation of Dreams*, 201.

[164] Ibid., 400.   [165] Ibid., 400.   [166] Ibid., 400.

[167] Freud to Fliess, 9 June 1899, in Masson, *The Complete Letters*, 354.

front is that the two forms of repeated wishes, even though they both involve censorship and the resurrection of childhood material, operate in slightly different ways. The return of the repressed, which hinges on the sexual material, stems from Freud's studies of hysteria and refers primarily to the creation of symptoms and compromise formations in later adult life. These raise a particular relation to time and memory: the process of deferred or retroactive effect, *Nachträglichkeit*, which, as we saw in Chapter 3 has received particular attention within French psychoanalysis. The defining feature of the disturbances caused within adult mental life by a recurrence of the (unconscious) memory of sexual experiences obtained in childhood, is that the original experiences pre-dated puberty, and pre-dated an awareness of their sexual implication, so that the sexual nature of the experience is something which is conferred on it retroactively, in fantasy, by the adult. The experience occurs, as it were, in two stages – one carrying the memory of a scene forwards from child to adult, the other reactivating the original impression with adult emotions. The resulting disturbance is partly a product of this sequential inversion, so that the memory comes first, the emotional investment afterwards. As Jones quotes Freud, 'an inverted relation of this kind between real experience and memory appears to be the psychological condition of repression'.[168]

However, there is a problem with transferring this model directly to the recollection or representation of infantile selfishness. I have suggested that such 'egoic' wishes do not appear to be attached to the experience of the body in the same way as the sexual wishes. Moreover, it does not seem appropriate to make either the positive representation of autonomy or the negative representation of selfishness unassimilable to or unrecognisable by consciousness in the same manner as the sexual perversions. Can we, for instance, attribute to the emergence of egotism within the self the same kind of maturational delay as affects the development of sexual feelings? It seems hard, then, to press the temporal case for rejection, repression, discontinuity and traumatic re-emergence as a general feature of these kinds of childhood wishes, although Freud does hint at just such a model in a reference to the work of Meynert during a discussion of sibling rivalry: 'we may expect that within the lifespan we ascribe to children, stirrings of altruism and a sense of morality will awaken, and that, as Meynert puts it, a secondary ego will overlay the primary and inhibit it'.[169] Even so, it hardly seems appropriate to place the wish 'to be great', to be 'sovereign', under

---

[168] Jones, *Sigmund Feud*, vol. I, 280.
[169] Freud, *The Interpretation of Dreams*, 193.

the same kind of pathological censure as the more obviously sexual wishes. The boundary, even in Freud's own self-references, between aspects of egotism that must be abandoned in a 'normal' course of development, and aspects which would seem precisely to characterise an achieved or exemplary normality, is not nearly so easily determined as Freud wants to make it seem. Does not Freud himself admit that the dream of the 'Botanical Monograph' corresponds to something in his thinking which is 'a passionate and emotional plea for my freedom to act as I do and arrange my life in the way that seems right to me and me alone',[170] and go on to connect enmity arising from sibling rivalry with the child's 'first conscious stirrings for freedom and justice',[171] much as Winnicott saw childish protest as 'sticking up for the rights of the individual'.[172] Jones, too, stresses the independence Freud 'vehemently craved for': it is a word that 'constantly recurs'.[173] He also quotes some remarks that Freud made in later life in which he asserted 'there is scarcely anything to which I am so hostile as the thought of being someone's protégé',[174] recalling Fichte's liberal protest against subservience of a hundred years earlier. Such admissions seem wholly to invert the identification of the child with a negative 'rage for greatness' that must be left behind. Does not the writing of *The Interpretation of Dreams* itself, and the hope that one day there might be a public inscription – 'Here the secret of dreams was revealed to Dr. Sigm. Freud on July 24, 1895' – indicate the vindication of precisely such a childhood wish?[175]

My larger point here is that the meaning of what Freud has to say about 'egotism' and the I, and by implication the self's relation both to unconscious origins and the idea of autonomy, remains suspended because our reading of all these terms remains confused. There appear to be two different moral perspectives defining the self's relation to its own unconscious history. One emphasises interruption, repression, and the fragile transcendence of egotism (though, paradoxically, the repressed terms of 'self-love' or 'rage for greatness' seemingly replicate

---

[170] Ibid., 304–5.   [171] Ibid., 193.

[172] Compare also Neville Symington's comment that 'Bion believed in his own personal freedom to be in a group according to his own mode, to think his own thoughts and to be pursuing his own aims when conducting an analysis', 'The Possibility of Human Freedom', 97.

[173] Jones, *Sigmund Freud*, vol. I, 195.

[174] Ibid., 188.

[175] Freud, Letter to Fliess, 12 June 1900, Masson, *The Complete Letters*, 417.

rather than invert the mature features of individual identity). The other perspective has more of a need to foster continuity with the child, in order to derive the concept of an autonomous or authentic individuality holding the self together (though, paradoxically, this continuity must be invisible, submerged, and unconscious). Beneath this ambivalence in both the structure and content of Freud's theory of the wish there is an ambiguity over the distinctions between egotism, independence, selfhood and autonomy. This in turn holds the relations between wishing, childhood and the unconscious in suspense. These relations have become ambiguous, not because Freud has set out like Schelling, or indeed Jung, to use the alternative topographical dimensions of the psyche as a space in which to unfold an ulterior account of the process of individuation, or of the person's original freedom, or of the ultimately 'unthinkable' nature of psychic internality. Rather they are ambiguous precisely because they are *not* an object of enquiry; because Freud leaves the issue of the self to one side in his investigation of psychic processes.

And here we arrive at a crucial differentiation. Psychoanalytic inquiries into the structure of the psyche attempt to elucidate the function of its different topographical domains, or to determine their genesis and their role within the developmental processes of childhood. In either case, whatever theoretical instabilities or obscurities are encountered are to be resolved by the more complex elucidation of psychic processes themselves. This will take place, for instance, in Freud's metapsychological papers of 1915 and more significantly in his major reformulation of the original theoretical framework in the early 1920s. But there are other kinds of instabilities affecting the boundaries and interrelationships between terms such as autonomy and selfishness, which are not properly developmental or psychical in origin. Rather they arise from instabilities in the social definition of these terms – not only through socio-political tensions, but also instabilities stemming from the piecemeal depiction of 'individuality' emerging out of various competing disciplines or modes of belief: psychology, literature, religion, nascent sociology, philosophy, anthropology and political science.

What I want to suggest is that the inquiry into psychic structure – the status of psychoanalysis itself as an autonomous project – must at some points remain unresolved, not only because of the profound complexities which the 'unconscious' introduces into the theoretical account of psychology, but because of profound historical ambiguities and social tensions over the ultimate status of the self, and therefore the conditions of self-knowledge in modern society. When Jones suggests that

'Freud found the origin of the ego the most obscure problem of all', or when Freud himself admits in 1920 that the analysis of the ego has made little headway,[176] we have to ask: how much have these obscurities to do with the ego's relation to the unconscious, and how much instead with instabilities in the wider concept of the 'ego' itself? Despite Freud's attempt to pin down the reference points of a psychic system, certain fundamental terms of the system – in fact, precisely those pertaining to notions of autonomy, individuality, independence, the nature of the self – cannot be made watertight within Freud's account. In some respects they cannot be clarified with respect to some of their most basic associations, because they are theoretical objects of a particularly ambiguous kind whose meanings are implicated in both historically shifting and sociologically contested accounts of selfhood. In the following chapter, I will expand on these kinds of problems emerging in the context of a wider crisis in liberal self-definition, before returning to consider the representation of paternal and political authority in *The Interpretation of Dreams*.

[176] Jones, *Sigmund Freud*, vol. I, 391; Freud, *Beyond the Pleasure Principle*, *SE*, vol. XVIII, 53.

7   The liberal unconscious

What has been manifesting itself as either a structural instability over genetic sequence in the psyche, or equally an ambivalence over the nature of unconscious wishes, wears a different face if we simply ask: how clearly defined are the general features of selfhood for Freud at this stage? Immediately we are confronted with a polyphony of voices – and I mean not the eventual subdivision of 'internal' voices within the psyche into id, ego and superego, but the multiple versions of the self which emerge from the conflicting interpretations of *Ich* and *Ich-heit*.[1] Straight off, we can identify at least one major dichotomy in the 'I', which is the way it refers in *The Interpretation of Dreams* to both that principle which is identified with rational consciousness, but also to what we might call the selfhood of the self as an independently motivated being. The first of these covers a range of different assumptions: the *Ich* can imply for Freud an abstract 'reality principle', a kind of objectivity we might say, though one grounded in general experience. It is this association that emerges from Freud's description of the primary and secondary processes which he will elaborate further in a paper of 1911, 'Formulations on the Two Principles of Mental Functioning'.[2] With a slightly different kind of emphasis it can refer to the civilised aspect of consciousness. Bruno Bettelheim suggests that 'when Freud names the reasonable, conscious aspects of our mind the I, we feel subtly flattered that our *real* I is what we value most highly in ourselves'.[3] More strongly than this it can imply rationalism: a specific adherence to transparency and logic in conscious thinking, contrasted with the anti-logic of the unconscious.

---

[1] In the following analysis I will stick to the German term *Ich* – I – because this is the term Freud himself uses, and because it carries a more general set of connotations than the term 'ego' allows for. As Laplanche and Pontalis suggest, Freud's early writings use the term '*Ich*' 'in a rather unspecific way' (Laplanche and Pontalis, *The Language of Psychoanalysis*, 131).

[2] Freud, 'Formulations on the Two Principles of Mental Functioning', *SE*, vol. XII, 213–26.

[3] Bettelheim, *Freud and Man's Soul*, 55.

Eric Fromm, for instance, draws this implication out when illustrating Freud's model of mind: 'If all that is real were conscious, then indeed man would be a rational being; for his rational thought follows the laws of logic.'[4] But these comprise only one set of meanings for the I, all of which are to some extent related to each other.

The second alternative connotation of the *Ich*, as the individual self, can also be taken in a number of different ways. It can imply most simply self-consciousness (Michel Henry, for instance, posits a foundational relation between Freud's *Ich* and the philosophical tradition of the Cartesian cogito),[5] or alternatively something more like a 'designation for the personality as a whole'.[6] At some points in his work the I implies something like an organ or an agency that 'controls the approaches to motility' and 'supervises all its own constituent processes'.[7] In a more psychological vein it might be that part of the mind which identifies with *being* a self; Laplanche and Pontalis mention the ego of La Rochefoucauld's *amour-propre* in this respect.[8] Staying with this more strongly individuated sense of the I one might link it with a basic account of individualism in liberal philosophy – supposing a conflict of independent wills as part of the nature of human society, in relation to which I assert the moral right to be 'for myself'. Fromm sees Freud's man as a 'variant of the classic *homo economicus*' and as 'primarily an isolated being, whose primary interest is the optimal satisfaction of both his ego and his libidinous interest'.[9] Even more emphatically than this, Philip Rieff hears the Hobbesian words '*Homo homini lupus*' echo through Freud's social psychology.[10]

Taking these sets of meanings altogether, it is clear that, though some of them are merely implicit, Freud's *Ich* mediates both notions of a general rational subjectivity *and* a robust liberal sense of the self's independence – that is, the very ambivalence between the universal and the particular that set the German idealists stumbling and oscillating in their attempt to ground a secular theory of human being. In translation the ambivalence is compounded a notch further in that two terms that Freud is able to hold separate – the I (*Ich*) and egotism (*egoistisch*), the latter implying in Freud's usage an anti-social component to be rejected – are more readily identified with each other in English,

---

[4] Fromm, *The Crisis of Psychoanalysis*, 50.
[5] Henry, 2–102.
[6] Laplanche and Pontalis, *The Language of Psychoanalysis*, 131.
[7] Freud, *The Ego and the Id*, *SE*, vol. XIX, 17.
[8] Laplanche and Pontalis, *The Language of Psychoanalysis*, 131.
[9] Fromm, *The Crisis of Psychoanalysis*, 45.
[10] Rieff, *Freud*, 221–2.

as ego and egotism. Thus Bettelheim has laboured to extract a 'good' Freudian connotation of ego, meaning existentially independent, from a bad one – egotism – which he feels has arisen through the translation of *Ich* by 'ego'.[11] 'What the story of the Sphinx seems to emphasize is that the answer to the riddle of life is not just man, but each person himself … we must know ourselves in order to free ourselves from destructive powers'.[12] If anything, for Bettelheim, 'the German *Ich* is invested with stronger and deeper personal meaning than the English "I"'.[13]

For the French interpreter of Freud, working in the shadow of the debates between structuralism and phenomenology in the 1950s and 1960s, yet further possibilities suggest themselves. Borch-Jacobsen finds that if the dream-wish undergoes distortion, it is because it is 'inadmissable, irreconcilable, with the conscious, social, orderly ego';[14] but the ego also relates to thinking, and thus to a 'cogitatio' which 'overflows consciousness at every turn, where consciousness is understood as certainty and presence of self in representation'. This certainty of self again picks up a slightly different, more phenomenologically individuated resonance from the 'conscious, social, orderly ego'. But in a further move, 'the subject-conscious-of-itself' is never dislodged from its 'privileged and central position … except to the benefit of an other subject – one that is deeper'.[15] This takes the relationship between conscious and unconscious back towards a more Schellingian use of the term in which the unconscious conceals a more absolute subject – hence the I (as the 'subject') is now identified with two separate poles of a divide in consciousness. It will turn out 'to be the most opaque to consciousness'.[16]

The concept of the I, in Freud's usage, slips ambiguously between the idea of general objectivity and specifically individual (self-)consciousness; and also between something socially cohesive (common sense, objective reality) and something radically subversive of social coherence. It straddles the very crises which drove Schelling to formulate a theory of the self's unconscious basis in the first place – can a society of independent individuals claim some absolute support, or underlying ground, on which to found a collective narrative of its own moral and subjective experience? But because our attention is drawn towards the unconscious, we tend to be distracted from such radical instabilities in the 'I'/'ego'. The Jungian psychologist James Hillman saw Freud as

---

[11] Bettelheim, *Freud and Man's Soul*, 53–5.
[12] Ibid., 27.   [13] Ibid., 55.
[14] Mikkel Borch-Jacobsen, *The Freudian Subject* (Basingstoke and London: Macmillan, 1982), 2.
[15] Ibid., 6.   [16] Ibid., 8.

attempting to wrestle his way out of Cartesian individualism by appeal-
ing to the universal parameters of Oedipal theory. But at the same time
Freud remained trapped in the apprehension that man is 'an individual
creature in a horde led by a chief'.[17] This description is a good example
of the way in which, quite apart from the internal, metapsychological
extrapolation of the self's psychic constituents, there are uncertainties
about what selfhood implies under normal circumstances which potentially unhinge or subvert the meaning of that 'internal' account.

To give a few more examples of the radical differences which this
indeterminacy can introduce into interpretations of Freud's model: if
the I is taken as a rational or general subject, the unconscious wish
might appear to preserve the possibility of a self whose authenticity is
threatened by integration with the general identity of 'selves'. We have
seen something like this in Bettelheim and Winnicott, and also in Jung's
'The Plight of the Individual in Modern Society', but it is an idea which
has had wider currency in critical theory and philosophy, for instance
in Herbert Marcuse's critique of 'one-dimensional' man, or Michel
Henry's suggestion that, when 'objectivity ceaselessly extends its reign
of death over the devastated universe', then 'life has no refuge but the
Freudian unconscious', and psychoanalysis is 'the soul of a world without soul'.[18] Alternatively, in a more orthodox Freudian approach, the
unconscious can be taken as that instinctual part of the self which must
be repressed in order for civilised life to be maintained.[19]

On the other hand, if the I is taken to indicate an ultimately isolated and self-motivated self or the kind of selfhood belonging to 'an
average businessman of the nineteenth century'[20] – from one kind
of liberal perspective, the foundational unit of modern society – the
unconscious might appear as a more unbounded and general current of
natural instinct *against* which civilised independence must be defended
(this would bring Freud's unconscious closer to Schopenhauer's notion
of the generalised and blindly driven will).[21] From yet another point
of view, the unconscious might appear as a second, determining law
which helps complete the rational account of human behaviour –
making it amenable once more to the rationalistic image of the ego.

[17] James Hillman, 'Man Is by Nature a Political Animal'': or Patient as Citizen', in Sonu
    Shamdasani and Michael Münchow (eds.), *Speculations After Freud: Psychoanalysis,
    Philosophy and Culture* (London: Routledge, 1994), 32.
[18] Herbert Marcuse, *One Dimensional Man: Studies in the Ideology of Advanced Society*
    (London: Routledge & Kegan Paul, 1968); Henry, *The Genealogy of Psychoanalysis*, 7.
[19] See, for instance, Freud, '"Civilized" Sexual Morality and Modern Nervous Illness',
    SE, vol. IX, 177–204.
[20] Fromm, *The Crisis of Psychoanalysis*, 47.
[21] For Freud's relation to Schopenhauer, see Chapter 1.

This is in effect the way Ernest Jones reads it: 'If unconscious motivation is taken into account, therefore, the rule of determinism is of general validity.'[22]

If one turns to Lacan, the entire range of associations here fall out differently again, for now the key concept within which *Ich-heit* must be oriented is 'the Subject' and the unconscious itself is 'homologous with what occurs at the level of the Subject'.[23] The whole set of further difficulties which arise when one attempts to position the Freudian I in relation to the philosophy of the subject has been admirably explored by Mikkel Borch-Jacobsen: 'the cleavage or division of the subject that psychoanalysis keeps talking about takes place against a background of unity, a *unitary* subject'; '*Who* is thinking, in this instance (who, then, is thinking me)?'[24]

But one can also pose these questions differently, and ask simply: whose version of the self lurks behind Freud's concepts of the I? Is it Goethe's robust independence, Freud's favourite point of cultural reference? Is it Darwin and Malthus? Is it Hobbes, as Phillip Rieff suggests, or Bentham – according to Edwin Boring, 'Freud's pleasure principle is derived from the utilitarian's hedonism'.[25] Paul Roazen makes the case for an image of man derived from a combination of J. S. Mill, Nietzsche and Dostoevsky;[26] Fromm suggests Benjamin Franklin, but also Spinoza's absolute and La Mettrie's *l'homme machine* as the basis for the Freudian self.[27] For Peter Gay Freud's idealisation of rational and passionate independence places him in proximity to Voltaire and Diderot as the last *philosophe*;[28] while for Andrew Bowie Freud's 'I' implicitly revives the conceptions of Fichte and Schelling.[29]

Freud's ego has become essentially a prism for the many different tensions in modern theories of the self. As perhaps it should, if psychoanalysis is to be a general science of the human individual. Laplanche and Pontalis thus make a case for the need to hang on to all the implications of the I: 'For Freud *exploits* traditional usages: he opposes organism to environment, subject to object, internal to external, and so on,

---

[22] Jones, *Sigmund Freud*, vol. I, 366.

[23] Jacques Lacan, *The Four Fundamental Concepts*, 24.

[24] Borch-Jacobsen, *The Freudian Subject*, 6, 4.

[25] Edwin Boring, *A History of Experimental Psychology* (New York: Appleton-Century-Crofts, 1950), 693.

[26] Paul Roazen, *Political Theory and the Psychology of the Unconscious* (London: Open Gate, 2000).

[27] Fromm, *The Crisis of Psychoanalysis*, 45–7.

[28] See Chapter 1, Peter Gay, *A Godless Jew: Freud Atheism and the Making of Psychoanalysis* (New Haven, CT: Yale University Press, 1987).

[29] Bowie, *Aesthetics and Subjectivity*, 58–60.

while continuing to employ "*Ich*" at these different levels'. What is more, they add, 'he plays on the ambiguities thus created, so that none of the connotations normally attaching to "ego" or "I" ("*Ich*") is forgotten'.[30] But if the most basic connotations of the 'I' are ambiguous (conceptually, historically, ethically, existentially) does this not radically unsettle any attempt to pin down a psychic history of the self's relation to autonomy – how it is lost, where it is gained; where it is fantasied, where it is real – within the psychoanalytic account? If the wider account must be left in suspense, then one must also acknowledge that the structural problems in completing the account of the apparatus are not just incidental and empirical. They reach back towards ontological crises generated by the complexities of social existence.

The first and sole authority

After all, it is my father I have to thank for what I feel is, perhaps, my one secure possession: my sense of inner freedom.[31]

There remains one more angle from which to approach the contradictions over autonomy in *The Interpretation of Dreams*, one more closely related to the social and moral contexts of individuality just outlined, and this is the relationship with the father, so repeatedly staged in this text, which dramatises a very explicit agon over selfhood, subservience and self-determination: 'The authority that characterises the father provoked the child's criticism early on; the strict demands he made caused the child to keep a keen eye open for his father's every weakness.'[32] Here, again, I will show that structural instabilities seemingly internal to the psychoanalytic account – representative of purely psychic processes – in fact conceal more profound instabilities at a historical and sociological level. That is to say, the instabilities are not ones that psychoanalysis will be able to master simply through clearer technical elucidations of its own psychological account.

In *The Interpretation of Dreams* it is specifically the father who most often provides an axial point around which the disparate intimations of childhood and selfhood can turn. Some of the grounds for this lie in the crucial role played by the death of Freud's own father in inaugurating his self-analysis, which would in turn lead to the discovery of the Oedipus complex. In a letter to Fliess of November 1896, Freud admitted that, 'by one of those dark pathways behind the official consciousness the

[30] Laplanche and Pontalis, *The Language of Psychoanalysis*, 131–2.
[31] Stefan Zweig, *The World of Yesterday* (London: Pushkin Press, 2009), 31.
[32] Freud, *The Interpretation of Dreams*, 278.

old man's death has affected me deeply … in [my] inner self the whole past has been reawakened by this event';[33] likewise in the preface to the book's second edition, Freud is explicit that the work as a whole was also 'a portion of my own self-analysis, my reaction to my father's death – that is to say … the most important event, the most poignant loss, of a man's life'.[34] The many references to *Hamlet* which punctuate the text, seemingly incidentally, likewise keep up an ingenious subliminal commentary on the theme of the paternal transference of power and life's guilty returns. Freud at one point even identifies his own book with *Hamlet*, emphasising that Shakespeare wrote the play 'immediately after his father's death', when his 'mourning for his father was still fresh, and when presumably his childhood feelings towards him were revived'.[35]

Examining Freud's recollections of the father appears to move us on to very different terrain from the investigation of the psychic apparatus. Certainly, the father provokes a meditation on the nature of law and obedience, but there is at most, we might think, a metaphorical connection between the issue of determinism in the psyche and these revived memories of paternal authority (though both may concern the operation of forces on the psychic life of the individual). And yet, just as the wish potentially hinged together Freud's different psychological and energetic narratives of selfhood, so the father occupies a nodal position at the limits of self-recollection *and* the inception of psychic structures, while also mediating the imagination of authority per se. What appears from one point of view as a product of Freud's scientific investigation of functions within the psyche – the reawakening of the past; the recollection of childhood; the analysis of conflict – appears, in the light of Freud's statements above, as a response to the death of the father: it is *he* who has awakened the past by 'one of those dark pathways behind the official consciousness'; it is *his* disappearance which, in a continuation of that quote, makes Freud 'feel quite uprooted'.[36]

One thinks here of the way the absolute in Schelling, that principle which represents the ultimate underpinning of law in a universe whose own principles appear to be shifting historically, is represented through the language of paternity. And how this paternity behind the being of the individual, its prior grounds, is already underway from a Christian idealisation of the notion of God to an anthropic principle located within

---

[33] Freud to Fliess, 2 November 1896, Masson (ed.), *The Complete Correspondence*, 202.
[34] Freud, *The Interpretation of Dreams [SE]*, vol. IV, xxvi.
[35] Freud, *The Interpretation of Dreams*, 204.
[36] Masson (ed.), *The Complete Correspondence*, 202.

the person, as their unconscious grounds, their 'ownmost' nature. For Schelling, Schubert and later Carus, the unconscious will form the theoretical basis for a new dynamic account of the psyche which folds the question of paternity and authorship into the depths of the individual itself. Does the father here in Freud fulfil a similar theoretical role – a cipher for the issue of how law inheres in the individual (along with all the ambivalence in that question) shrunk down to an empirical feature of psychic history? If this were so, an analysis of the role of the father in *The Interpretation of Dreams* might provide a missing link to that crisis in the liberal theorisation of the self on which our hunt for the meaning of the I foundered.

Within this larger context of the evolving frameworks of nineteenth-century self-description per se – the need for an empirical science of the individual mind, rather than merely Freud's autobiographical self-description – there are important precedents for this structural emphasis on the father. Turning again to the associationist tradition: as an ultimate causal priority gravitates, within that paradigm, towards the original laying down of impressions and ideas in the mind, so an ultimate moral function gravitates towards the father–son relation. Whatever has happened in childhood in relation to the father has somehow conditioned the future person – has laid down the law. One thinks of J. S. Mill's *Autobiography*, in which both the utilitarian theory of selfhood and the psychological experience of his own self-formation are traumatically implicated in each other. J. S. Mill's was 'the only mind directly formed by [James Mill's] instructions'.[37] In a similar way, Freud admits to Fliess that 'much in my life was fashioned by him'.[38] In comparison with Schelling, Freud is less able to explore the foundations of the self by proposing transcendental or ideal dimensions of that enquiry. He has no wish to ply back and forth between metaphysics and empirical experience in that way. But for that very reason, having been purged of idealist elements, the empirical account of how authority emerges in relation to the father takes on a crucial theoretical importance. 'The father is the oldest, first, and sole authority for the child'[39] is how Freud justifies this attention in his analysis of the dream of Count Thun. The father is thus both a spur to Freud's own self-analysis and a theoretical object located at the foundations of a more general scientific account of the psyche. Perhaps if the relations between the I, individuality and

[37] Mill, *Autobiography*, 63.
[38] Masson (ed.), *The Complete Correspondence*, 202.
[39] Freud, *The Interpretation of Dreams*, 167.

egotism seem indeterminate in the abstract, exploring the relation to the father may offer some clearer way of anchoring the self.

However, the representation of the father in *The Interpretation of Dreams* is invaded by odd forms of parallax, precisely because of the nature of the psyche as object of investigation. From one kind of empirical perspective, as we have seen, the father is plausibly located at the inception of personal development, in the form of an original encounter with the nature of authority. He is at least partly implicated in laying down or instigating the psychic apprehension of law (later with Klein this role will shift to the mother), and is perhaps also the origin of memory traces from which may derive important features of the unconscious mind.[40] On the other hand, the very window which Freud opens on to childhood, in order to understand the developmental structure of the self and its origins, is provided by unconscious memories as they emerge in dreams. Yet we are told that the dream has no means of representing logical relations,[41] while the unconscious system operates under a different, inverted concept of law. Thus the attempt to stabilise an understanding of how law inheres in the self, via the figure of the father, at the same time radically destabilises the image of the father's authority. *The Interpretation of Dreams*, though latterly respectfully dedicated to the father, both records for posterity the painful moment of his public humiliation and subjects his mental afterlife to further humiliation at the hands of unconscious fantasy. The father who once reprimanded the infant Freud for urinating in the bedroom appears one-eyed, feeble and urinating into a bottle held by the son.[42] We are reminded by Freud that Cronos devoured his children, but Zeus castrated his father.[43] A dream in which Freud fantasises that his father played a leading role in Magyar politics leads on to observations about his intestinal obstruction in real life, and a recollection of how his dead body was evacuated of stools.[44]

From one point of view that kind of phantasmal oscillation between reverence and obedience, and resentment and acts of humiliation, is an effect of the 'principle of ambivalence' at the heart of psychic life. One might thus wish to construct, outside of these specifically psychic distortions, the 'real' empirical situation which has determined the mind in a particular way – though this way might be disguised from the individual itself. But on the other hand, the object of Freud's study here is

---

[40] Parental involvement in the institution of psychic law, particularly the inception of conscience in the child, will become more explicit as Freud develops the concept of the superego in the early 1920s.

[41] Freud, *The Interpretation of Dreams*, 237.

[42] Ibid., 167.   [43] Ibid., 197.   [44] Ibid., 274.

precisely the psyche itself, the manifestation of its *own* internal laws and consistencies. Freud is not concerned with the reality of the father, but the reality of his existence within the *unconscious*. It is the unconscious that represents the 'heart of our being'[45] and the 'true reality of the psyche',[46] and dreams are thus one of our most concrete point of access to it. It is in the unconscious, too, that the father both persists as an item of imaginative identification and continues to act upon the self, irrespective of his presence or absence in the world outside. So how should the father, in principle, appear? Before the psyche, determining it, instigating a movement towards reality and maturation? Or internally, existing by virtue of the psyche, and subjected to its inversions and transformations? How does this 'heart' relate to that 'beginning', and what connotation does either carry for the logic of individual autonomy? We can see how this indeterminacy in effect repeats, and perhaps more starkly, the ambivalence that clung to the notion of obscene or affirmatory selfishness in the ego. The father is both the sole and first authority for the self and authority's hysterical vanishing point within it.

In this connection, the genetic account of paternal authority takes on all the complexities and hesitations that we saw emerging in Schelling over the causal relation between the self and an external embodiment of the law. We saw in those earlier chapters how the burial of knowledge of the self's original inception – the sinking of that act of the absolute into 'unconsciousness' – established both the emergence of the individual as an autonomous entity and a certain kind of bar on the recognition or recovery of this relationship. For Freud, as also for Mill, a certain veil falls over this original relationship with the father: 'The impressions that had the greatest influence upon us, from earliest youth, hardly ever become conscious.'[47] There is a parallel here with Freud's description of the distorted way in which the adult recalls the childhood experience of being held aloft in later dreams of flying: 'years afterwards, they create the repetition in their dreams, but in their dreams they leave out the hands that held them, so that now they hover and fall freely'.[48] Likewise, and again as with Schelling, to unearth this forgotten relationship threatens to re-open that theoretical wound in self-understanding – not just because it links the individual foundationally to someone other than itself, but because it foregrounds the problems of beginning and linking per se. One wonders, then, how much of the hostility towards the father results from an original emotive fact, forgotten

---

[45] Ibid., 398.   [46] Ibid., 405.
[47] Ibid., 352. This intuition will be further extended in Freud's later notion of a repressed 'primal scene'.
[48] Ibid., 209.

but now remembered (once the Oedipal wishes have been revealed, 'there is little doubt we would all rather turn our gaze away from the scenes of our childhood')[49] and how much it is a symbolic fabrication deriving from the need to formulate an account of the self as independently motivated, and therefore predicated on the subversion or negation of prior authority figures.

This analysis of the father–son relation is incomplete, however, in one important respect. In both the structural description of paternal authority and the recollection of the father in dreams Freud is drawn to mediate that relationship, and the notion of contested autonomy, via associations with political authority, both as a metaphor and as a historical reality. These mediations attempt to tether the terms of autonomy to more specific cultural and political contexts. A key instance of this occurs in Freud's footnote to the dream of 'Count Thun', at the end of the section in Chapter 5 which examines material from infancy as a source of dreams.[50] It is noteworthy for being the longest footnote in the book's first edition, but also for the way it attempts to bridge issues of patriarchal and political authority, childhood and kingship. The dream itself occurs partly in response to a daytime altercation over aristocratic privilege which inspires the dreamer to return at night to the revolutionary climate of 1848. One of the most interesting points in the passage is Freud's suggestion that

The prince is called *Landesvater* and the father is the oldest, first and sole authority for the child, from whose absolute power the other social authorities have proceeded in the course of the history of human culture (insofar as "Matriarchy" does not impose limits on this proposition).[51]

['*Der Fürst heißt Landesvater, und der Vater ist die älteste, erste, für das Kind einzige Autorität, aus deren Machtvollkommenheit im Laufe der menschlichen Kulturgeschichte die anderen sozialen Obrigkeiten hervorgegangen sind (insofern nicht das "Mutterrecht" zur Einschränkung dieses Satzes nötigt).*'][52]

There are a number of interesting collisions in this sentence. It links in to the series of *Hamlet* references, which in their own way provoke comparisons between the childish and princely conflict over authority. But there is also a complex point about the psychic life of power, and about the father's relation both to the child and to the cultural foundations of authority per se. Just as with Freud's schematic diagrams of the psychic apparatus in chapter 7 of *The Interpretation of Dreams*, one senses that too many different reference-points are being integrated here by too slender means. We shift from the metaphorical depiction of the *prince*

[49] Ibid., 203.   [50] Ibid., 167.   [51] Ibid., 167.
[52] Sigmund Freud, *Die Traumdeutung* (Frankfurt am Main: Fischer, 2000), 225.

as father (*Landesvater*), to the father as sole authority for the *child*, and then from the father as first authority for the child, to the father as original authority from which all other social authorities have proceeded. There is a point of parallax here around the shift from kingdom to family and from family to the cultural origins of authority. The attributive grammar of the sentence is awry, and indeed there are discrepancies in the interpretation of Freud's syntax here. Whereas the ordering of Crick's 'oldest, first and sole authority for the child' centralises the child in the derivation of authority, implying that it is in relation *to the child* that the father is the oldest and first authority, Strachey's *Standard Edition*, which here matches the German more closely, has 'A Prince is known as the father of his country; the father is the oldest, first, and for the children the only authority ...',[53] which implies instead that the father is the oldest and first authority in general, and then introduces the clause 'and for the children the only authority' as an aside.

There is a disturbance here caused by bringing the child's idealisation of the father into proximity with the general political derivation of authority itself. Insofar as the father–son relation is triangulated through the 'outer' point of the history of princes, the absolute nature of that familial relationship appears to be grounded and culturally verified. But insofar as the notion of prince is triangulated through the 'inner' point of the child's idealisation of the father, it is potentially distorted by the mythologising and self-aggrandising tendencies of childhood. In this second case, the statement would present us with the fantasy, not the reality, of worldly authority: the fantasy that in modernity there could be a 'sole' authority. One might compare here the crucial qualification made later by Melanie Klein concerning the child's relation to paternal authority: 'Permanent submission to the authority principle, permanent greater or less intellectual dependency and limitation, are based on this first and most significant experience of authority, on the relationship between the parents and the little child'.[54] What is important here is the negative emphasis on 'dependency'. John Phillips comments on this passage that, although authority is something the child cannot do without, 'the influence of authority in the development of the child is harmful from the beginning', it is 'already the first barrier to the child's freedom and independence of thought', therefore 'the aim of child analysis is to reduce it'.[55] Furthermore, the danger for the child is

[53] Freud, *The Interpretation of Dreams [SE]*, 217.
[54] Melanie Klein, 'The Development of a Child', *Love, Guilt and Reparation and Other Works, 1921–1945* (London: Hogarth Press, 1975), 35–6.
[55] John Phillips, 'The Fissure of Authority: Violence and the Acquisition of Knowledge', in John Phillips and Lyndsey Stonebridge (eds.) *Reading Melanie Klein* (London: Routledge, 1988), 161.

its inability to disentangle idealised or persecuting visions of the superego – the violence of its own internal phantasy – from the 'real' object
of the parent. Development is possible 'when the infant discovers that
authority is based on a false or counterfactual attribution';[56] that is to
say, the child gradually learns to separate its own phantasy of authority (which may be extreme, monolithic or all-powerful) from the more
limited and fallible empirical reality.

In the *Landesvater* passage in the Freud, there is by contrast an attempt
to make two different investigations into the grounds of individuality – its
psychological experience and its historical and socio-political underpinnings – fit within the frame of a single relationship. The father, abstracted
by associationist psychology as the primal educator of the child, is here
projected into an embodiment of the grounds of social authority per se.
But this sandwiching together of ancient and early modern rulership
with the modern bourgeois father pastes over a crisis in the political history of authority itself. Not just the slipping away of the liberals from
governmental power in Austria – the end of the Liberal era in Austria,
as Schorske and others frequently term the timing of *The Interpretation
of Dreams* – but also that ideological crisis which beset the attempts at
the end of the eighteenth century to think the transition from absolute
to self-given power. It was here that this book began, with the attempt to
stabilise theoretically, through a philosophy of human nature or a science
of mind, the individual's relation to order and to freedom.

The same dream occasions another peculiar elision around autonomy, politics and fatherhood, this time with respect to aristocratic
and liberal representations of authority. It concerns Freud's confusion and frustration at being the only person unable to solve a pair
of after-dinner riddles at a social gathering to which he was invited.
Capable, like Oedipus, of solving the riddle of the Sphinx, the solution
to these simple verses escapes him. The first revolves around a pun on
the German word for ancestor – *Vorfahren* – which can equally mean to
drive on ahead (*vorfahren*), as a coachman might be ordered to do:

> The master commands it,
> The driver does it,
> Everyone has it,
> It lies in the grave.[57]

There are, in fact, three riddles here in relation to Freud. First of all,
the 'intended' play on '*Vorfahren*', which is the 'official' solution to the
puzzle. Secondly, the verse contracts in a few short lines the images

---

[56] Ibid., 162.
[57] Freud, *The Interpretation of Dreams*, 276.

of subservience and the death of the father: two issues which, each in their own way, haunt Freud's attempt to negotiate the boundaries of the psychic apparatus. This we might term a 'private' riddle, in relation to *The Interpretation of Dreams* itself, and which might explain why Freud found the solution particularly obscure. But there is a third puzzle, or a disturbance, which concerns Freud's own associations to the terms of aristocracy and ancestry.

Freud links the image of masters and drivers back to the person of Count Thun whom he had witnessed earlier in the day using his aristocratic privilege to brush aside a ticket inspector, while Freud stood waiting on the Westbahnhof platform.[58] It is therefore Thun who is 'driving ahead so imperiously' in the riddle, and Freud adds that it is 'the only merit of these grandees that they had taken the trouble to be born (that they were descendents)'.[59] He identifies himself, in contrast, with 'we middle-class plebians',[60] and extracts from the dream the further unconscious assertion: 'It's nonsense to be proud of one's forebears. I prefer to be a forebear myself, an ancestor'.[61] There are many interesting things going on in this liberal defiance of privilege. In the first place, the digression into the world of class conflict curves inexorably back to the terms of 'familial' authority: for Freud explicitly identifies himself with the position of a father – as forebear – and demotes Count Thun to the position of a child, who is merely, passively born. But there is a further more political puzzle, in that Freud does not simply, in a radical gesture, invert the conventional hierarchical associations of aristocrat and middle-class individual; he subtly switches their identities. Freud's aristocrat is reduced to a condition of mediocrity, of average or mere abstract 'individuality', while Freud wrests to his 'plebian' self the equivalent of a radically aristocratic substance. Behind the 'I prefer to be a forebear myself, an ancestor', there is surely, partially, an identification with the aristocrat's autonomy and patrilineage, the desire to be a dynastic founder.[62]

The tone here is remarkably similar to Fichte's 'I want to be independent – not to be in and through another but to be something for myself',[63] or Schelling's: 'let someone accept subordination as necessary, and hence as original … What would he have? He would be finished'.[64] However,

---

[58] Ibid., 160.   [59] Ibid., 276.
[60] Ibid., 275.   [61] Ibid., 277.
[62] See Hanns Sachs, *Freud, Master and Friend* (London: Imago, 1945), 24–8, for an amusing account of Vienna's masquerade of democracy, and the attempts of the middle class to pattern their behaviour on the style of the privileged class: 'The thing was to dress and act in such a way as to be taken for a member of the aristocracy', 26–7.
[63] Fichte, *Vocation*, 21.   [64] Schelling, *Ages*, 180.

unlike Fichte and Schelling, Freud does not acknowledge the resulting instability of individual identity freed from any preceding authority. Instead he naively invests the liberal ideal with the substance of a certain privileged autonomy, and holds it off from any awareness of the more destructive elements of conflict and social competition associated with middle-class existence, though lower down the page he does gloss the thoughts of another dreamer: 'this is a demented world and a deranged society. The deserving don't get their due, and the ones who don't care get it all'.[65] This is all taking place, it must be remembered, around the time of the electoral success of the Christian Social Party in 1897, which enabled the appointment of the anti-Semitic Carl Lueger as mayor of Vienna and in turn heralded the implosion of Austrian liberal ideals.

A third passage, again in the chapter on the material sources of dreams, gives a clearer instance of the way in which Freud attempts to corroborate the 'agon' of authority in the psyche with a contest over absolute political authority. Freud is here touching on the crucial question of Oedipal conflict as a factor of general significance and turns to the 'primeval days' of human society for supporting evidence: 'The more absolute the father's rule in the ancient family, the more the son as *rightful successor* is forced into the position of enemy, and the greater his impatience to come to power through the death of the father.'[66] But he dovetails this conflict over the transference of power in ancient Greece into a description of the modern bourgeoisie: 'Even in our middle-class families, by refusing his son his independence and the wherewithal to support it, the father is helping to develop the natural seeds of enmity in him. The physician is often enough in a position to notice that in his grief at the loss of his father, the son cannot suppress his satisfaction at gaining his freedom at last.'[67]

What Freud elides in this portrait of the modern father, who keeps a grip 'on the remnants of the dreadfully antiquated *potestas patris familias*',[68] is that the autonomy that is at stake here in father–son relations cannot have the same political import as in the classical model, cannot yield the same social substance to the son, except insofar as it is triangulated through an unconscious fantasy of power – a 'rage for greatness' – that allows an ideal of sovereignty to echo through the more lacklustre and increasingly fragile socio-political conditions of the liberal middle class. Again, Hanns Sachs' image of the attempts of the middle class to ape the aristocracy through 'cavalier' fictions is significant.[69]

---

[65] Freud, *The Interpretation of Dreams*, 277.
[66] Ibid., 197.   [67] Ibid., 197.   [68] Ibid., 197.
[69] Sachs, *Freud*, 27.

As Hannah Arendt suggested in *The Human Condition*: 'Throughout the whole of occidental antiquity it would indeed have been self-evident that even the power of the tyrant was less great, less "perfect" than the power which the *paterfamilias*, the *dominus*, ruled over his household of slaves and family'.[70] But in modern society, the nature of both that household, and the public realm of the *polis*, have been through several seismic reformulations which have drastically inverted, rather than sustained, the terms of patriarchal authority. For Tocqueville in 1840, the notion of autonomous individuality in modern democracy was itself a fantasy, born out of the habit of thinking about oneself in isolation: 'Among democratic peoples new families continuously rise from nothing while others fall, and nobody's position is quite stable.'[71] However, the inversions of autonomy become particularly acute as one approaches the era of mass society. Here, one-man, monarchical rule, 'which the ancients stated to be the organizational device of the household', is transformed 'into a kind of no-man rule'.[72] For Arendt, the experience of the political yields to the rule of bureaucracy. Correspondingly, the power of the family is absorbed into the 'social', which is characterised by conformism and the strength of common interest.[73] Adorno and Horkheimer would likewise read Freud's work in precisely this context of the decline of the role of the father in modern society.[74]

In each of these three examples from *The Interpretation of Dreams*, Freud has elided or blurred something to do with the nature of modern autonomy, while attempting to set the content of the unconscious psyche in a wider political context. There are two different accounts one could give of these distortions. In the first place, there is the possibility that the comparisons with princes and kings are not first and foremost political or historical derivations, but identifications which to some degree express and sustain the force of infantile idealisation. The father, the self and the political in modernity are being inflated by Freud into absolute expressions of power, and as such succumb to the very forms of pathological idealisation they are intended to elucidate. The father is *Landesvater*; the son, in a later text, is His Majesty the Ego;[75] the

---

[70] Hannah Arendt, *The Human Condition* (University of Chicago Press, 1998), 27.

[71] Tocqueville, *Democracy in America*, 507.

[72] Arendt, *The Human Condition*, 40.

[73] Ibid., 40. Compare Tocqueville: 'Individuals are forgotten, and the species alone counts', *Democracy in America*, 451.

[74] Theodor Adorno, 'Freudian Theory', 125; Max Horkheimer, 'Authoritarianism and the Family Today', in R. N. Anshen (ed.), *The Family: Its Function and Destiny* (New York: Harper Brothers, 1949).

[75] Sigmund Freud, 'Creative Writers and Day-Dreaming', *The Standard Edition*, vol. IX *(1906–1908): Jensen's 'Gradiva' and Other Works*, 150.

familial generational contest is compared with the impatience of Henry V to come to the throne.[76] A second possibility is to locate the source of such idealisation not in the fantasy life of the individual, but in the scientific account itself. The ideal and abstracted representation of the father bears some resemblance, one can argue, to the prince, the *Landesvater*, but mainly by virtue of his position not at the head of a principality, but at the head of the psychical enquiry into the self. It is by virtue of his insertion at the root of the ontogenetic account of the I that the real father comes to acquire a kind of absolute 'constitutional' status, and this in turn facilitates comparisons with the absolute ruler in history, or with ancient patriarchal authority. In either case, these ambiguities around the idealised status of the father once more open up a host of unintended ironies within the psychoanalytic account of identity: where, or how, is authority *really* located, and where is it being fantasied?

The key issue here is not one concerning the 'internalisation' of the political in Freud's account of the psyche. Some work has been done on examining *The Interpretation of Dreams* in its political context and analysing the extent to which the crises of Viennese liberalism find their way into the book – both at the level of everyday descriptions, and at a theoretical level. William J. McGrath, for instance, explores the way in which Freud's adolescent experience of politics had a formative effect on his psychoanalytic discoveries.[77] In a different way, Carl Schorske has levelled a powerful critique at Freud, arguing that he takes the stress points of liberal politics in *fin-de-siècle* Vienna and ferries them back into the details of dream narratives, where they concern, ultimately, the elucidation of a primary conflict with the father. For Schorske, at a time when the Austrian Reichsrat had fallen 'deep into political hysteria' and the Habsburg Empire was 'pulling apart at the seams internally', *The Interpretation of Dreams* reduces the struggle with Austrian socio-political reality to 'an epiphenomenal manifestation of psychic forces'.[78] Examining in particular the dream of Count Thun, Schorske finds a political fact of the utmost importance in Freud's situation of these details in a section devoted to 'infantile material'. The dream leads Freud away from the figure of the Count towards an image of his ailing and humiliated father. For Schorske, 'as the father replaces the prime minister on the station platform, patricide replaces politics' and 'psychoanalysis overcomes history'.[79]

---

[76] Freud, *The Interpretation of Dreams*, 315.

[77] William McGrath, 'Freud and the Force of History', in T. Gelford and J. Kerr (eds.), *Freud and the History of Psychoanalysis* (Mahwah, NJ: The Analytic Press, 1992), 79–97.

[78] Carl Schorske, 'Politics and Patricide in Freud's *Interpretation of Dreams*', 182–3.

[79] Ibid., 197.

But I am struck by something else in Freud's relation to the political. Schorske's charge (in some ways comparable to Marquard's critique of *Naturphilosophie*) is that Freud's project becomes one of ideological fabrication – he converts an unmanageable political reality into an equivocal personal victory. However, both Schorske's assertion that Freud internalises and displaces a problem with authority that is 'outside', and McGrath's that Freud's youthful experience of politics informs the development of his own self-analysis, miss something fundamental in the historical undertow beneath Freud's scientific project. In their concentration on the personal element in Freud's self-analysis, they miss the wider question of what a psychological science is doing there in the first place. The very attempt to flesh out the structure of internal life, as a detached entity for scientific investigation, is itself enmeshed in that longer-range project of self-description, self-justification and self-objectification within the post-Enlightenment sciences of man. Insofar as this wider nineteenth-century project attempted to humanise and stabilise a description of the self that would be free of the trappings of religious and metaphysical dogmatism, and to endow a notionally 'autonomous' selfhood with a certain substance or consistency of its own, Freud's turn to the inner life is itself already political.

This leads back, once more, to that wider anxiety over selfhood with which this book began. This is one place where the investigation of the unconscious itself leads, not just to the sexual, but to specific, though conflicting, intuitions concerning liberal individuality in modernity: ego and egotism, robust and pathological autonomy, conformity and the freedom to be oneself. It appears that selfhood in *The Interpretation of Dreams* is both a neutral, background assumption – a quality of I-ness that must be taken for granted in order to begin the exploration of specific anomalies in psychic life – and is itself one of the most troubling objects within the framework of the study. It is barely explicitly encountered as a problem, and yet *its* internal contradictions jostle through the accounts of inner life, of thinking, wishing and remembering oneself.

At the opening of the twentieth century psychoanalysis engendered a new science of psychopathology, or a new version of that science, centred on the role of unconscious memories and unconscious instinctual (libidinal) factors in certain kinds of mental disturbance. From at least the work of Alfred Adler onwards, questions were also raised about the weight that should be given to external socio-political factors in psychic life, alongside the internal and 'libidinal' ones. At first this concerned the extent to which psychoanalysis might be sensitive to the impact of class tensions, or the exigencies of life in a mass society, on its analytic subjects. These two different kinds of factors (the instinctual and the social or experiential) constitute two different kinds of pathology impinging on the character of individual life, of which psychoanalysis has tended to emphasise the first dimension, the internal one. But there is a third factor that should be taken into account, which might be described as the disruptive effect on psychoanalytic theory of complex 'pathologies' within the liberal account of individuality itself. What is the individual called upon to be in modern society, and how coherent or universal is the model account, against which the experience of particular individuals might be measured? How to establish such a norm of 'liberal' individuality, when its ideals are contested and undergoing historical change? One obvious example of this is Freud's implicit and explicit gendering of autonomy. In Freud's time there was widespread resistance to female emancipation and to avenues of self-development for women, and changing sociologies of gender in the course of the century have not failed to impact on some of the original assumptions about the formation of male and female individuality within psychoanalysis.[80] All three of these sets of 'traumas' (psychological, historical/social, cultural/ideological) are implicated in any attempt to settle the basis of the psychoanalytic unconscious. The unstable relationship between the experience and the *definition* of individuality in particular, will keep the ground of psychoanalytic theory moving under its own feet throughout the twentieth century.

---

[80] See, for instance, Juliet Mitchell, *Psychoanalysis and Feminism* (London: Allen Lane, 1974); Elaine Showalter, *The Female Malady: Women, Madness and English Culture, 1830–1980* (London: Virago Press, 1987); Charles Bernheimer and Claire Kahane (eds.), *In Dora's Case: Freud – Hysteria – Feminism* (New York: Columbia University Press, 1990); and Lisa Appignanesi and John Forrester, *Freud's Women* (Harmondsworth: Penguin, 2000).

Conclusion

> While psychology always denotes some bondage of the individual, it also presupposes freedom in the sense of a certain self-sufficiency and autonomy of the individual.[1]

> Freud released us all to be continually mysterious to ourselves and others.[2]

My goal in this book has not been, like Schelling's, to ground history in unconsciousness, but to give the unconscious a history. The conventional view of Freud is that he overturned the theory of selfhood, so that the I is no longer master in its own house; but this gesture had already been made many times throughout the nineteenth century, at the very least by Schelling, Schopenhauer, Carus and von Hartmann. For Schelling and Carus this 'overturning' of consciousness, self or I paradoxically served the purpose of preserving the notional autonomy of the individual. Much of the work of this book has been directed towards shifting our understanding of the unconscious, backwards from the epoch of psychoanalysis, to encompass this earlier history in which the concept is rooted, and its connections to German Romantic and idealist precursors. This has meant tracing the way the unconscious became an increasingly central term, and finally an explicit principle, in the post-Kantian philosophy of the subject. At the same time I have wanted to establish how unconsciousness and its correlates become inscribed more broadly within the early nineteenth-century human sciences, and specifically in the technical descriptions of the psyche in Romantic psychology.

In this account of the movement of the unconscious between philosophy and psychology, from a theory of the subject to a theory of the psyche, it has transpired that the unconscious is both an object of empirical enquiry *and* a solution to the dilemmas of describing the ontology of the

---

[1] Adorno, 'Freudian theory and the pattern of fascist propaganda', 136.
[2] Christopher Bollas, *The Mystery of Things* (London: Routledge, 1999), 1.

individual. It is ambiguously both part of the experience of selfhood and, theoretically, a way of representing the autonomy of selfhood, a building block within modern theories of human identity. Perhaps for this reason, the drive towards the theorisation of autonomous selves in modern culture has placed an increasing weight of attention on the self's unconscious interior – 'our ownmost and most genuine nature';[3] 'the inward forces which make [human nature] a living thing';[4] the 'heart of our being'.[5]

I have also considered how Romantic and modern psychologists for-mulate the notion of the psyche as the medium of the explicitly *individual* mind. The overlap between the psychological and the ontological or philosophical implications of the unconscious has characteristically centred on the way in which the unconscious allows *individuality* to be described. Certain aspects of the unconscious common to both Romantic psychology and psychoanalysis – its resistance to objectification, or to representation in terms of temporal or causal sequence[6] – allow for the inscription of an inner logic of the self as *causa sui*. Likewise, the cen-tring of psychic life on conditions of historicity, on unconscious origins or repressed foundations, appears to be less purely the result of empir-ical observation of the self, and as much allied to a complex of theor-etical assumptions designed to displace eighteenth-century notions of mechanical system and determinacy. The unconscious grounds of the psyche develop early in the nineteenth century partly as a way of over-coming the paradoxical confrontation between concepts of order, con-nectedness and freedom and between social unity and individuality, all of which were to be installed as key components in an emerging liberal account of the self.

This leads me to a further aspect of the book, which locates both Schelling's and Freud's unconscious in relation to the broader crises of liberal self-description. Seen from one perspective, the travels of the unconscious from Fichte's I, to Schelling's psyche, to Freud's psychic apparatus, present the gradual detachment of the ontology of the indi-vidual from absolute and metaphysical claims regarding the unity of the world, which might be associated in turn with philosophical, political or theological absolutism. It records the way theories about the foun-dation of life shift from ideas of its universal and rational organisation,

---

[3] Carus, 'Über Lebensmagnetismus', 153.
[4] Mill, 'Liberty', 188.
[5] Freud, *The Interpretation of Dreams*, 398.
[6] 'We have learnt that unconscious mental processes are in themselves "timeless". This means in the first place that they are not ordered temporally', Freud, *Beyond the Pleasure Principle*, 299.

through more differentiated and organic philosophies of nature and history, towards the depiction of structures governing the individual as an independent unit. This narrative is very particular to German intellectual culture in the nineteenth century and its transition from idealism towards empiricism, and from absolute to relative concepts of order (in England, to some extent, this movement is reversed). We have seen how Schelling's descriptions of the psychical and historical experience of the I seek to safeguard metaphysical assumptions concerning both the substance of the self and its moral integration in a coherent world, to free the self from external causation yet provide it with enigmatic links to an absolute foundation through the unconscious. To draw a parallel to Adorno's study of Kierkegaard, which deals with the same period of historical transition: 'Through conjuration a mythically self-enclosed subjectivity undertakes to rescue "fundamental human relations" and their meaning, ontology.'[7]

Freud's psychic apparatus no longer seems to fit such characterisation, insofar as the unconscious no longer masks a clandestine 'theology' of the individual. Freud does not identify the individual with a secret or emergent freedom or an intangible 'spirit' of individuality, or assume any overarching unifying principle within the world, other than general physical laws governing the concentration and displacement of energy – 'the dominating tendency of mental life, and perhaps of nervous life in general, is the effort to reduce, to keep constant or to remove internal tension due to stimuli'.[8] What stood out in Schelling's work as a displacement of divine or absolute organisation in the world behind the screen of the unconscious, transmutes in Freud to a more technical concern with the structure and dynamics of thought association, libidinal energy, censorship and resistance as empirical phenomena for the scientific investigation of mental life. Not metaphysics, but at most 'metapsychology'. This despite the penumbra of Romantic ideology which has surrounded the terms of psychoanalysis from its inception and which has continually been recovered and renegotiated, both within and outside the psychoanalytic tradition, including in the work of Jung, Rank, Binswanger and many others.

And yet, as observed throughout Chapter 6, *The Interpretation of Dreams* implies a certain shoring up of individuality all the same – not so much in what is attributed existentially or ontologically to the unconscious, but in the attempt to isolate and materialise certain laws (generic infantile wishes; the pleasure principle; the Oedipus complex;

---

[7] Adorno, *Kierkegaard*, 57.
[8] Freud, *Beyond the Pleasure Principle*, 55–6.

primal repression) through which the psychical experience of a self and its world are constituted. First of all, one might remark that the very isolation of the individual as a psychical or biological unit ratifies one liberal version of the foundational autonomy of the self. Accounts of experience, motivation, character and desire are centred on that individuated basis, and other kinds of social, cultural, political and religious phenomena are derived from it via a series of permutations of instincts. Of course, Freud everywhere radically complicated this notion of isolated individuality, not the least by making it historically a composite of the influences and identities of others. As he famously remarks at the opening of his work on *Group Psychology and the Analysis of the Ego*, 'in the individual's mental life someone else is invariably involved', and therefore, from the very first, individual psychology 'is at the same time social psychology as well'.[9] The Freudian individual appears in many ways to be a compound of other lives (the Kleinian individual even more so). Nevertheless, the very frame which scientific analysis places around the psyche assumes the coherent detachment of the individual as an autonomous object of investigation, and a primarily internal axis for its anxieties over self-constitution. This is an individual that is assumed to assimilate 'others' to an internal logic of desire; it is driven to repeat its own past, and to seek its own enjoyment; to preserve itself, and to destroy itself in its own way; to be hostile or indifferent to its neighbours. There are political and sociological assumptions about individuality built in to the supposedly neutral scientific description of the psyche as an autonomous system.

But this very assumption of an unconscious, instinct-driven logic to the individual (which was originally a background assumption in psychoanalysis, rather than an overt 'project') also becomes one of the major faultlines within it. First of all, it is notions of the self, of the I and of individuality which provide the weak points around which many of the early major splits in the psychoanalytic movement take place. It indicates the site of rifts not only with Adler's 'individual psychology', Stekel's 'Beloved Ego', and Jung's teleology of the individual, but also between Anna Freud and Melanie Klein (particularly over the formation of the ego and superego, and the task of analysis in relation to them), and between American ego-psychology and the Lacanian 'subject'. Disagreements emerge over the basic interpretations of individuality, its motivation and socialisation, whether it is autonomous or dependent, coherent or incoherent, and later on over whether characterisations of autonomous individuality are a function of specifically

---

[9] Freud, *SE*, vol. XVIII, 69.

Western, bourgeois or patriarchal societies. Looked at from this angle, whatever psychoanalysis was formerly meant to be about (for instance, as a delimited technics of psychical processes), it has not ceased to develop itself in the direction of multiple theories of the self: 'In a striking sense, psychoanalysis has become a theory of personal identity' and 'the analysis of a person's moral being';[10] psychoanalytic theory 'is of vital importance for understanding the fundamental conditions of selfhood'; it investigates the 'hidden self' 'lurking behind all forms of self-organisation'.[11]

Secondly, in relation to Freud's development of his own models of psychic functioning, what I elicited as a set of submerged ambiguities over the self and its autonomy in *The Interpretation of Dreams* becomes an ever more explicit and critical structural issue. The more perfectly psychoanalysis attempts to present the genesis of the individual – the more it aspires towards a complete developmental psychology of the unconscious – the more it provokes indeterminacies over how this self begins, what is its basis, and what are its real and fantasised elements. This is borne out by the way in which it is the renegotiation of the I, rather than the unconscious, which will provoke the major reorganisations in Freud's own metapsychology, first of all with the introduction of the concept of 'narcissism' in 1914, and then again with the complete reformulation of the theory in the 1920s around the tripartite structure of id, ego and superego. At this late stage in his career Freud noted that, 'pathological research has directed our interest too exclusively to the repressed. We should like to learn more about the ego, now that we know it, too, can be unconscious in the proper sense of the world'.[12]

Not only do such reformulations of psychic structure introduce major shifts into the way in which I and self are theorised, but the attempt to stabilise these successive models continues to generate confusion, both over how the I originates, and what the primary reference point for the concept is. For example, Richard Wollheim points out that Freud's formulation of narcissism is 'dangerously ambiguous', because it is conceived 'sometimes as an attraction to one's own person, sometimes as an attraction to one's own body'.[13] Similar criticisms are made by Jean Laplanche, for whom 'On Narcissism: An Introduction' constitutes 'a

---

[10]   Hinshelwood, *Therapy or Coercion*, 6, 3.
[11]   Anthony Elliott, *Psychoanalytic Theory: an Introduction* (Oxford: Blackwell, 1994), 2, 6.
[12]   Freud, *SE*, vol. XIX, 19. In 1920 he likewise complained 'the analysis of the ego has made so little headway', *SE* vol. XVIII, 53.
[13]   Wollheim, *Freud*, 118.

calling into question of the theory in its entirety'; it 'quickly came to be considered incomplete, if not monstrous' by Freud.[14]

I will follow Laplanche's exposition of the ambiguities over 'narcissism' a little further, because it articulates very well how some of the hazards that emerge around autonomy in *The Interpretation of Dreams* become even more pronounced as Freud attempts to determine the origins of selfhood more accurately. For Laplanche, the 'problematic of the ego' concerns two competing derivations of selfhood which come to the fore intermittently in Freud's work on narcissism. On the one hand, Freud frequently theorises narcissism in relation to a primary biological unit – prior even to the differentiation of an ego – and perhaps associated with the intrauterine state. This is one version of the self's most basic foundation, which assumes a certain ultimate 'individuality' in the form of 'a primal state, closed in upon itself, the prototype of the state of sleep and of dreaming'.[15] The image returns in *Beyond the Pleasure Principle* where Freud traces the origin of consciousness from a primal monadic entity: an increasingly defended 'living vesicle' suspended 'in the middle of an external world charged with the most powerful energies'.[16] On the other hand, Freud equally investigates selfhood through a specifically psychical formation – the differentiation and development of the ego within the human organism. What is at stake in this second version is an originary 'libidinal cathexis' of the I, which itself forms only part of the systems of conscious and unconscious mental processes.[17] Selfhood is here tied to a form of sexual self-love, to narcissism.

Both of these modes of description might designate the site of an origin of the 'self', but their connotations are rather different. Does individual subjectivity derive from a biological or a psychical condition, from a material property of being self-enclosed, or from a gratificatory investment of the I? Is it objectively or only subjectively present? Is the formation of the ego a step on the way from primal dreaming to the negotiation of reality, or is the ego itself the site of a narcissistic distortion of external relations? There seems to be an inherent problem over how to locate the basis of 'selfhood' – a problem not just of articulating the relevant dynamic processes in the unconscious, but of how the concept itself attaches to the organism. Strachey comments that '"ego" seems sometimes to correspond to the "self" and 'it is not always easy

---

[14] Jean Laplanche, *Life and Death in Psychoanalysis* (Baltimore, MD: Johns Hopkins University Press, 1976), 67. See also Neville Symington, *Narcissism: a New Theory* (London: Karnac, 1993), 5, 'for most of us who are psychoanalysts ... the model we have of the mind is inadequate to explain the phenomenon of narcissism'.

[15] Laplanche, *Life and Death*, 70.

[16] Freud, *SE*, vol. XVIII, 298.   [17] Laplanche, *Life and Death*, 72.

... to draw a line between these two senses of the word'.[18] Hinshelwood locates a similar ambiguity in Klein's usage of the concept: 'If the "ego" stands for a part of the structure of the mind objectively described, "self" tends to stand for the subject *in his own phantasies* described from a subjective point of view.' However, 'ego, self and subject are loosely interchangeable in Klein's writings'.[19] Laplanche further underscores the contradiction in any attempt to conceptualise the 'subjectivity' of a biological system, or 'to retrace the genesis of that "for itself"'.[20] The problem of being or becoming an 'I', one might add, is there as much for Freud as it is for Jung, and will continue to be investigated through many competing models, in the work of Melanie Klein and other object relations theorists.

What all these hesitations over the emergence of the individual demonstrate, is that the nature of the relation between the self, the I and the unconscious remains technically 'disturbed' throughout the history of the psychoanalytic movement, whether this unconscious aspect is conceived as the repressed (early Freud); as the id (later Freud); as unconscious phantasy (Klein); as the submerged totality of the self (Jung); the discursive structure of the Subject (Lacan); the quality of maternal 'holding' (Winnicott); or the unthought known (Bollas). And this means that the functional and technical description of the psyche, under various systems, is liable to be accompanied by a sense, either of the complexities and uncertainties of our knowledge of psychic structure, or of the unconscious basis of the self as being, beyond certain limits, intractably obscure, enigmatic, or hidden. Something of this kind takes place with Freud's introduction of the 'id'. The id in many ways displaces the 'unconscious' (which Freud recognised as having become too conceptually diffuse) as the primal, instinctual foundation, out of which the emergence of both selfhood and the I must ultimately be theorised. But in 1920 Freud acknowledged both that the internal sources of excitation were 'at once the most important and the most obscure element of psychological research' and that psychology forced him to adopt a figurative language which rendered his descriptions of instinct 'bewildering and obscure'.[21] Three years later, as he attempted to explicate and materialise the id as a bundle of particular drives and instincts, he also described it as a withdrawn and fundamentally obscure kernel of selfhood: 'We shall now look upon an individual as a psychical id,

---

[18] James Strachey, Editor's Introduction to 'The Ego and the Id', *SE*, vol. XIX, 8.

[19] R. D. Hinshelwood, *A Dictionary of Kleinian Thought* (London: Free Association Books, 1991), 285.

[20] Laplanche, *Life and Death*, 72.   [21] Freud, *SE*, vol. XVIII, 60.

unknown and unconscious, upon whose surface rests the I, developed from its nucleus the Pcpt. System.'[22] Quoting Georg Groddeck, Freud observed, 'we are "lived" by unknown and uncontrollable forces'.[23]

It is this kind of concession to the obscurity of the self's foundation which keeps psychoanalysis permeable to ontological uses – descriptions of the enigma of *being* a self – in contrast to the more instrumental accounts of selfhood given in mainstream psychology. The unconscious basis of the self, constantly under threat of becoming methodologically invisible, is always capable of being reinvested with metaphysical functions. Christopher Bollas' work, for instance, develops Winnicott's notion of an area of 'essential aloneness', a part of the inevitable and necessary solitude of any one self, in much the same way as Schelling uses the unconscious psyche, both to counter the notion of external causation, and to compensate for an excessively instrumental or objectified model of individuality. Bollas' notion of the 'idiom' of the self, from the late 1980s, is intended to represent 'the expression of any self's destiny', the aim of which is 'to realise one's own form of being through experience'.[24] The unconscious, for Bollas, both sustains individuality in this way, and provides a dimension through which integration with a wider universe can be thought. The self's experience of the 'cosmology creating work of the unconscious ego psychically substantiates the conviction that we live inside a mysterious intelligence'.[25] As with Fichte's obscure bond of the will, Bollas' notion of the unconscious mysteriously bridges self and other in such a way that the autonomy of neither is compromised. The analytic encounter is 'a paradoxical meeting. So deep and yet so impossible to describe'.[26] Certain statements by Bollas also recall Schelling's turn to negative theology to frame the origins of self: it is from the experience of the noumenal encounter of two minds in the analytic situation 'that we construct a theory of God from which we originate'.[27]

A more obvious example of this metaphysical turn within psychoanalysis is provided by Wilfred Bion's later work, particularly from

---

[22] Freud, *SE*, vol. XIX, 24.   [23] Ibid., 23.

[24] Bollas, *The Mystery of Things*, 3.

[25] Ibid., 7.   [26] Ibid., 10.

[27] Ibid., 10. Bollas here comes close to Jung's perception that the individual 'will never find the real justification for his existence, and his own spiritual and moral autonomy' except in 'an extra-mundane principle capable of relativizing the overpowering influence of external factors', Jung, *The Undiscovered Self*, 16. But both are re-traversing arguments of Schelling's about the need to root individuality in some kind of mysterious and absolute ground, whether this is conceived of as God, gravity, the past or the unconscious. Nothing in the universe is 'oppressed, purely dependent or in subjection, for everything is in itself absolute, and hence also in the absolute', *Ideas*, 159.

Transformations (1965) onwards, which again is concerned with establishing the existence of personal freedom, and the freedom to think one's own thoughts. Such freedom is everywhere under threat from social pressures or states of compulsion or automatism which, operating at unconscious levels, hold the will in bondage.[28] As with Bollas, Bion makes ontological use of the unconscious. It is that through which one might theorise the potential for freedom of multiple individuals, whose experiences are coevally embedded in an unknowable 'dark ground' of reality, out of which subjective experience is articulated. Bion, like Schelling, drew on Meister Eckhart for this notion of the ground, which he termed 'O'.[29] 'O' denotes 'the ultimate reality represented by terms such as ultimate reality, absolute truth, the godhead, the infinite, the thing-in-itself'.[30] O is 'darkness and formlessness', it 'can be "become"', but it cannot be "known"'.[31] Every object known by humans is an evolution of the unknowable O, while interpretation in the analytic session 'is an actual event in the evolution of O that is common to analyst and analysand'.[32]

The investigations of psychical individuality in Winnicott, Bollas and Bion take place on very different grounds from Fichte and Schelling's work. The latter would hardly recognise the framework of assumptions operating in the former. And yet, insofar as psychoanalysts set out to articulate the origins or nature of the self, or to derive a rationale for the self's autonomy, they find themselves faced with similar conceptual dilemmas which necessitate the rooting of individuality in the unconscious. These tendencies, even at the end of the twentieth century, have kept the psychoanalytic unconscious functionally in touch with those earlier Romantic investigations into human freedom and the ontology of the psyche.

This book has only been able to allude very briefly to the fortunes of psychoanalytic theory as Freud's work and the movement itself progressed beyond its initial articulations in *The Interpretation of Dreams*. Freud's thinking through of the nature of individual and social life was complex and extensive and, in the hands of later psychoanalytic developers, continues to afford new insights into the nature of psychological and social existence. But as a way of closing this account, and reflecting back on the relation between Freud's work and Schelling's, I want to turn to Freud's work of 1920, *Beyond the Pleasure Principle*,

---

[28] See Neville Symington, 'The Possibility of Human Freedom', 96–7.

[29] See Gérard Bléandonu, *Wilfred Bion: His Life and Works 1897–1979* (New York: Other Press, 1994), 211–12.

[30] Wilfred R. Bion, *Attention and Interpretation* (London: Karnac, 1984), 26.

[31] Ibid., 26.   [32] Ibid., 27.

for one last glimpse of the way the dilemmas of 'individuality' work themselves out in psychoanalytic thought. Of all Freud's writings, it is this later text, which notoriously introduced the 'death drive', and the war between life and death drives as a new basis for the psychoanalytic comprehension of instincts, which is most often linked with a return to the excesses of Romantic speculation on the metaphysical basis of life. In Freud's own terms it contains 'often far-fetched speculation' and at points gives 'the impression of mysticism', while some of the hypotheses (for instance that drawn from Aristophanes' account of the origins of human life in Plato's *Symposium*) provide us with 'myth rather than a scientific explanation'.[33] It is not only this highly speculative tendency which causes this work to be regarded 'as a throwback to the days of *Naturphilosophie*'.[34] It is also the way Freud structures the operations of nature in terms of polarities – constructive and destructive, life and death instincts, vacillating rhythms of existence, 'our views have from the very first been *dualistic*'[35] – which cannot help but conjure up the influence of Schelling's philosophy of nature, with its complex patterns of integration and disintegration and its dialectics of unity and freedom.[36] Likewise the way in which Freud is tempted to address the largest questions, 'the origin of consciousness' or to solve 'the riddle of life'.[37]

To be sure, the terms in which this is done is not really Schellingian, or if it is a *Naturphilosophie* it is one fundamentally altered through having taken on the 'Helmholtzian' commitment to energetic principles, for which Gustav Fechner (cited as a forerunner in the text) might provide a transitional example. But when Freud argues that 'the attributes of life were at some time evoked in inanimate matter by the action of a force of whose nature we can form no conception' but which may have been similar 'to that which later caused the development of consciousness in a particular stratum of living matter', the whole framework of enquiry is brought into proximity with the idealist attempt to derive the origins of subjectivity.[38] Freud's narratives of the notional beginnings of individuated life in primitive protista and germ-cells seem little different from the notional *Ur-Typen* and *Ur-Zellen* which provide the building blocks of life for Schelling's followers in the nineteenth century biological sciences, such as Lorenz Oken.

[33] Freud, *SE*, vol.XVIII, 24, 37, 57.
[34] Hannah S. Decker, quoted in Mark Luprecht, *'What People Call Pessimism*, 69.
[35] Freud, *SE*, vol. XVIII, 53.   [36] See Chapter 2.
[37] Freud, *SE*, vol., XVIII, 25, 60.   [38] Ibid., 38.

It is instructive to compare *Beyond the Pleasure Principle* with a work like May Sinclair's *Defence of Idealism*, published in 1917, which likewise drew on psychoanalytic and evolutionary theory, to see how close Freud comes to a more metaphysical text. Sinclair's work is intent on fathoming the enigma of selfhood, made more mysterious by the new philosophies of the unconscious stemming from Henri Bergson, Samuel Butler and Freud. Like Freud, Sinclair tries to comprehend the nature of human individuality by turning to the bedrock of biological life on which that individuality is founded. Evolution encompasses a myriad different selves which all go to achieve 'the work of the proud individuality we now are'.[39] The 'difficulties of the hypothesis of independent selfhood are great',[40] but Sinclair pursues it by analysing accounts such as Butler and Ewald Hering's of the first forms of individuation: the 'humble self-contained existence' of the simplest organism 'cannot satisfy its unquenchable longing to appear', Sinclair argues, and so 'it compels its organism to reproduce itself'.[41] Sinclair makes use of the psychoanalytic concept of sublimation in her search to identify a teleology within life, an evolving project of 'individuality'. The 'purified spirit of psychoanalysis', the truth underlying its theory, is 'the deliverance of the Will-to-live from its bondage to the Unconscious'.[42] If this in some ways appears to anticipate Freud's 'where id was there ego shall be' of the later *New Introductory Lectures*, Sinclair's vision is perhaps closer to Schelling's, in that it sees the history of nature as a preparation for human freedom.

However, even though Sinclair sees herself as developing tendencies within Freud's work, *Beyond the Pleasure Principle* sets out to argue a very different case. In fact, the latter half of Freud's text seems specifically designed to quash such teleological illusions. 'There is unquestionably no universal instinct towards higher development observable in the animal or plant world', Freud writes, even though it may be difficult 'to abandon the belief that there is an instinct towards perfection at work in human beings'.[43] Freud's goal is the opposite of Sinclair's, in that he seeks consciously to distinguish himself from any strain of optimism, or quasi-Romantic principle of emergent freedom or cosmic harmonisation. Where Sinclair finds 'the original speck of protoplasm' sufficient as a starting point for life but 'absurdly insufficient to carry on with',[44] the principle Freud is most keen to establish is not a life-enhancing one,

---

[39] Sinclair, *A Defence of Idealism*, 35.
[40] Ibid., 33.   [41] Ibid., 34.
[42] Ibid., 11.   [43] Freud, *SE*, vol. XVIII, 41–2.
[44] Sinclair, *A Defence of Idealism*, 34.

but the death drive – a counter-principle to Eros, which keeps his biological units particulate and isolated.

What brings Freud's work into association with Schelling's, however,
is not a Romantic vision of the unity of nature. It is that Freud, like
Sinclair, makes a detour through biological and evolutionary theory
in order to fix the ultimate basis of human individuality. The turn to
nature, and the attempt to reconstruct a logic of separation and conjuga-
tion in life's most elementary units, is everywhere shadowed by tensions
in the modern and liberal theory of individuality, and by the anxieties
of the contemporary world. Freud speculates, for instance, on the characteristics which enable germ cells 'to have an independent existence'.[45]
At times such germ cells are represented as behaving 'in a completely
"narcissistic" fashion', but they are also compelled 'into a vital association', or may suggest a vision of life 'torn apart into small particles,
which have ever since endeavoured to reunite'.[46] *Group Psychology*, published a year later, but with which Freud had been preoccupied since
1919, draws at length on Gustave le Bon's *The Psychology of Crowds*,
which at times appears to integrate political history in the wake of the
French Revolution with elementary biology. The crowd, formed out of
a provisional combination of heterogeneous elements, is able to generate a new being through a process of reunion, 'exactly as are the cells
which constitute a living body'.[47] Ten years later Freud would think this
process in reverse, arguing that, in consequence of the 'primary mutual
hostility of human beings, civilised society is perpetually threatened
with disintegration'.[48]

If these overtones of liberal socio-political anxiety seem merely incidental (the problem of being an individual is by no means the core
issue with which Freud is engaged in this text, one might argue), it
must be remembered that the point from which *Beyond the Pleasure
Principle* starts, the point from which the whole panorama of biological
speculation flows, is an attempt to account for a shortcoming in the
experience of psychoanalytic therapy. People are sometimes resistant
to being cured, Freud acknowledges, and specifically to being cured
of their passivity, their submissiveness which 'has its roots deep in [an]

---

[45] Freud, *SE*, vol. XVIII, 40.
[46] Ibid., 50, 58.
[47] Gustave le Bon, *The Crowd* (New Brunswick, NJ: Transaction, 1995), 47. In the
same work Freud quotes 'a valuable remark' from W Trotter's *Instincts of the Herd
in Peace and War* 'to the effect that the tendency towards the formation of groups is
biologically a continuation of the multicellular character of all the higher organisms',
Sigmund Freud, *Group Psychology, SE*, vol. XVIII, 87.
[48] Freud, *Civilization and Its Discontents, SE*, vol. XX, 112.

unconscious parental complex'.[49] Even when such patients comprehend that this passivity is a compulsive repetition of their infantile life, they may not be persuaded to abandon it. That is, in the therapeutic relation they may remain in the thrall of an authority figure (the physician) and unable or unwilling to achieve the independent individuality which Freud sees as fundamental to healthy life. The passage through the Oedipus complex has left them with 'a permanent injury to self-regard in the form of a narcissistic scar', and this constitutes the 'sense of inferiority' common in neurotics.[50] It is the attempt to understand why people should fail to *be* individuals, to be autonomous in the strong 'liberal' sense, that sends Freud back to this hypothetical investigation of 'living vesicles', 'special envelopes', 'protective shields', and basic or exaggerated forms of self-sufficiency, almost as an attempt to prove, at a biological level, that individuation is what life is ultimately about.[51] The very conflict of life and death instincts might be seen as an attempt to manage the competing tendencies in life, but also in society, towards unification and separation, withdrawal and connection, and to attain some final vision of a balance of forces undergirding human life, within which the drive towards individuality maintains a permanent presence. Freud is engaged in an analysis of how individuated units arise; what keeps them separate, or static; how life shifts from passive defence to active relating; what the binding forces are in society; what the forces are that bind autonomous units together or pull them apart. As the evolutionist Ernst Haeckel had suggested already in 1899: 'We can only arrive at a correct knowledge of the structure and life of the social body, the State, through a scientific knowledge of the structure and life of the individuals who compose it, and the cells of which they are in turn composed.'[52] For Haeckel, the study of 'protists' provides an essential grounding in social relations.

The point about Sinclair and Schelling, then, is not that Freud is theorising an emergent unity in life, but that all three are trying to embed desired aspects of individual autonomy within a transcendental fabric of nature. For some, autonomy will indicate 'creative self-development', or the freedom and evolution of the human will; but it can equally mean, as it does so often for Freud, the preservation of the self as an autonomous and separate unit, living and dying in one's own way, the defence of the concept of individuality. Both features became prevalent

---

[49] Freud, *SE*, vol. XVIII, 20.
[50] Ibid., 20–1.   [51] Ibid., 27.
[52] Ernst Haeckel, *The Riddle of the Universe* (London: Watts, 1929), 6.

as competing traditions or emphases within liberal philosophy in the nineteenth century, as Isaiah Berlin famously propounded.[53]

The pathos here lies in the way in which the issue of selfhood and society – the tendency towards fragmentation, the drive to combine – needs to be embedded, as it was for Schelling, in an account of nature as a whole, a theory of general natural organisation. There is pathos, too, in Freud's attempts to abstract and finalise a certain foundational vision of the laws of individuality and combination at precisely the time when the political authority and the political foundations of liberal selfhood were being eroded. Theodor Adorno would later read Freud's theories of group psychology and of the 'ego ideal' and 'superego', developed in the 1920s, as a prescient index of political life in the 1930s. The weakening of the function of the 'ego' in Freud's later work, according to Adorno, represents the real loss of political substance of 'selfhood' for the middle classes, and the emergence of the fascist or mass individual, who, no longer capable of self-motivation, identifies with the dictates of idealised leader figures to the impoverishment of autonomous inner life. At this point in modernity, Adorno argues, psychological processes, though they persist in each individual, 'have ceased to appear as the determining forces of social processes', and this indicates the abolition of psychological motivation 'in the old, liberalistic sense'.[54] Meanwhile the superego 'anticipates almost with clairvoyance the postpsychological de-individualised social atoms which form the fascist collectivities'.[55] What Freud was embedding in the most elementary account of nature, was soon being read for its relevance as an ideological response to contemporary political crises.

As central Europe headed into an even more calamitous undermining of the liberal ideal than had overshadowed the dream book, Freud felt the need to slip the theoretical basis of psychoanalysis from its empirical mooring within the system of the individual, and to anchor the emergence of individuality itself in a wider, metaphysically conceived fabric of nature. As *Beyond the Pleasure Principle* attempts to drive the justifications for the psychic structure of the person deeper and deeper into a notional primordial bio-history, to triangulate the instabilities of identity through that absolute basis, so Freud's account does seem finally to approach the grandiose mythologisations of the *Naturphilosophie*. Schelling's scientific and philosophical 'mythologies' of human structure were themselves elaborated in the midst of, and

---

[53] Isaiah Berlin, *Two Concepts of Liberty. An Inaugural Lecture Delivered Before the University of Oxford on 31 October 1958* (Oxford: Clarendon Press, 1958).
[54] Adorno, 'Freudian Theory and the Pattern of Fascist Propaganda', 118–37, 136.
[55] Ibid., 136.

in response to, another set of calamitous upheavals in the experience of society, religion and government, following the developments of the Enlightenment and the French Revolution, and then again during the course of the Napoleonic invasion and the attempts to rebuild political structure in the early decades of the nineteenth century. In its own way, Freud's text is a poignant index of the later collapse of a certain ideal of liberal autonomy. That final desire to found the structure of the psyche more absolutely, matched only by Freud's late foray into the history of myth and religion in *Moses and Monotheism*, cannot be detached from the need to preserve the imagined foundational structure of a certain ideal of civilised individuality itself.

Bibliography

Abrams, M. H., *Natural Supernaturalism: Tradition and Revolution in Romantic Literature* (New York: Norton, 1971).

Adorno, Theodor W., *Kierkegaard: Constructions of the Aesthetic* (Minneapolis: University of Minnesota, 1989).

'Freudian Theory and the Pattern of Fascist Propaganda', in Andrew Arato and Eike Gebhardt (eds.), *The Essential Frankfurt School Reader* (New York: Continuum, 1993), 118–37.

Metaphysics: Concepts and Problems (Cambridge: Polity, 2001).

Alexander, F. G. and S. T. Selesnick, *The History of Psychiatry: an Evaluation of Psychiatric Thought and Practice from Prehistoric Times to the Present* (New York: Harper & Row, 1966).

Amacher, Peter, 'Freud's Neurological Education and Its Influence on Psychoanalytic Theory', *Psychological Issues*, 4, 4, Monograph 16 (New York: International University Press, 1965).

Andersson, Ola, *Studies in the Prehistory of Psychoanalysis: The Etiology of Psychoneuroses and Some Related Themes in Sigmund Freud's Scientific Writings and Letters, 1886–1896* (Stockholm: Svenska, 1962).

Anzieu, Didier, *Freud's Self-Analysis*, trans. Peter Graham (Madison, CT: International Universities Press, 1986).

Appignanesi, Lisa and John Forrester, *Freud's Women* (Harmondsworth: Penguin, 2000).

Arendt, Hannah, *The Human Condition* (University of Chicago Press, 1998).

Aristotle, *A New Aristotle Reader*, ed. J. L. Ackrill (Oxford University Press, 1987).

Askay, Richard and Jensen Farquhar, *Apprehending the Inaccessible: Freudian Psychoanalysis and Existential Phenomenology* (Evanston, IL: Northwestern University Press, 2006).

Baader, Franz von, 'On the Analogy between the Knowledge-drive and the Procreative-drive', in A. F. Marcus and F. W. J. Schelling (eds.), *Jahrbücher der Medicin als Wissenschaft*, vol. III, part 1 (Tübingen: J. G. Cotta, 1808), 113–24.

Bachofen, Johann Jakob, *An English Translation of Bachofen's Mutterrecht (Mother Right) (1861), A Study of the Religious and Juridicial Aspects of Gynecocracy in the Ancient World, vol. I: 'Lycia', 'Crete' and 'Athens'*, abr. and trans. David Partenheimer (Lewiston, Queenston and Lampeter: Edwin Mellen, 2007).

Beck, Lewis White, *Early German Philosophy: Kant and his Predecessors* (Cambridge, MA and London: Belknap/Harvard University Press, 1969).

Beierwaltes, Werner, *Platonismus und Idealismus* (Frankfurt am Main: Vittorio Klostermann, 1972).

Beiser, Frederick C., *The Fate of Reason: German Philosophy from Kant to Fichte* (Cambridge, MA: Harvard University Press, 1987).

Enlightenment, Revolution, and Romanticism: the Genesis of Modern German Political Thought, 1790–1800 (Cambridge, MA: Harvard University Press, 1992).

German Idealism: the Struggle Against Subjectivism 1781–1801 (Cambridge, MA: Harvard University Press, 2002).

Bell, Matthew, *The German Tradition of Psychology in Literature and Thought, 1700–1840* (Cambridge University Press, 2005).

Benjamin, Walter, *Illuminations*, ed. Hannah Arendt (New York: Schocken, 1968).

The Origin of German Tragic Drama (London: Verso, 1985).

'The Life of Students', in *Selected Writings, vol. I: 1913–1926* (Cambridge, MA: Belknap/Harvard University Press, 1996).

'Surrealism: the Last Snapshot of the European Intelligentsia', in *Selected Writings, vol. II: 1927–1934* (Cambridge, MA: Belknap/Harvard University Press, 1999).

The Arcades Project (Cambridge, MA: Belknap/Harvard University Press, 1999).

Beres, David, 'Psychoanalysis, Science and Romanticism', in *Drives, Affects, Behavior: Essays in Honor of Marie Bonaparte*, vol. II, ed. Max Schur (New York: International Universities Press, 1965), 397–417.

Berlin, Isaiah, *Two Concepts of Liberty. An Inaugural Lecture Delivered Before the University of Oxford on 31 October 1958* (Oxford: Clarendon Press, 1958).

'The Apotheosis of the Romantic Will', in Henry Hardy and Roger Hausheer (eds.), *The Proper Study of Mankind: An Anthology of Essays* (London: Pimlico, 1998).

Bernfeld, S., 'Freud's Earliest Theories and the School of Helmholtz', *Psychoanalytic Quarterly*, 13 (1994), 341–62.

Bernheimer, Charles and Claire Kahane (eds.), *In Dora's Case: Freud – Hysteria – Feminism* (New York: Columbia University Press, 1990).

Bettelheim, Bruno, *Freud and Man's Soul* (London: Hogarth Press, 1983).

Binswanger, Ludwig, *Being-in-the-World: Selected Papers of Ludwig Binswanger*, trans. Jacob Needleman (New York and Evanston, IL: Harper & Row, 1968).

Bion, Wilfred R., *Attention and Interpretation* (London: Karnac, 1984).

Bléandonu, Gérard, *Wilfred Bion: His Life and Works 1897–1979* (New York: Other Press, 1994).

Bobbio, Noberto, *Liberalism and Democracy* (London: Verso, 1990).

Böhme, Jakob, *The High and Deep Searching Out of the Threefold Life of Man*, trans. John Sparrow (London: Watkins, 1909, Kessinger reprint).

Bollas, Christopher, *The Mystery of Things* (London: Routledge, 1999).

Borch-Jacobsen, Mikkel, *The Freudian Subject* (Basingstoke and London: Macmillan, 1982).

Boring, Edwin, *A History of Experimental Psychology* (New York: Appleton-Century-Crofts, 1950).

Bosanquet, Bernard, *The Value and Destiny of the Individual* (London: Macmillan, 1923).

Bowie, Andrew, *Aesthetics and Subjectivity: From Kant to Nietzsche* (Manchester University Press, 1990).

Schelling and Modern European Philosophy (London: Routledge, 1993).

Bredekamp, Horst, 'From Walter Benjamin to Carl Schmitt, via Thomas Hobbes', *Critical Inquiry*, 25, 2 (Winter 1999), 247–66.

Breton, André, *Communicating Vessels* (Lincoln: University of Nebraska Press, 1990).

Breuer, Josef and Sigmund Freud, *Studies on Hysteria* (1893–95), *SE*, vol. II.

Britton, Ronald, *Belief and Imagination: Explorations in Psychoanalysis* (London: Routledge, 1998).

Bronfen, Elizabeth, *The Knotted Subject: Hysteria and Its Discontents* (Princeton University Press, 1998).

Brown, Robert F., *The Later Philosophy of Schelling: the Influence of Boehme on the Works of 1809–1815* (Lewisburg, PA: Bucknell University Press, 1977).

Buchholz, Michael B. and Günter Gödde (eds.), *Macht und Dynamik des Unbewussten: Auseinandersetzungen in Philosophie, Medizin und Psychoanalyse*, in the series *Das Unbewusste*, 3 vols. (Gießen: Psychosozial-Verlag, 2005).

Budd, Susan, 'The Shark Behind the Sofa: the Psychoanalytic Theory of Dreams', *History Workshop Journal*, 48 (Autumn 1999), 133–50.

Burkhardt, Jakob, *History of Greek Culture* (London: Constable, 1964).

Caputo, John D., *The Mystical Elements in Heidegger's Thought* (New York: Fordham University Press, 1986).

Carus, Carl Gustav, 'Über Lebensmagnetismus und über die magischen Wirkungen überhaupt', in *Denkwürdigkeiten aus Europa* (Hamburg: Marion von Schröder, 1963).

Psyche, On the Development of the Soul. Part One: The Unconscious (Dallas, TX: Spring Publications, 1970).

Caygill, Howard, *A Kant Dictionary* (Oxford: Basil Blackwell, 1995).

'The Shared World – Philosophy, Violence, Freedom', in Darren Sheppard, Simon Sparks, Colin Thomas (eds.), *On Jean-Luc Nancy* (London: Routledge, 1997).

Chéniex-Gendron, Jacqueline, *Surrealism* (New York: Columbia University Press, 1990).

Cobban, Alfred, 'The Revolt Against the Eighteenth Century', in Harold Bloom (ed.), *Romanticism and Consciousness: Essays in Criticism* (New York: W. W. Norton, 1970).

Coleman, William, *Biology in the Nineteenth Century* (New York: John Wiley, 1971).

Coleridge, S. T., *The Collected Works of Samuel Taylor Coleridge,* vol. XII, *Marginalia, Part 2: Camden to Hutton*, ed. H. J. Jackson and George Whalley (Princeton University Press, 1984).

The Collected Works of Samuel Taylor Coleridge, vol. XII, *Marginalia, Part 4: Pamphlets to Shakespeare*, ed. H. J. Jackson and George Whalley (Princeton University Press, 1998).

Darnton, Robert, *Mesmerism and the End of Enlightenment in France* (New York: Schocken, 1970).

Derrida, Jacques, *Force de loi: Le 'Fondement mystique de l'autorité'* (Paris: Galilée, 1994).

    Spectres of Marx: The the State of the Debt, the Work of Mourning, and the New International (London: Routledge, 1994).

    Resistances of Psychoanalysis (Stanford University Press, 1998).

Dews, Peter, *Logics of Disintegration* (London: Verso, 1987).

Dietrich, Paul A., 'The Wilderness of God in Hadewijch II and Meister Eckhart and His Circle', in Bernard McGinn (ed.), *Meister Eckhart and the Beguine Mystics* (New York: Continuum, 1994).

Dixon, Thomas, *From Passions to Emotions: the Creation of a Secular Psychological Category* (Cambridge University Press, 2003).

Doerner, Klaus, *Madmen and the Bourgeoisie: A Social History of Insanity and Psychiatry*, trans. Joachim Neugroschel and Jean Steinberg (Oxford: Basil Blackwell, 1991).

Eagleton, Terry, *The Ideology of the Aesthetic* (Oxford: Basil Blackwell, 1990).

Ecker, Alexander, *Lorenz Oken: a Biographical Sketch*, trans. Alfred Tulk (London: Kegan Paul Trench, 1883).

Eliot, George, *The Lifted Veil/Brother Jacob* (Oxford University Press, 1999).

Ellenberger, Henri F., *The Discovery of the Unconscious: the History and Evolution of Dynamic Psychiatry* (London: Fontana Press, 1994).

Elliott, Anthony, *Psychoanalytic Theory: an Introduction* (Oxford: Blackwell, 1994).

Emerson, Ralph Waldo, *The Journals and Miscellaneous Notebooks of Ralph Waldo Emerson*, vol. IX: *1843–47*, ed. Ralph H. Orth and Alfred R. Ferguson (Cambridge, MA: Harvard University Press, 1971).

Engels, Friedrich, 'Schelling and Revelation' [1842] in *Karl Marx Frederick Engels: Collected Works*, vol. II: *Frederick Engels 1838–42* (London: Lawrence & Wishart, 1975).

Eschenmayer, C. A., *Versuch die Scheinbare Magie des Thierischen Magnetismus aus Physiologischen und Psychischen Gesetzen zu Erklären* (Vienna: Haas'schen Buchhandlung, 1816).

    Über Besessenseyn und Zauber, published in Justinus Kerner, *Geschichten Besessener euerer Zeit. Beobachtungen aus dem Gebiete Kako-Dämonisch-Magnetischer Erscheinungen* (Karlsruhe: G. Braun, 1835).

Esposito, Joseph L., *Schelling's Idealism and Philosophy of Nature* (London: Associated University Press, 1977).

Fackenheim, Emil L., *The God Within: Kant, Schelling, and Historicity*, ed. John Burbidge (University of Toronto, 1996).

Faflak, Joel, *Romantic Psychoanalysis: The Burden of the Mystery* (Albany, NY: State University of New York Press, 2008).

Fanning, Stephen, *Mystics of the Christian Tradition* (London: Routledge, 2001).

Fechner, Gustav, *Life After Death* (New York: Pantheon Books, 1943).

Ferenczi, Sandor, 'Philosophie und Psychoanalyse (Bemerkungen zu einem Aufsatze des H. Professors Dr. James S. Putnam)', in *Imago, Zeitschrift für Anwendung der Psychoanalyse auf die Geisteswissenschaften*, vol. I, 1912 (Nendeln/Liechtenstein: Kraus Reprint, 1969), 519–26.

'Stages in the Development of the Sense of Reality', in *First Contributions to Psycho-Analysis* (London: Karnac, 1994), 213–39.

Feuerbach, Ludwig, *Thoughts on Death and Immortality* (Berkeley, CA: University of California Press, 1980).

ffytche, Matt, 'F. W. J. Schelling and G. H. Schubert: Psychology in Search of Psyches', *Romantic Psyche and Psychoanalysis* issue, *Romantic Circles Praxis Series* (December 2008), www.rc.umd.edu/praxis/psychoanalysis/ffytche/ffytche.html.

'The Modernist Road to the Unconscious', in Peter Brooker, Andrzej Gasiorek, Deborah Longworth and Andrew Thacker (eds.), *The Oxford Handbook of Modernisms* (Oxford University Press, 2010).

Fichte, J. G., *Addresses to the German Nation* [1807–08], ed. G. A. Kelly (New York and Evanston, IL: Harper & Row, 1968).

Fichte-Schelling Briefwechsel, ed. Walter Schulz (Frankfurt am Main: Suhrkamp Verlag, 1968).

Science of Knowledge: With the First and Second Introductions [1794], trans. Peter Heath and John Lachs (Cambridge University Press, 1982).

The Vocation of Man [1800] (Indianapolis, IN: Hackett, 1987).

Introductions to the Wissenschaftslehre and Other Writings (1797–1800), ed. Daniel Breazeale (Indianapolis, IN: Hackett, 1994).

Reclamation of the Freedom of Thought from the Princes of Europe, Who Have Oppressed It Until Now [1793], trans. Thomas E. Wartenberg, in James Schmidt (ed.), *What Is Enlightenment?: Eighteenth-Century Answers and Twentieth-Century Questions* (Berkeley, CA: University of California Press, 1996).

Flournoy, Theodor, *From India to the Planet Mars*, ed. Sonu Shamdasani (Princeton University Press, 1994).

Forrester, John, *Dispatches from the Freud Wars: Psychoanalysis and Its Passions* (Cambridge, MA: Harvard University Press, 1997).

Foucault, Michel, *The Order of Things: an Archaeology of the Human Sciences* (London: Tavistock, 1980).

Frank, Manfred and Gerhard Kurz (eds.) *Materialen zu Schellings philosophischen Anfängen* (Frankfurt am Main: Suhrkamp, 1975).

Freud, Sigmund, *The Standard Edition of the Complete Psychological Works of Sigmund Freud*, under the general editorship of James Strachey in collaboration with Anna Freud, assisted by Alix Strachey and Alan Tyson, 24 vols. (London: The Hogarth Press and the Institute of Psychoanalysis, 1953–74) [*SE*].

'The Aetiology of Hysteria' (1896), in *SE*, vol. III *(1893–1899): Early Psycho-Analytic Publications*, 191–221.

The Interpretation of Dreams (1900), *SE*, vol. IV, 5.

'On Dreams' (1901), in *SE*, vol. V *(1900–1901): The Interpretation of Dreams (Second Part) and On Dreams*, 629–86.

'Creative Writers and Day-Dreaming' (1908), in *SE*, vol. IX *(1906–1908): Jensen's 'Gradiva' and Other Works*, 141–54.

'Formulations on the Two Principles of Mental Functioning' (1911), *SE*, vol. XII (*1911–1913*): *The Case of Schreber, Papers on Technique and Other Works*, 213–26.

Totem and Taboo: Some Points of Agreement between the Mental Lives of Savages and Neurotics (1913), *SE*, vol. XIII (*1913–1914*): *Totem and Taboo and Other Works*, vii–162.

'The Unconscious' (1915), in *SE*, vol. XIV (*1914–1916*): *On the History of the Psycho-Analytic Movement, Papers on Metapsychology and Other Works*, 159–215.

Introductory Lectures on Psychoanalysis (1916), *SE*, vol. XV, 16.

From the History of an Infantile Neurosis (1918), in *SE*, vol. XVII (*1917–1919*): *an Infantile Neurosis and Other Works*, 1–24.

Beyond the Pleasure Principle (1920), in *SE*, vol. XVIII (*1920–1922*): *Beyond the Pleasure Principle, Group Psychology and Other Works*, 1–64.

Group Psychology (1921), in *SE*, vol. XVIII, 65–144.

'Two Encyclopaedia Articles' (1923), in *SE*, vol. XVIII, 233–60.

The Ego and the Id (1923), in *SE*, vol. XIX (*1923–1925*): *The Ego and the Id and Other Works*, 1–66.

'The Loss of Reality in Neurosis and Psychosis' (1924), *SE*, vol. XIX, 181–8.

'A Short Account of Psycho-Analysis' (1924), in *SE*, vol. XIX, 189–210.

Civilization and Its Discontents (1930), in *SE*, vol. XXI, (*1927–1931*): *The Future of an Illusion, Civilization and its Discontents, and Other Works*, 57–146.

Studienausgabe vol. I, *Vorlesungen zur Einführung in die Psychoanalyse und Neue Folge*, ed. Alexander Mitscherlich, Angela Richards and James Strachey (Frankfurt am Main: S. Fischer Verlag, 1982).

The Complete Letters of Sigmund Freud to Wilhelm Fliess 1887–1904, ed. Jeffrey Moussaieff Masson (Cambridge, MA: Harvard University Press, 1985).

The Letters of Sigmund Freud to Eduard Silberstein 1871–1881, ed. Walter Boehlich (Cambridge, MA: Harvard University Press, 1990).

The Interpretation of Dreams, trans. Joyce Crick (Oxford University Press, 1999).

Die Traumdeutung (Frankfurt am Main: Fischer, 2000).

Frie, Roger and Bruce Reis, 'Understanding Intersubjectivity: Psychoanalytic Formulations and Their Philosophical Underpinnings', *Contemporary Psychoanalysis*, 37 (2001), 297–327.

Fromm, Eric, 'Freud's Model of Man and its Social Determinants', in *The Crisis of Psychoanalysis: Essays on Freud, Marx and Social Psychology* (New York: Henry Holt, 1969).

Frosh, Stephen, *Key Concepts in Psychoanalysis* (London: The British Library, 2002).

Galdston, Iago, 'Freud and Romantic Medicine', *Bulletin of the History of Medicine*, 30 (1956), 489–507.

Gasking, Elizabeth, *Investigations into Generation 1651–1828* (London: Hutchinson, 1967).

Gerabek, Werner E., *Friedrich Wilhelm Joseph Schelling und die Medizin der Romantik* (Frankfurt am Main: Peter Lang, 1995).

Gmelin, Eberhard, *Ueber den Thierischen Magnetismus* (Tübingen: Jakob Friederich Heerbrandt, 1787).

Neue Untersuchungen über den Thierischen Magnetismus (Tübingen: Jakob Friederich Heerbrandt, 1789).

Gode-von Aesch, Alexander, *Natural Science in German Romanticism* [1941] (New York: AMS Press, 1966).

Goldmann, Stefan, 'Von der "Lebenskraft" zum "Unbewussten"; Stationen eines Konzeptwandels der Anthropologie', in Michael B. Buchholz and Günter Gödde (eds.), *Macht und Dynamik des Unbewussten: Auseinandersetzungen in Philosophie Medizin und Psychoanalyse* (Gießen: Psychosozial-Verlag, 2005).

Gould, Stephen Jay, *Ontogeny and Phylogeny* (Boston, MA: Harvard University Press, 1977).

Gray, John, *Liberalism* (Buckingham: Open University Press, 1995).

Grinstein, Alexander, *Sigmund Freud's Dreams* (New York: International Universities Press, 1980).

Grubrich-Simitis, Ilse, 'How Freud Wrote and Revised *The Interpretation of Dreams*: Conflicts Around the Subjective Origins of the Book of the Century', *Psychoanalysis and History*, 4, 2 (Summer 2002), 111–26.

Guntrip, Harry, *Psychoanalytic Theory, Therapy and the Self* (London: Karnak, 2001).

Habermas, Jürgen, *Theorie und Praxis* (Neuwied and Berlin: Luchterhand, 1963).

The Philosophical Discourse of Modernity (Cambridge: Polity Press, 1990).

'Martin Heidegger: On the Publication of the Lectures of 1935', in Richard Wolin (ed.), *The Heidegger Controversy* (Cambridge, MA: MIT Press: 1993).

Haeckel, Ernst, *The Riddle of the Universe* (London: Watts, 1929).

Hamilton, Paul, *Coleridge and German Philosophy* (London: Continuum, 2007).

Hartmann, Eduard von, *Philosophy of the Unconscious*, trans. William Chatterton Coupland (London: Kegan Paul, Trench, Trubner, 1931).

Heer, Friedrich, *The Intellectual History of Europe* (London: Weidenfeld & Nicholson, 1966).

Hegel, G. W. F., *Faith and Knowledge* [1802], trans. Walter Cerf and H. S. Harris (Albany, NY: State University of New York Press, 1977).

Phenomenology of Spirit [1807], trans. A. V. Miller (Oxford University Press, 1977).

Philosophy of Mind [1830], trans. William Wallace and A. V. Miller (Oxford University Press, 1971).

Hegel: the Letters, ed. Clark Butler and Christiane Seiler (Bloomington: Indiana University Press, 1984).

Heidegger, Martin, *An Introduction to Metaphysics* (New Haven, CT: Yale University Press, 1959).

'What Are Poets For?', *Poetry, Language, Thought*, trans. Albert Hofstadter (New York: Harper & Row, 1975).

Schelling's Treatise on the Essence of Human Freedom, trans. Joan Stambaugh (Athens, OH: Ohio University Press, 1985).

'The Self-Assertion of the University', in Richard Wolin (ed.), *The Heidegger Controversy* (Cambridge, MA: MIT Press, 1993).

Hölderlin's Hymn 'The Ister' (Bloomington: Indiana University Press, 1996).

Henrich, Dieter, 'Fichte's Original Insight', in Darrel Christensen (ed.), *Contemporary German Philosophy*, vol. I (University Park: Pennsylvania State University Press, 1982).

Henry, Michel, *The Genealogy of Psychoanalysis* (Stanford University Press, 1993).

Hillman, James, "Man Is by Nature a Political Animal": or Patient as Citizen', in Sonu Shamdasani and Michael Münchow (eds.), *Speculations After Freud: Psychoanalysis, Philosophy and Culture* (London: Routledge, 1994).

Hinshelwood, R. D., *A Dictionary of Kleinian Thought* (London: Free Association Books, 1991).

Therapy or Coercion: Does Psychoanalysis Differ from Brainwashing (London: Karnac, 1997).

Hobhouse, L. T., 'Liberalism', in *Liberalism and Other Writings* (Cambridge University Press, 1994).

Hoffmann, E. T. A., *E.T.A. Hoffmann Briefwechsel, Erster Band von Königsberg bis Leipzig 1794–1814*, ed. Hans von Müller and Friedrich Schnapp (Munich: Winkler, 1967).

Tagebücher, ed. Hans von Müller and Friedrich Schnapp (Munich: Winkler, 1971).

Holbach, Baron d', *The System of Nature, Volume One*, trans. H. D. Robinson (Manchester: Clinamen Press, 1999).

Horkheimer, Max, 'Authority and the Family', in *Critical Theory: Selected Essays* (New York: Herder and Herder, 1972).

Horn, Friedemann, *Schelling and Swedenborg: Mysticism and German Idealism* (West Chester, PA: Swedenborg Foundation, 1997).

Humboldt, Wilhelm von, *The Limits of State Action* (Indianapolis, IN: Liberty Fund, 1993).

Hyppolite, Jean, *Genesis and Structure of Hegel's Phenomenology of Spirit* (Evanston, IL: Northwestern University Press, 1974).

Jaspers, Karl, *The Origin and Goal of History* (New Haven, CT: Yale University Press, 1953).

Schelling; Größe und Verhängnis (Munich: R. Piper, 1955).

The Philosophy of Existence (Philadelphia, PA: University of Pennsylvania Press, 1971).

Jones, Ernest, *The Life and Work of Sigmund Freud*, 3 vols. (New York: Basic Books, 1953–57).

The Life and Work of Sigmund Freud, ed. and abr. Lionel Trilling and Steven Marcus (London: Penguin, 1964).

Jung, C. G., References are to *The Collected Works of C. G. Jung [CW]*, Sir Herbert Read, Michael Fordham, Gerhard Adler and William McGuire (eds.) 20 vols. (London: Routledge & Kegan Paul; Princeton University Press, 1953–83).

'On the Psychology and Pathology of So-Called Occult Phenomena' (1902), *CW*, vol. I, *Psychiatric Studies*, 2nd edn (Princeton University Press, 1970).

Symbols of Transformation (1911–12/1952), *CW*, vol. V (London: Routledge & Kegan Paul, 1956).

Psychological Types (1921), *CW*, vol. VI (Princeton University Press, 1971).

'The Relations Between the Ego and the Unconscious' (1928), in *CW*, vol. VII, *Two Essays on Analytical Psychology*, 2nd edn (Princeton University Press, 1966), 121–241.

'The Structure of the Unconscious' (1916), in *CW*, vol. VII, 269–304.

'On the Nature of the Psyche' (1947/1954), in *CW*, vol. VIII, *The Structure and Dynamics of the Psyche* (Princeton University Press, 1972).

'Archetypes of the Collective Unconscious' (1934/1954), in *CW*, vol. IX, part 1, *The Archetypes and the Collective Unconscious*, trans. R. F. C. Hull, 2nd edn (London: Routledge, 1968).

'Individual Dream Symbolism in Relation to Alchemy' (1936), in *CW*, vol. XII, *Psychology and Alchemy*, 2nd edn (Princeton University Press, 1968).

Mysterium Coniunctionis: An Inquiry into the Separation and Synthesis of Psychic Opposites in Alchemy (1955–6), *CW*, vol. XIV, 2nd edn (Princeton University Press, 1977).

'The Aims of Psychotherapy' (1931), in *CW*, vol. XVI, *The Practice of Psychotherapy: Essays on the Psychology of the Transference and Other Subjects*, 2nd edn (London: Routledge & Kegan Paul, 1966).

'Sigmund Freud: "On Dreams"', in *CW*, vol. XVIII, *The Symbolic Life: Miscellaneous Writings* (Princeton University Press, 1980).

The Zofingia Lectures, Supplementary to CW, Vol. A (Princeton University Press, 1983).

Nietzsche's Zarathustra: Notes of the Seminar Given in 1934–9, Supplementary to CW, Seminar Papers, vol. II, 2 parts (London: Routledge, 1994).

'The Spirit of Psychology', in Joseph Campbell (ed.), *Spirit and Nature: Papers from the Eranos Yearbooks*, vol. I (London: Routledge & Kegan Paul, 1955), 371–444.

'Seven Sermons to the Dead', in Robert A. Segal (ed.), *The Gnostic Jung* (Princeton University Press, 1992) 181–93.

Memories, Dreams, Reflections (London: Fontana Press, 1995).

The Undiscovered Self (London: Routledge, 2002).

Synchronicity: An Acausal Connecting Principle (London: Routledge, 2008).

Kant, *Critique of Pure Reason* [1781/1787] trans. Norman Kemp Smith (Basingstoke: Macmillan, 1993).

Prolegomena to Any Future Metaphysics [1783], ed. Beryl Logan (London: Routledge, 1996).

Metaphysical Foundations of Natural Science [1786], in *Philosophy of Material Nature*, trans. James Ellington (Indianapolis, IN: Hackett, 1985).

Critique of Practical Reason [1788] in Mary J. Gregor (ed.), *Practical Philosophy, The Cambridge Edition of the Works of Immanuel Kant* (Cambridge University Press, 1996).

Critique of Judgement [1790], trans. J. H. Bernard (New York: Hafner Press, 1951).

Anthropology from a Pragmatic Point of View [1798] (Carbondale and Edwardsville, IL: Southern Illinois University Press, 1996).

Kaufmann, Walter, *Nietzsche; Philosopher, Psychologist, Antichrist* (New York: Vintage, 1968).

Kerner, Justinus, *Franz Anton Mesmer, aus Schwaben, Entdecker des thierischen Magnetismus* (Frankfurt am Main: J. Rütter, 1856).

Kerslake, Christian, 'Insects and Incest: From Bergson and Jung to Deleuze', *Multitudes: Revue Politique, Artistique, Philosophique*, 25 (22 October 2006) www.multitudes.samizdat.net/Insects-and-Incest-From-Bergson.

Kierkegaard, Søren, *The Concept of Irony*, trans. Howard V. Hong and Edna H. B. Hong (Princeton, NJ: Princeton University Press, 1989).

Klein, Melanie, 'The Development of a Child', *Love, Guilt and Reparation and Other Works, 1921–1945* (London: Hogarth Press, 1975).

Kojève, Alexandre, *Introduction à la lecture de Hegel* (Paris: Gallimard, 1947).

Kolakowski, Lezsek, *Main Currents of Marxism*, 3 vols. (Oxford University Press, 1978).

Krieger, Leonard, *The German Idea of Freedom, History of a Political Tradition* (Boston, MA: Beacon Press, 1957).

Lacan, Jacques, *The Four Fundamental Concepts of Psychoanalysis* (Harmondsworth: Penguin, 1977).

'Seminar XX', *Encore*, in Juliet Mitchell and Jacqueline Rose (eds.), *Feminine Sexuality, Jacques Lacan and the École Freudienne* (Basingstoke and London: Macmillan, 1982).

Écrits: a Selection (London: Routledge, 1985).

The Seminar of Jacques Lacan, Book II: The Ego in Freud's Theory and in the Technique of Psychoanalysis 1954–55, ed. Jacques-Alain Miller (New York: W. W. Norton, 1991).

The Psychoses: The Seminar of Jacques Lacan, Book III: 1955–1956, ed. Jacques-Alain Miller (London: Routledge, 1993).

Lacoue-Labarthe, Philippe and Jean-Luc Nancy, 'The Unconscious is Destructured like an Affect (Part I of "The Jewish People Do Not Dream")', *Stanford Literary Review*, 6, 2 (Fall 1989), 191–209.

Langen, August, *Der Wortschatz des Deutschen Pietismus* (Tübingen: Max Niemeyer, 1968).

Laplanche, Jean, *Hölderlin et la question du père* (Paris: Presses Universitaires de France, 1961).

Life and Death in Psychoanalysis (Baltimore, MD: Johns Hopkins University Press, 1976).

'Notes on Afterwardsness', in John Fletcher and Martin Stanton (eds.), *Seduction, Translation, Drives* (London: ICA, 1992).

Laplanche, Jean and J.-B. Pontalis, *The Language of Psychoanalysis* (London: Karnac, 1988).

La Vopa, Anthony J., *Fichte: The Self and the Calling of Philosophy, 1762–1799* (Cambridge University Press, 2001).

Lawrence, D. H., 'Psychoanalysis and the Unconscious' in *Fantasia of the Unconscious and Psychoanalysis of the Unconscious* (Harmondsworth: Penguin, 1971).

Leary, David E., 'Immanuel Kant and the Development of Modern Psychology', in William R. Woodward and Mitchell G. Ash (eds.), *The Problematic Science: Psychology in Nineteenth Century Thought* (New York: Praeger, 1982).

Le Bon, Gustave, *The Crowd* (New Brunswick, NJ: Transaction, 1995).

Leibbrand, Werner, *Die Spekulative Medizin der Romantik* (Hamburg: Claassen, 1956).

Leibniz, Gottfried, *Philosophical Writings* (London: Dent, 1973).

Levinas, Emmanuel, *Time and the Other* (Pittsburgh, PA: Duquesne University Press, 1987).

Lewes, G. H., *The History of Philosophy from Thales to Comte*, 2 vols. (London: Longmans, Green, 1880).

Lovecraft, H. P., 'The Case of Charles Dexter Ward', in *At the Mountains of Madness* (London: HarperCollins, 1999).

Lovejoy, Arthur O., *The Great Chain of Being* [1936] (Cambridge, MA: Harvard University Press, 1964).

Lukács, Georg, *History and Class Consciousness: Studies in Marxist Dialectics* (London: Merlin Press, 1971).
  Goethe and His Age (London: Merlin Press, 1979).
  The Destruction of Reason (London: The Merlin Press, 1980).

Lukes, Steven, *Individualism* (Oxford: Basil Blackwell, 1973).

Luprecht, Mark, *'What People Call Pessimism': Sigmund Freud, Arthur Schnitzler, and Nineteenth-Century Controversy at the University of Vienna Medical School* (Riverside, CA: Ariadne Press, 1991).

Makari, George, *Revolution in Mind: the Creation of Psychoanalysis* (London: Gerald Duckworth, 2008).

Mann, Thomas, 'Freud and the Future', *International Journal of Psychoanalysis*, 37 (1956), 106–15.

Marcus, A. F. and F. W. J. Schelling (eds.), *Jahrbücher der Medicin als Wissenschaft* (Tübingen: Cotta, 1806).

Marquard, Odo, *Transzendentaler Idealismus, Romantische Naturphilosophie, Psychoanalyse* (Cologne: Jurgen Dinter, 1987).

Marquet, François, *Liberté et existence: Études sur la formation de la philosophie de Schelling* (Paris: Gallimard, 1973).

Marx, Karl and Frederick Engels, *Collected Works*, vol. III (London: Lawrence & Wishart, 1975).

McFarland, Thomas, *Coleridge and the Pantheist Tradition* (Oxford: Clarendon Press, 1969).

McGinn, Bernard (ed.), *Meister Eckhart and the Beguine Mystics* (New York: Continuum, 1994).

McGrath, William, 'Freud and the Force of History', in T. Gelford and J. Kerr (eds.), *Freud and the History of Psychoanalysis* (Mahwah, NJ: The Analytic Press, 1992).

Meadowcraft, J. (ed.), *The Liberal Political Tradition: Contemporary Reappraisals* (Cheltenham: Edward Elgar, 1996).

Mill, J. S., *Gesammelte Werke*, ed. Theodor Gomperz, vol. XII: *Ueber Frauenemancipation. Plato. Arbeiterfrage. Socialismus*, trans. Sigmund Freud (Leipzig: Fues, 1880).

Autobiography (Oxford University Press, 1971).

The Collected Works of John Stuart Mill, vol. VIII: *A System of Logic Ratiocinative and Inductive, Books IV–VI* (University of Toronto Press, 1974).

'On Liberty', in M. Warnock (ed.), *Utilitarianism* (Glasgow: William Collins, 1979).

The Collected Works of John Stuart Mill, vol. IX: *An Examination of Sir William Hamilton's Philosophy* (University of Toronto Press, 1979).

Mitchell, Juliet, *Psychoanalysis and Feminism* (London: Allen Lane, 1974).

Müller-Tamm, Jutta, *Kunst als Gipfel der Wissenschaft: Ästhetische und Wissenschaftliche Weltaneignung bei Carl Gustav Carus* (Berlin: Walter de Gruyter, 1995).

Myers, F. W. H., 'The Subliminal Consciousness', *Proceedings of the Society for Psychical Research*, 7 (February 1892), 289–355.

Nagel, Thomas, *The View From Nowhere* (Oxford University Press, 1986).

Nancy, Jean-Luc, *The Experience of Freedom* (Stanford University Press, 1993).

Neuhouser, F., *Fichte's Theory of Subjectivity* (Cambridge University Press, 1990).

Nicholls, Angus and Martin Liebscher (eds.), *Thinking the Unconscious: Nineteenth-Century German Thought* (Cambridge University Press, 2010).

Nietzsche, Friedrich, *The Birth of Tragedy and The Genealogy of Morals* (New York: Anchor Books/Doubleday, 1956).

Noll, Richard, *The Jung Cult: Origins of a Charismatic Movement* (London: Fontana Press, 1996).

Norman, Judith and Alistair Welchman (eds.), *The New Schelling* (London and New York: Continuum, 2004).

Novalis, *The Novices of Sais*, trans. Ralph Manheim (New York: Archipelago Books, 2005).

Oetinger, Friedrich, *Biblisches und Emblematisches Wörterbuch* [1776], ed. Dmitrij Tschizewskij and Ernst Benz (Hildesheim: Georg Olms, 1969).

Oken, Lorenz, *Lehrbuch der Naturphilosophie* [1810], trans. Alfred Tulk as *Elements of Physio-Philosophy* (London: Ray Society, 1847).

O'Meara, Thomas F., *Romantic Idealism and Roman Catholicism: Schelling and the Theologians* (South Bend, IN: University of Notre Dame, 1982).

Perrot, Michelle (ed.), *From the Fires of Revolution to the Great War*, vol. IV, in Philippe Ariès and Georges Duby (eds.), *A History of Private Life*, 5 vols (Cambridge, MA: Harvard University Press, 1990).

Phillips, Adam, *Winnicott* (London: Fontana, 1988).

Phillips, John, 'The Fissure of Authority: Violence and the Acquisition of Knowledge', in John Phillips and Lyndsey Stonebridge (eds.), *Reading Melanie Klein* (London: Routledge, 1988).

Pinkard, Terry, *German Philosophy 1760–1860: The Legacy of Idealism* (Cambridge University Press, 2002).

Plato, *Phaedrus*, trans. Walter Hamilton (Harmondsworth: Penguin, 1973).

Plitt, Gustave Leopold, *Aus Schellings Leben in Briefen*, 3 vols. (Leipzig: Hirzel, 1869–70).

Plotinus, *The Enneads*, trans. Stephen MacKenna (Harmondsworth: Penguin, 1991).

Pocci, Franz (ed.), *Justinus Kerner und sein Münchener Freundeskreis: eine Sammlung von Briefen* (Leipzig: Insel, 1928).

Popper, K. R., *The Open Society and Its Enemies*, vol. II: *The High Tide of Prophecy: Hegel, Marx and the Aftermath* (London: Routledge, 1993).

Rank, Otto, *Truth and Reality* (New York and London: W. W. Norton, 1964).

Psychology of the Soul: a Study of the Origin, Conceptual Evolution, and Nature of the Soul [1930] (Baltimore, MD: Johns Hopkins University Press, 1998).

Rayner, Eric, *The Independent Mind in British Psychoanalysis* (London: Free Association Books, 1990).

Reed, Edward S., *From Soul to Mind: the Emergence of Psychology from Erasmus Darwin to William James* (New Haven, CT: Yale University Press, 1997).

Richards, Graham, *Mental Machinery: the Origins and Consequences of Psychological Ideas, 1600–1850* (Baltimore, MD: Johns Hopkins University Press, 1992).

Richards, Robert J., *The Romantic Conception of Life* (University of Chicago Press, 2002).

Richardson, Michael and Krysztof Fijałkoski (eds.), *Surrealism Against the Current* (London: Pluto Press, 2001).

Richter, Jean Paul, *Titan: a Romance*, 2 vols., trans. Charles Brooks (London: Trübner, 1863).

Jean Paul: a Reader, ed. Timothy J. Casey (Baltimore, MD: Johns Hopkins University Press, 1992).

Ricoeur, Paul, *Freud and Philosophy: an Essay on Interpretation* (New Haven, CT: Yale University Press, 1970).

Rieff, Philip, *Freud: The Mind of the Moralist* (New York: The Viking Press, 1959).

Roazen, Paul, *Political Theory and the Psychology of the Unconscious* (London: Open Gate, 2000).

Rose, Gillian, *Hegel Contra Sociology* (London: Athlone, 1981).

The Broken Middle (Oxford: Blackwell, 1992).

'Of Derrida's Spirit', in David Wood (ed.), *Of Derrida, Heidegger and Spirit* (Evanston, IL: Northwestern University Press, 1993).

Rose, Jacqueline, *On Not Being Able to Sleep: Psychoanalysis and the Modern World* (London: Chatto & Windus, 2003).

Ross, David, *Aristotle* (London: Routledge, 1995).

Rousseau, Jean-Jacques, *The Confessions, and Correspondence, including the Letters to Malesherbes*, ed. Christopher Kelly, Roger D. Masters and Peter G. Stillman (Hanover, NH: University Press of New England, 1995).

Rylance, Rick, *Victorian Psychology and British Culture 1850–1880* (Oxford University Press, 2000).

Sachs, Hanns, *Freud, Master and Friend* (London: Imago, 1945).

Samuels, Andrew, Bani Shorter and Fred Plaut (eds.), *A Critical Dictionary of Jungian Analysis* (London: Routledge, 2003).

Sartre, Jean-Paul, *Being and Nothingness: an Essay on Phenomenological Ontology*, trans. Hazel E. Barnes (London: Routledge, 1993).

Schelling, F. W. J., 'Of the I as the Principle of Philosophy', in Fritz Marti (ed.), *The Unconditional in Human Knowledge: Four Early Essays (1794–1796)* (Lewisburg, PA: Bucknell University Press, 1980).

Ideas for a Philosophy of Nature [1797/1803] (Cambridge University Press, 1988).

Von der Weltseele, eine Hypothese der höheren Physik zur Erklärung des allgemeinen Organismus [On the World Soul; a Hypothesis of the Higher Physics, as an Explanation of the General Organism, 1798], in *Sämmtliche Werke*, part 1, vol. II, 345–651.

System of Transcendental Idealism [1800], trans. Peter Heath (Charlottesville, VA: University Press of Virginia, 1978).

The Philosophy of Art [1802–1804], trans. Douglas W. Stott (Minneapolis, MN: University of Minnesota Press, 1989).

System of the Whole of Philosophy and of Naturphilosophie in Particular [1804], in *Sämmtliche Werke*, part 1, vol. VI, 141–587.

'On the Relation Between the Plastic Arts and Nature' [1807] in *The Philosophy of Art; an Oration on the Relation Between the Plastic Arts and Nature*, trans. A. Johnson (London: John Chapman, 1845).

Philosophical Inquiries into the Nature of Human Freedom [1809], trans. James Gutmann (La Salle, IL: Open Court, 1985).

Philosophische Entwürfe und Tagebücher 1809–1813 (Hamburg: Felix Meiner, 1994).

'The Stuttgart Seminars' [1810], in *Idealism and the Endgame of Theory: Three Essays by F. W. J. Schelling*, trans. Thomas Pfau (Albany, NY: State University of New York Press, 1994).

Die Weltalter, Urfassungen, ed. Manfred Schröter (Munich: Biederstein/ Leibniz, 1946).

The Ages of the World [1813], in Slavoj Žižek/F. W. J. von Schelling, *The Abyss of Freedom/Ages of the World*, trans. Judith Norman (Ann Arbor: The University of Michigan Press, 1997).

The Ages of the World [1815] trans. Jason M. Wirth (State University of New York, 2000).

The Ages of the World [1815], trans. Frederick de Wolfe Bolman, Jr. (New York: Columbia University Press, 1942).

Treatise on 'The Deities of Samothrace': A Translation and an Interpretation [1815], trans. Robert F. Brown (Missoula, MT: Scholars Press, 1977).

On the History of Modern Philosophy [1827] (Cambridge University Press, 1994).

System der Weltalter: Münchener Vorlesung 1827/28 in einer Nachschrift von Ernst von Lasaulx (Frankfurt am Main: Vittorio Klostermann, 1998).

Philosophie der Mythologie [1842], in *Sämmtliche Schriften*, Abt. 2, vol. II.

Historical-critical Introduction to the Philosophy of Mythology [1842] (Albany, NY: State University of New York Press, 2007).

Das Tagebuch 1848, ed. Hans Jörg Sandkühler (Hamburg: Felix Meiner, 1990).

Sämmtliche Werke, ed. K. F. A. Schelling, I *Abtheilung* vols. I–X; II *Abtheilung* vols. I–IV (Stuttgart: Cotta, 1856–61).

Briefe und Dokumente, Band I 1775–1809, ed. Horst Fuhrmans (Bonn: H. Bouvier, 1962).

Schelling, Karl, 'Grundsätze zu einer Künftigen Seelenlehre', *Jahrbücher der Medicin als Wissenschaft*, 2, 2 (Tübingen: Cotta, 1807).

Schiller, Friedrich, 'Das Verschleierte Bild zu Sais', in Julius Petersen and Friedrich Beissner (eds.), *Schillers Werke Nationalausgabe*, vol. I (Weimar: Hermann Böhlaus Nachfolger, 1943), 245–56.

Schlegel, Friedrich, *The Philosophy of Life, and Philosophy of Language*, trans. Rev. A. J. W. Morrison (London: Bohn, 1847).

Friedrich Schlegel's Lucinde and the Fragments, trans. Peter Firchow (Minneapolis: University of Minnesota Press, 1971).

Schopenhauer, Arthur, *The World as Will and Representation*, trans. E. F. Payne, 2 vols. (New York: Dover, 1966).

'Essay on Spirit Seeing and Everything Connected Therewith', in *Parerga and Paralipomena*, vol. I, trans. E. F. J. Payne, 2 vols. (Oxford University Press, 1974).

Schorske, Carl E., *Fin-de-Siècle Vienna: Politics and Culture* (London: Weidenfeld and Nicholson, 1979).

Schubert, G. H., *Ahndungen einer allgemeinen Geschichte des Lebens*, 2 vols. (Leipzig: Reclam, 1806–21).

Ansichten von der Nachtseite der Naturwissenschaft [Views of the Nightside of Natural Science] (Darmstadt: Wissenschaftliche Buchgesellschaft, 1967).

Der Erwerb aus einem Vergangenes und die Erwartungen von einem Zukünftigen Leben: eine Selbstbiographie, 3 vols. (Erlangen: J. J. Palm u. Ernst Enke: 1854–6).

Shamdasani, Sonu, 'From Geneva to Zürich: Jung and French Switzerland', *Journal of Analytical Psychology*, 43 (1998), 115–26.

Jung and the Making of Modern Psychology (Cambridge University Press, 2003).

Shils, Edward, *The Virtue of Civility: Selected Essays on Liberalism, Tradition and Civil Society*, ed. Steven Grosby (Indianapolis, IN: Liberty Fund, 1997).

Showalter, Elaine, *The Female Malady: Women, Madness and English Culture, 1830–1980* (London: Virago Press, 1987).

Sinclair, May, 'Clinical Lectures on Symbolism and Sublimation', part 2, *Medical Press* (16 August 1916), 142–5.

A Defence of Idealism: Some Questions and Conclusions (London: Macmillan, 1917).

Sismondi, Jean Charles Léonard de, *Italian Republics, or, the Origins, Progress and Fall of Italian Freedom* (Paris: A. and W. Galignani, 1841).

Solms, Mark, 'Controversies in Freud Translation', *Psychoanalysis and History*, 1, 1 (1998), 28–44.

'Freud, Luria and the Clinical Method', *Psychoanalysis and History*, 2, 1 (February 2000), 76–109.

Southern, R. W., *Western Society and the Church in the Middle Ages* (Harmondsworth: Penguin, 1979).

Spinoza, Benedict de, *The Ethics* (Harmondsworth: Penguin, 1996).

Stekel, Wilhelm, *The Beloved Ego: Foundations of the New Study of the Psyche* (London: Kegan Paul, Trench, Trubner, 1921).

Sulloway, Frank J., *Freud, Biologist of the Mind: Beyond the Psychoanalytic Legend* (New York: Basic Books, 1979).

Symington, Neville, 'The Possibility of Human Freedom and its Transmission (With Particular Reference to the Thought of Bion)', *International Journal of Psycho-Analysis*, 71 (1990), 95–106.

Narcissism: a New Theory (London: Karnac, 1993).

Tauler, Johannes, *Sermons*, trans. Maria Shrady (New York: Paulist Press, 1985).

Taylor, Charles, *Hegel* (Cambridge University Press, 1975).

Sources of the Self: The Making of the Modern Identity (Cambridge University Press, 1989).

The Ethics of Authenticity (Cambridge, MA: Harvard University Press, 1991).

Tilliette, Xavier (ed.), *Schelling im Spiegel Seiner Zeitgenossen* (Torino: Bottega d'Erasmo, 1974).

'Die "Höhere Geschichte"', in Ludwig Hasler (ed.), *Schelling, Seine Bedeutung für eine Philosophie der Natur und der Geschichte* (Stuttgart: Frommann-Holzboog, 1981), 193–204.

'Une philosophie en deux', in Jean-François Courtine and Jean-François Marquet (eds.), *Le Dernier Schelling* (Paris: J. Vrin, 1994).

Tocqueville, Alexis de, *Democracy in America* (London: Fontana Press, 1994).

Tsouyopoulos, Nelly, 'Der Streit zwischen Friedrich Wilhelm Joseph Schelling und Andreas Röschlaub über die Grundlagen der Medizin', *Medizinhistorisches Journal*, 13 (1978), 229–46.

Vincent, Andrew, 'Liberalism and Postmodernism', in James Meadowcraft (ed.), *The Liberal Political Tradition* (Cheltenham: Edward Elgar, 1996).

Walzel, Oskar, *Deutsche Romantik* (Leipzig: B. G. Teubner, 1908).

Warnock, Mary (ed.), *Utilitarianism* (London: Collins, 1962).

Weber, Max, *The Protestant Ethic and the Spirit of Capitalism* (London: Unwin University Books, 1930).

Weber, Samuel, 'Taking Exception to Decision: Walter Benjamin and Carl Schmitt', *Diacritics*, 22, 3–4 (Fall–Winter 1992), 5–18.

The Legend of Freud (Stanford University Press, 2000).

Whyte, Lancelot Law, *The Unconscious Before Freud* (New York: Anchor Books, 1962).

Winnicott, D. W., 'What Do We Mean by a Normal Child?', in *The Child and the Family: First Relationships* (London: Tavistock, 1957).

'Communicating and Not Communicating', in *The Maturational Processes and the Facilitating Environment: Studies in the Theory of Emotional Development* (London: Hogarth Press, 1965).

Playing and Reality (London and New York: Routledge, 1991).

Winterstein, Alfred von, 'Psychoanalytische Anmerkungen zur Geschichte der Philosophie', *Imago: Zeitschrift für Anwendung der Psychoanalyse auf die Geisteswissenschaften*, 2, (1913) (Nendeln/Liechtenstein: Kraus Reprint, 1969).

Wirth, Jason M. (ed.), *Schelling Now: Contemporary Readings* (Bloomington, IN: Indiana University Press, 2005).

Wittgenstein, Ludwig, *Philosophical Investigations* (Oxford: Basil Blackwell, 1989).

Wollheim, Richard, *Freud* (London: HarperCollins, 1991).

Wood, David (ed.), *Of Derrida, Heidegger and Spirit* (Evanston, IL: Northwestern University Press, 1993).

Wordsworth, William, 'Ode: Intimations of Immortality from Recollections of Early Childhood', in E. de Selincourt and H. Darbishire (eds.), *Wordsworth's Poetical Works*, vol. IV (Oxford University Press, 1947), 279–85.

Zaretsky, Eli, *Secrets of the Soul: a Social and Cultural History of Psychoanalysis* (New York: Alfred A. Knopf, 2004).

Žižek, Slavoj, *The Indivisible Remainder: An Essay on Schelling and Related Matters* (London: Verso, 1996).

Žižek, Slavoj and F. W. J. von Schelling, *The Abyss of Freedom/Ages of the World*, trans. Judith Norman (Ann Arbor: The University of Michigan Press, 1997).

Index